www.wadsworth.com

wadsworth.com is the World Wide Web site for Wadsworth Publishing Company and is your direct source to dozens of online resources.

At *wadsworth.com* you can find out about supplements, demonstration software, and student resources. You can also send e-mail to many of our authors and preview new publications and exciting new technologies.

wadsworth.com
Changing the way the world learns®

Morals, Marriage, and Parenthood

An Introduction to Family Ethics

LAURENCE D. HOULGATE
California Polytechnic State University

Wadsworth Publishing Company
I(T)P® An International Thomson Publishing Company

Belmont, CA • Albany, NY • Boston • Cincinnati • Johannesburg • London • Madrid
Melbourne • Mexico City • New York • Pacific Grove, CA • Scottsdale, AZ
Singapore • Tokyo • Toronto

For Jack and Karen

Philosophy Editor: Peter Adams
Assistant Editor: Kerri Abdinoor
Editorial Assistant: Mindy Newfarmer
Marketing Manager: Dave Garrison
Print Buyer: Stacey Weinberger
Permissions Editor: Yanna Walters
Production: Matrix Productions
Copy Editor: Victoria Nelson

Cover Design: Cassandra Chu
Cover Image: Paul Klee, Wandbild-aus
   dem Tempel der Sehnsucht Dorthin,
   Metropolitan Museum of Art.
   Christie's Images/SuperStock.
Compositor: R&S Book Composition
Printer: Transcontinental Printing

Printed in Canada
1 2 3 4 5 6 7 8 9 10

For more information, contact Wadsworth Publishing Company, 10 Davis Drive,
Belmont, CA 94002, or electronically at http://www.wadsworth.com

International Thomson Publishing Europe
Berkshire House
168-173 High Holborn
London, WC1V 7AA, United Kingdom

Nelson ITP, Australia
102 Dodds Street
South Melbourne
Victoria 3205 Australia

Nelson Canada
1120 Birchmount Road
Scarborough, Ontario
Canada M1K 5G4

International Thomson Publishing Southern Africa
Building 18, Constantia Square
138 Sixteenth Road, P.O. Box 2459
Halfway House, 1685 South Africa

International Thomson Editores
Seneca, 53
Colonia Polanco
11560 México, D.F. México

International Thomson Publishing Asia
60 Albert Street
#15-01 Albert Complex
Singapore 189969

International Thomson Publishing Japan
Hirakawa-cho Kyowa Building, 3F
2-2-1 Hirakawa-cho, Chiyoda-ku
Tokyo 102 Japan

Library of Congress Cataloging-in-Publication Data
Houlgate, Laurence D.
   Morals, marriage, and parenthood: an introduction to family ethics/Laurence D. Houlgate.
      p.   cm.
   Includes bibliographical references.
   ISBN 0-534-55157-2 (alk. paper)
   1. Family. 2. Family—Moral and ethical aspects. 3. Social values.   I. Title.
HQ518.H68 1998
306.85—dc21   98-28477

 This book is printed on acid-free recycled paper.

Contents

Preface

Morals, Marriage, and Parenthood is the first anthology of essays entirely devoted to the general theme of ethical problems in marriage and family relationships. Several previous anthologies on contemporary moral problems have contained a single chapter of essays on family ethics, and there have been some anthologies on children's rights and parental responsibilities, but nothing has yet been published that collects and brings together classical and contemporary sources on the wide range of ethical issues presented in this volume.

This is surprising for two reasons. First, my experience has been that the moral problems of the family excite student interest much more than most of the ethical issues presented for study in applied ethics courses. I believe that this is because most of the moral problems we encounter in our everyday lives concern or affect those persons who are closest to us: our spouse, siblings, parents, children, and other family members. We worry about such intensely personal topics as whether to have an extramarital affair, whether a couple should bear a second or third child instead of adopting, whether to get a divorce or keep our marriage intact when our children are young, whether to place our elderly parents in a long-term care facility instead of bringing them home to live with us, or whether to spank our child instead of choosing a noncorporal means of punishment. University students are as concerned with these issues as anyone, not only because they still are closely attached to their parents and siblings, but because most will someday have families of their own.

The other reason for surprise that this is the first family ethics anthology to be published is that a great deal of excellent writing on the problems of family ethics has been produced in the past twenty years. Some has been reprinted in scattered social ethics anthologies, but much of it has languished in relatively inaccessible philosophy journals. It is time, therefore, to gather these essays (and some previously unpublished work as well) into one volume and consider them together as part of a single discipline.

This brings me to the second objective of this anthology: to introduce philosophers, sociologists, and others who share a professional interest in marriage and family to a new subfield of applied ethics: family ethics. Family ethics should stand on its own beside medical ethics, environmental ethics, and business ethics as a distinct area of study, as deserving of its own course in the university curriculum as these other subfields. As the material in this anthology amply testifies, not only is there a large body of excellent writing on the many problems of family ethics, but the writing comes from classical as well as contemporary sources, it includes work from several disciplines, and it is culturally diverse, touching at several points on issues of race and gender.

The essays included in this anthology have been gathered together into several distinct problem areas, beginning with several chapters that debate the nature and justification of the institutions of marriage and family. However, any of the chapters can be read as a separate unit—for example, as an introduction to a particular problem of family ethics (e.g., the ethics of adultery and divorce). This feature makes the volume particularly useful for those who wish to adopt it as a text for a general philosophy course in contemporary moral problems or as a supplement of relevant readings for standard sociology courses in marriage and family.

Each chapter is devoted to a particular question or a related set of problems. Chapter 1 introduces students to the field of family ethics, describes a method for resolving problems of family ethics, and discusses some of the theoretical issues related to this and other methods.

Chapters 2 and 3 raise several preliminary questions that must be answered before further ethical questions about the family can be raised: What is the family? How shall this term be defined? How have previous generations understood the ethical relationships among family members? How do persons of other cultures conceive these relationships?

The essays in Chapter 4 raise several questions about traditional marriage, including the question of whether and how it is a justifiable institution and the heavily debated contemporary question of whether it is justifiable to disallow marriages between persons of the same sex.

Chapter 5 looks at some of the criticisms of traditional family, beginning with Plato's suggestion that the private family should be eliminated in the ruling class of the state, and concluding with the contemporary feminist claim that the traditional allocation of roles according to gender in marriage is unjust.

Does the rising rate of adultery, divorce, and single-parent families indicate that the family is in decline? What assumptions about the family do we make when we say that these factors are evidence of family breakdown? Are such assumptions defensible? These questions are the topic of Chapter 6.

Is adultery justifiable? Why is faithfulness a virtue in marriage? Is it ever permissible for the parents of young children to divorce? Chapter 7 includes essays giving opposing answers to these questions.

Chapter 8 is about spousal violence, child abuse, and marital rape. Although few would defend any of these acts, essayists look at why some legislative bodies have been reluctant to make marital rape a crime and how the idea that the family is "private" has slowed attempts to intervene in cases of spousal violence and child abuse.

Chapters 9, 10, and 11 look at the several moral problems arising out of the relationship between children and their parents. Chapter 9 begins with the ethics of childbearing: Why have children at all? Are there any motives for having a child that are morally suspect? Is it ever unfair to have a child? This chapter then moves to the question of whether adults have a "natural right" to have children and, if so, whether it would be practical to "license" parents as a condition for having children.

Adults take liberty rights for granted, but most would deny that children have such basic liberties as the right to decide where to live, what to eat, whether or not to attend school, and what time to be in bed at night. This position is defended by some authors and opposed by others in Chapter 10.

Is there an ethics of raising children? Can we discover a moral principle that will guide parents in making childrearing decisions? Is it permissible for parents to raise children in such a way that they will be constrained to choose one sort of life rather than another when they become adults, or does this exertion of influence wrongly violate the future autonomy of the child? What kind of person should we teach our children to become—egoists or altruists? These are some of the questions raised in Chapter 11.

Chapter 12 concludes the anthology with three essays that discuss the ethical relationship between *adult* children and their elderly parents: Do adult children have an obligation to "honor and respect" their parents? What is the ground for this obligation? Are there any conditions under which parents do not deserve the honor and respect of their adult children?

Most of the material in this anthology has been presented and "field tested" in classes at California Polytechnic State University, San Luis Obispo. In return I have received many helpful criticisms. I would like to thank all of my students in these classes for agreeing to serve in this experiment in learning. They have helped me to launch a new and exciting subfield of ethics. I also wish to thank the reviewers: Professor Susan Armstrong, Humboldt State University; Professor Raymond Belliotti, SUNY Freedonia; Professor Julie Van Camp, California State University, Long Beach; and Professor Rosalind Ladd, Wheaton College.

1

What Is Family Ethics?

Introduction
Family Ethics and Applied Ethics
How Do We Do Applied Ethics?
Ethical Theory and the Family

When a teenage girl confided to police at a traffic stop that her father, who was driving the car, had a bag of cocaine hidden under the seat, it drew attention to some of the most difficult problems of ethics: Does family loyalty have any moral limits? Is it morally right to inform on a family member who has committed a crime? If we think that it is justifiable, and even praiseworthy, to inform on a stranger who has committed a crime, then why shouldn't we make a similar moral evaluation of this girl's behavior? Do we have different or more stringent obligations to family members than the obligations that we have to others?

Family ethics is the name for a group of ethical problems that arise when persons interact as members of families or when persons intend to join, create or dissolve families. Thus, the moral problem of physician-assisted suicide ("Is it ever morally permissible for a physician to assist someone in the attempt to end their life?") is *not* a problem of family ethics because it does not necessarily affect persons as actual or intending members of families. But the problem faced by the teenage girl in the preceding example does qualify as a problem of family ethics. The question "Is it justifiable to inform on my father?" posed a much more serious problem for her than it would have if the man driving the car had been a stranger, an acquaintance, or even a friend. And the question had this high degree of stringency precisely because this man is her father; they are members of the same family. Similarly, questions such as "Is adultery ever permissible?" only arise for persons who are

From *Kindred Matters: Rethinking the Philosophy of the Family* (1993), ed. Meyers, et al. Used by permission of Cornell University Press.

married—that is, for persons in the specific family relationship referred to as "marriage." And for the same reasons, all of the following questions would also qualify as problems of family ethics: Is monogamous marriage a justifiable form of human relationship? Is it permissible for parents of young children to divorce? Why is incest regarded as always morally wrong? Is a man ever justified in forcing his wife to have sexual intercourse? Are there any motives for having a child that are morally unacceptable? Should children have the right to be free from the control of their parents? What obligations do grown children have to their elderly parents? and so on. In each case, the moral problem is about persons interacting with other persons as members of the same family.

FAMILY ETHICS AND APPLIED ETHICS

Following a trend in the recent history of ethics, the questions of family ethics would be classified under the general heading of *applied ethics,* along with such other ethics disciplines as business ethics, medical ethics, and environmental ethics. Although the name is new, applied ethics is something that has been done by philosophers and by most thinking humans since we have been capable of formulating and deliberating about moral problems. "Doing applied ethics," as I define it here, means finding or attempting to find rational solutions to specific moral problems. Most of us would like to think that "rational thinking" is what we do when we are faced with an ethical question arising in everyday life. That is, we would like to think that at least some of our moral decisions are made on the basis of reasons that are relevant to and support the decision rather than on the basis of mere subjective "taste" or prejudice. If this is what is meant by "applied ethics," then most of us do applied ethics everyday.

However, in the past thirty years a distinction has been made by philosophers between applied ethics and ethical theory, giving rise to a different definition of applied ethics than the one just provided. *Ethical theory* is a discipline that attempts to ask such general questions as: What makes an action (any action) morally right or morally wrong? The answers to these questions are put in the form of highly general moral principles—for example, the *principle of utility* ("Act so as to promote the greatest good for the greatest number"), the *categorical imperative* ("Act so as to treat other persons, including oneself, always as an end, never merely as a means"), the *theory of natural law* ("Act so as to conform one's conduct to the natural inclinations of one's species"), or the *Divine Command theory* ("Act so as to conform one's conduct to the commands of God"). Applied ethics, then, is a dependent discipline that applies the principles developed out of theoretical ethics to the ethical problems that are specific to a determinate area of human activity, such as business, medicine, the environment, or the family. For example, using this approach in medical ethics, when it is asked whether it is morally right for a physician to perform a late-term abortion, the solution would be reached through a correct application of a relevant theoretical principle. If we believe that utility is the only thing that makes an action morally permissible or a duty, then questions about abortion are entirely resolved by application of the *utility* principle to particular cases of abortion; we have only to ask whether a particular abortion would promote the greatest good for the greatest number. On the other hand, if we have arrived at natural law as the foundation of morality, then the abortion question will be resolved quite differently, through an application of the appropriate natural law principle. In the case of abortion, this would be the principle that says that we must always act so as to preserve innocent human life (because it is understood that self-preservation is a natural inclination of the human species). It does not take much thought to understand why someone using this principle would come to a different conclusion about the morality of a late-term abortion than would a utilitarian.

It appears, then, that if we are going to do applied ethics, it would be important to resolve the main questions of theoretical ethics as a necessary first step. And only when this task is accomplished could we turn to the task of applying the general principles that result from our theorizing to specific topics. Hence, we would have as many applied ethical theories of the family (or medicine, business, law, the environment) as there are ethical theories: utilitarian family ethics, natural law family ethics, Kantian family ethics, and so on.

But a brief look at the essays collected in this volume indicates that most of our authors have declined to take this tedious route to the resolution of ethical problems concerning the family. Although the questions they raise about marriage and family relationships might eventually lead us to ask general or theoretical questions about the nature of the right and the good, it is important to see that most of our authors neither raise these (theoretical) questions nor give more than passing reference to fundamental ethical principles as a first step to finding an answer to the applied questions. In most cases, as these essays indicate, applied ethics can be and is satisfactorily done without answering the more general questions—indeed, without the reader ever knowing anything about theoretical ethics and the principles developed thereby.[1]

Let me explain how this simplified approach to the applied ethics of the family is accomplished.

HOW DO WE DO APPLIED ETHICS?

Suppose that you are a woman, thirty-two years old, an executive in a small computer software company. You have been married for five years, but your marriage has not been going well in the past year. Both you and your husband seem to be growing apart, developing separate interests, and moving within different circles of friends and acquaintances. The spark has grown out of your marriage. Neither of you seems to have the fun with each other that you once had when you first married. You are now seriously contemplating separation and even dissolution of the marriage. You have also met another man, a colleague with whom you work and see every day at the software firm. You have shared many of your personal problems with him over long lunch breaks and you and he have begun to develop a strong friendship. You know that with a bit of encouragement your friendship could develop into something much more.

At the same time, you have always thought of yourself as a good person. You want to do the morally right thing. You do not want to do the act that would satisfy only your own interests; you regard that as selfish and as somehow contrary to morality. You believe that you have some obligation to think about the effects of your actions on others. However, you are not quite sure what it would be morally right or wrong to do in the current circumstances. Would it be wrong to have an extramarital affair when your marriage is nearly at an end? Is it wrong to go ahead with a divorce if your husband refuses to consent?

Philosophers would point out that these questions presuppose another: How do we make a rational decision about an ethical question? Here is one decision procedure: First, if the question is an ethical one, then the act affects the interests of others besides ourselves. If the only person whose interests are affected by what we do is ourselves, then the question of whether we ought to do it is a *prudential,* not an *ethical* question. The question would not be: Is it morally right to do this act? but: Is it wise or prudent to do this? For example, suppose that you are about to go for a long Sunday drive by yourself in an area that lacks service stations, but you haven't calculated to determine whether you have enough fuel in the gas tank of your car. The question: Should I check my gas gauge and determine whether I have enough gas? is, under normal circumstances, a prudential, not an ethical, question because the consequences of not checking your gas gauge involve only yourself. The question is: Would it be prudent to check my fuel? not: Do I have a moral obligation to check my fuel? Of course, we can imagine circumstances under which the moral question would arise, but the circumstances would be those in which your act involves the interests of others—for example, you have passengers and they depend on you to get them home.

Second, if you have determined that the interests of others besides yourself are affected by what you do, then the next step is to determine *how* they are affected. If what we do does not harm another or others, does not cause anyone to be unjustly treated, or does not violate a special obligation to particular persons, then it would be odd for someone to question the morality of our behavior. For example, if I propose to take my child to the amusement park for the day, then the moral question "Ought you to do that?" would ordinarily not arise. If it did arise, then we would expect the person asking it to indicate that taking the child to the park might cause her or others some kind of harm (perhaps the amusement park has defective equipment). If our inquisitor admits that he not only sees no harm in taking the child to the park, but he thinks that this is beneficial, then we might ask him whether he implies by his question that my conduct is unjust (perhaps he means that there is another child equally deserving of this benefit). If he again denies that this is what he had in mind, then we might press ahead and ask him whether he believes that I am neglecting a special obligation to another person (for example, a promise that I have made to do something for someone else which I cannot fulfill if I take my child to the amusement park). If my inquisitor admits that none of these conditions obtains and continues to ask whether my conduct is morally permissible, then I can only conclude that he does not grasp the meaning of the words "morally permissible."

Moral problems arise when factual circumstances and a relevant rule of morality combine to suggest that our conduct might be *impermissible*. In the preceding case, a number of relevant moral rules were proposed: rules prohibiting harm to others, rules requiring just conduct, and rules requiring that we keep our promises. Moral rules generate rights and duties. For example, the rule that tells us to refrain from acts that cause harm to others creates a moral *duty* not to harm others and a reciprocal *right* not to be harmed. There are a number of different ways of classifying these rights and duties, but one classification I have found particularly helpful in thinking about the moral problems that arise in married and family life is the following[2]:

1. Duties of nonmaleficence
2. Duties of fidelity
3. Duties of gratitude
4. Duties of nondeception
5. Duties of personal relationships
6. Duties to respect autonomy
7. Duties of justice

The duties listed here are *prima facie*. This means that the duty is conditional in the sense that there may be other moral considerations that intervene. Hence, the fact that an act might violate one of these duties does not yet mean or imply that the act is morally wrong. On further investigation, we may discover that there are other circumstances justifying the conduct in question. For example, that I have a duty to keep my promises (a duty of fidelity) is always valid as a rule of *prima facie* duty. This means that I must keep my promise if no other moral considerations intervene; if I break my promise, then the burden is on me to show that these other considerations have intervened.

In what follows I will indicate in parentheses the names of some of the authors in this volume who mention the highlighted duty in the context of their discussion.

Duties of Nonmaleficence

Duties of nonmaleficence are the duties that every person has not to harm or to affect detrimentally the interests of others.[3] This is perhaps the largest category of moral duties because of the many different ways in which our conduct might cause harm to another person or persons. The first and most obvious way is conduct that causes or threatens to cause *physical harm*. Most cases of violence in the family are believed to be wrong or impermissible because they involve violations of moral rules prohibiting physical harm (Lee, hooks, Jackson, Archard). Second, there is conduct that causes or threatens to cause *emotional* or *psychological harm*. Some types of parental behavior (e.g., incest, divorce, giving birth to an impaired infant) are condemned on the grounds that they threaten this type of harm (Russell, Houlgate, Steinbock). Third, there is conduct that causes or threatens to cause *harm to a valuable institution;* for example, some authors refer in their arguments to conduct that harms the nuclear family (Plato, Wasserstrom). Fourth, there is conduct that harms or threatens to cause *harm to future persons;* for example, alcoholic mothers are believed to cause harm to infants that are not yet born, implying harm to future generations of human beings (Steinbock).

Duties of Fidelity

Duties of fidelity are obligations we incur because of a previous voluntary act of our own, such as making a promise. Unlike duties of nonmaleficence, I must have voluntarily performed some past act (e.g., making a marital promise to be faithful) if my present conduct (e.g., having sexual relations with a woman who is not my wife) is alleged to be morally wrong. The promise that we break may be one that we have expressly made or it may be implied by other things that we do. Violations of marriage vows are an obvious example of this type of conduct giving rise to moral problems in the family (Martin, Wasserstrom).

Duties of Gratitude

Duties of gratitude are duties that rest on previous acts of other persons, such as a favor done for me by another. Some philosophers (Locke, Narveson) have argued that it is from the general duty of gratitude that we are to derive the obligation of grown children to honor their parents.

Duties of Nondeception

Duties of nondeception are obligations we undertake not to knowingly deceive others. Acts of deception might also be classified as a kind of harm (deceptive acts invade our interest in knowing the truth), and they may also be classified as acts that restrict or deny others their autonomy (by lying to them we restrict their options for future action), but it is useful to make such acts into a separate and distinct category. Examples relevant to family ethics include parents who lie to their children (Jecker) and persons who deceive their spouse about their adulterous behavior (Wasserstrom).

Duties of Personal Relationships

Duties of personal relationships arise from the noncontractual relationships that we have with other persons. Some of these relationships are *voluntary*—that is, we are free to create them or to end them (for example, friendship). Other kinds of personal relationships are *nonvoluntary* since it is not through a voluntary act of our own that the relationship was created (for example, sibling relationships).

Some philosophers contend that there are moral rules that uniquely apply to conduct within the family (Schoeman). For example, parents have obligations to their own children that they do not have to other children, grown children have obligations to their elderly parents that they do not have to other elderly persons, and siblings have obligations to each other that they do not have to nonsiblings. Although the rules that create these obligations are *general* rules—that is, they apply generally to situations that share certain features in common (e.g., to all those who are parents of young children)—they still apply uniquely to situations that arise within the context of family relationships, not to other kinds of relationships (for example, the relationship between a lawyer and her client).

Second, duties of personal relationships include the *duty of beneficence*. The duty of beneficence is the duty to promote the welfare or good of others. Although some philosophers classify it as a duty separate and distinguishable from other duties, here it is treated as a subclassification of the duties of personal relationships. Although we may not be required to provide a justification for a failure to promote the good or welfare of a stranger, we would certainly be called upon to justify our failure to promote the good of our parent, child, or sibling. Indeed, the duty to promote the good of a family member is a paradigm case of what it means to have a duty of a personal relationship.

Duties to Respect Autonomy

We have a *prima facie* duty not to limit the freedom of others to perform self-regarding actions. An act is "self-regarding" if the (good or bad) consequences of the act concern or affect the interests of no one other than the actor. Moral problems arise when we restrict or deny freedom of self-regarding action to those who have the capacity for rational choice. In the history of the family, these problems arise when men restrict the self-regarding behavior of their wives (Firestone, Okin) and when parents restrict the behavior of their older children (Cohen, Brennan and Noggle).

Duties of Justice

It is sometimes the case that conduct within families is unjust. This may occur when a benefit or burden is distributed among family members, such as a father who "plays favorites," denying his adopted child benefits that he regularly gives to his biological children, or imposing burdens on her that he does not impose on them. Questions of justice may also arise when parents punish their children (Hoekema) and when social roles are distributed in families on the basis of gender rather than choice (Okin, Simmons, Engels).

I have said that moral problems arise when factual circumstances and a relevant moral rule combine to give rise to the question: Is it permissible to do that? For example, divorce, adultery, and corporal punishment of children are problems of family ethics because each type of conduct appears to violate one or more of the general duties listed here. It is the task of the moral philosopher to determine whether this is true and, if so, whether there might be other moral considerations justifying the conduct in question. For example, the fact that the divorce of parents of young children might cause the children to suffer emotional harm gives rise to the moral question: Is it permissible for them to divorce? Their conduct appears to violate both their duty of nonmaleficence and their duty of personal relationship to their children. Before we morally condemn such divorces, however, we need to know the answer to several other questions: What harm do unhappily married parents cause their children by remaining married? Is this harm avoidable? How can they mitigate or avoid the harm that they would cause by getting a divorce? Do parents have other *prima facie* moral duties that conflict with and outweigh their duty to their children?

There is no simple formula for answering these questions. The last question seems to be particularly vexing. What are we to do if the *prima facie* duties come into conflict in actual situations? Is there a ranking of the *prima facie* duties that would always tell us when one takes precedence over the others? None of the authors provides a general criterion by which to tell what considerations are *always* to be taken into account in determining what is morally right or wrong. This is not to say that no criterion or general principle can be formulated and defended; it is only to point out that the preceding set of rules of duty is an important one that most of the authors in this book appear to accept and use in the course of their argument. Morever, they use these rules without relying on or attempting to rank them or to derive them from a single basic principle or general ethical theory. If there is a common method of ethics to be found in this volume, it appears to be the one suggested by John Stuart Mill in the opening chapter of *Utilitarianism:* to provide the reader with "considerations capable of determining the intellect to give its assent" to the proposed solutions. A solution is correct if the considerations presented by the author suffices to persuade the reader, at least unless and until others can come up with reasons why the arguments provided should no longer compel assent.

[Beginning students of ethics may want to delay their reading of the following theoretical section until they finish some of the essays in Parts III and IV—ED.]

ETHICAL THEORY AND THE FAMILY

A common criticism of the preceding approach to family ethics is that it either cannot account for or positively distorts ethical relationships within families and other forms of interpersonal groupings. When moral conduct is assumed to be a matter of rule following, then all moral relationships appear to consist entirely of duties and rights defined by rules. "Is there a right to _____?" and "Do I have a duty to _____?" are assumed to be the only ways to frame an ethical question. As a result, our view of ethical issues arising in the family context and how to go about resolving them might be said to be unduly narrow and dogmatic.[4] For example, if I am attempting to decide whether I should donate one of my kidneys to my seriously ill sister, I am not trying to determine whether my sister has a right to one of my kidneys. Even if I should concede that she has no such right, I would still be left wondering whether I ought to proceed with the donation.

Similar conclusions about the inadequacy of traditional rule-based theories to account for the morality of interpersonal relationships have been reached in recent years by Ferdinand Schoeman,[5] Francis Schrag,[6] Lawrence Becker,[7] Carol Gilligan,[8] and Christina Hoff Sommers.[9] Schoeman contends that the problem can be traced to the fact that "moral and social philosophy have concentrated almost exclusively on abstract relationships among people, emphasizing either individual autonomy or general social well-being." However, in this process, "certain key

aspects of our moral experience—those aspects which deal with intimate relationships—have been virtually ignored"[10] Sommers goes further and insists that
contemporary philosophers have been *hostile* to the family.[11] Moral commitment
to specific individuals are usually analyzed in terms of promises, contracts, and
other voluntary agreements. She calls this "the volunteer theory of moral obligation" and argues that it is "generally fatal" to family morality. "For it looks upon
the network of felt obligation and expectation that binds family members as a sociological phenomenon that is without presumptive moral force."[12] The reason
that the volunteerist dogma is accepted by contemporary moral philosophers, she
writes, is "an uncritical use of the model of promises as the paradigm for obligations."[13] Sommers argues that there is no reason to opt for this paradigm. We
would reach strikingly different conclusions about family morality if we were to
expand our list of paradigms to include kinship and other family relationships.

What conclusions? In the following sections, I want to look at some possible
answers, showing why some might account for what Sommers calls "family
morality" and why others fail.

The Ethics of Rights

It seems clear that an important function of the idea of family is to support demands and claims. We say, for example, "You are a member of our family, therefore you should (may) do X," or "You are a member of our family, therefore, you
should (may) relate to Y in manner Z." The social relationship that the idea of
family points to provides the basis for special opportunities and privileges on one
hand and special responsibilities and duties on the other. Consider the following
example: You see a stranger being dropped off from a car with three heavy laundry bags. You know that the nearby laundromat is closed for renovation. You are
late for an appointment. Should you hurry across the street and inform the
stranger before the car drives off? It would seem to be the decent thing to do, but
it is not clear that this is something that you ought to do. Moreover, the stranger
certainly has no right to your making this special effort to inform her about the
closed laundromat. Now change the example. Suppose that the person who is
being dropped off is your mother. It seems much too weak to say that telling her
about the closed laundromat is the decent thing to do. I think that most of us
would insist that you *ought* to tell her, this is your duty and she has a right to this
extra effort from you, even though we would admit that an act such as this would
be supererogatory in a situation involving a stranger.

Another case. On a cold winter day you notice a derelict who has passed out
on the sidewalk. No one else is around. Should you try to help him? Of course,
there are degrees of help, from calling the police to staying with the man until they
arrive to bundling him into your car and taking him home. We might say that you
should at least make a phone call, but we would think it exceedingly generous of
you to take the derelict home. But now suppose that when you give the man a
closer look, you discover that he is your brother, driven to alcoholic excess by the
recent death of his wife and the loss of his job. I doubt that we would hesitate any
longer in our moral judgment. Of course you should take him home; this is your
duty. He is your brother, not a stranger. To leave him there, or even to limit your

help to a phone call would not be merely uncharitable. It would be wrong, a serious breach of moral obligation.

By an *ethics of rights* I mean a theory of morality that takes the notion of rights as a basic moral category. Such theories have a number of important features. First, the obligations that people have to do or refrain from doing certain actions is limited to those obligations that correspond to rights. For example, there is a (general) obligation not to interfere with the freedom of action of competent adult persons only because they have the right not to have their liberty interfered with by others.

Second, an ethics of rights divides morality into two parts, one *mandatory* (i.e., obligatory) and the other *elective* (i.e., superogatory). The part that is mandatory is sometimes referred to as *acts of justice* and the part that is elective is referred to as *acts of benevolence* or *charity*. This division is made because there are many acts that we think do not rest on anyone's rights but that should be part of one's conception of morality. To return to the example cited at the beginning of this section, if I notice the woman emerging from the car with the heavy bags of laundry, it is not her right that I cross the street to tell her the laundromat is closed for renovation. If, nonetheless, I do cross the street and tell her, then what has been done is something over and beyond the call of duty—it is an act of kindness and generosity.

The third feature of a rights-based ethics concerns the mandatory, nonelective part of morality, which is further divided into two parts: general rights and specific rights. *General rights* are those rights that everyone has equally, such as rights to life, liberty, and property. *Specific rights* are those possessed by particular persons. Some arise from the voluntary acts of others, such as from an explicit or implicit promise to do something in our behalf. Thus, I have a right to your care or solicitude only if you have explicitly or tacitly promised to show me this care and solicitude. Other kinds of specific rights arise from the nonvoluntary acts of another; for example, John accidentally spills coffee on a book that he borrowed from Joan. Joan now has a specific right (of reparation) to receive a new book or the money to buy a new book from John.

There are other features of an ethics of rights—for example, that rights impose certain moral requirements on third parties—but the features just listed suffice to show that an ethics of rights is obviously defective as an account of ethical relationships within the family or (indeed) within any sort of personal relationship such as that between friends or between members of the same community. First, it is clear that informing my mother about the closed laundromat is not an act of charity for which I should be praised. As noted, I have an obligation to cross the street and inform her about the closed laundromat. It is the sort of act that is expected of a son and thus it would not ordinarily be referred to as an act of kindness. But to explain why it is that I have an obligation to inform my mother about the closed laundromat or why I have an obligation to take care of my sick brother, the ethics of rights would have us say that this obligation derives either from a general right or a specific right.

My obligation derives from a general right only in the sense that all similarly situated mothers have a right to the help of their children. And yet, although my mother has this right against me, a stranger does not. The right to benevolence attaches only to persons in interpersonal relationships; that is, it seems to be some sort of specific right. But if it is a specific right, then (according to the ethics of rights) this right could derive only from a (tacit or explicit) promise that I have made or it is the consequence of my own past behavior. But the obligation to give aid to our parents or siblings is not (usually) something that any of us have ever voluntarily assumed. I may recognize an obligation to give aid to my sick brother even though I have never said or implied anything in word or deed that could be construed as a promise to give him (or any other family relation) my aid. Nor can my obligation to my brother be traced to something I have done to him (or he has done for me) in the past that gives him the right to my aid. I do not give aid to my brother because I see this as an act of gratitude, or as a way of repairing damage that I have caused by a previous act of mine, but (simply) because *he is my brother.*

The Ethics of Sentiment

A deeper criticism of the ethics of rights is that the concept of rights and the related notion of justice are inappropriate ways of characterizing the family and other types of personal relationships. David Hume was one of the first to advance this argument. Hume conceived the family as nearly a "complete instance of . . . enlarged affections" among persons,

> . . . and the stronger the mutual benevolence is among the individuals, the nearer it approaches; till all distinction of property be, in a great measure, lost and confounded among them. Between married persons, the cement of friendship is by the laws supposed so strong as to abolish all division of possessions; and has often, in reality, the force ascribed to it.[14]

Similar observations about "mutual benevolence" in the family have been made by several contemporary philosophers. Thus, Michael Sandel argues that an appeal is made to rights only in those situations in which "there is sufficient discord to make the accommodation of conflicting interests and aims the overriding moral and political consideration."[15] But if discord and conflict is rarely in evidence, as in an ideal family, then we remove the conditions that are the prerequisite for an appeal to rights. In such families, "relations are governed in large part by spontaneous affection and . . . in consequence, the circumstances of justice prevail to a relatively small degree."[16]

> Individual rights and fair decision procedures are seldom invoked, not because injustice is rampant but because their appeal is preempted by a spirit of generosity in which I am rarely inclined to claim my fair share. Nor does this generosity necessarily imply that I receive out of kindness a share that is equal to or greater than the share I would be entitled to under fair principles of justice. I may get less. The point is not that I get what I would otherwise get, only more spontaneously, but simply that the questions of what I get and what I am due do not loom large in the overall context of this way of life.[17]

Sandel's point is that the family cannot be characterized by an ethics of justice and rights because the family is an intimate group, held together by love and identity of interests. It is not a "political association" in which interests differ and goods to be distributed are scarce.

The problem with this argument is that not all families meet this ideal. Sandel and Hume rely upon "an idealized, even mythical, account of the family."[18] Families are not always harmonious social groups, and when interests diverge demands may be made by individuals within the family for the observance of their rights. Moreover, even within families that outwardly appear to be harmonious, we need to know whether the circumstances of justice prevail in order to assess them morally. For example, "even if wives never had occasion to ask for their just share of the family property, due to the generosity and spontaneous affection of their husbands, we would be unable to assess the families in which they lived from a moral point of view unless we knew whether, if they did ask for it, they would be considered entitled to it."[19]

Finally, the theory of rights does not imply that the primary motive for one family member's provision of care and loving attention to another is a desire to perform a duty or to recognize the rights of another. It is agreed that such motives are inimical to the natural affection and sympathy that family members feel for each other. If my only motive for feeding my young child is a desire to do my duty, then something psychologically essential is missing from our relationship. But the theory of rights is not about the motivation of conduct. It does not say that we should always act from the inducement of respecting the rights of others. Indeed, it does not assert that we should act from any particular motive. To quote John Stuart Mill from another context, to assert otherwise "is to mistake the very meaning of a standard of morals and confound the rule of action with the motive of it."[20] The rights theorist recognizes that most conduct within the family is done from motives other than a feeling of duty, such as benevolence, care, and sympathy, "and rightly so done if the rule of duty does not condemn them." According to the ethics of rights, the *rule of duty* is the obligation not to violate the rights of others. Hence, it is certainly possible for a man, motivated by a sympathetic concern for his wife, to lie to her, to break a promise, or to deny her certain liberties. In such cases it is not only appropriate, it is essential to indicate that it is the violation of his wife's *rights,* not his benevolent motive, that provides the ground for our assessment of the morality of his conduct.

Some ethical issues in the family can be framed in the language of rights—for example, my child has a right against me that I provide him with food and shelter, my wife has a right to an equal share of the family property. What is wrong with the ethics of rights is not that it mistakenly assumes that the category of rights can be used to characterize some ethical issues that arise in the family, but that it makes the false assumption that *all* moral obligations, including those that arise in the family, are based on specific rights arising either from voluntary agreements or other kinds of previous acts of others. However, as argued in the previous section, many family obligations are not grounded in specific rights.

The Ethics of Giving and Receiving

The ethical or logical consequences of membership in a family include the *prima facie* privilege of being a recipient of acts of benevolence performed by other members of the family to which one belongs and the duty to perform acts of benevolence when other family members are in need. These acts of benevolence are mandatory since not to help a family member is wrong and contemptible. Moreover, the mere existence of need gives a family member the right to ask and to expect to be helped by other members of his family as something that is his due. This is a privilege of membership in a family.

To what ethical theory can we turn to explain the latter fact? What makes it morally obligatory to help a member of my family who is in need of help in situations in which it would not be obligatory to help a stranger? Why is it that what would ordinarily be pure acts of benevolence, or imperfect duties when one is dealing with strangers, become perfect duties toward other members of the family to which one belongs?

One answer to these questions has been provided by John Ladd, who proposes an "ethics of giving and receiving." The ethics of giving and receiving is an ethics that provides "a moral principle that bases the rightness of giving and receiving, of helping and being helped, on *other kinds* of relationships than those representing rights or entitlements."[21] The principle says:

A ought to do X for B because A is related to B (ArB) and B needs X.

For example, a father ought to feed his infant because it is his infant and the infant needs to be fed. If it is raining, my neighbor is not at home, and her front door has blown open, letting in the rain, then I ought to shut the door because she is my neighbor and she needs (would want) the door shut.

Ladd calls this the "principle of giving and receiving," hereafter referred to as GR. Ladd argues that it differs in two important ways from the principle concerned with the ethics of rights. First, GR is *not universalizable*. It holds only between specific persons who are already related to each other in a specific way, as members of families, villages, neighborhoods, communities. In other words, GR is personal; it binds particular persons to particular persons rather than persons to persons generally. A father is morally required to care for and nurture *his* child but not other people's children. Second, although in many cases in which we would invoke GR as a source of our duty to give help to another, the duty is *peremptory* (i.e., it can be demanded as a right), in some cases this is not true. For example, my neighbor cannot assert a right that I shut her front door, although I would not hesitate to say that this is an act that I ought to do. Third, Ladd holds that his principle is *deontological,* meaning only that it does not reduce ethical requirements and relationships to dispositions or tendencies to promote value or ends. Nor is it derived from a right inherent in the person toward whom one has the obligation. It is found *only* in the relationship.

It follows that there is such a thing as filial duty per se (e.g., the special duty of a child to his mother), and generally there is a morality of special family or kinship relations and, presumably, a morality of communal relationships generally (e.g., of neighbors, members of the same village, scholars). And this, according to Ladd, Sommers and other philosophers, conforms to what most people think:

> For most people think that we do owe special debts to our parents even though we have not voluntarily assumed our obligations to them. Most people think that what we owe to our own children does not have its origin in any voluntary undertaking, explicit or implicit, that we have made to them, or to society at large,

to care for them. And, "preanalytically," many people believe that we owe special consideration to our siblings even at times when we may not *feel* very friendly to them.[22]

I hasten to add that the preceding observation is certainly not new. Moreover, it is quite wrong to contend (as Sommers does) that traditional ethical theory has ignored interpersonal relations. John Stuart Mill explicitly points to interpersonal relations as furnishing proof that showing favor and preference toward others is more often something that we believe we ought to do than something that would be regarded as unjust: "A person would be more likely to be blamed than applauded for giving his family or friends no superiority in good offices over strangers when he could do so without violating any other duty."[23] W. D. Ross argued in 1930 that a morally significant relation in which other people may stand to me is that of "wife to husband, of child to parent, of friend to friend, of fellow countryman to fellow countryman, and the like; and each of these relations is the foundation of a *prima facie* duty, which is more or less incumbent on me according to the circumstances of the case."[24] A. C. Ewing echoed these sentiments when he wrote that "it is very much of a paradox to say that a man is no more under a special obligation to . . . his own parents, children, or wife than to a total stranger . . . It is felt that people should . . . be regarded . . . as being in special individual relations to the agent."[25]

But is this "common belief" best explained in terms of Ladd's ethical principle? We need to clarify the notion of "is related to" in GR. How are we to tell when one person, A, "is related to" another person, B, and when A is *not* related to B? Ladd does not tell us. But it is certainly not sufficient to leave this decision up to intuition. Intuition might inform me that we are *all* related to one another in a certain significant way, in that all human beings constitute a community, bound by social feelings. Indeed, as Mill has eloquently argued, the social feelings of humankind—analyzed as "the desire to be in unity with our fellow creatures"—is a powerful psychological principle in human nature. Not all of us have these feelings, but a preponderant majority of us *must* have them if society between human beings is to exist at all.

> Not only does all strengthening of social ties, and all healthy growth of society, give to each individual a stronger personal interest in practically consulting the welfare of others, it also leads him to identify his *feelings* more and more with their good, or at least with an even greater degree of practical consideration for it. He comes, as though instinctively, to be conscious of himself as a being who *of course* pays regard to others. The good of others becomes to him a thing naturally and necessarily to be attended to, like any of the physical conditions of our existence.[26]

And yet, according to Ladd, persons who are merely members of the same society are *not* covered by the principle of giving and receiving, "for in the present context it is meant to hold only between particular persons who are already related to each other in a specific way." For example, Ladd has noted that "barring special circumstances such as a contractual agreement, a mother is morally required to feed her own baby, but not other people's babies; if she feeds other babies, she will be performing an act of supererogation."[27] What is it that makes the former situation an instantiation of GR and the latter not? What makes them dissimilar? Unfortunately, Ladd gives no clue other than the remark that the mother and her baby are "already related to each other in a specific way." But can't it be argued that the mother is also related to *other* babies in a specific way? If she comes upon an infant in great distress and she is available to help, then, all else being equal, she *does* have some obligation to help. She may say to herself: "It's none of my business—I don't know why this infant is here in this place, alone and crying; I might even aggravate its discomfort; there might be trouble later for me or for my family if I intervene; besides I'm late for my appointment; anyway, why should *I* be the one to stop? Maybe one of its parents is close by or someone else has already gone for help." As Herbert Fingarette argues, such an inner debate would be pointless if it were not for a *tacit initial assumption* that, all else being equal, we have an obligation to help a needy child who is in great distress if we are the one who is available to help.[28] In fact, she wouldn't run through all the *contrary* obligations and inconveniences in order to justify *not* helping the infant unless she tacitly assumes an obligation to help. Moreover, helping the infant-stranger is *not* something that she would regard as superogatory, an act of praiseworthy generosity on her part.

As noted, Ladd intends the principle of giving and receiving to have a limited scope—that is, he does not want it to apply to "relationships" between strangers, to society as a whole. But given the preceding considerations, it is difficult to see how the principle can be restricted. My argument has been that in an important sense we are *all* related to each other in a specific way. The very idea of being a "responsible person" seems to suggest that at a minimum a society of responsible persons will be related to one another through mutual trust, care, and respect.

In saying this, I do not wish to deny that there is a moral difference between the relationship in which we stand to strangers and the relationship in which we stand to family and friends. All other things being equal, it does make a difference that the person who is in need is a member of my family, and in many cases the help that I give to a stranger who is in need of help can be called a supererogatory act, an act of generosity. What I *do* wish to deny is that the special obligation I owe to members of my family can be derived from a general principle (GR) that says that I have an obligation to help them because I am related to them and they are in need of my help. The notion of "is related to" is much too broad to do the work that Ladd wants it to do.

The Principles of Family Beneficence

The source of the difficulty with Ladd's principle of giving and receiving is that it attempts to find a common feature or characteristic of all of those types of intimate or interpersonal relationships in which we recognize an obligation to help other persons in those same relationships. But why should we assume that there is a common feature? Couldn't it be the case that each relationship is distinct, having no more in common with one another than that each is the basis of a perfect duty of benevolence?

Let us try a narrower ethical principle, one that restricts itself to a particular kind of family relationship:

A ought to do X for B because B is a child, A is the parent of B (ApB), and B needs X.

I shall call this the *principle of parental beneficence,* or PB. There are several other principles, similar to PB, each of them prescribing for a particular kind of family relationship. Consider, for example, the *principle of filial beneficence* or FB:

A ought to do X for B because A is the grown child of B (AgB) and B needs X.

Or again, the *principle of sibling beneficence,* or SB:

A ought to do X for B because A is the sibling of B (AsB), and B needs X.

Let us refer to PB, FB, and SB collectively as the *principles of family beneficence.* These principles say that the mere fact that persons are in a particular kind of family relationship gives rise to the obligation to help a member of the same family if he or she is in need. PB, FB, and SB each have a more limited scope than GR; for in the present context they are meant to hold only between particular persons who are related to each other in a specific way (e.g., as parent and child) rather than being related to each other in some generic way. Second, contrary to Ladd's remarks about GR, PB, FB and SB are universalizable in the sense that they bind particular *kinds* of persons to other particular *kinds* of persons, e.g. parents to children, siblings to siblings.[29] Third, the duties are usually acts that can be demanded by the needy family member as a right, although at the same time, unlike acts of supererogation, the performance of these duties is not "imperfect," that is, a matter of choice. For example, the help that I give to my elderly father, although something he might expect from me as "his right," is an essential part of the parent-child relationship. I cannot choose not to help my father and assume that our relationship will remain the same.

Ross, Ladd, and Sommers argue for a deontological account of family morality and its principles of family beneficence. This means that the obligation of one family member to give help to another needy member (e.g., to care for that person's child) is *underivative* (i.e., it is not a conclusion derived from the goodness of this act) and that the truth of these principles is somehow self-evident. Thus, it is the duty of parents to care for their children not because, other things being equal, the life of society is somehow *better* because parents care for their children, but just because of the parent-child relationship. Ross in particular appears to claim that the obligation to help members of our family is read off directly, and with self-evident necessity, from the set of apparently neutral facts about the biological relationship.

I side with Brand Blanshard and other critics of Ross in observing that this conclusion does not seem credible.[30] It implies that if the practice of parents caring for their biological children should turn out to produce consequences that are demonstrably *worse* than an alternative practice of childrearing, it would still be a person's moral obligation to care for his or her biological children. Second, if the principles of family beneficence were self-evident, then it would be meaningless to ask *why* we have duties of benevolence toward members of our families. Suppose that giving help to a member of my family would bring a great deal of pain to others; for example, my brother, recently charged with embezzlement, wants me to help him obtain a highly skilled but expensive defense attorney. I am sure that my brother is guilty of the crime and I am even more certain that if he should be exonerated, he will commit even more serious crimes in the future, causing a great deal of misery to others. If I were reluctant to do something that might contribute to this misery, I might ask: Why should I take it as obligatory to perform an act (helping a member of my family who needs my help) that produces such pain? This is certainly a reasonable question, but it is a question that cannot be asked if a principle of family beneficence were self-evident. I take it that this is a logically unacceptable result.

Utilitarianism and Family Beneficence

In his essay *Utilitarianism,* John Stuart Mill presents the utilitarian theory of ethics in three parts. First, he postulates that happiness is the "ultimate end of human existence, with reference to and for the sake of which all other things are desirable (whether we are considering our own good or that of other people)." Second, happiness is defined as "an existence exempt as far as possible from pain, and as rich as possible in enjoyments." Third, our fundamental moral obligation is to bring about the greatest amount of happiness for all those who will be affected.

> [Happiness] being, according to the utilitarian opinion, the end of human action, is necessarily also the standard of morality, which may accordingly be defined, as the rules and precepts for human conduct, by the observance of which an existence such as has been described might be, to the greatest extent possible, secured to all mankind, and not to them only, but, so far as the nature of things admits, to the whole of sentient creation.

Most of those who have thought about ethical relationships within the family reject a utilitarian approach because it appears to "simplify unduly our relations to our fellows."[31] Ross argues that the essential defect of the utilitarian theory is that "it ignores, or at least does not do full justice to, the highly personal character of duty. If the only duty is to produce the maximum of good, the question who is to have the good—whether it is myself, or my benefactor, or a person to whom I have made a promise to confer that good on him, or a mere fellow man to whom I stand in no such special relation—should make no difference to my having a duty to produce that good. But we are all in fact sure that it makes a vast difference."[32]

Ross appears to direct his criticism at a primitive version of utilitarianism that would have us directly appeal to the principle of utility whenever we make a moral decision. He ignores the fact that utilitarians can easily accommodate the common-sense appeal to rules in moral decision making. Some of Mill's strongest words in *Utilitarianism* were reserved for those who assume that "the acknowledgement of a first principle is inconsistent with the admission of secondary ones."[33] To adopt utility or any other principle as the fundamental principle of morality requires subordinate principles to apply it by. This is no less true with the principles of family beneficence. Secondary or subordinate principles such as "Parents ought to nurture and educate their offspring," "We have duties of benevolence toward our siblings," and "Children have the duty to care for their elderly parents" are common to all moral systems. Moreover, the fact that no moral system can do without them is no argument against the system. That would be like contending that when I inform a traveler about her ultimate destination, I cannot at the same time inform her of signposts and landmarks on the way. "The proposition that happiness is the end and aim of morality does not mean that no road ought to be laid down to that goal."[34]

I believe that Mill would argue that one of these roads is indicated by the subordinate principles of family beneficence. To paraphrase Mill, we do not have to assume experience has taught us nothing about the tendencies of our actions. At this point in human history we have surely acquired a great deal of information about the effects of certain types of conduct on human happiness, including those acts and omissions that affect or concern members of our families. Thus, at the moment when one of us feels tempted to neglect our child or refuse the legitimate needs of a sibling or an elderly parent, it would be absurd to suggest that this is the first time we would be considering whether this would be injurious to the social good. We know this from past experience, and the summary of this experience comes down to us in the form of moral rules, rules that tell us that we must care for and nurture our children, that we must respond to the legitimate needs of our siblings, and that we have an obligation to help our elderly parents when they become too frail to care for themselves.

Let me return now to Ross's objection to the utilitarian analysis of family morality. Ross contends that there may be cases in which a utilitarian calculation could not distinguish morally between the act of giving aid to a family member and the act of helping a stranger. But this is absurd (Ross contends) because, as we all know, if we are faced with a choice between giving help to a stranger and giving help to a member of our family, all things being equal, we ought to give help to the family member, even if the utility score turns out to be equal. Therefore, according to Ross, Sommers, and other critics of utilitarianism, something other than consequences is relevant to determining rightness of conduct.

As I interpret Mill's words in *Utilitarianism,* the principles of family beneficence are mere "rules of thumb" that we use only to avoid the necessity of estimating the probable consequences of our actions at every step.[35] We are to guide our conduct by appeal to these and other moral rules, not because there is anything sacrosanct in the rules themselves but because moral decisions are frequently to be made in a hurry and we do not have time to do the required utility calculations. This means that in a situation in which I am caught in a conflict between giving help to my child and giving help to a stranger, I should give help to my child because the rule SB tells me that it is probable that this act is optimific (that is, it is the act that produces the greatest net utility).

I doubt that this argument will satisfy the critic of utilitarianism. Again, suppose that it is *not* true in the particular case that giving help to my child is optimific and that, in this instance, breaking the rule SB will have better results than keeping it. Then I must violate the rule SB and the original criticism advanced against the utilitarian stands. The only response that the utilitarian could have is that once we carefully examine the particular case, its counterintuitive aspect will tend to disappear. Consider the following example as illustrating one type of situation in which a person might go against one of the principles of family beneficence. My twenty-year-old son is a marginal student at the university. His grades have been poor largely because he devotes little time to study, preferring instead to fully indulge in the social side of university life. He asks me for money to pay for his next semester's tuition. I have just enough funds in my savings account to satisfy his request, but I decide that it would be better to give the money to a desperately poor but brilliant young woman who also needs financial aid. It may be argued that it is wrong to give the money to the young woman, but there are good grounds for contending that this ethical judgment may be irrational. First, it will do more good to give the money to the young woman than to my son. Second, this act will have little effect on the general inclination of other people to give aid to needy family members. Once the circumstances are understood, I suspect that many would agree with my decision. At the same time, they would take note that this *is* a special case. Thus, I doubt that my act of refusing to help my carefree son would lead to a general breakdown of the practice of giving help to family members who have genuine and pressing needs. Third, although I might feel some guilt at failing to satisfy my son's request, I may in fact impress on him the importance which I attach to his making a serious effort to succeed academically. This may, in turn, lead him to try harder next year.

The general conclusion the utilitarian wishes to impress on us is that in every case in which it is known that the keeping of the principle of family beneficence (or any other of the moral rules that apply to family relationships) has been in general optimific but such that in the special case at hand the optimific behavior is to violate the particular principle, then in these circumstances we should violate it. Moreover, once we examine the circumstances that dictate that we violate that principle, what we had at first thought to be counterintuitive will be found, after careful consideration, to conform to common sense.[36]

QUESTIONS FOR THOUGHT
AND DISCUSSION

1. What is family ethics? What are some examples of ethics questions that would be classified as questions of family ethics? What are some examples of ethics questions that would not be classified as questions of family ethics?
2. What is applied ethics? What is the distinction between applied and theoretical ethics?
3. Why do some scholars believe that in order to answer applied ethics questions we must first resolve some of the main questions of theoretical ethics?
4. How do we determine whether a question is an ethical question or a prudential question? What are some examples of both of these kinds of questions?

5. What are the rules of morality the violation of which suggests that a particular act might be morally wrong? What are some examples of such violations within the context of marital and family relationships?

6. Why have traditional ethical theories had difficulty dealing with the rights and duties of family membership? Explain, with particular reference to both utilitarian and nonutilitarian ethical theories.

7. Can utilitarian theories explain and accommodate the special duties of family membership?

8. Is the impartial nature of the utilitarian principle consistent with the general belief that it would not be unjust to give favor or preference to members of one's own family (for example, when deciding who to feed, clothe or shelter)? Explain.

FURTHER READING

John Hardwig, "In Search of an Ethics of Personal Relationships." In H. LaFollette and G. Graham, eds., *Person to Person*. Philadelphia: Temple University Press, 1989.

Nancy S. Jecker, "Impartiality and Special Relations." In D. T. Meyers, C. Murphy, and K. Kipnis, eds., *Kindred Matters: Rethinking the Philosophy of the Family*. Lewiston, NY: Edwin Mellen Press, 1993.

John Ladd, "The Idea of Community." *New England Journal* (American Institute of Planners, New England), 1972, vol. 1.

James Rachels, "Morality, Parents and Children." In H. LaFollette and G. Graham, eds., *Person to Person*. Philadelphia: Temple University Press, 1989.

Ferdinand Schoeman, "Rights of Children, Rights of Parents, and the Moral Basis of the Family." *Ethics* 91 (1980). [This paper is reprinted in this volume as Chapter 10.]

Christina Hoff Sommers, "Philosophers Against the Family." In H. LaFollette and G. Graham, eds., *Person to Person*. Philadelphia: Temple University Press, 1989.

NOTES

1. This is not an uncommon approach in the history of ethics. For example, when answering the objection that "there is not time" to do all the calculations necessitated by the utilitarian principle, John Stuart Mill answers that the calculations have already been done. The results of these calculations are embodied in our everyday moral rules. Mill recognizes and even recommends that we resolve our moral problems not by direct application of the utilitarian principle, but by using these moral rules. See later in this chapter for a theoretical defense of this approach to the ethics of the family.

2. The classification is a variation of that suggested by W. D. Ross, *The Right and the Good* (London: Oxford University Press, 1930), 21.

3. Duties to do good or to promote the welfare of others (duties of beneficence) are treated as a sub-class of category (5) duties of personal relationships, below.

4. Cf. John Ladd, "Is 'Corporate Responsibility' a Coherent Notion?" In W. M. Hoffman, ed., *Proceedings of the Second National Conference on Business Ethics* (Washington, DC: University Press of America, 1979), 4.

5. Ferdinand Schoeman, "Rights of Children, Rights of Parents, and the Moral Basis of the Family," *Ethics* 91 (1980). [This essay is reprinted in this volume in Chapter 10.]

6. Francis Schrag, "Children: Their Rights and Needs." In W. Aiken and H. LaFollette, eds. *Whose Child?* (New Jersey: Rowman and Littlefield, 1980).

7. Lawrence Becker, *Reciprocity* (London: Allen and Unwin, 1984).

8. Carol Gilligan, *In a Different Voice: Psychological Theory and Women's Development* (Cambridge, MA: Harvard University Press, 1982).

9. Christina Hoff Sommers, "Filial Morality," *The Journal of Philosophy* (1986): 439–456.

10. Schoeman, Chapter 10, 439.

11. Christina Hoff Sommers, "Philosophers Against the Family." In H. LaFollette and G. Graham, eds., *Person to Person* (Philadelphia: Temple University Press, 1989), 83.

12. Ibid., 96.

13. Ibid., 97.

14. David Hume, *A Treatise of Human Nature,* ed. L. Selby-Bigge. (Oxford: Oxford University Press, 1978), 17–18. [First published in 1777.]

15. Michael Sandel, *Liberalism and the Limits of Justice* (Cambridge: Cambridge University Press, 1982), 31.

16. Ibid., p. 33.

17. Ibid.

18. Susan Moller Okin, *Justice, Gender, and the Family* (New York: Basic Books, 1989), 29.

19. Ibid., 30–31.

20. John Stuart Mill, *Utilitarianism* (London: 1861), chap. 2.

21. John Ladd, "Legalism and Medical Ethics." In J. Davis, B. Hoffmaster, S. Shorten, eds., *Contemporary Issues in Biomedical Ethics* (New Jersey: The Humana Press, 1978), 22.

22. Sommers, "Philosophers Against the Family," 92.

23. Mill, *Utilitarianism,* chap. 5.

24. W. D. Ross, *The Right and the Good* (London: Oxford University Press, 1930), 19.

25. A. C. Ewing, *Ethics* (New York: Free Press, 1953), 70–71.

26. Mill, *Utilitarianism,* chap. 3.

27. John Ladd, "The Idea of Community," *New England Journal* (American Institute of Planners, New England, 1972), vol. 1, 24.

28. Herbert Fingarette, *On Responsibility* (New York: Basic Books, 1967), 146.

29. However, they are not universalizable in the sense that they do not bind persons to persons generally. That is, if the rule applies, one must be a parent, child, or sibling.

30. Brand Blandshard, *Reason and Goodness* (London: Allen and Unwin, 1961).

31. Ross, *The Right and the Good,* 19.

32. Ibid., 20.

33. Mill, *Utilitarianism,* chap. 2.

34. Ibid.

35. This account of the role of rules in ethical decision making is called act utilitarianism or extreme utilitarianism. See J. C. C. Smart, "Extreme and Restricted Utilitarianism," *The Philosophical Quarterly* 6 (1956): 344.

36. Parts of the preceding section of this chapter are reprinted from "Ethical Theory and the Family," by Laurence D. Houlgate in *Kindred Matters: Rethinking the Philosophy of the Family,* edited by D. Meyers, K. Kipnis and C. Murphy (Ithaca, NY: Cornell, 1993), pp. 59–73. Used by permission of Cornell University Press.

I

Preliminary Issues

2

The Nature and History
of the Family

T he authors in this and the next chapter ask three questions about the family that must be answered as an essential preliminary to the study of family ethics. Each question arises from a unique perspective on the family: definitional, historical, and multicultural. The first question is about the nature of the family: How should the word "family" be defined? Second, the historian wants to know about the changes, if any, in the family across generations: How do the ethical relationships between family members in contemporary culture compare to those in earlier times? And the student of comparative cultures is interested in the differences between family relationships across cultural groups: How do family relationships vary between Western and non-Western cultures and even within groups that are part of Western culture?

THE NATURE OF THE FAMILY

In 1980, the White House Conference on Families almost did not take place because representatives of the various constituencies attending the conference could not agree about the meaning of the word "family." Early in the planning stages, the name of the conference had been changed from "The White House Conference on the American Family" to "The White House Conference on Families" because a planning group had urged acceptance of a "neutral" model of the family rather

than the traditional biparental model suggested by the word "American."[1] They
did this largely because then President Jimmy Carter insisted that "this Conference
will clearly recognize the pluralism of family life in America." The president was
referring to the fact that in the late 1970s the so-called "traditional" American family of working father, homemaker mother, and two minor children accounted for
only 7 percent of husband-wife families. And yet, by the time that the conference
took place three years after Carter's remarks, the family traditionalists had tri-
umphed. "Recognizing the pluralism of family life antagonizes those to whom that
pluralism is anathema."[2] Hence, when the conference leadership slots were filled,
the only recognition given to pluralism was the inclusion of one widow (Coretta
Scott King) on the conference board of directors.

Almost from the moment the conference on families was conceived, trouble
was unavoidable "because diversity of family styles and traditionalism in family
style peacefully coexist only so long as neither one gains actual or symbolic advantage over the other."[3] It was the traditionalist's fear that diverse family forms
would be recognized through an endorsement of a broad definition of the word
"family" that almost sank the conference.

In the first reading in this chapter, sociologist William Goode stresses the need
to define the object of a study before one begins to do an empirical study. However, as he implies, the various attempts of the White House conference participants to give a "concrete" definition of family were doomed to fail. He means
that if we insist on a particular set of necessary and sufficient conditions, then we
will exclude many social groups that are commonly referred to as families. Thus,
if the presence of father, mother, and children are specified as necessary conditions
of family, then a widow or widower with children living at home would not constitute a family. On the other hand, if we use a set of characteristics typical of the
traditional family as our starting point and we eliminate each characteristic one by
one, then at some point in the process of elimination we will hesitate or even
refuse to refer to the social group as a family (for example, a person living alone
or two roommates living in a college dormitory for several months, rarely interacting with each other). There seems to be no clear dividing line between families and nonfamilies. Instead, Goode suggests that many social groups can be
thought of as "more or less" families, "as they are more or less similar to the traditional type of family."

Ruth Macklin expands on Goode's study by asking us to distinguish between
the *biological, legal, customary,* and *subjective intentional* determinants of the meaning
of the term "family." Macklin argues that the context may determine on any given
occasion how the word "family" is being used. Thus, a genealogist doing single-
name family history research, or a geneticist attempting to trace the progress of a
genetically inherited disease, will use the word "family" to refer to groups of
people who are genetically or biologically related to one another. Macklin's point
in making these distinctions is that when we pay attention to context we learn that
many different factors determine the conditions of membership in a family. This
observation might serve to explain why attempts to find what Goode refers to as
a "concrete definition" of the concept of family are "doomed to fail."

THE WESTERN FAMILY: 1500–1800

John Demos's description of family life in the seventeenth-century colony of Plymouth, Massachusetts indicates that if there were any difference between the households we live in during this century and the households of our ancestors, it is in the rich variety and the complexity of the extended households, not in a relative lack of households containing nuclear families. Demos also argues that the family no longer has the social importance it had in the early American colonies. There was a long period of time prior to the Industrial Revolution in which the family functioned within the community as a business, school, vocational institute, church, house of correction, and welfare institution. Since most of these functions have transferred out of the family to special public institutions, the importance of the family in contemporary times becomes personal and psychological, not social. That is, the family becomes important to the people who comprise it instead of its importance being tied to its peculiar functions within the larger society. In this respect, Demos's conclusions about the "advantages" of the family to its individual members should be compared to the remarks of William Goode.

In the next essay, Beatrice Gottlieb argues that there were hints of the emergence of the idea of the "affectionate" family prior to the eighteenth century, although "ideas about family roles were constantly being expressed." She means that emotional responses (fulfillment and delight, disappointment and rage) and the corresponding moral judgments of praise and blame were largely based on the extent to which a family member played his or her "role" of father, mother, brother, sister, wife, and so on. Gottlieb uses dramatic literature (especially the plays of Shakespeare) and several other sources to establish her conclusion that in the period 1500–1800, "to be a brother, a wife, or a son was to accept a role with set duties and a predetermined place in the family structure." There are few examples in this period of the post-1800 notion of family members who dynamically interact with each other as individual personalities.

Defining the Family: A Matter of More or Less

William J. Goode

William J. Goode is professor of sociology at Stanford University. He is the author of many books and essays on the family.

Since thousands of publications have presented research findings on the family, one might suppose that there must be agreement on what this social unit is. In fact, sociologists and anthropologists have argued for decades about how to de-

From William J. Goode, *The Family,* 2nd ed. (Englewood Cliffs, NJ: Prentice-Hall, © 1982). Reprinted by permission.

fine it. Indeed, creating a clear, formal definition of any object of study is sometimes more difficult than making a study of that object. If we use a *concrete* definition, and assert that "a family is a social unit made up of father, mother, and children," then only about 35 percent of all U.S. households can be classed as a family. Much of the research on the family would have to exclude a majority of residential units. In addition, in some societies, one wife may be married to several husbands, or one husband to several wives. The definition would exclude such units. In a few societies there have been "families" in which the "husband" was a woman, and in some, certain "husbands" were not expected to live with their "wives." In the United States, millions of households contain at least one child, but only one parent. In a few communes, every adult male is married to all other adult females. That is, there are many kinds of social units that seem to be *like* a family, but do not fit almost any concrete definition that we might formulate.

We can escape such criticisms in part by claiming that most adults eventually go through such a *phase* of family life; that is, almost all men and women in the United States marry at some time during their lives, and most of them eventually have children. Nevertheless, analysis of the family would be much thinner if we focused only on that one kind of household. In ordinary language usage, people are most likely to agree that a social unit made up of father, mother, and child or children is a genuine family. They will begin to disagree more and more, as one or more of those persons or social roles is missing. Few people would agree that, at the other extremes, a household with only a single person in it is a family. Far more would think of a household as a family if it comprised a widow and her several children. Most people would agree that a husband-wife household is a family if they have children, even if their children are now living somewhere else. However, many would not be willing to class a childless couple as a family, especially if that couple planned never to have children. Very few people would be willing to accept a homosexual couple as a family.

What can we learn from such ordinary language usage? First, that *family* is not a single thing, to be captured by a neat verbal formula. Second, many social units can be thought of as "more or less" families, as they are more or less similar to the traditional type of family. Third, much of this graded similarity can be traced to the different kinds of role relations to be found in that traditional unit. Doubtless the following list is not comprehensive, but it includes most of those relationships:

1. At least two adult persons of opposite sex reside together.

2. They engage in some kind of division of labor; that is, they do not both perform exactly the same tasks.

3. They engage in many types of economic and social exchanges; that is, they do things for one another.

4. They share many things in common, such as food, sex, residence, and both goods and social activities.

5. The adults have parental relations with their children, as their children have filial relations with them; the parents have some authority over their children, and both share with one another, while also assuming some obligation for protection, cooperation, and nurturance.

6. There are sibling relations among the children themselves, with, once more, a range of obligations to share, protect, and help one another.

When all these conditions exist, few people would deny that the unit is a family. As we consider households in which more are missing, a larger number of people would express some doubt as to whether it really is a family. Thus, if two adults live together, but do nothing for each other, few people would agree that it is a family. If they do not even live together, fewer still would call the couple a family.

Individuals create all sorts of relations with each other, but others are more or less likely to view them as a family to the extent that their continuing social relations exhibit some or all of the role patterns noted above. Most important for our understanding of the family is that in all known societies, and under a wide range of social conditions, some kinds of familistic living arrangements seem to emerge, with some or all of these traits. These arrangements can emerge in prisons (with homosexual couples as units), under the disorganized conditions of revolution, conquest, or epidemic; or even when political attempts are made to reduce the importance of the family, and instead to press people to live in a more communal fashion. That is, people create and recreate some forms of familistic social patterns even when some of those traditional elements are missing.

This raises the inevitable question: Why does this happen? Why do people continue to form familistic relations, even when they are not convinced that it is the ideal social arrangement? Why is *this* and not some other social pattern so widespread? Of course, this is not an argument for the *universality* of the conjugal family. Many other kinds of relations between individuals are created. Nevertheless, some approximation of these familistic relationships do continue to occur in the face of many alternative temptations and opportunities as well as counter pressures. Unless we are willing to assert that people are irrational, we must conclude that these relationships must offer some *advantages*. What are they?

We suppose that the most fundamental set of advantages is found in the division of labor and the resulting possibility of social exchanges between husband and wife (or members of a homosexual couple), as well as between children and parents. This includes not only economic goods, but help, nurturance, protection, and affection. It is often forgotten that the modern domestic household is very much an *economic* unit even if it is no longer a farming unit. People are actually producing goods and services for one another. They are buying objects in one place, and transporting them to the household. They are transforming food into meals. They are engaged in cleaning, mowing lawns, repairing, transporting, counseling—a wide array of services that would have to be paid for in money if some member of the family did not do them.

Families of all types also enjoy some small economies of scale. When there are two or more members of the household, various kinds of activities can be done almost as easily for everyone as for a single person; it is almost as easy to prepare one meal for three or four people as it is to prepare a similar meal for one person. Thus, the cost of a meal is less per person within a family. Fami-

lies can cooperate to achieve what an individual cannot, from building a mountain cabin to creating a certain style of life. Help from all members will make it much easier to achieve that goal than it would be for one person.

All the historic forms of the family that we know, including communal group marriages, are also attractive because they offer *continuity*. Thus, whatever the members produce together, they expect to be able to enjoy together later. Continuity has several implications. One is that members do not have to bear the costs of continually searching for new partners, or for new members who might be "better" at various family tasks. In addition, husband and wife, as well as children, enjoy a much longer line of social credit than they would have if they were making exchanges with people outside the family. This means that an individual can give more at one time to someone in the family, knowing that in the longer run this will not be a loss: the other person will remain long enough to reciprocate at some point, or perhaps still another member will offer help at a later time.

Next, the familistic mode of living offers several of the advantages of any informal group.[1] It exhibits, for example, a very short line of communication; everyone is close by, and members need not communicate through intermediaries. Thus they can respond quickly in case of need. A short line of communication makes cooperation much easier. Second, everyone has many idiosyncratic needs and wishes. In day to day interaction with outsiders, we need not adjust to these very much, and they may be a nuisance; others, in turn, are likely not to adjust to our own idiosyncrasies. However, within the familistic mode of social interaction, people learn what each other's idiosyncratic needs are. Learning such needs can and does make life together somewhat more attractive because adjusting to them may not be a great burden, but does give pleasure to the other. These include such trivia as how strong the tea or coffee should be, how much talk there will be at meals, sleep and work schedules, levels of noise, and so on. Of course with that knowledge we can more easily make others miserable, too, if we wish to do so.

Domestic tasks typically do not require high expertise, and as a consequence most members of the family can learn to do them eventually. Because they do learn, members derive many benefits from one another, without having to go outside the family unit. Again, this makes a familistic mode of living more attractive than it would be otherwise. In addition, with reference to many such tasks, there are no outside experts anyway (throughout most of world history, there have been no experts in childrearing, taking care of small cuts or bruises, murmuring consoling words in response to some distress, and so on). That is, the tasks within a family setting are likely to be tasks at which insiders are at least as good as outsiders, and typically better.

No other social institutions offer this range of complementarities, sharing, and closely linked, interwoven advantages. The closest possible exception might be some ascribed, ritual friendships in a few societies, but even these do not offer the range of exchanges that are to be found in the familistic processes.

We have focused on advantages that the *members* of families obtain from living under this type of arrangement. However, when we survey the wide range of family patterns in hundreds of societies, we are struck by the fact that this social unit is strongly supported by *outsiders*—that is, members of the larger society.

It is supported by a structure of norms, values, laws, and a wide range of social pressures. More concretely, other members of the society believe such units are necessary, and they are concerned about how people discharge their obligations within the family. They punish members of the family who do not conform to ideal behavior, and praise those who do conform. These intrusions are not simply whimsical, or a matter of oppression. Other members of the society do in fact have a stake in how families discharge their various tasks. More broadly, it is widely believed that the collective needs of the whole society are served by some of the activities individual families carry out. In short, it is characteristic of the varieties of the family that participants on an average enjoy more, and gain more comfort, pleasure, or advantage from being in a familistic arrangement than from living alone; and other members of the society view that arrangement as contributing in some measure to the survival of the society itself. Members of societies have usually supposed it important for most *other* individuals to form families, to rear children, to create the next generation, to support and help each other—whether or not individual members of specific families do in fact feel they gain real advantages from living in a familistic arrangement. For example, over many centuries, people opposed legal divorces, whether or not they themselves were happily married, and with little regard for the marital happiness of others.

This view of what makes up the "familistic social package" explains several kinds of widely observable social behavior. One is that people experiment with different kinds of arrangements, often guided by a new philosophy of how people ought to live. They do so because their own needs have not been adequately fulfilled in the traditional modes of family arrangements available to them in their own society. Since other people have a stake in the kinds of familistic arrangements people make, we can also expect that when some individuals or groups attempt to change or experiment with the established system, various members of the society will object, and may even persecute them for it. We can also see why it is that even in a high-divorce society such as our own, where millions of people have been dissatisfied or hurt by their marriages and their divorces, they nevertheless move back into a marital arrangement. That is, after examining various alternatives, the familistic social package still seems to offer a broader set of personal advantages, and the outside society supports that move. And, as noted earlier, even when there are strong political pressures to create new social units that give far less support for the individual family, as in China, Russia, and the Israeli kibbutzim, we can expect that people will continue to drift back toward some kind of familistic arrangement.

Our Understanding of the Family

Ruth Macklin

Ruth Macklin is professor of bioethics in the Albert Einstein College of Medicine. She is the author of *Mortal Choices: Bioethics in Today's World* (New York: Pantheon Books, 1987).

To begin, I offer three brief anecdotes. The first is a remark made by a long-married, middle-aged man at a wedding. The wedding couple were both about forty. The bride had been married and divorced once, the groom twice. During a light-hearted discussion about marriage and divorce, the middle-aged man remarked: "I could never divorce my wife. She's family!"

The second is a remark made by a four-year-old boy. I had just moved to the neighborhood and was getting to know the children. The four-year-old, named Mikey, was being tormented by a five-year-old named Timmy. I asked Mikey, "Is Timmy your brother?" Mikey replied: "Not any more. Not the way he acts!"

The third story appears in a case study presented as part of a bioethics project on everyday dilemmas in nursing home life. A resident, Mrs. Finch, is a constant complainer who seeks more choices and independence than the nursing home allows. A social worker at the home talked to Mrs. Finch about her adaptation, suggesting that she think of the residents and staff group as a large family where "we all make allowances for each other" and "we all pull our weight." Mrs. Finch responded that she is in the nursing home because she needs health care. She already has a family and does not want another one.

In my commentary on the case of Mrs. Finch, I gave an analysis that suggests some of the complexities in understanding the concept of the family. I wrote:

> Mrs. Finch is quite right to reject the social worker's suggestion that the nursing home be viewed as "a large family." A family is a well-defined social and cultural institution. People

From Ruth Macklin, "Artificial Means of Reproduction and Our Understanding of the Family," *Hastings Center Report* 21 (1991): 5–8. Reprinted by permission.

may choose to "adopt" unrelated persons into their own family, and biologically related family members may choose to "disown" one of their members (which doesn't sever the kinship ties, though it may sever relations). But an organization or institution does not become a "family" because members or residents are exhorted to treat each other in the way family members should. The social worker's well-intended chat with Mrs. Finch is an exhortation to virtue rather than a proper reminder about the resident's obligations to her new "family."[1]

It is possible, of course, to settle these conceptual matters simply and objectively by adopting a biological criterion for determining what counts as a family. According to this criterion, people who are genetically related to one another would constitute a family, with the type and degree of relatedness described in the manner of a family tree. This sense of *family* is important and interesting for many purposes, but it does not and cannot encompass everything that is actually meant by family, nor does it reflect the broader cultural customs and kinship systems that also define family ties.

What makes the first anecdote amusing is the speaker's deliberate use of the biological sense of family in a non biological context, that is the context of being related by marriage. In saying that he could never divorce his wife because "she's family," he was conjuring up the associations normally connected with biologically related family and transferring those associations to a person related by the convention of marriage. In a society in which the divorce rate hovers around 50 percent, being a family member related by marriage is often a temporary state of affairs.

What makes the second anecdote amusing is Mikey's denial, based solely on Timmy's behavior, that his biologically related sibling was his brother. When two people are biologically related, they cannot wave away that kinship relation on grounds of their dislike of the other's character or conduct. They can sever their relationship, but not their genetic relatedness. Whether family members ought to remain loyal to one another, regardless of how they act, is an ethical question, not a conceptual one.

The third story also relies on the *biological notion of family*. Mrs. Finch construed the concept literally when she insisted that she already had a family and "didn't need another one." When I observed in my commentary that a family is a well defined social and cultural institution, I meant to rebut the social worker's implication that anything one wants to call a family can thereby become a family. Yet considered from a moral perspective, our conception of the family does draw on notions of what members owe to one another in a functional understanding of the family:

> Families should be broadly defined to include, besides the traditional biological relationships, those committed relationships between individuals which fulfill the functions of family.[2]

It seems clear that we need a richer concept than that of biological relatedness to flesh out our understanding of the family. Although the biological concept is accurate in its delineation of one set of factors that determine what is a family, it fails to capture other significant determinants. . . .

In addition to the biological meaning, there appear to be three chief determinants of what is meant by family. These are law, custom, and what I shall call subjective intentions. All three contribute to our understanding of the family. The effect of artificial means of reproduction on our understanding of the family will vary, depending on which of these three determinants is chosen to have priority. There is no way to assign a priori precedence to any one of the three. Let me illustrate each briefly.

Law as a Determinant of the Family

Legal scholars can elaborate with precision and detail the categories and provisions of family law. This area of law encompasses legal rules governing adoption, artificial insemination by donor, foster placement, custody arrangements, and removal of children from a home in which they have been abused or neglected. For present purposes, it will suffice to summarize the relevant areas in which legal definitions or decisions have determined what is to count as a family.

Laws governing adoption and donor insemination stipulate what counts as a family. In the case of adoption, a person or couple genetically unrelated to a child is deemed that child's legal parent or parents. By this legal rule, a new family is created. The biological parent or parents of the child never cease to be genetically related, of course. But by virtue of law, custom, and usually emotional ties, the adoptive parents become the child's family.

The Uniform Parentage Act holds that a husband who consents to artificial insemination by donor (AID) of his wife by a physician is the legal father of the child. Many states have enacted laws in conformity with this legal rule. I am not aware of any laws that have been enacted making an analogous stipulation in the case of egg donation, but it is reasonable to assume that there will be symmetry of reasoning and legislation.

Commenting on the bearing of family law on the practice of surrogacy, Alexander M. Capron and Margaret J. Radin contend that the "legal rules of greatest immediate relevance" to surrogacy are those on adoption. These authors identify a number of provisions of state laws on adoption that should apply in the case of surrogacy. The provisions include allowing time for a "change of heart" period after the agreement to release a child, and prohibition of agreements to relinquish parental rights prior to the child's birth.

Capron and Radin observe that in the context of adoption, "permitting the birth mother to reclaim a child manifests society's traditional respect for biological ties." But how does this observation bear on artificial reproduction, where the biological tie can be either genetic or gestational?

Consider first the case of the gestational surrogate who is genetically unrelated to the child. Does society's traditional respect for biological ties give her or the genetic mother the right to "reclaim" (or claim in the first place) the child? Society's traditional respect is more likely a concern for genetic inheritance than a recognition of the depth of the bond a woman may feel toward a child she has given birth to.

Secondly, consider the case of egg donation and embryo transfer to the life of the man whose sperm was used in IVF. If the sperm donor and egg recipient were known to the egg donor, could the donor base her claim to the child on "society's traditional respect for biological ties"? As I surmised earlier, it seems reasonable to assume that any laws enacted for egg donation will be similar to those now in place for donor insemination. In the latter context, society's traditional respect for biological ties gave way to other considerations arising out of the desire of couples to have a child who is genetically related to at least one of the parents.

Custom as a Determinant of Family

The most telling examples of custom as a determinant of family are drawn from cultural anthropology. Kinship systems and incest taboos dictated by folkways and mores differ so radically that few generalizations are possible. Ruth Benedict writes: "No known people regard all women as possible mates. This is not in an effort, as is so often supposed, to prevent inbreeding in our sense, for over great parts of the world it is one's own cousin, often the daughter of one's mother's brother, who is the predestined spouse."[3] In contrast, Benedict notes, some incest taboos are

> extended by a social fiction to include vast numbers of individuals who have no traceable ancestors in common. . . . This social fiction receives unequivocal expression in the terms of relationship which are used. Instead of distinguishing lineal from collateral kin as we do in the distinction between father and uncle, brother and cousin, one term means literally "man of my father's group (relationship, locality, etc.) or his generation." . . . Certain tribes of eastern Australia use an extreme form of this so-called classificatory kinship system. Those whom they call brothers and sisters are all those of their generation with whom they recognize any relationship.[4]

One anthropologist notes that "the family in all societies is distinguished by a stability that arises out of the fact that it is based on marriage, that is to say, on socially sanctioned mating entered into with the assumption of permanency."[5] If we extend the notion of socially sanctioned mating to embrace socially sanctioned procreation, it is evident that the new artificial means of reproduction call for careful thought about what should be socially sanctioned before policy decisions are made.

Subjective Intention as a Determinant of Family

This category is most heterogeneous and amorphous. It includes a variety of ways in which individuals—singly, in pairs, or as a group—consider themselves a family even if their arrangement is not recognized by law or custom. Without an accompanying analysis, I list here an array of examples, based on real people and their situations.

- A homosexual couple decides to solidify their relationship by taking matrimonial vows. Despite the fact that their marriage is not recognized by civil law, they find an ordained minister who is willing to perform the marriage ceremony. Later they apply to be foster parents of children with AIDS whose biological parents have died or abandoned them. The foster agency accepts the couple. Two children are placed in foster care with them. They are now a family.

- A variation on this case: A lesbian couple has a long-term monogamous relationship. They decide they want to rear a child. Using "turkey-baster" technology, one of the women is inseminated, conceives, and gives birth to a baby. The three are now a family, with one parent genetically related to the child.

- Pat Anthony, a forty-seven-year-old grandmother in South Africa, agreed to serve as gestational surrogate for her own daughter. The daughter had had her uterus removed, but could still produce eggs and wanted more children. The daughter's eggs were inseminated with her husband's sperm, and the resulting embryos implanted in her own mother. Mrs.

Anthony gave birth to triplets when she was forty-eight. She was the gestational mother and the genetic grandmother of the triplets.

- Linda Kirkman was the gestational mother of a baby conceived with a sister's egg and destined to live with the infertile sister and her husband. Linda Kirkman said, "I always considered myself her aunt." Carol Chan donated eggs so that her sister Susie could bear and raise a child. Carol Chan said: "I could never regard the twins as anything but my nephews." The two births occurred in Melbourne within weeks of each other.[6]

My point in elucidating this category of heterogeneous examples is to suggest that there may be entirely subjective yet valid elements that contribute to our understanding of the family, family membership, or family relationships. I believe it would be arbitrary and narrow to rule out all such examples by fiat. The open texture of our language leaves room for conceptions of family not recognized by law or preexisting custom.

Posing the question, Who counts as family? Carol Levine replies: "The answer to this apparently simple question is by no means easy. It depends on why the question is being asked and who is giving the answer."[7]

Family Life in Seventeenth Century Massachusetts

John Demos

John Demos is the author of *Past, Present and Personal: The Family and the Life Course in American History* (New York: Oxford University Press, 1986).

The relationship between the inner workings of the family and the larger historical process is extremely intricate. Few scholars have attempted to chart its course through time—to discover, that is, at what rate and for what reasons changes in the one sphere have significant effects in the other. Of course, no such effort is feasible here. Still it may be useful to attempt a brief comparative review of the family then and now, if only as a means of pulling together the various materials from Plymouth.

It seems, in the first place, that the whole area of membership and underlying structure presents some striking instances of continuity. From the very beginning of settlement at Plymouth the family was nuclear in its basic composition and it has not changed in this respect ever since. One adult couple and their own children formed the core of each household—with the addition in some cases of an aged grandparent or "servant." Only the latter term introduces a real element of

difference from the pattern of our own day. Insofar as it designated children purposely "bound out" from some other family, it stands in some degree to confound us. Also (though less often) included among the servants were orphans and certain types of deviant or sick persons. But aside from this the typical domestic unit is easily recognized in our own terms. Moreover, the settlers' definition of kindred (beyond the immediate family), and the range of effective contacts between such people, seem equally similar.

Of course, families were considerably larger in the seventeenth century than they are today. And this difference is magnified by the further differences in typical house plans. Most Old Colony dwellings were extremely small by our own standards, and even so parts of them were not usable during the long winter months. Thus there was little privacy for the residents, and little chance to differentiate between various portions of living space. Life in these households was much less segmented, in a formal sense, than it usually is for us; individuals were more constantly together and their activities meshed and overlapped at many points.

Still, despite this rather different set of physical arrangements, the usual alignment of roles and re-

From John Demos, *The Little Commonwealth: Family Life in Plymouth* (New York: Oxford University Press, 1970), pp. 180–190. Reprinted by permission.

sponsibilities within the family was basically similar to the modern American pattern. The husband was head of the household and, at least in theory, the final arbiter of its affairs. Yet the wife had her own sphere of competence and a corresponding measure of authority. In certain most important areas of family life—the sale of real property or the disposition of children—the couple would make decisions together.

Possibly the lines of authority between parent and child were much tighter and more formal than in our own society; but the evidence on this point is not conclusive. In any case, the experience of childhood and growth through time did follow a course more distinctively its own. Childhood as we know it did not last much beyond the age of six or seven years. After that, participation in adult activities began in earnest. There was little schooling of the kind—the institutional kind—which in our own day helps to set apart a very broad age group. Instead children spent most of their time working (and relaxing) alongside older people, and were generally perceived as "little adults." If six or seven marked a turning point of greater import in the seventeenth than in the twentieth century, the opposite was true of adolescence. At Plymouth the "teens" formed a period of relative calm and steady progress toward full maturity. Courtships began at this stage and, though officially restricted by requirements of parental approval, they seem in many respects to have followed the lines of personal inclination. Marriage came somewhat later than it does now and needed at the outset substantial gifts of property from both sets of parents. But such gifts were never withheld, and were often framed so as to establish the complete autonomy of the recipients. The later years of life in Plymouth Colony brought, in most cases, no new departures of a major kind. The process of managing a family, and tending an estate, provided an essential continuity. Positions of power and prestige came chiefly to those over forty, and might indeed be retained to a very advanced age. Most men yielded reluctantly to "old age" proper, "retiring" only when forced to do so by real infirmity.

The foregoing survey has focused chiefly on issues and trends internal to the family. But it is also important to consider the whole field of relationships joining the family with the community at large. And in doing so we reach at last an area where the contrasts between the Plymouth pattern and our own are far more striking than the continuities.

Consider, for a start, the range of *function*—material, psychological, social, and otherwise—performed by the family then and now. Of course, there is an underlying core common to both sides of the comparison, and indeed to virtually all systems of family life. It comprises the fulfillment of certain basic and universal needs—most obviously, those for shelter, food, and sexual release. But beyond this lies a great variety of other possibilities—a vast territory of social purpose and activity in which the family may or may not be involved. And, broadly speaking, the history of the family in America has become a history of contraction and withdrawal; its central theme is the gradual surrender to other institutions of functions that once lay very much within the realm of family responsibility. Plymouth Colony, as much as any place, marks the beginning of this story. . . .

The Old Colony family was, first of all, a "business"—an absolutely central agency of production and exchange. Each household was more or less self-sufficient; and its various members were inextricably united in the work of providing for their fundamental material wants. Work, indeed, was a wholly natural extension of family life and merged imperceptibly with all of its other activities.

The family was also a "school." "Parents and masters" were charged by law to attend to the education of all the children in their immediate care—"at least to be able duly to read the Scriptures." Most people had little chance for any other sort of education, though "common schools" were just beginning to appear by the end of the Old Colony period.

The family was a "vocational institute." However deficient it may have been in transmitting the formal knowledge and skills associated with literacy, it clearly served to prepare its young for effective, independent performance in the larger economic system. For the great majority of persons—the majority who became farmers—the process was instinctive and almost unconscious. But it applied with equal force (and greater visibility) to the various trades and crafts of the time.

The ordinary setting for an apprenticeship was, of course, a domestic one.

The family was a "church." To say this is not to slight the central importance of churches in the usual sense. Here, indeed, the family's role was partial and subsidiary. Nonetheless, the obligation of "family worship" seems to have been widely assumed. Daily prayers and personal meditation formed an indispensable adjunct to the more formal devotions of a whole community.

The family was a "house of correction." Idle and even criminal persons were "sentenced" by the Court to live as servants in the families of more reputable citizens. The household seemed a natural setting both for imposing discipline and for encouraging some degree of character reformation.

"The family was a welfare institution"; in fact, it provided several different kinds of welfare service. It was occasionally a "hospital"—at least insofar as certain men thought to have special medical knowledge would receive sick persons into their homes for day-to-day care and treatment. It was an "orphanage"—in that children whose parents had died were straightaway transferred into another household (often that of a relative). It was an "old people's home"—since the aged and infirm, no longer able to care for themselves, were usually incorporated into the households of their grown children. And it was a "poorhouse" too—for analogous, and obvious, reasons.

Since the entire community had an interest in the smooth performance of these various tasks, it seemed only natural that there should be a certain amount of direct governmental supervision over the family. When a given family failed in some area, or experienced serious conflict among its individual members, the authorities might decide to intervene. The "harmony" of husband and wife, the subordination of children to parents—even such internal matters as these came, in theory, under official scrutiny. The government was also empowered to determine *who* might head a household in the first place.[1] Undesirables could, if necessary, be warned away.[2] One quite early statute ordered that "no servant coming out of England or elsewhere . . . be admitted his freedom or to be for himself untill he have served forth his tyme either with his master or some

other although he shall buy out his tyme, except he have beene a housekeeper or master of a famyly or meete and fitt to bee so."[3] A contract of servitude was not, in short, simply a business arrangement, in which the servant might substitute cash for labor in order to obtain immediate freedom. It was also a kind of apprenticeship in householding: a young man could learn how to be head of a family by living in one for a time. The sole exception to these provisions was—quite logically—the servant who had previously been a head-of-household ("or meete and fitt to bee so").

The very different situation of the modern family requires no such extended review. But clearly most of the functions enumerated above have long since been transferred out of the family—transferred to other institutions specially contrived for the purpose. One could say, therefore, that the family now occupies far less social "space," that profound environmental pressures have worked relentlessly to reduce its importance in the overall scheme of things.

And yet the situation has another side as well. For while the family is now less important from a social standpoint, it may well be *more* important from a psychological one. The crucial factor here is a certain feeling of connectedness, or isolation, with regard to the community at large—the degree to which individual persons sense that their life in a family makes a natural whole with other aspects of their experience. At Plymouth, we have seen, the family was joined to other institutions and other purposes in an intricate web of interconnections. It did not stand out in any special way from adjacent parts of the social backdrop; it acquired no distinctive aura of emotional or ideological significance. Its importance, while impossible to doubt, was more assumed than understood—was, indeed, so basic and so automatic as to be almost invisible. Family and community, private and public life, formed part of the same moral equation. The one supported the other, and they became in a sense indistinguishable.

The point becomes clearer when set in contrast to the situation that obtains in our own time. No longer can one feel such an essential continuity between the various spheres of experience; the central threads in the invisible web have been broken. Partial connections unquestionably remain, but they seem conspicuous on that very account. And in some overall reckoning elements of disjunction loom largest by far.

The family, in particular, stands quite apart from most other aspects of life. We have come to assume that, whenever a man leaves his home "to go out into the world," he crosses a very critical boundary. Different rules, different values, different feelings apply on either side, and any failure to appreciate this brings, inevitably, the most painful kind of personal distress. The contrast has, of course, a pejorative character. The family becomes a kind of shrine for upholding and exemplifying all of the softer virtues—love, generosity, tenderness, altruism, harmony, repose. The world at large presents a much more sinister aspect. Impersonal, chaotic, unpredictable, often characterized by strife and sometimes by outright malignity, it requires of a man that he be constantly "on his guard." It goads and challenges him at every point, and occasionally provokes responses of a truly creative sort; but it also exhausts him. So it is that he must retreat periodically within the family circle, in order to rest and to marshal his energies for still another round. In this instance the family is important not so much as the foundation for an ideal social order, but as the foil to an actual state of so-

cial disorder. It forms the bulwark against the outside world—destroy it, and anarchy reigns everywhere. It forms, too, a bulwark against anxieties of the deepest and most personal kind. For we find in the family, as nowhere else in our "open society," an indispensable type of protection against the sense of utter isolation and helplessness. Given all these circumstances family life is bound to seem somewhat more intense, more contrived, and far more self-conscious.

The source of these changes between the seventeenth century and our own is to some extent implicit in the foregoing discussion. The biggest single factor seems to have been the separation of work from the individual household, in connection with the growth of an urban, industrial system. This it was that gave profound meaning to the sense of an "outside" or "public" world. But in the American setting there was the added factor of mobility, geographical and social—all the competitive pressures generated by an expansive and democratic social order. Men had reason to feel somewhat anxious and insecure in the world of work: here, indeed, was the price they paid for the chance to better themselves—a whole darker side of "the American experience." The family, meanwhile, was increasingly set off; and it was also invested with that special sort of moral halo which it still retains.

The Emotional Significance of the Family in the Western World before the Industrial Age

Beatrice Gottlieb

Beatrice Gottlieb is a scholar and translator living in New York City.

Our experiences in families seem to be intensely personal. Each relationship with another family member has its own unique mixture of positive and negative feelings, of contacts and avoidances.

At the same time, none of us are oblivious to the requirements of family roles. Fathers are supposed to act one way, brothers another. When a father says, "I'm a big brother to my son," or a girl says, "My mother and I are really like sisters," they are recognizing norms in the very act of tampering with them. The emotional significance of the family has come to reside more and more in personal interactions rather than the feelings and beliefs connected with the religious aspect of the family. . . . A feeling not unlike religious emotion, based on an extremely positive view of these interactions, has come to the fore.

> And here being thus together,
> We are an endless mine to one another;
> We are one another's wife, ever begetting
> New births of love; we are father, friends,
>   acquaintance;
> We are, in one another, families.
> I am your heir and you are mine. This place
> Is our inheritance.

This is Shakespeare in *The Two Noble Kinsmen,* sounding rather modern in his only reference to "family" that is not political. He seems to be saying that a family is an assortment of individuals tied to each other by frequent contact and a shared concern about the future ("I am your heir"). Nothing here about power, public image, glory of ancestors. In their adversity the speaker must rely on his cousin as he would on the people in his household, his near relations, and his neighbors. The "friends" and "acquaintances" are perhaps not so modern, since they represent the intrusion of nonkin, but this passage comes about as close as anything in the early seventeenth century to a general statement about the emotional significance of the family. The passage operates on the small scale of personal interactions and embraces household and kin without distinction.

Using the word "family" when talking about such things was as rare in the past as it is common today, although talking about them was not rare. Ideas about family roles were constantly being expressed. Whether the subject was a nonspecific role like "kinsman" or a specific one like "father," "brother," "wife," and so on, it was freighted with expectations that were for the most part good, although there were some roles of which the worst seemed to be expected: "stepmother," for example. Expectations formed the basis for a wide range of emotional responses. At one extreme was the possibility of fulfillment and delight, at the other the possibility of disappointment and rage.

This is the stuff of literature, the split between appearance and reality, ideals and behavior. Imaginative literature in the Western world has often dealt with family relationships, and in dramatic literature from the sixteenth century on the distortion of family roles was a favorite subject. Dramatists and poets can tell us, if anyone can, what people thought about the emotional role of the family. I rely mainly on Shakespeare, on the assumption that his large output and wide, lasting appeal are something of a guarantee of the currency of his ideas. If Shakespeare had not been as interested as he was in how family members behaved to each other, we probably would not be reading him still. Like so many other writers in these centuries, he perceived the whole world as a tissue of family relationships. I am not advocating that we read him or any of his literary contemporaries as a reliable source of realistic observations. Rather, he is a mine of ideas, all presented with emotional coloring—exactly what we are looking for.

There is another class of writing, less enjoyable to read, that can be considered together with imaginative literature. It comprises the normative statements about family roles in religious confessors' handbooks, advice to householders, moral polemics, and educational theory. . . . They can help us interpret the literary work, often by drawing our attention to the fact that literary works focused on some relationships to which the advice-givers paid little attention. Toward the end of the period there was an increasing abundance of another kind of writing: personal letters and diaries. They show us people in the midst of playing family roles, responding to them, and even from time to time telling us what they thought about them.

What emerges from all these sources does not add up to a full-blown ideology, like the ideology that appeared in the period after 1800, which assumed that a family was centered on a romantically involved couple whose responsibilities were clearly divided between husband and wife and whose children were emblems of love warmed by orderly affection. Much of what scholars today say about the nineteenth century stresses the newness of this image, but it is possible to see many of its elements in the centuries before 1800.

The balance between "individual relationships" and "standard roles" was skewed in most of what was written before 1800. The proper performance of standard roles got much more attention than love and friendship between the individuals in a family. Alberti may not have been typical but, since he was one of the few who were not silent, we can take note of the fact that for him the model of disinterested personal affection was friendship, which he exhorted kinship to imitate. "If," says one of the interlocutors in *Della famiglia,* "you must share every thought, possession, and fortune with your friends and undergo inconveniences, hardships, and fatigue for those who love you, you certainly owe much more to your father. . . ." because he is your father, not because you and he feel like friends.

Still, there are occasional glimmers of the idea that being in a family meant being able to let one's guard down in an atmosphere of warmth and intimacy. They come late in the period, when a sharp line was being drawn between family and servants, who were now being housed in segregated quarters and were supposed to appear only when summoned by a bell. . . . [T]he houses of the wealthy were being built with family dining rooms and sitting rooms separated from public reception areas. At the very end of the period, an obscure Virginian wrote, "When relations whom we love visit us we have no reserves, ceremony is discarded, & what is all important, they visit us in times of Trouble and Sickness, when common acquaintances are apt to neglect us."

"Relations whom we love" tips the balance away from standard roles to individual relationships. If people in earlier times thought that such relationships were among the satisfactions provided by family life, they did not say so. I suspect they had the experience without conceptualizing it as people did later. The idea of finding emotionally satisfying personal relationships in the family emerged only slowly. It seems to have started with marriage, which was talked about mainly as a means to family formation, but it was hard for any sexual relationship to be completely untouched by the ideas of romantic love found in the chivalric literature that was already widely diffused before 1350 and the Petrarchan poetry that flourished throughout the period, both of which spread even more with the development of printing. By the end of the seventeenth century, the sister-in-law of Louis XIV could observe that if

men wanted loving relationships with their wives (and she assumed they did), there were better ways than making lots of babies: "Trust, respect, and tenderness are a hundred times more apt to produce the affection and harmony that are so desirable in marriage." Marriage was becoming a relationship thought of as an end in itself, or at least as one whose end was emotional satisfaction. "Happiness" and "peace" were the words that people used. Ordinary French couples, when asked why they wanted to marry, more and more often stated that they were in search of happiness and peace.

Before long, these things were connected with the family in general. "How often when travelling in dark nights & bad roads did I reflect on the peaceful happy circle I had left behind," wrote one Virginian in the early Republic. "Without thee and the rest of our beloved family & a few friends," wrote another, "this world would cease to have a charm for me. To these do I look for the little happiness which may be destined for me in this life." A religious aura associated with these feelings was starting to surround the family. Wetenhall Wilkes in 1740 had declared that married love was "the completest image of heaven we can receive in this life." Later, people sometimes thought of heaven as an image of the family—in the words of an American in 1808, "the happy seats above where there will be no sorrow, no more pain, no more parting, there we [the man, his wife, and their family] shall live together in everlasting love."

It is a far cry from these late effusions, well on the way to nineteenth-century ideology, to the tone of earlier literature on family relations. There the balance was tipped in favor of standard roles, and the subject most often addressed was how roles might be bungled and distorted. If good role-players were depicted, they were invariably set against bad role-players: no Griselda without her cruel husband, no Cordelia without Goneril and Regan, no good son like Sheridan's Charles Surface without Joseph Surface. The extreme horror of Jacobean drama derived not only from the relentless depiction of physical cruelty but also from what was, to put it mildly, inappropriate role playing. The duchess of Malfi was done in by a most unnatural brother. This was shocking stuff, as were all the patricides, fratricides, adulteries, and rejections of children in imaginative literature.

The relationships most commonly depicted were almost never treated as dynamic interactions of individual personalities. Rather, they were performances—good, bad, sincere, perfunctory. The conjugal relationship was a matter of husbands and wives following or not following appropriate role patterns, the relationship of parents and children a matter of what fathers and mothers were supposed to be like and what sons and daughters were supposed to be like, and the fraternal relationship a matter of what brothers and sisters owed each other and how they honored their obligations.

In the conjugal relationship the role of the wife got more attention than that of the husband. It was on her that the happiness of a marriage was said to depend, perhaps because the writers almost always took a man's point of view. In Alberti, who always spoke of the family as essentially masculine, this attitude was particularly exaggerated. A wife was, above all, supposed to be fertile, "a woman suited to childbearing," someone who was "prolific and [would] bring peace and honesty to your house." One of the interlocutors in *Della famiglia* says he told his wife shortly after they were married, "Three things will please me above everything else. The first is . . . that you will never wish for any other man in this bed but me." In other words, the first requirement after fertility was that she not misuse her sexuality. Being chaste was one way, presumably, that she brought honesty to the house. As for "peace," this speaker says the second thing that will please him is for her to care for the family "modestly in peace and tranquillity." He concludes by saying that she should see to it that "our household goods would not be wasted." Says another speaker, "The woman shall preserve what the man brings home."

Ben Jonson commends Penshurst for being in the charge of a lady who is such a good manager that a royal visitor could drop in without advance notice: ". . . not a roome but drest, / As if it had expected such a guest!" But, like Alberti, Jonson is mindful of the wife's sexual function: "Thy lady's noble, fruitful, chaste withall. / His children

thy great lord may call his owne; / A fortune, in this age, but rarely knowne." A wife was supposed to be fruitful, efficient, and submissive, but the quality that provoked the most emotional comment was chastity. It was closely linked to the other wifely qualities, especially submissiveness. She subordinated herself to her husband and kept things running smoothly. The last thing a wife was supposed to be was exciting. In the words of *Della famiglia,* "We must . . . seek a woman suited to childbearing and *pleasant enough* to be our constant companion" (my emphasis). The image of the ideal wife in all such utterances was remarkably consistent.

Jonson could not resist the cynical observation that chastity was "in this age but rarely known" and the dramatic situations in Shakespeare remind us that men were not confident that wives would be what they wanted them to be. Wifely qualities are often put to the test in Shakespeare's plays. Many of the women in Shakespeare are of course not yet wives and there is a considerable contrast between the role of lover and that of wife. Courtship, a common subject in the plays, seems to be less about getting a wife, as wives were usually portrayed, than about another side of the relationship between the sexes. It was when a woman became a wife that the familiar role requirements appeared. The wives in Shakespeare, with few exceptions, are submissive and chaste, sometimes heroically so. The least submissive is the proverbial shrew Kate, who is at the center of a comedy that exudes the values and atmosphere of a charivari, a noisy entertainment aimed at putting things back into their proper order. The merry wives of Windsor seem not to be submissive but in fact are, and they are impeccably chaste. It is their husbands who are uneasy about their wives' chastity, like husbands in some of the more serious plays. The wives in those plays are treated unfairly by their husbands, and they respond with extraordinarily reassuring demonstrations of submissiveness and chastity. "I must be patient," says Hermione in *The Winter's Tale,* and defends herself from the charge of adultery by saying to her husband: "I lov'd him as in honour he requir'd; / . . . with a love even such, / So and no other, as yourself commanded."

Desdemona has the same reassuring combination of qualities. "Whate'er you be, I am obedient," she says, and an onlooker remarks, "Truly, an obedient lady," when he hears her say to Othello, "I will not stay to offend you." Emilia undercuts the reassurance by reminding the men in the audience that "the ills we do, their [men's] ills instruct us so," but Desdemona is the one who has heroic stature and embodies the ideal. She is content to be what she is supposed to be:

> If e'er my will did trespass 'gainst his love,
> Either in discourse of thought or actual deed,
> Or that mine eyes, mine ears, or any sense
> Delighted them in any other form,
> Or that I do not yet, and ever did,
> And ever will (though he do shake me off
> To beggarly divorcement) love him dearly,
> Comfort forswear me! Unkindness may do
>   much;
> And his unkindness may defeat my life,
> But never taint my love.

In the relationship between parents and children, fathers and sons got the most attention. A good father was strong, wise, and honorable. A good son was respectful and obedient. The conversations in Alberti's *Della famiglia* take place while such a good father is on his deathbed. He is described as loving his sons "more than anyone else." "I believe," says one of the speakers, "there is no love so powerful, so constant, so complete, and so great as to equal a father's love for his children." Later, someone says the duty of an "upright, good, prudent father" is to risk everything "for the honor of our house and our family." Not surprisingly, the duty to the house in general, rather than to individual sons, receives emphasis in Alberti, and such a father is called "the model of family love." Sons, like wives, were supposed to be submissive. The Bible commanded everyone to "honor thy father and thy mother," and for a long time commentaries on this commandment had almost nothing to say about the obligations of parents to children. This gradually changed, but the generally recognized qualities of a good father did not, since they could easily be understood to include concern for children.

When mothers were mentioned in normative works, they were hardly differentiated from fa-

thers. If the father was the model of every manly virtue, the mother was the model of every womanly virtue, and it was usually left at that. The responsibility for "parenting" was the father's. Of course, what we call parenting is not exactly what people in the past were usually talking about. They may have been aware of a more motherly kind of parenting, but they rarely mentioned it, except in connection with very little children, who were not a common subject for discussion. Expectations about the mother's role can be glimpsed indirectly in some aspects of the cult of the Virgin Mary, especially her role as merciful intercessor.

The attitude toward disobedient, disrespectful sons, as expressed in drama, was akin to the attitude toward anything that upset the natural order. Daughters in Shakespeare tend to be more reliable than sons. *The Tempest* has a particularly warm, harmonious, idyllic father-daughter pair and Timon of Athens addresses his daughter as "cordial of mine age" and "dearer than my soul." Hamlet is a good son, bent on avenging his father's death and ready at any moment to sing his praises ("Where every god did seem to set his seal"). He struggles to be obedient, since he has received a "dread command" from his father's ghost. His fault (which makes the play more complex and interesting than an ordinary revenge play) is that he is not as quick to act as the impetuous and less intelligent Laertes, son of a father on whom every god had not set his seal, yet convinced that any "drop of blood that's calm proclaims me bastard" and ready to show himself his "father's son in deed more than in words."

Although obedience is almost always the note sounded in the parent-child relationships in Shakespeare, much depends on how fathers play their roles. When the disappointing son, Prince Hal, turns into the reassuringly reformed King Henry, he addresses a father-surrogate as follows:

> You shall be as a father to my youth;
> My voice shall sound as you do prompt
>   my ear,
> And I will stoop and humble my intents
> To your well-practis'd wise directions.

Fathers who do not give "wise directions" can upset the natural order as much as disobedient sons can. The romantic comedies of the two centuries after Shakespeare often turn on the foolish decisions of deluded parents. There are many such examples in Moliere and Sheridan, very few in Shakespeare. *King Lear* is the magnificent, ambiguous exception. Cordelia is punished for properly understanding the filial role: "You have begot me, bred me, lov'd me; I Return those duties back as are right fit, / Obey you, love you, and most honour you." This will be quite enough when Lear becomes helpless and dependent and the exaggerated protestations of his other daughters have shown themselves to be false. Meanwhile Lear suffers for his unwise directions. The play hovers on the brink of the dangerous idea that he deserves what he gets, which contributes to the mysterious power of this disturbing work. It is brought back from the brink by the unremitting wickedness and generally unnatural behavior of Goneril and Regan, who are no better wives than they are daughters, and by the more accessible situation of Gloucester and his two sons. Gloucester is a worthy father. Edgar is a worthy son. Edmund, the unworthy son, is a bastard. Everyone is reassuringly true to type in this trio, and the worthy father, no less than Lear (the unworthy father?), suffers from filial disloyalty.

Lear, which is, I suppose, the most "family" of all Shakespeare's plays, also has something to tell us about sisters and brothers. This is one subject that the normative literature passed over in relative silence. Writers of that literature tended to talk about authority in the household or obligations to the abstract entity of "house," neither of which directly involved the relationship of siblings to each other. The speech about "family" in *The Two Noble Kinsmen* does not mention brothers or sisters. Still, they were a subject hard to avoid anywhere else, either in literature or life. Their relationships were fraught with ambivalence, being associated with both cooperation and competition, often in the same breath. Ideal brothers loved each other selflessly, real brothers were likely to vie for parental favors. Alberti says little, taking it for granted that the fraternal relationship is an extremely close one. The dying father in *Della famiglia* hands over the care of his sons to his brother with his last breath. One of the speakers says that brothers should live together under the same roof.

Shakespeare's plays show a number of warm, loving relationships between brothers, which often extend to each other's children, so that uncles are shown to be as important as they surely were in reality. Sisters and brothers are also shown in close relationships, full of concern for each other, as in *Twelfth Night,* and sometimes too easily making assumptions about their obligations to each other, as in *Measure for Measure.*

The dark side of the fraternal relationship is, however, much more evident in Shakespeare. Bad brothers seem to have had an endless fascination for audiences. To be a bad brother was a clear sign of villainy and, conversely, villains were bad brothers. Plots take their starting points from fraternal betrayals and usurpations, as in *The Tempest* and *As You Like It.* Bad brothers move the action along in *Much Ado about Nothing, Lear,* and, of course, *Richard III.* Richard is a perfect villain in every one of his family roles, but most strikingly as a brother and, in the role that is its corollary, as an uncle. The ghosts of the princes murdered in the Tower cry out, "Thy nephews' souls bid thee despair." He sums up his treachery to his brothers as follows: "The sons of Clarence have I pent up close, / His daughters meanly have I match'd in marriage, / The sons of Edward sleep in Abraham's bosom." Referring to people by their family roles instead of their names is a constant reminder of implied obligations. What the obligations of a brother are is constantly suggested, more often by how they are honored in the breach. Here is a sampling of such loaded statements: "False to thy gods, thy brother, and thy father." (*Lear,* V, iii, 134); "That a brother should be so perfidious!" (*The Tempest,* I, ii, 67); "Tell me / If this might be a brother." (*The Tempest,* V, 130-131); "He . . . bars me the place of a brother." (*As You Like It,* the opening speech of the play by Orlando); "A secret and villainous contriver against me his natural brother." (*As You Like It,* I, i, 150); "Your brother (no, no brother! yet the son—/ Yet not the son—I will not call him son / Of him I was about to call his father)." *As You Like It,* II, iii, 119–121); "I am his brother, and I love him well." *(Richard III,* I, iv, 232); "Who spoke of brotherhood? Who spoke of love?" (*Richard III,* II, i, 108); "Brother, for in that name doth nature plead." (*Titus Andronicus,* I, i, 373).

To be a brother, a wife, or a son was to accept a role with set duties and a predetermined place in the family structure. Every one of these roles was nevertheless the focus of deep feeling, especially when its requirements were ignored. I think there is more to be said about the feelings people thought were connected with family relationships, but we have to become more accustomed to detaching ourselves from our present-day ideas on the subject before that can be done.

Several decades into the nineteenth century a European traveler in the United States thought he perceived an important difference between the Old World and the New in the hold that the family had on people's loyalties. In contrast to France, he said, the United States had no tradition of powerful families who might resist the ambitions of a tyrant, and instead relied on strong communities and a belief in the importance of the individual. Alexis de Tocqueville was a political thinker, and his was a political perspective, but he chose to use the vocabulary of emotion when he spoke of the family:

> As long as family feeling was kept alive, the opponent of oppression was never alone; he looked about him and found his clients, his hereditary friends, and his kinfolk. If this support was wanting, he felt himself sus-

tained by his ancestors and animated by his posterity. But when patrimonial estates are divided, and when a few years suffice to confound the distinctions of race, where can family feeling be found?

Where indeed? The implication is that only "good families" had family feeling—a message that comes to us from countless sources in the four hundred and more years preceding this statement. Defined in Tocqueville's terms, it was a feeling from which most people in the past were excluded. I have suggested that they might not have been excluded from a whole array of other family feelings that were, however, rarely characterized as such.

A statement like Tocqueville's illustrates how hard it is to get beyond the intellectual and class bias of even the best writers if we want a really broad picture of the past. He may have been blind to the values and feelings of some of his own fellow countrymen whose traditions had more in common with Americans than he thought. His is a useful statement, however, because it so backward-looking. At the very moment when a different set of ideas about family life was crystallizing he summed up the older ideas in terms so lapidary they could be carved on a tombstone.

QUESTIONS FOR THOUGHT
AND DISCUSSION

1. What does William Goode mean when he asserts that it is impossible to give a concrete definition of the word "family"? Are there any groups that everyone would agree are families? Are there any groups of persons that everyone would agree are *not* families?

2. According to Goode, what are some of the advantages of the institution of family? Are there any disadvantages of this institution, either to family members or to others? Would we be better off if we did not have this institution?

3. The *nuclear family* consists of a mother and father and their children. The *extended family* includes all the other relatives who are living in the same house—for example, grandparents, aunts and uncles. Why do some people defend extended families as better for the individuals who were a part of them than nuclear families? Why do some people take the opposite point of view and defend nuclear families as better than extended

families? Which of these positions do you think is the most plausible? Explain.

4. According to Ruth Macklin, what are the four determinants of the concept of family? How does recognition that there are several determinants affect the search for a definition of family? Would Macklin support Goode's claim that it is impossible to provide a concrete definition of family?

5. Why does John Demos argue that the relationships of the family with the community at large were much different in the seventeenth-century English colony at Plymouth, Massachusetts than they are today? What factors explain these differences?

6. What are the various functions of the family in contemporary America? How do these functions differ from family functions in the seventeenth century?

7. What are the advantages of the family? Compare and contrast the answers of William Goode and John Demos to this question.

8. What does Beatrice Gottlieb mean by the "emotional significance" of the family? What conclusions does she reach about the emotional significance of the family in the periods before and after the Industrial Age in western Europe?

9. Compare and contrast John Demos's observations about the emotional significance of the family in seventeenth-century Plymouth with Beatrice Gottlieb's conclusions about the emotional significance of the family in western Europe prior to the Industrial Revolution.

FURTHER READING

Laurence D. Houlgate, *Family and State*. Totowa, NJ: Rowman and Littlefield, 1988.

W. K. Lacey, *The Family in Classical Greece*. Ithaca, NY: Cornell University Press, 1968.

Irene Levin and Jan Trost, "Understanding the Concept of Family." *Family Relations* (July 1992): 348–351.

Nicholas Javuchi and William J. Goode, eds., *The Family Through Literature*. New York: Oxford University Press, 1973.

NOTES

Introduction

1. Paper prepared by the Department of Health, Education and Welfare Family Impact Task Group, January 10, 1977.

2. Gilbert Y. Steiner, *The Futility of Family Policy* (Washington, DC: The Brookings Institution, 1981), p. 37.

3. Ibid.

William Goode

1. For further comparisons of bureaucracy and informal groups, see Eugene Litwak, "Technical Innovation and Theoretical Functions of Primary Groups and Bureaucratic Structures," *American Journal of Sociology,* 73 (1968), pp. 468–481.

Ruth Macklin

1. "Changing Conceptions of Motherhood," *Law, Medicine and Health Care* 16 (Spring/Summer, 1988): 35.

2. A. Capron and M. Radin, "Choosing Family Law over Contract Law," *Law, Medicine and Health Care* 16 (Spring/Summer 1988), p. 35.

3. Ruth Benedict, *Patterns of Culture* (New York: Mentor Books, 1934), p. 29.

4. Ibid., p. 30.

5. Melville J. Herskovits, *Cultural Anthropology* (New York: Alfred A. Knopf, 1955), p. 171.

6. R. Alta Charo, "Legislative Approaches to Surrogate Motherhood," *Law, Medicine and Health Care* 16 (Spring/Summer 1988), p. 104.

7. Levine, "AIDS and Changing Concepts of Family," *Milbank Quarterly* 68, supp 1 (1990), p. 35.

John Demos

1. In 1636 the Court ordered "that none be allowed to be housekeeps, or build any cottags, till such time as they be allowed and approved by the Govr & Cowncell." *Records of the Colony of New Plymouth, in New England,* ed. Nathaniel B. Shurtleff and David Pulsifer (Boston, 1855–61), I, 44. The procedures for securing such approval were slightly altered as time went on, but the principle remained the same. Occasionally one sees it operating in a specific case—for example, in the following entry in the Court Orders of April, 1638: "Willm Maycumber, of Dorchester, coop, is lycensed to dwell within this govment, at Plymouth or elsewhere, upon the testymony of his good behavior thee heath brought with him." Ibid., 82.

2. In 1668, at a town meeting in Plymouth "it was . . . agreed that John Emerson be forthwith warned to depart the towne with all Convenient speed." *Records of the Town of Plymouth* (Plymouth, 1889), 106. For the record of a similar case at Marshfield, see Lysander S. Richards, *History of Marshfield* (Plymouth, Mass., 1901), p. 82.

3. William Brigham, *The Compact with the Charter and Laws of the Colony of New Plymouth* (Boston, 1836), p. 65.

3

Multicultural
Perspectives

Introduction
Lin Yutang, "On Growing Old in China"
Richard Brandt, "Hopi Family Ethics"
Nathan Murillo, "The Mexican-American Family"
Patricia Hill Collins, "Bloodmothers, Othermothers and
Women-Centered Networks in African-American Communities"

There is much to learn about the ethics of the family from the comparative study of families across cultures. This chapter features four short essays describing and analyzing some of the ethical attitudes within families that are typical of Chinese, Native American (Hopi), Mexican–American, and African–American cultures.

The essay by philosopher Lin Yutang is about the contrast between the Chinese and Western family systems' treatment of the elderly. In pre-1930s China, he writes, there was a desire to grow old and to appear old because of "the premium generally placed upon old age." Young adults had a strong sense of obligation to care for their old parents. This was "expressly defended on the sole ground of gratitude" for the many sacrifices their parents made for them when they were young. Yutang writes that the idea of personal service to one's elderly parents was also based on the Chinese "conception of life [that] is based upon mutual help within the home." This contrasts sharply with the Western notion of individualism, which he thinks the elderly carry to a "foolish extent," including their feeling ashamed of someday being dependent upon their children.

In the second essay in this section, philosopher and anthropologist Richard Brandt makes some brief observations about the Hopi attitude toward family relationships. His main point is that the individual Hopi's main obligation is to his or her clan, not to the nuclear family. The clan, in turn, is maternal, that is, a child belongs to the clan of his mother. As a result, Brandt writes, when a man grows old and infirm, his biological children, the persons with whom ties of affection are strongest, feel less responsibility to care for him, whereas those charged with this responsibility (members of his clan) will ordinarily feel less affection. One unfortunate consequence is that poor elderly people (especially men) in the Hopi tribes are less well off than their white counterparts and much less well off than elderly persons in traditional Chinese society.

In the third essay Nathan Murillo writes that although there is strong respect for the elderly in Mexican-American families: "Due to the patrilineal factor, relatives on the father's side of the family may be considered more important than those from the mother's side." Murillo does not indicate whether this favoritism translates into an expectation of less respect and attention to the needs of the mother's elderly parents than to those of the father's parents.

Another feature of Mexican-American family relationships that Murillo stresses is male domination. Although this old tradition is undergoing rapid change consistent with the changing roles of women in North American society, there is still the expectation among many Mexican-American families that "the husband and father is the autocratic head of the household" and his wife the revered but ever-obedient caregiver. However, Murillo writes, "fewer and fewer women . . . are willing to accept the traditional role assigned to them according to traditional values."

Finally, Patricia Hill Collins writes about the cultural tradition of the African-American *extended* family in which "grandmothers, sisters, aunts, or cousins act as othermothers by taking on child-care responsibilities for one another's children."[1] The tradition continues to this day, despite the fact that it is "under assault in many inner-city neighborhoods, where the very fabric of African-American community life is being eroded by illegal drugs." For those who point to inner-city families headed by a single woman as evidence of the "breakdown" of the African-American family, Collins would force them to explain why community-based child care in those African-American communities would have worse consequences for children than traditional child care in intact two-parent working families in the more affluent white communities.

On Growing Old in China

Lin Yutang

Lin Yutang (1895–1976) was professor of English at Beijing National University, Dean of Arts at Amoy University, and later in his life was head of the Arts and Letters Division of UNESCO. He is the author of over thirty-five books in English.

In my efforts to compare and contrast Eastern and Western life, I have found no differences that are absolute except in this matter of the attitude towards age, which is sharp and clearcut and permits of no intermediate positions. The differences in our attitude towards sex, toward women, and toward

From *The Importance of Living* by Lin Yutang (William Heinemann, 1931).

work, play, and achievement are all relative. The relationship between husband and wife in China is not essentially different from that in the West, nor even the relationship between parent and child. Not even the ideas of individual liberty and democracy and the relationship between the people and their ruler are, after all, so very different. But in the matter of our attitude toward age, the difference is absolute, and the East and West take exactly opposite points of view. This is clearest in the matter of asking about a person's age or telling one's own. In China, the first question a person asks the other on an official call, after asking about his name and surname is, "What is your glorious age?" If the person replies apologetically that he is twenty-three or twenty-eight, the other party generally comforts him by saying that he has still a glorious future, and that one day he may become old. But if the person replies that he is thirty-five or thirty-eight, the other party immediately exclaims with deep respect, "Good luck!"; enthusiasm grows in proportion as the gentlemen is able to report a higher and higher age, and if the person is anywhere over fifty, the inquirer immediately drops his voice in humility and respect. That is why all old people, if they can, should go and live in China, where even a beggar with a white beard is treated with extra kindness. People in middle age actually look forward to the time when they can celebrate their fifty-first birthday, and in the case of successful merchants or officials, they would celebrate even their forty-first birthday with great pomp and glory. But the fifty-first and the seventy-first is still happier and grander, while a man able to celebrate his eighty-first birthday is actually looked upon as one specially favored by heaven. The wearing of a beard becomes the special prerogative of those who have become grandparents, and a man doing so without the necessary qualifications, either of being a grandfather or being on the other side of fifty, stands in danger of being sneered at behind his back. The result is that young men try to pass themselves off as older than they are by imitating the pose and dignity and point of view of the old people, and I have known young Chinese writers graduated from the middle schools, anywhere between twenty-one and twenty-five, writing articles in the magazines to advise what "the young men ought and ought not to read," and discussing the pitfalls of youth with a fatherly condescension.

This desire to grow old and in any case to appear old is understandable when one understands the premium generally placed upon old age in China. In the first place, it is a privilege of the old people to talk, while the young must listen and hold their tongue. "A young man is supposed to

have ears and no mouth," as a Chinese saying goes. Men of twenty are supposed to listen when people of thirty are talking, and these in turn are supposed to listen when men of forty are talking. As the desire to talk and to be listened to is almost universal, it is evident that the further along one gets in years, the better chance he has to talk and to be listened to when he goes about in society. It is a game of life in which no one is favored, for everyone has a chance of becoming old in his time. Thus a father lecturing his son is obliged to stop suddenly and change his demeanor the moment the grandmother opens her mouth. Of course he wishes to be in the grandmother's place. And it is quite fair, for what right have the young to open their mouth when the old men can say, "I have crossed more bridges than you have crossed streets!" What right have the young got to talk?

In spite of my acquaintance with Western life and the Western attitude toward age, I am still continually shocked by certain expressions for which I am totally unprepared. Fresh illustrations of this attitude come up on every side. I have heard an old lady remarking that she has had several grandchildren, but "It was the first one that hurt." With the full knowledge that American people hate to be thought of as old, one still doesn't quite expect to have it put that way. . . .

I have no doubt that the fact that the old men of America still insist on being so busy and active can be directly traced to individualism carried to a foolish extent. It is their pride and their love of independence and their shame of being dependent on their children. But among the many human rights the American people have provided for in the Constitution, they have strangely forgotten about the right to be fed by their children, for it is a right and an obligation growing out of service. How can any one deny that parents who have toiled for their children in their youth, have lost many a good night's sleep when they were ill, having washed their diapers long before they could talk and have spent about a quarter of a century bringing them up and fitting them for life, have the right to be fed by them and loved and respected when they are old? Can one not forget the individual and his pride of self in a general scheme of home life in which men are justly taken care of by their parents and, having in turn taken care of their children, are also justly taken care of by the latter? The Chinese have not got the sense of individual independence because the whole conception of life is based upon mutual help within the home; hence there is no shame attached to the circumstance of one's being served by his children in the sunset of one's life. Rather it is considered good luck to have children who can take care of one. One lives for nothing else in China.

In the West, the old people efface themselves and prefer to live alone in some hotel with a restaurant on the ground floor, out of consideration for their children and an entirely unselfish desire not to interfere in their home life. But the old people have the right to interfere, and if interference is unpleasant, it is nevertheless natural, for all life, particularly the domestic life, is a lesson in restraint. Parents interfere with their children anyway when they are young, and the logic of noninterference is already seen in the results of Behaviorists, who think that all children should be taken away from their parents. If one cannot tolerate one's own parents when they are old and comparatively helpless, parents who have done so much for us, whom else can one tolerate in the home? One has to learn self-restraint anyway, or even marriage will go on the rocks. And how can the personal service and devotion and adoration of loving children ever be replaced by the best hotel waiters?

The Chinese idea supporting this personal service to old parents is expressly defended on the sole ground of gratitude. The debts to one's friends may be numbered, but the debts to one's parents are beyond number. Again and again, Chinese essays on filial piety mention the fact of washing diapers, which takes on significance when one becomes a parent himself. In return, therefore, is it not right that in their old age, the parents should be served with the best food and have their favorite dishes placed before them? The duties of a son serving his parents are pretty hard, but it is sacrilege to make a comparison between nursing one's own parents and nursing a stranger

in a hospital. For instance, the following are some of the duties of the junior at home, as prescribed by Tu Hsishih and incorporated in a book of moral instruction very popular as a text in the old schools:

> In the summer months, one should, while attending to his parents, stand by their side and fan them, to drive away the heat and the flies and mosquitoes. In winter, he should see that the bed quilts are warm enough and the stove fire is hot enough, and see that it is just right by attending to it constantly. He should also see if there are holes or crevices in the doors and windows, that there may be no draft, to the end that his parents are comfortable and happy.
>
> A child above ten should get up before his parents in the morning, and after the toilet go to their bed and ask if they have had a good night. If his parents have already gotten up, he should first curtsy to them before inquiring after their health, and should retire with another curtsy after the question. Before going to bed at night, he should prepare the bed, when the parents are going to sleep, and stand by until he sees that they have fallen off to sleep and then pull down the bed curtain and retire himself.

Who, therefore, wouldn't want to be an old man or an old father or grandfather in China?

This sort of thing is being very much laughed at by the proletarian writers of China as "feudalistic," but there is a charm to it which makes many old gentlemen inland cling to it and think that modern China is going to the dogs. The important point is that every man grows old in time, if he lives long enough, as he certainly desires to. If one forgets this foolish individualism which seems to assume that an individual can exist in the abstract and be literally independent, one must admit that we must so plan our pattern of life that the golden period lies ahead in old age and not behind us in youth and innocence. For if we take the reverse attitude, we are committed without our knowing to a race with the merciless course of time, forever afraid of what lies ahead of us—a race, it is hardly necessary to point out, which is quite hopeless and in which we are eventually all defeated. No one can really stop growing old; he can only cheat himself by not admitting that he is growing old. And since there is no use fighting against nature, one might just as well grow old gracefully. The symphony of life should end with a grand finale of peace and serenity and material comfort and spiritual contentment, and not with the crash of a broken drum or cracked cymbals.

Hopi Family Ethics

Richard Brandt

Richard Brandt (1910–1997) was professor of philosophy at the University of Michigan and the author of many influential books and essays on ethics. He wrote *Hopi Ethics* early in his career, after living with the Hopi in 1946 and returning to the Hopi reservation in the summers of 1947 and 1948.

Clan and Nuclear Family Relationships

A very important institution among the Hopi is the clan system. Every Hopi is born a member of a certain clan—Spider, Coyote, and so on—the clan of his mother. That is to say, each Hopi is regarded as affiliated with a certain group of persons and as at least distantly related to them. He is also thought to be connected in some special way with the clan *wuya*—some animal, plant, etc., to which the legends of his clan explain a special relationship of that group. Clan members enjoy a certain amount of prestige which comes to the clan because of its position in the religious ceremonies— each ceremony being property passed along within the membership of a single clan. Each clan also cherishes its own traditions: about its origin; its path of wandering, eventually leading to its present location; the incidents connected with its affiliation within the village; its ceremonies; and so on. A person cannot marry (or have sexual relations with) a member of his own clan; hence a man will always be of a different clan from his children. Members of the same clan have certain rights and duties respecting each other, and a Hopi feels close to persons in the same clan, including members of the same clan from a different Hopi town or even a New Mexico pueblo.

The woman is an important person in a Hopi household, partly because the children are of her clan and feel themselves especially close to her blood relatives. The women of a household also own the house and the household utensils; even if a Hopi man constructs a new house for his family, it belongs to his wife. After a woman's death, ownership of her house passes to her daughters or other close female relatives; if she had no close female relatives, traditionally it is considered the property of her lineage or clan. Ownership of the best strips of land is also associated with the female line; that is, the right to use land passes from a woman to her daughters, never, in theory, from a man to his children. If a woman has no children or sisters (i.e., if the household line runs out), at her death the land reverts to the clan, to be reallocated by the clan "head." A boy will be given some rights and duties with respect to land belonging to his household, and he may continue to cultivate such a parcel after marriage. But at marriage, by tradition, he joins the household of his wife and will cultivate a portion of the fields belonging to his wife's household, very often continuing, however, to cultivate the parcel of land associated with his own (his mother's) lineage. Offices in the clan and ceremonial "property" are inherited along the woman's line; the custom is for a man to select one of his sister's sons whom he regards as best fitted and train him to take over his office or responsibility after his death. . . .

Relationships of Affection and Acceptance

There are reasons in the Hopi social system for expecting that the average Hopi will develop attachments for a wider group of persons, and concentrate them less on members of the nuclear family, than is true in the average white American family. For, according to the traditional Hopi arrangements, a household includes not only one's parents and siblings but one's mother's sisters and their children; and even if this traditional group is split into separate households, the relationships normally remain very intimate. Moreover, a Hopi normally lives in the same town as a great many relatives on his father's side. In addition, he must have a "ceremonial father" to induct him into the tribal societies, and he may be "adopted" by someone during or after a serious illness. His relations with these "fathers" will not be purely formal; each will perform services for the other, and some affection will normally develop.

It is an interesting question what effect this arrangement actually has on attachments between members of the nuclear family. One is impressed by instances of affection between mothers and daughters and between siblings; and Hopi generally seem quite fond of their children. There is some evidence, however, which suggests only a moderate degree of affection. Dorothy Eggan reports that, of twenty individuals studied by her, only two showed affection for the primary family comparable to that familiar in white American society. Again, it is well known that old people are often neglected by the Hopi. For instance, one informant mentioned that his mother was living with a sister of his [nearby]. To inquiry whether he ever visited her, he replied, "Oh, no. She can't talk very well any more either; or at least, I can hardly understand her." . . .

What happens to the aged among the Hopi depends on individual circumstances. A man or woman with ceremonial position or some other basis for respect is more likely to be well treated; and, of course, those with affectionate near relatives can depend on them. The prospects of others are more bleak, even for a woman with daughters living in what is theoretically her house. Men are apt to be in an especially disagreeable situation because of Hopi theory that responsibilities lie primarily with *clan* relatives. This means that one's own children, the persons with whom ties of affection are strongest, feel less responsibility, whereas those charged with responsibility will ordinarily feel less affection.

The Mexican-American Family

Nathan Murillo

Nathan Murillo is Professor Emeritus at California State University, Northridge, where he was a counsellor and taught courses in psychology and Chicano studies. He has served as a consultant to the Peace Corps in Central and South America and Southeast Asia.

For the Chicano, the family is likely to be the single most important social unit in life. It is usually at the core of his thinking and behavior and is the center from which his view of the rest of the world extends. Even with respect to identification

From Nathan Murillo, "The Mexican American Family," in Carrol A. Hernandez, Marsha J. Haug, and Nathaniel N. Wagner, eds., *Chicanos: Social and Psychological Perspectives*, 2nd ed. (Saint Louis: C. V. Mosby, 1976), pp. 19–24.

the Chicano *self* is likely to take second place after the family. For example, an individual is seen first as a member of the Ruiz or Mendoza family before he is seen as Juan or Jose—that is, before he obtains his more personal acceptance. Thus to a significant extent the individual Chicano may view himself much of the time as an agent or representative of his family. In many respects this means that he must be careful of his behavior lest his actions somehow reflect adversely on his family bringing them dishonor or disgrace . . .

The importance of the family to a Chicano and the close interpersonal ties that exist among family members, including those of the extended family, are not often appreciated in the Anglo society. To the Chicano, family needs and demands have the highest priority. If his help is required by the family, he may temporarily forego job, school, or any other activity that might prevent him from meeting his family obligation.

The family maintains its position of prominence within the psychological space of the Chicano individual, I believe, primarily by virtue of its ability to provide emotional and material security. A Chicano in need of emotional support, guidance, goods, or money expects and is expected to turn to his family first in order to have such needs met. Only in unusual circumstances, dire need, or when there is no alternative will a Chicano attempt to seek help from others. This often occurs at great expense to the pride and dignity of both the individuals or families to seek professional help for medical and emotional problems . . .

The strength of the family, resting as it does on the foundation of providing security to its members, is sometimes expressed through a sharing of material things with other relatives even when there might be precious little to meet its own immediate needs. This sometimes causes Anglos bewilderment and provokes them to criticism when there is a lack of understanding of this aspect of the Chicano family feeling. This is especially true with some welfare workers who are trying to help a family make ends meet and discover that the family is sharing what they have with others outside the immediate home environment. . . .

Within the Chicano or Mexican American concept of family there are two subconcepts. These are the *nuclear* family, consisting of husband, wife, and children, and the *extended* family, which encompasses grandparents, uncles, aunts, and cousins. Due to the patrilineal factor, relatives on the father's side of the family may be considered more important than those from the mother's side. In addition to these members, the extended family concept also includes compadres who are the godparents of the children. For each child there may be a different set of compadres. The relationship between parents and compadres is very similar to that between the parents and other adult relatives where there is mutual respect and interchange of help and advice.

[There are] two dimensions under which the interpersonal patterns within the family are usually organized. The first is respect and obedience to elders and the second is male dominance . . .

The husband and father is the autocratic head of the household. He tends to remain aloof and independent from the rest of the family. Few decisions can be made without his approval or knowledge. He is free to come and go as he pleases without explanation to or questions by other family members. In essence the father represents authority within the family. All other family members are expected to be respectful of him and to accede to his will or direction . . .

The wife-mother is supposed to be completely devoted to her husband and children. Her role is to serve the needs of her husband, support his actions and decisions, and take care of the home and children. In substance she represents the nurturant aspects of the family's life. Although she is usually highly respected and revered, her personal needs are considered to be secondary to those of the other family members. Her life tends to revolve around her family and a few close friends . . .

There is presently much confusion and conflict among Chicanos, as well as Anglos, as to the role of the woman in society. There are fewer and fewer women who are willing to accept the traditional role assigned to them according to traditional values. Chicanas are struggling for greater equality not only in the Anglo society but also in comparison to the Mexican American male. The Chicana has the difficult task of gaining for herself more flexibility in carrying out a greater variety of activities that traditionally have been denied her in the Mexican American culture. . . . The old concept of male-female roles in Chicano society is requiring a painful examination and reevaluation of what is important and what is less important in the functional roles between man and woman.

Bloodmothers, Othermothers and Women-Centered Networks in African-American Communities*

Patricia Hill Collins

Patricia Hill Collins is a professor of African-American Studies at the University of Cincinnati.

In African-American communities, fluid and changing boundaries often distinguish biological mothers from other women who care for children. Biological mothers, or bloodmothers, are expected to care for their children. But African and African-American communities have also recognized that vesting one person with full responsibility for mothering a child may not be wise or possible. As a result, othermothers—women who assist bloodmothers by sharing mothering responsibilities—traditionally have been central to the institution of Black motherhood.[1]

The centrality of women in African-American extended families reflects both a continuation of West African cultural values and functional adaptations to race and gender oppression.[2] This centrality is not characterized by the absence of husbands and fathers. Men may be physically present and/or have well-defined and culturally significant roles in the extended family and the kin unit may be woman-centered. Bebe Moore Campbell's parents separated when she was small. Even though she spent the school year in the North Philadelphia household maintained by her grandmother and mother, Campbell's father assumed an important role in her life. "My father took care of me," Campbell remembers. "Our separation didn't stunt me or condemn me to a lesser humanity. His absence never made me a fatherless child. I'm not fatherless now."[3] In woman-centered kin units such as Campbell's—whether a mother-child household unit, a married couple household, or a larger unit extending over several households—the centrality of mothers is not predicated on male powerlessness.[4]

Organized, resilient, women-centered networks of bloodmothers and othermothers are key

in understanding this centrality. Grandmothers, sisters, aunts, or cousins act as othermothers by taking on child-care responsibilities for one another's children. When needed, temporary child-care arrangements can turn into long-term care or informal adoption.[5] Despite strong cultural norms encouraging women to become biological mothers, women who choose not to do so often receive recognition and status from othermother relationships that they establish with Black children.

In African-American communities these women-centered networks of community-based child care often extend beyond the boundaries of biologically related individuals and include "fictive kin."[6] Civil rights activist Ella Baker describes how informal adoption by othermothers functioned in the rural southern community of her childhood:

> My aunt who had thirteen children of her own raised three more. She had become a midwife, and a child was born who was covered with sores. Nobody was particularly wanting the child, so she took the child and raised him . . . and another mother decided she didn't want to be bothered with two children. So my aunt took one and raised him . . . they were part of the family.[7]

Even when relationships are not between kin or fictive kin, African American community norms traditionally were such that neighbors cared for one another's children. Sara Brooks, a southern domestic worker, describes the importance that the community-based child care a neighbor offered her daughter had for her: "She kept Vivian and she didn't charge me nothin either. You see, people used to look after each other, but now its not that way. I reckon its because we all was poor, and I guess they put theirsell' in the place of the person that they was helpin."[8] Brooks's experiences demonstrate how the African-American cultural value placed on

From Patricia Hill Collins, *Black Feminist Thought: Knowledge, Consciousness, and the Politics of Empowerment* (Boston: Unwin Hyman, 1990), pp. 119–123. Reprinted by permission of Routledge, New York.

cooperative child care traditionally found institutional support in the adverse conditions under which so many Black women mothered.

Othermothers are key not only in supporting children but also in helping bloodmothers who, for whatever reason, lack the preparation or desire for motherhood. In confronting racial oppression, maintaining community-based child care and respecting othermothers who assume child-care responsibilities serve a critical function in African-American communities. Children orphaned by sale or death of their parents under slavery, children conceived through rape, children of young mothers, children born into extreme poverty or to alcoholic or drug-addicted mothers, or children who for other reasons cannot remain with their bloodmothers have all been supported by othermothers, who, like Ella Baker's aunt, take in additional children even when they have enough of their own.

Young women are often carefully groomed at an early age to become othermothers. As a ten-year-old, civil rights activist Ella Baker learned to be an othermother by caring for the children of a widowed neighbor: "Mama would say, 'You must take the clothes to Mr. Powell's house, and give so-and-so a bath.' The children were running wild. . . . The kids . . . would take off across the field. We'd chase them down, and bring them back, and put 'em in the tub, and wash 'em off, and change clothes, and carry the dirty ones home, and wash them. Those kind of things were routine."[9]

Many Black men also value community-based child care but exercise these values to a lesser extent. Young Black men are taught how to care for children (Young 1970; Lewis 1975). During slavery, for example, Black children under age ten experienced little division of labor. They were dressed alike and performed similar tasks. If the activities of work and play are any indication of the degree of gender role differentiation that existed among slave children, "then young girls probably grew up minimizing the difference between the sexes while learning far more about the differences between the races."[10] Differences among Black men and women in attitudes toward children may have more to do with male labor force patterns. As

Ella Baker observes, "my father took care of people too, but . . . my father had to work."[11]

Historically, community-based child care and the relationships among bloodmothers and othermothers in women-centered networks have taken diverse institutional forms. In some polygynous West African societies, the children of the same father but different mothers referred to one another as brothers and sisters. While a strong bond existed between the biological mother and her child—one so strong that, among the Ashanti for example, "to show disrespect towards one's mother is tantamount to sacrilege,"[12] children could be disciplined by any of their other "mothers." Cross-culturally, the high status given to othermothers and the cooperative nature of child-care arrangements among bloodmothers and othermothers in Caribbean and other Black societies gives credence to the importance that people of African descent place on mothering.[13]

Although the political economy of slavery brought profound changes to enslaved Africans, cultural values concerning the importance of motherhood and the value of cooperative approaches to child care continued. While older women served as nurses and midwives, their most common occupation was caring for the children of parents who worked.[14] Informal adoption of orphaned children reinforced the importance of social motherhood in African-American communities.[15]

The relationship between bloodmothers and othermothers survived the transition from a slave economy to post emancipation southern rural agriculture. Children in southern rural communities were not solely the responsibility of their biological mothers. Aunts, grandmothers, and others who had time to supervise children served as othermothers.[16] The significant status women enjoyed in family networks and in African-American communities continued to be linked to their bloodmother and othermother activities.

The entire community structure of bloodmothers and othermothers is under assault in many inner-city neighborhoods, where the very fabric of African-American community life is being eroded by illegal drugs. But even in the most troubled communities, remnants of the othermother tradition endure. Bebe Moore Campbell's 1950s North Philadelphia neighborhood underwent some startling changes when crack cocaine flooded the streets in the 1980s. Increases in birth defects, child abuse, and parental neglect left many children without care. But some residents, such as Miss Nee, continue the othermother tradition. After raising her younger brothers and sisters and five children of her own, Miss Nee cares for three additional children whose families fell apart. Moreover, on any given night Miss Nee's house may be filled by up to a dozen children because she has a reputation for never turning away a needy child.[17]

Traditionally, community-based child care certainly has been functional for African-American communities and for Black women. Black feminist theorist bell hooks suggests that the relationships among bloodmothers and othermothers may have greater theoretical importance than currently recognized:

> This form of parenting is revolutionary in this society because it takes place in opposition to the ideas that parents, especially mothers, should be the only child rearers. . . . This kind of shared responsibility for child care can happen in small community settings where people know and trust one another. It cannot happen in those settings if parents regard children as their "property," their possession.[18]

The resiliency of women-centered family networks illustrates how traditional cultural values—namely, the African origins of community-based child care can help people cope with and resist oppression. By continuing community-based child care, African-American women challenge one fundamental assumption underlying the capitalist system itself: that children are "private property" and can be disposed of as such. Notions of property, child care, and gender differences in parenting styles are embedded in the institutional arrangements of any given political economy. Under the property model stemming from capitalist patriarchal families, parents may not literally assert that their children are pieces of property, but their parenting may reflect assumptions analogous to those they make in connection with property.[19] For example, the exclusive parental "right" to discipline children as parents see fit, even if discipline borders on abuse, parallels the widespread assumption that property owners may dispose of their property without consulting members of the larger community. By seeing the larger community as responsible for children and by giving othermothers and other nonparents "rights" in child rearing, African-Americans challenge prevailing property relations. It is in this sense that traditional bloodmother/othermother relationships in women-centered networks are "revolutionary."

QUESTIONS FOR THOUGHT AND DISCUSSION

1. Lin Yutang argues that there is a great difference between traditional Chinese and contemporary American adult attitudes of respect and behavior toward their elderly parents. What do you think explains this difference?

2. According to the essays by Lin Yutang and Richard Brandt, there are remarkable differences between the degree to which Chinese and Hopi adults respect and care for their elderly parents. What are these differences? What do you think explains this difference?

3. According to Brandt, what are the differences between the obligations of a Hopi toward his or her clan and his or her nuclear family?

4. After reading Nathan Murillo's essay, what do you think are the main differences between the way in which members of Mexican-American families

conceive the role of husbands and wives within the family and the way in which members of your own family (and/or families in your cultural group) conceive them?

5. According to Patricia Hill Collins, what is an "othermother"? How does she distinguish between the obligations toward children of an othermother and a bloodmother?

6. How does the African-American custom of seeing the larger community as responsible for children and by giving othermothers and other nonparents "rights" in childrearing "challenge prevailing property relations"?

FURTHER READING

Hammadah Abd al Ati, *The Family Structure in Islam*. Lagos, Nigeria: American Trust Publications, 1977.

Ruth Benedict, *Patterns of Culture*. New York: Mentor Books, 1934.

Maria Hong, ed., *Growing Up Asian American: An Anthology*. New York: W. Morrow, 1993.

Robert Joseph Taylor, James S. Jackson, and Linda M. Chatters, eds., *Family Life in Black America*. Thousand Oaks, CA: Sage, 1997.

Norma Williams, *The Mexican American Family: Tradition and Change*. Dix Hills, NY: General Hall, 1990.

NOTES

Introduction

1. Compare the communal childrearing model suggested by Plato in Chapter 5 with Firestone's suggestions for an alternative family form in Chapter 6.

Patricia Hill Collins

1. Rosalie Riegle Troester, "Turbulence and Tenderness: Mothers, Daughters and 'Othermothers' in Paule Marshall's *Brown Girls, Brownstones*," *Sage: A Scholarly Journal on Black Women*, vol. 1 (1984): pp. 13–16.

2. Bernice Johnson Reagon, "African Diaspora Women: The Making of Cultural Workers," in *Women and Africa and the African Diaspora* ed. R. Terborg-Penn, Sharon Harley, and A.B. Rushing (Washington, D.C.: Howard University Press, 1987), 167–180.

3. Bebe Moore Campbell, *Growing Up with and without My Dad* (New York: Putnam, 1989).

4. Nancy Tanner, "Matrifocality in Indonesia and Africa and among Black Americans," in *Woman, Culture, and Society*, ed. M. Z. Rosaldo and L. Lamphere (Stanford: Stanford University Press, 1974), pp. 129–156.

5. Carol D. Stack, *All Our Kin: Strategies for Survival in a Black Community* (New York: Harper & Row, 1974).

6. Ibid.

7. Ellen Cantarow, *Moving the Mountain: Women Working for Social Change* (Old Westbury, NY: Feminist Press, 1980), p. 59.

8. Thordis Simonsen, ed., *You May Plow Here: The Narrative of Sara Brooks* (New York: Touchstone, 1986), p. 181.

9. Cantarow, op. cit.

10. Deborah Gray White, *Ar'n't I a Woman? Female Slaves in the Plantation South* (New York: W. W. Norton, 1985), p. 94.

11. Cantarow, op. cit., p. 60.

12. Meyer Fortes, "Kinship and Marriage among the Ashanti," in *African Systems of Kinship and Marriage,* ed. A. R. Radcliffe-Brown and Daryll Forde (New York: Oxford University Press, 1950), p. 263.

13. Niara Sudarkasa, "Interpreting the African Heritage in Afro-American Family Organization," in *Black Families,* ed. Harriette Pipes McAdoo (Beverly Hills, CA: Sage, 1981), pp. 37–53.

14. White, op. cit.

15. Herbert Gutman, *The Black Family in Slavery and Free-*

dom, 1750–1925 (New York: Random House, 1976).

16. Molly C. Dougherty, *Becoming a Woman in Rural Black Culture* (New York: Holt, Rinehart and Winston, 1978).

17. "Children of the Underclass," *Newsweek,* September 11, 1989, pp. 16–27.

18. bell hooks, *From Margin to Center* (Boston: South End Press, 1984), p. 144.

19. Janet Farrell Smith, "Parenting as Property," in *Motherhood: Essays in Feminist Theory,* ed. Joyce Trebilcot (Totowa, N.J.: Rowman and Allanheld, 1983), pp. 199–212.

II

Criticisms and Defense of the Family

4

Marriage, Monogamy, and Sexual Preference

Introduction
A. John Simmons, "Locke on Rights and the Family"
Barbara Herman, "Kant on Sex and Marriage"
Michael D. Bayles, "In Defense of Monogamous Marriage"
James Q. Wilson, "Against Homosexual Marriage"
Richard D. Mohr, "The Case for Gay Marriage"

There is not as much dispute about the meaning of the term "marriage" as there is about the term "family." Most would agree that marriage is a contract. Hence, the duties that arise are self-imposed by the individuals who enter into the marital relationship. Marriage is an institution that societies have created to enable individuals to place themselves under an obligation to act in particular ways. In this respect, it is like any other duty that arises from a contract, and unlike the duties that arise from, say, the moral obligation not to injure or harm others. For example, even if I never agreed not to harm my neighbor, I am under an obligation not to do her injury.

Is marriage more than a contract? In refusing to annul a marriage in Pennsylvania, Judge James Bok remarked that "marriage is not only a contract but a status and a kind of fealty to the State as well" [*Bove* v. *Penciotti*, 46 Pa. D.&C.159 (C.P. 1942)]. Rejecting the position of one of his colleagues who had theorized that marriage is no more than a civil contract, Judge Bok responded that marriage is "at least a civil contract, with status and the State's interest added to it." Since the concept of status applies only to personal conditions over whose creation the individual has had no control and that are not the results of a contract (e.g., being a child), perhaps Judge Bok simply meant that a marriage bargain entails consequences the two parties cannot control, even by their mutual assent. For example, since marriage is of indefinite duration, persons who marry cannot stipulate the precise period of time that their marriage will last. Of course, this does not make the marriage contract any different from other kinds of agreements, the terms of which are regulated by the state (for example, employment contracts cannot be for less than a particular wage established by the state).

The seventeenth-century English philosopher John Locke agreed that marriage is at least a contract. Locke tells us that "conjugal society [that is, marriage] is made by voluntary compact between man and woman." But it is also a status. Since the chief purpose of marriage is "such a communion and right in one another's bodies as is necessary to its chief end, procreation," people who marry cannot escape the duty to provide for any offspring of their union. Although Locke claims that the purpose of marriage is procreation, he thinks that all of the other aspects of the marriage contract can be changed by mutual agreement between husband and wife.

In his essay on Locke, A. John Simmons defends Locke against those who claim that he attempts to justify the fact that marriage in seventeenth-century England placed men and women in an unequal moral relationship, making women "subject to their husbands." Simmons claims that this is a misreading of Locke. Although it is true that Locke holds to the standard sexist assumption of his day that men are superior decision makers, he does not think that this superiority should be made an unalterable feature of every marriage contract. A marriage contract between a man and a woman could include a provision that gives the wife the "last determination" on all marital decisions.

In the eighteenth century, German philosopher Immanuel Kant also regarded marriage as a voluntary agreement between a man and a woman, but he did not believe that producing and educating children was a necessary part of marriage. Instead, marriage is "the union of two persons of different sex for life-long reciprocal possession of their sexual faculties."

Is this how we should conceive the ethical relationship between sex and marriage? In her essay on Kant, Barbara Herman considers this question in the context of Kant's claim that persons involved in consensual premarital sexual relationships violate the moral law that we ought not to treat persons as mere means to the satisfaction of our desires. She shows the similarity of Kant's argument to the arguments of some contemporary feminists that sexual intercourse between a man and a woman turns women into things, mere objects for male sexual satisfaction. Herman also explains Kant's obscure theory that legal marriage makes sexual intercourse morally permissible by creating a "unity of will" between husband and wife. She leaves it to the reader to decide whether this would satisfy feminist objections about heterosexual intercourse.

In the third essay in this chapter, Michael Bayles provides a contemporary defense of monogamous marriage. He defends the traditional position that the institution of marriage promotes society's interest and responsibility with respect to procreation and the rearing of children. However, Bayles provides a defense of monogamous marriage that was not noted by philosophers of the seventeenth and eighteenth centuries. He argues that marriage is unique in promoting the most valuable of all human relationships: those that are based on intimacy and affection. Before making this ringing endorsement of marriage, however, Bayles argues that one cannot object to the absence of laws recognizing homosexual marriages on the ground that it deprives same-sex partners of the freedom to do what heterosexual persons are able to do. Instead, "it merely fails to provide legal recourse to enforce the agreements of the parties to such unions." He concludes that if homosexuals have ground for complaint, it must reside in the fact that homosexuals are being treated unequally by not being allowed to enter into enforceable marriage contracts. However, Bayles warns, not all cases of unequal treatment are unjustified.

Should partners of the same sex be allowed to marry? Some have answered this question affirmatively, on the grounds that state prohibitions on same-sex marriages is a violation of the constitutional requirement that no person shall be denied "equal protection of the laws." They say that denying access to a marriage license by two people of the same sex is no different from denying access to two people of different races. In "Against Homosexual Marriages," James Q. Wilson rejects this analogy on the ground that "marriage is a different issue than social integration."

In his essay "A Case for Gay Marriage," Richard Mohr tries a different approach. He argues (against Wilson and others) that marriage is not a mere creation of the law. Although the law provides a definition of marriage and of the terms "husband" and "wife," Mohr agrees with John Locke that marriage is primarily a *moral* relationship between persons. However, he disagrees with Locke that procreation is a defining feature of a marital relationship. Instead, "marriage is intimacy given substance in the medium of everyday life, the day-to-day." Mohr contends that there is nothing in this definition that excludes marital partners from being of the same gender. Indeed, studies of permanent gay and lesbian relationships show that they "fulfill in an exemplary manner" the terms of Mohr's definition. Moreover, contrary to the views expressed by Wilson, Mohr claims that gays provide a home environment that is at least as conducive to successful childrearing as that provided by heterosexual couples.

Other questions about marriage will be answered in subsequent chapters. In Chapter 7, Richard Wasserstrom examines the nature of marriage and the prohibition on extramarital sex and Mike W. Martin discusses the rationale for the virtue of faithfulness in marriage. In Chapter 5, Susan Moller Okin indicates why traditional sex roles within contemporary marriage place an unjust burden on women.

Locke on Rights and the Family

A. John Simmons

A. John Simmons is professor of philosophy at the University of Virginia.

Conjugal society, Locke writes, "is made by a voluntary compact between man and woman" (II, 78) . . . Locke is clearly speaking here of marriage as a *moral,* not a legal, relationship (II, 83; I, 123), and one whose terms are thus not to be thought of

From A. John Simmons, *The Lockean Theory of Rights* (Princeton University Press: Princeton, NJ: 1992), pp. 170–175. Reprinted by permission. References are to the *First Treatise on Government* (I) or to the *Second Treatise on Government* (II).

as constrained by any particular legal (or other) rules or conventions (II, 83). Husband and wife may promise to love, honor, cherish, and obey one another, or they may bind themselves by different and more specific agreements. The contract must be consistent with the ends of conjugal society, or else it cannot count as a marriage contract; but all else can "be varied and regulated by that contract which unites man and wife" (II, 83). There is thus a wide range of possible contracts between a woman and a man, ranging from purely economic (nonmarital) contracts, through "standard" marriage contracts, to quite individual and unconventional marriage contracts. For Locke, of course, the end or point of conjugal society is procreation and the care of the "common offspring" (II, 78, 83); so any marriage contract necessarily must be understood to include an agreement to care for and educate any children resulting from the union, and to "support and assist" one another during the time that the rearing of children takes place (II, 78, 83). For those of us who may disagree with this (or any other essentialist) account of marriage, however, Locke's contractualist view of marriage can still be accepted, with marriage contracts only exhibiting certain "family resemblances" to one another.[1]

Locke is, I think, correct in supposing that the rights (and duties) of spouses (or of any other persons involved in long-term, monogamous relationships) are primarily determined by consent, as the appropriate source of bonds between equals.[2] While there need not be anything so formal as a contract, voluntary agreements or understandings may distribute the rights and duties within the relationship as the partners please. That is the fundamental moral component of marriage. Religious and legal recognition of certain unions, the profound emotional ties that usually accompany them, and the function such unions play in social interaction do not alter this fundamental component, nor do other moral aspects of marriage that may add to it.[3] That marriage aims, in a sense, at overcoming the partners' preoccupation with their moral rights and duties with respect to one another, in no way suggests that they lack these rights and duties or that they are not based in a voluntary undertakings.[4] A more troubling problem, however, is that the "contractual" undertaking between wife and husband may be uninformed, seriously underspecified, or amorphous, leaving it uncertain just how the rights and duties within a marriage ought to be distributed. In such cases the natural solution is to favor equality between the parties; but it is in this context that Locke's least liberal (and most sexist) views on marriage are expressed.[5]

While a husband has no *absolute* power (right, authority) over his wife[6] Locke argues (I, 48; II,

82–83), he does have a certain "priority" over her (she "owes" him a limited "subjection" [I, 48]). Every husband has the right "to order the things of private concernment in his family, as proprietor of the goods and land there, and to have his will take place before that of his wife in all things of their common concernment" (I, 48). In disagreements between husband and wife, the man has the right of "last determination" in "things of their common interest and property" (II, 82). Why this priority of the man's will? Aside from references to God's punishment of women for Eve's transgressions (I, 47) (which, I argue below, Locke does *not* intend as a source of man's authority *over* woman), Locke says only this: when husband and wife disagree, it "being necessary that the last determination, i.e., the rule, should be placed somewhere, it naturally falls to the man's share, as the abler and stronger" (II, 82).

Even supposing (falsely) that men (individually or as a group) are "abler and stronger" than women, it is hard to see why Locke should have thought this fact a ground for unequal rights between husband and wife. After all, other natural inequalities in strength or ability (those between adult males, for instance) do not seem to justify inequalities in *their* rights, on Locke's view. . . . This apparent inconsistency seems easy to explain if we simply ascribe to Locke a firm commitment to the natural superiority and dominion of men over women, a prephilosophical commitment that his general philosophical principles cannot budge (even at the price of inconsistency). We could then argue that for Locke the "natural dominion of one sex over the other" is so obvious that it "does not even have to be justified."[7] Locke may say conjugal society is consensual; but given Locke's view of women's weakness and inequality, any contract of marriage would border on unconscionability.[8] In the end, the argument goes, Locke's real view is that men enjoy a *natural* (not contractual) dominion over women, both in and out of marriage. He should not be credited with having espoused a more "liberal attitude toward marriage and the relation of the sexes."[9]

This reading of Locke, I think, is unfair to him, for he quite specifically denies that man has any natural dominion over woman. God never gave him any such dominion: He never gave "any authority to Adam over Eve, or to men over their wives."[10] Women are not naturally subject to their husbands, although, Locke "grants," there is "a foundation in nature for it" (I, 47). What is this natural "foundation" for an artificial authority? It is quite clearly meant to be man's superior strength and ability—not as the source of his authority, but as a natural fact to which man's achievement of conventional authority is connected. What, then, is the relevance of this natural superiority? First, of course, it is natural (not *obligatory*) to defer in certain ways to those who are abler, stronger, wiser, older, or more virtuous (as Locke says elsewhere—e.g., II, 54). As a result, it is natural (and, subsequently, conventional) for women to *give* men greater authority than they reserve for themselves in their free marriage contracts. This is natural and conventional, not necessary—for Locke mentions instances in which women have elected *not* to give their husbands this authority (e.g., I, 47; II, 65). And *because* it is natural (and thus inevitably conventional), Locke assumes, if the marriage contract does not specify alternative arrangements, we may understand it to give greater authority to the husband. But Locke has, I think, a second reason for his belief that husbands typically have (limited) authority over their wives. In voluntary unions between persons that do not involve a precise specification of the methods for settling disputes, the right to determine the body's actions must be understood to lie with the greatest "force" in the body. This is an important principle for Locke, for it underlies his defense of majority rule as the understood rule of resolution for *political* unions: "it being necessary to that which is one body to move one way; it is necessary the body should move that way whither the greater force carries it, which is the consent of the majority: or else it is impossible it should act or continue one body" (II, 96). Locke's reasoning about the husband's right of "last determination" in a marriage proceeds similarly: this right must "be placed somewhere," so it "naturally falls to the man's share, as the abler and stronger" (II, 82).

Locke's argument is in neither case very convincing.[11] But the important point to note here is that he is in neither case arguing for a natural authority (of majorities or husbands). In both cases he is trying to give reasons for interpreting an inexplicit contract in a certain way, for understanding where the artificial authority to make decisions for a body must be taken to lie, when it has not been explicitly stated in the contract. And in both cases he allows that if there *has* been an explicit agreement on some alternative arrangement for decision-making, this agreement overrides the reasoning he has advanced. Thus, political bodies may "expressly agree" to require more than a simple majority for binding decisions (II, 99); and, presumably, this means they may opt for different procedures altogether (e.g., lottery, weighted lottery, plural voting for the more able, etc.). Similarly, every aspect of the marriage contract (except the responsibility to provide for offspring) may be varied by express agreement (II, 83). Wives may have the right of "last determination" themselves, if this is agreed on, or the mates may decide conflicts by lottery or by taking turns, and so on. The authority of husbands is neither natural nor necessary.

Where, then, does this leave a Lockean contractual account of "marital morality"? If we deprive the account of its false factual assumptions (about man's superior strength and ability), it seems not at all unreasonable or illiberal. Marriage contracts may distribute rights and duties between the partners as they specify. In the absence of explicit specification by or understanding of the partners, we should take the contract to have the conventional form.[12] In Locke's day, this meant a superior position for the husband; but the voluntariness and fairness of marriage contracts in Locke's day were typically undermined by the vastly inferior bargaining position of the woman (based on her economic dependency and social limitations).[13] Fairness, then, would have dictated that we interpret inexplicit contracts more equitably than the conventions of Locke's day would have suggested. Today, when conventions are more egalitarian and women's dependency on male approval less profound, the problem of unfair contracts is less dramatic. Women can, if they wish, accept a traditional or limited role in family decision-making; or they can insist on equal (or greater than equal) rights in this area as a condition of the marriage contract. Only unfairness and duress (etc.) involved in entry into a marriage will require us to question the terms of an explicit contract or interpret an inexplicit one in other than conventional terms.[14]

Kant on Sex and Marriage

Barbara Herman

Barbara Herman is professor and chair of the department of philosophy at the University of California, Los Angeles.

Why Is Sex Morally Problematic for Kant?

Kant argues that there is something about what happens in human sexual relations that leads to a condition compromising the moral standing of the partners.[1] Kant argues that there is such a sex-based moral problem and that it can be resolved only through the legal institution of marriage. He claims that within civil society it is possible to establish and secure the equality and autonomy of the partners in a sexual relationship by defining them, under the law, as husband and wife—that is, as equal juridical persons with public standing.[2] The argument for marriage follows the form of the argument concerning the necessity of the institution of property. (Of course, not just any legal institution of marriage could be cast in the role of preserving autonomy. One that regards the wife as the property of the husband only reflects the assault on autonomy that is [as Kant saw it] inherent in the sexual relation itself.)

The natural response of many to such an argument is, first, to heap scorn on the institution of marriage and, second, to claim that surely it is possible to have sex without moral difficulty—meeting in the moral state of nature, as it were, as free and equal persons sharing the pleasure of one another's bodies. Kant's argument has to be (and is) that there is something about the nature of persons and about the nature of the sexual relationship that makes a will to love well insufficient to guarantee the autonomy and equality of sexually involved persons.

The feature of sexual activity that Kant most frequently identified as the source of moral difficulty is the fact (as he saw it) that sexual interest in another is not interest in the other as a person.[3] Insofar as one is moved by sexual appetite, it is the sex (the eroticized body, the genitalia) of the other that is the object of interest. But since the body is an inseparable part of the person ("in its togetherness with the self it constitutes the person" (*Lectures on Ethics* 166), the sexual appetite, in taking the body as the object of its interest, compels regard of the person as an object (or blocks regard for the body as the body of a person). According to Kant, the objectification of the other is both natural and inevitable in sexual activity. Let me string together some passages from *Lectures on Ethics* to give the flavor of Kant's remarks.

> Taken by itself [sexual love] is a degradation of human nature; for as soon as a person becomes an Object of appetite for another, all motives of moral relationship cease to function, because as an Object of appetite for another a person becomes a thing and can be treated and used as such by every one.

> Because sexuality is not an inclination which one human being has for another as such, but is an inclination for the sex of another, it is a principle of the degradation of human nature,

From Barbara Herman, "Could It Be Worth Thinking about Kant on Sex and Marriage?" in *Mind of One's Own: Feminist Essays on Reason and Objectivity* (Boulder, CO: Westview Press, 1993), 55–63. Copyright © 1992 by Westview Press. Reprinted by permission of Westview Press.

in that it gives rise to the preference of one sex to the other, and to the dishonoring of that sex through the satisfaction of desire. The desire which a man has for a woman is not directed towards her because she is a woman; that she is a human being is of no concern to the man; only her sex is the object of his desires. Human nature is thus subordinated. Hence it comes that all men and women do their best to make not their human nature but their sex more alluring and direct their activities and lusts entirely towards sex. Human nature is thereby sacrificed to sex. If then a man wishes to satisfy his desire, and a woman hers, they stimulate each other's desire; their inclinations meet, but their object is not human nature but sex, and each of them dishonors the human nature of the other. (163–164)

Sex and the Subordination of Women

Talk about degradation and dishonor offends our sexually liberated ears. We might say, surely Kant confuses sexuality gone wrong with sex itself. But before yielding to the comfort of such a response, let us look at some other passages.

> There is a deep recognition in culture and in experience that intercourse is both the normal use of a woman, her human potentiality affirmed by it, and a violative abuse, her privacy irredeemably compromised, her selfhood changed in a way that is irrevocable, unrecoverable. And it is recognized that the use and abuse are not distinct phenomena but somehow a synthesized reality—both are true at the same time as if they were one harmonious truth instead of mutually exclusive contradictions. . . . By definition, she [has] a lesser privacy, a lesser integrity of the body, a lesser sense of self, since her body can be physically occupied and in the occupation taken over. By definition . . . this lesser privacy, this lesser integrity, this lesser self, establishes her lesser significance. She is defined by how she is made, that hole, which is synonymous with entry; and intercourse, the act fundamental to existence, has consequences to her being that may be intrinsic, not socially imposed.

> It is especially in the acceptance of the object status that her humanity is hurt: it is a metaphysical acceptance of lower status in sex and in society; an implicit acceptance of less freedom, less privacy, less integrity. In becoming an object so that he can objectify her so that he can fuck her, she begins a political collaboration with his dominance; and then when he enters her, he confirms for himself and for her what she is: that she is something, not someone; certainly not someone equal.

> What does it mean to be the person who needs to have this done to her: who needs to be needed as an object; who needs to be entered; who needs to be occupied; who needs to be wanted more than she needs integrity or freedom or equality? . . . The brilliance of objectification as a strategy of dominance is that it gets the woman to take the initiative in her own degradation (having less freedom is degrading) . . . she takes on the burden, the responsibility, of her own submission, her own objectification. . . . The pleasure of submission does not and cannot change the fact, the cost, the indignity, of inferiority.

This, to be sure, is not Kant. This second set of passages is from Andrea Dworkin's recent book, *Intercourse.*[4] The differences in what Kant and Dworkin say are sharp enough: Dworkin's focus is on the objectification of women, on the effects on women of sexuality as-we-know-it, and in particular, on the meaning and inherent violence of the act of intercourse. Still, her key ideas are, one might say, very Kantian. Sex (intercourse) turns women into things; the pleasures of sex lead women to volunteer to be treated as things; sex is not compatible with the standing of the partners as equal human beings. It was this degree of similarity with the parts of Kant that we are supposed to reject out of hand, combined with the power of Dworkin's account on its own terms, that suggested to me that adopting a different attitude toward Kant's treatment of sexuality might prove worthwhile.

. . . If there is no need to explain why Kantian ethics could not tolerate an activity in which persons are treated as objects, something needs to be offered in support of Kant's reasons for thinking sexuality is such an activity. Kant says the sexual regard is for the body or body part, not the person. The voice of erotic language often speaks of love for the beloved's body: lips, eyes, ears, feet— whatever. But must it? Is there room in sexual language for the terms of moral regard? It is a little odd to imagine sexual arousal as a moral deed— perhaps a bit less odd to be turned on by a quality of virtue, though some more than others: courage more easily than kindness (a cynic might see the marks of virility or maternity as the object here). Certainly the language and imagery of pornography support Kant's view, especially if one holds with those radical feminists who see pornography as an accurate expression of sexual reality.[5]

It is because Kant regards the sexual appetite per se as the cause of objectification that individual or private escape is not possible. Dworkin may similarly be inclined to accept a kind of sexual moral fatalism, given the asymmetry of power between men and women in intercourse. She sees no route of possible escape through private consensual acts. As she says:

> [Even visionary sexual reformers fail to face] the fundamental questions about intercourse as an act with consequences, some perhaps intrinsic. [Even with intercourse contingent on consent, and the conditions of consent the woman's desire,] the woman could not forcibly penetrate the man. The woman could not take him over as he took her over and occupy his body physically inside. His dominance over her expressed in the physical reality of intercourse has no real analogue in desire she might express for him in intercourse: she simply could not do to him what he could do to her.[6]

Human Love and Sexual Love

Suppose—in the light of this—we allow Kant's claim that the sexual appetite in itself is directed at the body. (There are of course, questions to be asked about what it might mean to think of an appetite "in itself," but we will have to leave those aside for now.) Is there any reason to think it follows that the *person* whose sexuality is aroused cannot see the object of sexual interest as a person?

Kant's reasons for thinking it does follow can be seen in the contrast he draws between what he calls human love and sexual love.

> Human love is good will, affection, promoting the happiness of others and finding joy in their happiness. But it is clear that when a person loves another purely from sexual desire, none of these factors enter into love. Far from there being any concern for the happiness of the loved one, the lover, in order to satisfy his desire, may even plunge the loved one into the depths of misery. Sexual love makes of the loved person an Object of appetite; as soon as that appetite has been stilled, the person is cast aside as one casts away a lemon that has been sucked dry. *(Lectures on Ethics* 163)

> if . . . a man wishes to satisfy his desire, and a woman hers, they stimulate each other's desire; their inclinations meet, but their object is not human nature but sex. *(Lectures on Ethics* 164)

Why can't human love transform sexual love? Does Kant think this because he regards appetites as untransmutable original existences?

We have, one would suppose, an appetite for food per se that can be transformed into a taste for and appreciation of fine food. But the structure of an appetite for food remains: hunger and satiety marking its boundaries and, as we might say, the appetite itself remaining an appetite for food. (The possibility of the perversion or inversion of an appetite, or instinct, does not change this.) So the appetite for sex can develop into an appetite for refined or exotic sex, but it is still an appetite for sex in the sense that its object is pleasure of a certain sort to be had from the sexual use of someone's body.[7]

Human love is an interest in a person as an agent with a life (with moral capacities and so forth). Although it could include an interest in another's having sexual satisfaction as a component of a good life, it does not have as its object pleasure and so is not structured by the analogues of hunger and satiety. Kant says: "Sexual love can, of course, be combined with human love and so carry with it the characteristics of the latter, but taken by itself and for itself, it is nothing more than appetite" (*Lectures on Ethics* 163). "Carry with it" is not the language of transformation. Frequently we love as persons those we love sexually, and our concern for their well-being may control and shape the expression of sexual appetite. But for Kant this gets us no further than the fact that absent property, we might not take what was of use to someone we cared about. This would not give the loved one claim or title to the object of use, just as our human love cannot transform the object of sexual love into a subject (a person).

Kant makes the further claim that in satisfying sexual desire one party surrenders use of a part for the purposes of gain or pleasure, giving the other a right of disposal over that part.[8] And since "a human being is a unity," the right gained thereby is over the whole person. But we cannot have rights of disposal over persons because persons are not things. That is why agreement about use does not provide a remedy: The problem is not one of force. One cannot give a right of disposal over a part for it is not a right we have. Thus, Kant argues, unless it is possible to have rights of disposal over persons, sexual activity is morally impermissible.[9] In a full treatment of Kant's views, three claims would need to be examined: first, that objectification leads to a right of disposal; second, that rights over a part of the body are in effect rights over the whole and that a right of disposal of the sexual part is a right of disposal over the person; and third, that we are not the sorts of things over which anyone (including ourselves) can have rights of disposal.

A right of disposal, I presume, is a right of free use (in the sense of having something at my disposal). We can take it as obvious that, and why, Kantian theory holds that we cannot freely use persons in this sense. But how do we get to a right of disposal from the fact that sexual interest is in and for a body (or for the pleasure to be had from sexual engagement with another's sexuality)? Kant seems to take it as given that sexual activity involves mutual surrender, so that to enjoy a person sexually is to enjoy a thing given to us. (The difficulty in getting agreement on limits of use for things we possess suggests the intuition that if an object is in my power, that I have a right of disposal over it is not without foundation.) Certainly there is much talk of possession, surrender, and use in erotic language.

In any case, I am here less interested in defending the odd metaphysics of Kant's claims about parts and wholes than I am in marking the fact that just such views about sexual use are integral to the kind of feminist argument both Dworkin and MacKinnon present. Their central programmatic task is to demonstrate that the effect of sexual regard or relationship cannot be partial—mere sex—but that the very categories of gender, of who we are as men and as women, are functions of objectifying sexual regard.

Although in Kant's view sexuality creates a morally impermissible relation between the sexual partners, it is neither desirable nor possible to forbid sexual activity. Sexual intercourse is the now standard (then necessary) means for procreation, and love relations with sexual components are essential to happiness (for many). So we have a kind of relationship that we cannot forego (as the kind of beings we are) but that is not morally acceptable. Marriage is supposed to solve the problem—resetting the moral stage so that there is a morally permissible way for sexual life to take place without inevitable moral loss or danger.

How Does Marriage Make Sex Morally Permissible?

We have reason to be dubious about any social institution's ability to restore or preserve what may be threatened or lost in intimate relations. We have special reasons to be dubious about the institution of "marriage" as it reflects and sustains just the exploitative and agency-demeaning features of moral concern. Rather than support the institution of marriage as-we-know-it, Kantian ethics should give reasons to judge that institution impermissible.

The institution of marriage as-we-know-it involves the State's acknowledgment of only certain relationships, entered into in only certain ways, creating thereby certain State-enforced rights and liabilities. It allows the State some security about property and children—someone is responsible for getting the kids to school and in condition for minimal socialization, and property is cared for through the regulatory role of the divorce courts.[10] Marriage encourages the creation of small, isolated, economically insecure units vulnerable to the vagaries of the market. It protects the chief arena of abuse of women and children, it endorses sexual inequality (protecting the sexual and social advantages of men), and it penalizes gay men and lesbians. The institution of marriage as-we-know-it is a nasty thing. If sexuality carries a moral burden, marriage hardly seems to be the arena of its resolution. Before thinking that what is needed is a reform of the institution of marriage, we want to wonder about the very idea of casting a social institution in this sort of morally creative role. Is it even possible to have a legal form of marriage that does not merely reinforce the moral damage of sexual relations between men and women as-we-know-them? How could the legal construction of the relationship recreate what practice has destroyed (or preserve what is endangered)? Kant has two different answers to these questions, one of which deserves some further attention.

In his *Lectures on Ethics,* Kant argues that

the sole condition on which we are free to make use of our sexual desire depends upon the right to dispose over the person as a whole—over the welfare and happiness and generally over all the circumstances of that person. . . . [I obtain these rights over the whole person (and so have the right of sexual use of that person)] only by giving the person the same rights over myself. This happens only in marriage. Matrimony is an agreement between two persons by which they grant each other equal reciprocal rights, each of them undertaking to surrender the whole of their person to the other with a complete right of disposal over it. (167)

Now the part that does the work:

But if I yield myself completely to another and obtain the person of the other in return, I win myself back; I have given myself up as

the property of another, but in turn I take that other as my property, and so win myself back again in winning the person whose property I have become. In this way the two persons become a unity of will. . . .
Thus sexuality leads to a union of human beings, and in that union alone is its exercise possible. (167)

Marriage solves the problem because each grants the other "equal reciprocal rights" and no one loses anything. Why suppose that if I give myself and get someone else back, that I get myself? Perhaps it goes this way: I give myself (or rights over myself) and you give yourself, but since you have me, in giving yourself to me you give me back to me. And so on. The idea might be this: Suppose I give you every pencil I own or will come to own knowing that (or on condition that) you will give me every pencil that you own or will come to own. One could say that we thereby create a community of pencil ownerships—a unity of will about pencils.

But even if this makes some sense, a unity of will out of two persons or a "union of human beings" does not. Although one sees what Kant may have wanted—a kind of romantic blending of self into a new and larger self—it is not possible for him to get what he wants. If the problem with sex is that we are embodied selves, and use of the body implies title over a self, things are not greatly improved if we become parts of a new self that has two bodies (and sex would then be what?). The threat to the autonomous agent would seem to be increased rather than resolved in the surrender to the new union of persons, a threat that is especially acute to women, who are not likely to share equally in the direction of the new union.[11]

Furthermore, the account is a mess in Kant's own terms—for it does not even make sense to "grant reciprocal rights" over a self when one's self is not the sort of thing over which there can be rights. Nor is there any need for marriage as a public institution, because the granting of reciprocal rights, if one had them, would be a matter of free contract.

In Defense of Monogamous Marriage

Michael D. Bayles

Michael Bayles was professor of philosophy at the University of Kentucky and at Florida State University. He was the author of several essays and books in ethics, philosophy of law, and professional ethics.

Historically, the official aims of marriage, according to the Catholic Church (which was the only church during the period of the establishment of monogamous marriage in Western society) were procreation and companionship. There was also a tendency to view it as a legitimate outlet for man's sinful nature. . . . In addition to the avowed purposes of marriage there were the actual social functions that it performed. The family unit was the basic social unit, not only for the education of children (that is, socialization, not formal schooling—which has only become widespread during the past century), but also for the production of necessities, including food and clothing, and for recreation. These historical functions of the extended family unit based on monogamous marriage have been undermined by the development of industrial, urban society. Consequently, the moral and legal status and functions of marriage require reexamination in the light of current social conditions.

The Rules of Marriage and Inequality

Before undertaking such a reexamination it is necessary to distinguish between rules of marriage and attendant social rules. They are mixed together in the traditional social institution of monogamous marriage, but there is no necessity for this mix and it is probably unjustified. In particular one must distinguish between penal laws prohibiting various forms of sexual union—homosexual, premarital, adulterous—and private arranging laws granting legal recognition to the marital relationship. Private arranging laws do not prescribe punishment for offenses; instead, they enable people to carry out their desires. People

are not punished for improperly made marriages; instead, the marriages are invalid and unenforceable. Laws against fornication, prostitution, cohabitation, and homosexuality are almost always penal. Objections to them cannot be transferred directly to the marriage relationship. All of these penal laws could be abolished and monogamous marriage could still be retained.

It may be claimed that despite their nonpenal form, marriage laws do in fact penalize those who prefer other forms of relationship. If homosexual and polygamous relationships are not legally recognized as "marriages," then persons desiring these forms of relationship are being deprived of some degree of freedom. When considering freedom one must be clear about what one is or is not free to do. Consider, for example, the case of gambling. One must distinguish between laws that forbid gambling and the absence of laws that recognize gambling debts. The latter does not deprive people of the freedom to contract gambling debts; it simply does not allow the use of legal enforcement to collect them. Similarly, the absence of laws recognizing polygamous and homosexual marriages does not deprive people of the freedom to enter polygamous and homosexual unions. Instead, it merely fails to provide legal recourse to enforce the agreements of the parties to such unions. The absence of laws recognizing such marriages does not deprive people of a freedom they previously had, for they were never able to have such agreements legally enforced. Nor have people been deprived of a freedom they would have if there were no legal system, for in the absence of a legal system no agreements can be legally enforced. If there is a ground for complaint, then, it must be one of inequality—that one type of relationship is legally recognized but others are not. However, a charge of inequality is warranted only if there are no relevant reasonable grounds for distinguishing between relationships.

From Michael D. Bayles, "Marriage, Love and Procreation," in R. Baker and F. Elliston, eds., *Philosophy and Sex* (Buffalo, NY: Prometheus, 1975). Reprinted by permission of Marjorie Bayles.

To settle that issue one must be clear about the state's or society's interests in marriage.

The rest of this essay is concerned with the purposes or functions of the marriage relationship in which society has a legitimate interest. It is not possible here to set out and to justify the purposes for which governments may legislate. It is assumed that the state may act to facilitate citizens' engaging in activities that they find desirable and to protect the welfare and equality of all citizens, including future ones. Government has an especially strong responsibility for the welfare of children. Of course, these legitimate governmental or social interests and responsibilities must be balanced against other interests and values of citizens, including those of privacy and freedom from interference.

There is no attempt or intention to justify penal laws prohibiting forms of relationship other than monogamous marriage. Indeed, it is generally assumed that they ought not be prohibited and that more people will enter into them than has been the case. In such a context, monogamous marriage would become a more specialized form of relationship, entered into by a smaller proportion of the population than previously. Underlying this assumption are the general beliefs that many people are unqualified or unfit for a marital relationship and ought never to enter one and that many people marry for the wrong reasons. If true, these beliefs may explain why both marriage and divorce rates have been steadily rising in most Western countries during this century.

Promoting Interpersonal Relationships

Alienation from others and loss of community are perceived by many to be among the most serious ills of modern, mass society. In such a situation it seems unlikely that many would deny the need for intimate interpersonal relationships of affection. The importance of such relationships for a good or eudaemonistic life have been recognized by philosophers as diverse as Aristotle and G. E. Moore. In considering such interpersonal relationships to be among the most valuable elements of a good life, one must distinguish between the value of a good and the strength of the desire for it. Many people have a stronger desire for life than

for such interpersonal relationships, but they may still recognize such relationships as more valuable than mere life. Life itself is of little value, but it is a necessary condition for most other things of value.

Among the most valuable forms of interpersonal relationship are love, friendship, and trust. These relationships are limited with respect to the number of persons with whom one can have them. Classically, there has been a distinction between agapeic and erotic love. Agapeic love is the love of all mankind—general benevolence. The concept of erotic love is more limited. In today's world erotic love is apt to be confused with sexual desire and intercourse. But there can be and always has been sex without love and love without sex. Personal love is more restricted than either agapeic love or sexual desire. It implies a concern for another that is greater than that for most people. Hence, it cannot be had for an unlimited number of other people. Similar distinctions must be drawn between friendship and acquaintance, trust of a political candidate and trust of a friend.

Such interpersonal relationships require intimacy. Intimacy involves a sharing of information about one another that is not shared with others. Moreover, it often involves seclusion from others—being in private where others cannot observe. In some societies where physical privacy is not possible, psychological privacy—shutting out the awareness of the presence of others—substitutes. Consequently, these valuable interpersonal relationships require intimacy and usually physical privacy from others, and at the very least nonintrusion upon the relationship. Moreover, these forms of interpersonal relationship require acts expressing the concern felt for the other person. In most societies acts of sexual intercourse have been such expressions of love and concern. It is not physically or psychologically necessary that sexual intercourse have this quasi-symbolic function, but it is a natural function of sexual intercourse. All that is here meant by "natural" is that in most societies sexual intercourse has this function, for which there is some psychological basis even though it is not contrary to scientific laws for it to be otherwise. Intercourse usually involves an element of giving of oneself, and one's sexual identity is frequently a central element of one's self-image. It is not, however, sexual intercourse that is intrinsically valuable but the feelings and attitudes, the underlying interpersonal relationship, that it expresses. Nonsexual acts also currently express such relationships, but sexual intercourse is still one of the most important ways of doing so. If sexual intercourse ceases to have this function in society, some other act will undoubtedly replace it in this function. Moreover, sexual intercourse will have lost much of its value.

If these interpersonal relationships of personal love and trust are of major value, it is reasonable for the state to seek to protect and foster them by according legal recognition to them in marriage. The specific forms of this recognition cannot be fully discussed. However, there is some basis for treating the partners to a marriage as one person. Historically, of course, the doctrine that the parties to a marriage are one person has supported the subjugation of women in all sorts of ways, for example, in their disability from owning property. But there is an underlying rationale for joint responsibility. Two people who, without a special reason such as taxes, keep separate accounts of income and expenditures do not have the love and trust of a couple who find such an accounting unnecessary. Moreover, in such a joint economic venture there is no point to allowing one party to sue the other. Only the advent of insurance, whereby neither spouse, but a third party, pays, makes such suits seem profitable. Another recognition of these relationships—albeit one not frequently invoked—is that one is not forced to testify against his or her spouse. More important is that neither party is encouraged to violate the trust and intimacy of the relationship, for example, by encouraging one to inform authorities about bedroom comments of his or her spouse.

The character of these valuable forms of interpersonal relationship provides an argument against according marriages of definite duration legal recognition equal to that accorded those that are intentionally of indefinite duration. For it to be "intentionally of indefinite duration," neither partner may, when entering the marriage, intend it to be for a specific period of time, for example, five years, nor may the marriage contract specify such a period. The following argument is not to show that

marriages for a definite duration should not be recognized, but merely to show that they should not have equal standing with those intentionally of indefinite duration. The basic reason for unequal recognition is that interpersonal relationships that are not intentionally of indefinite duration are less valuable than those that are.

Suppose one were to form a friendship with a colleague, but the two mutually agree to be friends for only three years, with an option to renew the friendship at that time. Such an agreement would indicate a misunderstanding of friendship. Such agreements make sense for what Aristotle called friendships of utility, but in the modern world these friendships are business partnerships. While there is nothing wrong with business friendships, they do not have the intrinsic value of personal friendships. In becoming close personal friends with someone, one establishes a concern and trust that would be seriously weakened or destroyed by setting a time limit to the friendship. It is sometimes claimed that time limits may be set because people will only be together for a while. But one need not see a person every day or even every year to remain friends. However, extended separation usually brings about a withering away of the friendship.

Similarly, the personal relationship of love and trust in marriage is of lesser value if it is intentionally for only a definite period of time. Moreover, the entering into a relationship that is intentionally of indefinite duration and legally recognized symbolizes a strength of commitment not found in other types of relationships. While two unmarried people may claim that there is no definite limit to their mutual commitment, their commitment is always questionable. Entering into a marital relationship assures the commitment more than does a mere verbal avowal.

There are two common objections to this argument. First, it is sometimes said that there may be special reasons for making marriages of short, definite duration, for example, if one partner will only live in the area for a while. But a personal love that is not strong enough to overcome difficulties of moving to another area and possible sacrifices of employment is not as close and strong as a love that can. Many married couples make such compromises and sacrifices. Second, it is sometimes claimed that commitment is in fact stronger when not legally reinforced, when one does not need the law to support the relationship. However, this claim overlooks the fact that when a married couple's relationship rests substantially upon their legal obligations, their relationship has already begun to deteriorate. The strength of commitment is established by the willingness to enter into a legal relationship that cannot be broken simply, without any difficulties. A person who is not willing to undertake the risk of the legal involvement in divorce should he desire to terminate the relationship is probably unsure of his commitment. Moreover, the legal relationship provides security against a sudden and unexpected change in one's life—the breakup of the social aspects will take some time, giving one a chance to prepare for a new style of life. Even then the change is often very difficult. Hence, if marriage is for the purpose of providing legal recognition of some of the most valuable interpersonal relationships, it should grant more protection and recognition to those intentionally of indefinite duration than to others. Such a conclusion does not imply that divorce should be impossible or exceedingly difficult. Friendships frequently do not last forever despite their not being intended for a limited period of time. The same may happen to a marital relationship. So while this argument supports not according legal recognition to relationships intended to be of definite duration equal to that accorded those intended to be of indefinite duration, it does not support restrictions on divorce in the latter case. Moreover, the average length of time of marriages has increased considerably since the seventeenth century. When a couple married then, one of them was likely to die within twenty years. With today's increased life expectancy, both parties may live close to fifty years after they marry.[18] Obviously, with such an increased possible length of marriage, there is a greater chance for marital breakdown and divorce. One may expect more divorces in marriages that have lasted twenty to twenty-five years simply because there are more such marriages. Nevertheless, such marriages are intentionally of indefinite duration—for life.

Protecting the Welfare of Children

Another area of pervasive social interest that has historically centered in marriage concerns the procreation and raising of children. Society has an interest not only in the number of children born but their quality of life. This fact is in deep conflict with the current emphasis on the freedom of individuals to make reproductive decisions unfettered by social rules and restrictions. Moreover, it is an area in which social control has traditionally been weak. Child abuse is widespread, and efforts to prevent it are mediocre at best. There are few general legal qualifications or tests for becoming a parent. Yet parenthood is one of the most potentially dangerous relationships that one person can have with another. If one is a poor college teacher, then at worst a few students do not receive a bit of education they might have. But as a parent one potentially can ruin completely the lives of one's children. At the least, they may develop into psychological misfits incapable of leading responsible and rewarding lives.

Essentially, there are three areas of social interest and responsibility with respect to procreation and the raising of children. First, there is a social interest in the sheer number of children born. The current emphasis on population control makes this interest abundantly clear. Second, there is a social interest in the potentialities of children. This area includes concern for genetic and congenital birth defects and abnormalities. Over 5 percent of all children born have a genetic defect. The possibility of genetic control of those who are born will soon take on major significance. Already, approximately sixty genetic diseases as well as almost all chromosomal abnormalities can be detected *in utero,* and adult carriers of about eighty genetic defects can be identified. Given the possibility of genetic control, society can no longer risk having genetically disadvantaged children by leaving the decision of whether to have children to the unregulated judgment of individual couples. Some social regulations with respect to genetic screening and, perhaps, eugenic sterilization are needed. While potential parents have interests of privacy and freedom in reproductive decisions, the social interests in preventing the suffering and inequality of possibly defective children may outweigh them in certain types of cases.

Third, the care and development of those who are born is a social interest and responsibility. This interest has been recognized for some time in the form of children's homes and compulsory education. However, increasing knowledge about childhood development extends the area in which social interests and responsibility may be reasonably involved. To give an example at the most elementary level, the nutritional diet of children during their first three years is crucial for their future development. So also is their psychological support. The welfare of future generations is not a private but a social matter. It is a proper task of society, acting through its government, to ensure that the members of the next generation are not physical or psychological cripples due to the ignorance, negligence, or even indifference of parents.

Historically, society has attempted to control procreation through the institution of marriage. Society's means were primarily to stigmatize children born out of wedlock and to encourage the having of many children. It is now recognized that no useful purpose is served by stigmatizing children born out of wedlock as illegitimate. (However, some useful purpose may be served by not according children born out of wedlock all the rights of those born in wedlock, for example, inheritance without parental recognition.) The emphasis on having as many children as one can has also disappeared. It is not this historical concern with procreation that is misplaced in modern society but the forms that the concern has taken.

If society has the responsibility to protect the welfare of children, then some social regulation and control of human reproduction and development is justified. Such regulation and control need not be effected by penal laws. For example, social concern has traditionally been expressed in adoptions through regulations to ensure that those who adopt children are fit to care for them. That some regulations have been inappropriate and not reasonably related to the welfare of children is not in question. Rather, the point is that there has been regulation without penal laws, or at least without resorting primarily to penal laws. Nor can social regulation and control be solely by legislation. Legislation alone is usually ineffective; it must be supported by informal social rules and expectations.

Not only has modern biomedicine made sex possible without procreation; it has also made procreation possible without sex. The techniques of artificial insemination and fertilization, embryo transfer, ova donation, ectogenesis, and cloning now, or soon will, make it possible for people to reproduce without sexual intercourse. Hence, not only may one have sex for pleasure, but one may reproduce for pleasure without sexual intercourse. Not only may people reproduce outside marriage; they are not even biologically required to have intercourse. Thus, sex and marriage may become dissociated from reproduction.

However, there are strong reasons for restricting procreation primarily to marriages of indefinite duration, which does not imply that such marriages should be restricted to procreation. Marriage has traditionally been the central social institution concerned with procreation. Consequently, if society is to exercise some control over procreation in the future, it would involve the least change in conditions to do so through marriage.

Moreover, there is considerable evidence that the disruption of family life contributes to juvenile delinquency. Whether divorce or marital breakdown (with or without divorce) is a prime cause of such delinquency does not matter. The point is that the disruption of home life does seriously affect the development of children. The chance of such disruption outside of a marriage that is intentionally of indefinite duration is higher than for that within. Moreover, there is some reason to believe that the presence of both mother and father is instrumental in the psychological development of children. In any case, the presence of two people rather than one provides the security that there will be someone to care for the children should one of the parents die. Generally, children are better off being with one parent than in a state orphanage, but better off still with both parents. Hence, for the welfare of children it seems best that procreation and child rearing primarily occur within the context of marriages intentionally of indefinite duration.

While society has a responsibility for the care and development of children, this general responsibility is best carried out if specific adults have obligations to care for specific children. In the past, the biological parent-child relation has reinforced the allocation of responsibility for specific children and has been a major factor in monogamy. The separation of reproduction and sexual intercourse threatens disruption of this assignment. For example, if gestation occurs in an artificial womb in a laboratory, there may be no "parents," only a scientific research group. More realistically, if a woman has an embryo from ova and sperm donors transferred to her uterus, it is unclear who are the child's parents. However, if there is to be optimal care for children, specific adults must have obligations for specific children. It cannot be left to somebody in general, for then nobody in particular is likely to do it. "Let George do it" is too prevalent and careless an attitude to allow with regard to children.

[The] contention that monogamy restricts the care for children if there are no specific adults responsible for this is not well founded. First, if there are no specific adults responsible for children, they may become "lost" in large groups and victims of the "it's not my job" syndrome. Second, monogamy per se does not cut children off from the support and care of others. One must distinguish the marital relationship from living arrangements. It is the isolated situation of the family that deprives children of such support. In many married-student housing complexes children have access to other adults. Even in general residential neighborhoods with separate family housing units, such support is available if there is a sense of community in the neighborhood.

Given the social interests in and responsibility for the procreation and development of children, some more effective controls of parenthood appear desirable. If the primary locus of reproduction is to be within marriages of intentionally indefinite du-

ration, then the easiest way to institute controls is to add requirements for people to enter such marriages. A few requirements such as blood tests are already generally prevalent. Alternatively, one might have a separate licensing procedure for procreation. Nonmarried couples and single people might also qualify for such licenses. Moreover, couples who want to marry but not have children would not have to meet requirements. However, the only requirements suggested below that might bar marriages are almost as important for those couples who do not have children as for those who do. If the requirements were tied to marriage they would be easier to administer. The only drawback is that unmarried people would not have to meet them. However, such requirements can and should be part of the medical practice of the "artificial" techniques of reproduction—artificial insemination and embryo transfer. And there are few if any effective methods, except generally accepted social rules, to control procreation outside of marriage.

One obvious requirement would be genetic screening. With modern medical techniques genetic problems do not imply that couples cannot become married, but they might be expected not to have children who are their genetic offspring. Artificial insemination and embryo transfer make it possible for almost everyone to have children, even though the children might not be genetically theirs. A general distinction between biological and social parenthood should be made, with legal emphasis on the latter.

More important, perhaps, is some general expectation of psychological fitness for family life and the raising of children. The difficulty with such an expectation is the absence of any clear criteria for fitness and reliable methods for determining who meets them. Perhaps, however, some formal instruction in family relations and child rearing would be appropriate. The Commission on Population Growth and the American Future has already called for an expansion of education for parenthood.[23] It is only a bit further to require some sort of minimal family education for marriage. Probably the easiest method for ensuring such education would be to make it a required subject in secondary schools. If that were done, few people would have difficulty meeting this requirement for marriage.

There should not be any financial or property qualifications for marriage. Society's interest in and responsibility for the welfare of the population in general is such that governments should ensure an adequate standard of living for all persons. Were that to be done there would be no reason to impose any financial restrictions on marriage. Nonetheless, prospective parents should have more concern for their financial situation than is now frequently the case. The adequate care of children is an expensive task, financially as well as psychologically and temporally.

Conclusion

It may be objected that neither the argument from interpersonal relations nor that from the welfare of children specifically supports monogamous marriage. While loving relationships cannot extend to an indefinite number of people, they can extend to more than one other person. Also, a polygamous union may provide a reasonable environment for procreation. Hence, neither of the arguments supports monogamous marriage per se.

Logically, the objection is quite correct. But it is a misunderstanding of social philosophy to expect arguments showing that a certain arrangement is always best under all circumstances. The most that can be shown is that usually, or as a rule, one social arrangement is preferable to another. Practically, polygamous marriage patterns will probably never be prevalent. For centuries they have been gradually disappearing throughout the world. If a disproportionate sex distribution of the population occurs in some areas or age groups (such as the elderly), then they may increase in significance. Unless that occurs, most people will probably continue to prefer marital monogamy.

More important, the burden of this essay has not been to defend the traditional ideal of marital union or even the current practice. Many of the traditional rules of marriage have been unjust, for example, the inequality between the sexes, both legally and in terms of social roles. Instead, it has been to defend social recognition of marriage of intentionally indefinite duration as a unique and socially valuable institution that society has interests in promoting and regulating. In particular, society has interests in and responsibility for promoting a certain form of valuable interpersonal relationship and protecting the welfare of children. Both of these purposes can be well served by monogamous marriage.

The image, then, is of a society with various forms of living together, but one in which marriage of intentionally indefinite duration would have a distinctive though lessened role as a special kind of socially and legally recognized relationship. There would not be laws prohibiting nonmarital forms of cohabitation. Divorce would be based on factual marital breakdown or mutual consent, with due regard for the welfare of children. Monogamous marriage would recognize a special form of personal relationship in which reproduction and child rearing primarily occur. Given the social interest in decreasing procreation, many people might marry but not have children, and others might not marry at all. Details of the legal marital relationship have not been specified, nor could they be in this brief essay except with respect to the main social interests. Questions of inheritance, legal residence and name, social-security benefits, and so on, have not been specified. Changes in laws with respect to many of these matters can be made without affecting the arguments for the value of, social responsibility for, and interests in marriage. Above all, it is an image in which sexual intercourse plays a much smaller role in the conception of marriage and the good life in general, a society in which vulgar hedonism has at least been replaced by a broader-based *eudaemonism*.

Against Homosexual Marriage

James Q. Wilson

James Q. Wilson is Collins Professor of Management and Public Policy at the University of California, Los Angeles. He is the author of *Moral Sense* (New York: Free Press, 1993) and more recently, *Moral Judgment* (New York: Basic Books, 1997).

Our courts, which have mishandled abortion, may be on the verge of mishandling homosexuality. As a consequence of two pending decisions, we may be able to accept a homosexual marriage.

In 1993 the supreme court of Hawaii ruled that, under the equal-protection clause of that state's constitution, any law based on distinctions of sex was suspect, and thus subject to strict judicial scrutiny. Accordingly, it reversed the denial of a marriage permit to a same-sex couple, unless the state could first demonstrate a "compelling state interest" that would justify limiting marriages to men and women. A new trial is set for early this summer. But in the meantime, the executive branch of Hawaii appointed a commission to examine the question of same-sex marriages; Its report, by a vote of five to two, supports them. The legislature, for its part, holds a different view of the matter, having responded to the court's decision by passing a law unambiguously reaffirming the limitation of marriage to male-female couples.

No one knows what will happen in the coming trial, but the odds are that the Hawaiian version of the equal-rights amendment may control the outcome. If so, since the United States Constitution has a clause requiring that "full faith and credit" shall be given to the public acts, records, and judicial proceedings of every other state, a homosexual couple in a state like Texas, where the population is overwhelmingly opposed to such unions, may soon be able to fly to Hawaii, get married, and then return to live in Texas as lawfully wedded. A few scholars believe that states may be able to impose public-policy objections to such out-of-state marriages. Utah has already voted one in, and other states may follow—but only at the price of endless litigation.

That litigation may be powerfully affected by the second case. It concerns a Colorado statute, already struck down by that state's supreme court, that would prohibit giving to homosexuals "any claim of minority status, quota preferences, protected status, or claim of discrimination." The U.S. Supreme Court is now reviewing the appeals. If its decision upholds the Colorado supreme court and thus allows homosexuals to acquire a constitutionally protected status, the chances will decline of successful objections to homosexual marriage based on considerations of public policy.

Contemporaneous with these events, an important book has appeared under the title *Virtually Normal*. In it, Andrew Sullivan, the editor of the *New Republic,* makes a strong case for a new policy toward homosexuals. He argues that "all public (as opposed to private) discrimination against homosexuals be ended. . . . *And that is all.*" The two key areas where this change is necessary are the military and marriage law. Lifting bans in those areas, while also disallowing anti-sodomy laws and providing information about homosexuality in publicly supported schools, would put an end to the harm that gays have endured. Beyond these changes, Sullivan writes, American society would need no "cures to [of homophobia] or reeducations, no wrenching private litigation, no political imposition of tolerance."

It is hard to imagine how Sullivan's proposals would, in fact, end efforts to change private behavior toward homosexuals, or why the next, inevitable, step would not involve attempts to accomplish just that purpose by using cures and reeducations, private litigation, and the political imposition of tolerance. But apart from this, Sullivan—an English Catholic, a homosexual, and someone who has on occasion referred to himself as a conservative—has given us the most sensible and coherent view of a program to put homosex-

From James Q. Wilson, "Against Homosexual Marriage," *Commentary* 101 (March 1996): 34–39. Copyright © 1996 by the American Jewish Committee. Reprinted by permission.

uals and heterosexuals on the same public footing. His analysis is based on a careful reading of serious opinions and his book is written quietly, clearly, and thoughtfully. In her review of it in *First Things* (January 1996), Elizabeth Kristol asks us to try to answer the following question: What would life be like if we were not allowed to marry? To most of us, the thought is unimaginable; to Sullivan, it is the daily existence of declared homosexuals. His response is to let homosexual couples marry.

. . . As we have seen, the Hawaiian supreme court ruled that any state-imposed sexual distinction would have to meet the test of strict scrutiny, a term used by the U.S. Supreme Court only for racial and similar classifications. In doing this, the Hawaiian court distanced itself from every other state court decision—there are several—in this area so far. A variant of the suspect-class argument, though, has been suggested by some scholars who contend that denying access to a marriage license by two people of the same sex is no different from denying access to two people of different sexes but also different races. The Hawaiian supreme court embraced this argument as well, explicitly comparing its decision to that of the U.S. Supreme Court when it overturned state laws banning marriages involving miscegenation.

But the comparison with black-white marriages is itself suspect. Beginning around 1964, and no doubt powerfully affected by the passage of the Civil Rights Act of that year, public attitudes toward race began to change dramatically. Even allowing for exaggerated statements to pollsters, there is little doubt that people in fact acquired a new view of blacks. Not so with homosexuals. Though the campaign to aid them has been going on vigorously for about a quarter of a century, it has produced few, if any gains in public acceptance, and the greatest resistance, I think, has been with respect to homosexual marriages.

Consider the difference. What has been at issue in race relations is not marriage among blacks (for over a century, that right has been universally granted) or even miscegenation (long before the civil-rights movement, many Southern states had repealed such laws). Rather, it has been the routine contact between the races in schools, jobs, and neighborhoods. Our own history, in other words, has long made it clear that marriage is a different issue from the issue of social integration.

There is another way, too, in which the comparison with race is less than helpful, as Sullivan himself points out. Thanks to the changes in public attitudes I mentioned a moment ago, gradually race was held to be not central to decisions about hiring, firing, promoting, and schooling, and blacks began to make extraordinary advances in society. But then, in an effort to enforce this new view, liberals came to embrace affirmative action, a policy that said that race *was* central to just such issues, in order to ensure that *real* mixing occurred. This move created a crisis, for liberalism had always been based on the proposition that a liberal political system should encourage, as John Stuart Mill put it, "experiments in living" free of religious or political direction. To contemporary liberals, however, being neutral about race was tantamount to being neutral about a set of human preferences that in such matters as neighborhood and schooling left groups largely (but not entirely) separate.

Sullivan, who wisely sees that hardly anybody is really prepared to ignore a political opportunity to change lives, is not disposed to have much of this either in the area of race or in that of sex. And he points out with great clarity that popular attitudes toward sexuality are anyway quite different from those about race, as is evident from the fact that wherever sexual orientation is subject to local regulations, such regulations are rarely invoked. Why? Because homosexuals can "pass" or not, as they wish; they can and do accumulate education and wealth; they exercise political power. The two things a homosexual cannot do are join the military as an avowed homosexual or marry another homosexual.

The result, Sullivan asserts, is a wrenching paradox. On the one hand, society has historically tolerated the brutalization inflicted on people because of the color of their skin, but freely allowed them to marry; on the other hand, it has given equal opportunity to homosexuals, while denying them the right to marry. This, indeed, is where Sullivan draws the line. A black or Hispanic child, if heterosexual, has many friends, he writes, but a gay child "generally has no one." And that is why the social stigma attached to homosexuality is different from that attached to race or ethnicity—"because it attacks the very heart of what makes a human being human—the ability to love and be loved." Here is the essence of Sullivan's case. It is a powerful one, even if (as I suspect) his pro-marriage sentiments are not shared by all homosexuals.

Let us assume for the moment that a chance to live openly and legally with another homosexual is desirable. To believe that, we must set aside biblical injunctions, a difficult matter in a profoundly religious nation. But suppose we manage the diversion, perhaps on the grounds that if most Americans skip church, they can as readily avoid other errors of (possibly) equal magnitude. Then we must ask on what terms the union shall be arranged. There are two alternatives—marriage or domestic partnership.

Sullivan acknowledges the choice, but disparages the domestic-partnership laws that have evolved in some foreign countries and in some American localities. His reasons, essentially conservative ones, are that domestic partnerships are too easily formed and too easily broken. Only real marriages matter. But—aside from the fact that marriage is in serious decline, and that only slightly more than half of all marriages performed in the United States this year will be between never-before-married heterosexuals—what is distinctive about marriage is that it is an institution created to sustain child-rearing. Whatever losses it has suffered in this respect, its function remains what it has always been.

The role of raising children is entrusted in principle to married heterosexual couples because after much experimentation—several thousand years, more or less—we have found nothing else that works as well. Neither a gay nor a lesbian couple can of its own resources produce a child; another party must be involved. What do we call this third party? A friend? A sperm or egg bank? An anonymous donor? There is no settled language for even describing, much less approving of, such persons.

Suppose we allowed homosexual couples to raise children who were created out of a prior heterosexual union or adopted from someone else's

heterosexual contact. What would we think of this? There is very little research on the matter. Charlotte Patterson's famous essay, "Children of Gay and Lesbian Parents" (*Journal of Child Development,* 1992), begins by conceding that the existing studies focus on children born into a heterosexual union that ended in divorce or that was transformed when the mother or father "came out" as a homosexual. Hardly any research has been done on children acquired at the outset by a homosexual couple. We therefore have no way of knowing how they would behave. And even if we had such studies, they might tell us rather little unless they were conducted over a very long period of time.

But it is one thing to be born into an apparently heterosexual family and then many years later to learn that one of your parents is homosexual. It is quite another to be acquired as an infant from an adoption agency or a parent-for-hire and learn from the first years of life that you are, because of your family's position, radically different from almost all other children you will meet. No one can now say how grievous this would be. We know that young children tease one another unmercifully; adding this dimension does not seem to be a step in the right direction.

Of course, homosexual "families" with or without children, might be rather few in number; just how few, it is hard to say. Perhaps Sullivan himself would marry, but, given the great tendency of homosexual males to be promiscuous, many more like him would not, or if they did, would not marry with as much seriousness.

That is problematic in itself. At one point, Sullivan suggests that most homosexuals would enter a marriage "with as much (if not more) commitment as heterosexuals." Toward the end of his book, however, he seems to withdraw from so optimistic a view. He admits that the label "virtually" in the title of his book is deliberately ambiguous, because homosexuals as a group are not "normal." At another point, he writes that the "openness of the contract" between two homosexual males means that such a union will in fact be more durable than a heterosexual marriage because the contract contains an "understanding of *the need for extramarital outlets*" (emphasis added). But no such "understanding" exists in heterosexual marriage; to suggest that it might in homosexual ones is tantamount to saying that we are now referring to two different kinds of arrangements. To justify this difference, perhaps, Sullivan adds that the very "lack of children" will give "gay couples greater freedom." Freedom for what? Freedom, I think, to do more of those things that heterosexual couples do less of because they might hurt the children.

The courts in Hawaii and in the nation's capital must struggle with all these issues under the added encumbrance of a contemporary outlook that makes law the search for rights, and responsibility the recognition of rights. Indeed, thinking of laws about marriage as documents that confer or withhold rights is itself an error of fundamental importance—one that the highest court in Hawaii has already committed. "Marriage," it wrote, "is a state-conferred legal-partnership status, the existence of which gives rise to a multiplicity of rights and benefits. . . ." A state-conferred legal partnership? To lawyers, perhaps; to mankind, I think not. The Hawaiian court has thus set itself on the same course of action as the misguided Supreme Court in 1973 when it thought that laws about abortion were merely an assertion of the rights of a living mother and an unborn fetus.

I have few favorable things to say about the political system of other modern nations, but on these fundamental matters—abortion, marriage, military service—they often do better by allowing legislatures to operate than we do by deferring to courts. Our challenge is to find a way of formulating a policy with respect to homosexual unions that is not the result of a reflexive act of judicial rights-conferring, but is instead a considered expression of the moral convictions of a people.

The Case for Gay Marriage
Richard D. Mohr

Richard D. Mohr is professor of philosophy at the University of Illinois–Urbana. He is the author of *The Platonic Cosmology* (Leiden: E. J. Brill, 1985), *Gay Justice* (New York: Columbia University Press, 1988), *Gay Ideas* (Boston: Beacon Press, 1992), and *A More Perfect Union: Why Straight America Must Stand Up for Gay Rights* (Boston: Beacon Press, 1994).

In this article, I advocate for the legalization of gay marriage. My analysis does not in the main proceed by appeal to the concept of equality; in particular, nothing will turn on distinctive features of Equal Protection doctrine. Rather the analysis is substantive and turns on understanding the nature and meaning of marriage itself . . .

Social and Legal Attempts to Define Marriage

Usually in religious, ethical, and legal thinking, issues are settled with reference to a thing's goodness. Yet oddly, the debate over gay marriage has focused not on whether the thing is good but on whether the thing can even exist. Those opposing gay marriage say that the very definition of marriage rules out the possibility that gay couples can be viewed as married.[1]

If one asks the average jo(e) on the street what marriage is, the person generally just gets tongue-tied. Try it. The meaning of marriage is somehow supposed to be so obvious, so entrenched and ramified in daily life, that it is never in need of articulation.

Standard dictionaries, which track and make coherent common usages of terms, are unhelpfully circular. Most commonly, dictionaries define marriage in terms of spouses, spouses in terms of husband and wife, and husband and wife in terms of marriage.[2] In consequence, the various definitions do no work in explaining what marriage is and so simply end up rawly assuming or stipulating that marriage must be between people of different sexes.

From Richard D. Mohr, "The Case for Gay Marriage," *Notre Dame Journal of Law, Ethics & Public Policy* 9 (1995): 216–229. © 1996 by Richard D. Mohr. Reprinted by permission of the author.

Legal definitions of marriage fare no better. Many state laws only speak of spouses or partners and do not actually make explicit that people must be of different sexes to marry.[3] During the early 1970s and again in the early 1980s, gays directly challenged these laws in four states, claiming that in accordance with common-law tradition, whatever is not prohibited must be allowed, and that if these laws were judicially construed to require different-sex partners, then the laws constituted unconstitutional sex or sexual orientation discrimination.[4] Gays lost all these cases, which the courts treated in dismissive, but revealing, fashion.[5]

The courts would first claim that the silence of the law notwithstanding, marriage automatically entails gender difference. The best-known of these rulings is the 1974 case *Singer v. Hara,* which upheld Washington State's refusal to grant a marriage license to two males. The case defined marriage as "the legal union of one man and one woman as husband and wife."[6] This definition has become *the* legal definition of marriage, since it has been taken up into the standard law dictionary, *Black's Sixth Edition,* where the case is the only citation given in the article on marriage.[7]

Yet the *Singer* definition tells us nothing whatever of the content of marriage. First, the qualification "as husband and wife" is simply circular. Since "husband" and "wife" *mean* people who are in a marriage with each other, the definition, as far as these terms go, presupposes the very thing to be defined. So what is left is that marriage is "the legal union of one man and one woman." Now, if the term "legal" here simply means "not illegal," then notice that a kiss after the prom can fit its bill: "the legal union of one man and one woman." We are told nothing of what "the union" is that is supposed to be the heart of marriage. The formulation of the definition serves no function other than to exclude from marriage—whatever it is—the people whom America views as destroyers of the American family, same-sex couples and polygamists: "*one* man and *one* woman." Like the ordinary dictionary definitions, the legal definition does no explanatory work.[8]

Nevertheless, the courts take this definition, turn it around, and say that since this is what marriage *means,* gender discrimination and sexual-orientation discrimination is built right into the institution of marriage; therefore since marriage itself is permitted, so too must be barring same-sex couples from it. Discrimination against gays, they hold, is not an illegitimate discrimination in marriage, indeed it is necessary to the very institution: No one would be married if gays were, for then marriage wouldn't be marriage. It took a gay case to reveal what marriage is, but reveals it, at least as legally understood, to be nothing but an empty space, delimited only by what it excludes—gay couples. And so it has all the marks of being profoundly prejudicial in its legal treatment of gays.

Gender in Marital Law

If we shift from considering the legal definition of marriage to the legal practices of marriage, are there differences of gender that insinuate themselves into marriage, so that botched definitions aside, marriage does after all require that its pairings be of the male-female variety? There used to be major gender-based legal differences in marriage, but these have all been found to be unjust and have gradually been eliminated through either legislative or judicial means. For example, husbands used to have an obligation to take care of their wives' material needs without their wives (no matter how wealthy) having any corresponding obligation to look after their husbands (however poor). Now both spouses are mutually and equally obliged.[9] At one time a husband could sell his wife's property without her consent; the wife had no independent power to make contracts. But these laws have not generally been in force since the middle of the last century and are now unconstitutional.[10] It used to be that a husband could *by definition* not rape his wife—one could as well rape oneself, the reasoning went. Now, while laws governing sexual relations between husbands and wives are not identical to those governing relations between (heterosexual) strangers, they are nearly so, and such differences as remain are in any case cast in gender-neutral terms.[11] Wives are legally protected from ongoing sexual abuse from husbands—whatever the non-legal reality.

Now that gender distinctions have all but vanished from the legal *content* of marriage, there is no basis for the requirement that the legal *form* of marriage unite members of different sexes. The legal definition of marriage—"union of one man and one woman"—though doggedly enforced in the courts, is a dead husk that has been cast off by marriage as a living legal institution.[12]

Babies in Marital Law

Perhaps sensing the shakiness of an argument that rests solely on a stipulative definition of little or no content, the courts have tried to supplement the supposedly obvious requirement for gender disparity in access to marriage with appeal to reproduction. By assuming that procreation and rearing of children is essential to married life, the courts have implicitly given marriage a functional definition designed to eliminate lesbians and gay men from the ranks of the marriageable.[13] "As we all know" (the courts self-congratulatorily declare), lesbians are "constitutionally incapable" of bearing children by other lesbians, and gay men are incapable of siring children by other gay men.

But the legally acknowledged institution of marriage in fact does not track this functional definition. All states allow people who are over sixty to marry each other, with all the rights and obligations marriage entails even though biological reality dictates that such marriages will be sterile. In Hawaii, the statute that requires women to prove immunity against rubella as a condition for getting a marriage license exempts women "who, by reason of age or other medically determined condition are not and never will be physically able to conceive children."[14] In 1984, Hawaii also amended its marriage statute to delete a requirement that "neither of the parties is impotent or physically incapable of entering into the marriage state."[15] This statutory latitude belies any claim that the narrow purpose of marriage is to promote and protect propagation.[16]

The functional definition is too broad as well. If the function of marriage is only to bear and raise children in a family context, then the state should have no objection to the legal recognition of polygamous marriages. Male-focused polygamous families have been efficient bearers of chil-

dren; and the economies of scale afforded by polygamous families also make them efficient in the rearing of children.[17]

So given the actual scope of legal marriage, reproduction and childrearing cannot be its purpose or primary justification.

This finding is further confirmed if we look at the rights and obligations of marriage, which exist independently of whether a marriage generates children and which frequently are not even instrumental to childbearing and rearing. While mutual material support might be viewed as guarding (indirectly) the interests of children, other marital rights, such as the immunity against compelled testimony from a spouse, can hardly be grounded in child-related purposes. Indeed, this immunity is waived when relations with one's own children are what is at legal stake, as in cases of alleged child abuse.[18]

The assumption that childrearing is a function uniquely tethered to the institution of heterosexual marriage also collides with an important but little acknowledged social reality. Many lesbian and gay male couples already are raising families in which children are the blessings of adoption, artificial insemination, surrogacy, or prior marriages. The country is experiencing something approaching a gay and lesbian baby boom.[19] Many more gays would like to raise or foster children. A 1988 study by the American Bar Association found that eight to ten million children are currently being raised in three million gay and lesbian households.[20] This statistic, in turn, suggests that around six percent of the U.S. population is made up of gay and lesbian families with children.[21] We might well ask what conceivable purpose can be served for these children by barring to their gay and lesbian parents the mutual cohesion, emotional security, and economic benefits that are ideally promoted by legal marriage.[22]

Marriage as a Creature of the State

If the desperate judicial and social attempts to restrict marriage and its benefits to heterosexual parents are conceptually disingenuous, unjust, and socially inefficient, the question arises: what is left of marriage? Given the emptiness of its standard justifications, should marriage as a legal institution simply be abolished? Ought we simply to abandon the legal institution in favor of a family policy that simply and directly looks after the interests of children, leaving all other possible familial relations on the same legal footing as commercial transactions?

Not quite; but to see what is left and worth saving, we need to take a closer look at the social realities of marriage. Currently state-sanctioned marriage operates as a legal institution that defines and creates social relations. The law creates the status of husband and wife; it is not a reflection of or response to spousal relations that exist independently of law. This notion that the law "defines and creates social relations" can be clarified by looking at another aspect of family law, one which ordinary people might well find surprising, even shocking. If Paul consensually sires a boy and raises the boy in the way a parent does, then we are strongly inclined to think that he is the boy's father in every morally relevant sense. And we expect the law to reflect this moral status of the father. But the law does not see things this way; it does not reflect and respond to moral reality. For if it turns out that at the time of the boy's birth, his mother was legally married not to Paul but to Fred, the boy is declared by law to be Fred's son, and Paul is, legally speaking, a stranger to the boy. If the mother subsequently leaves Paul and denies him access to the child, Paul has no right at all even to explore legally the possibility that he might have some legislated rights to visit the boy—or so the Supreme Court declared in 1989.[23] Here the law defines and creates the relation of father and son—which frequently, but only by legal accident, happens to accord with the moral reality and lived experience of father and son.

Similarly, in the eyes of the law, marriage is not a social form that exists independently of the law and which marriage law echoes and manages. Rather, marriage is entirely a creature of the law—or as Hawaii's Supreme Court recently put it: "Marriage is a state-conferred legal partnership status."[24]

If we want to see what's left in the box of marriage, we need to abandon this model of legal marriage as constitutive of a status, and rather look at marriage as a form of living and repository of norms independent of law, a moral reality that might well be helped or hindered, but not constituted by the law.[25] Further, current legal marriage, at least as conceptualized by judges, with its definitional entanglements with gender and procreation, is likely to distract us from perceiving lived moral reality.

A Fresh Approach: Marriage Defined

What is marriage? Marriage is intimacy given substance in the medium of everyday life, the day-to-day. Marriage is the fused intersection of love's sanctity and necessity's demand.

Not all loves or intimate relations count or should count as marriages. Culturally, we are disinclined to think of "great loves" as marriages. Antony and Cleopatra, Tristan and Isolde, Catherine and Heathcliff—these are loves that burn gloriously but too intensely ever to be manifested in a medium of breakfasts and tire-changes. Nor are Americans inclined to consider as real marriages arranged marriages between heads of state who never see each other, for again the relations do not grow in the earth of day-to-day living.

Friendships too are intimate relations that we do not consider marital relations. Intimate relations are ones that acquire the character they have—that are unique—because of what the individuals in the relation bring to and make of it; the relation is a distinctive product of their separate individualities. Thus, intimate relations differ markedly from public or commercial transactions. For instance, there is nothing distinctive about your sales clerk that bears on the meaning of your buying a pair of socks from him. The clerk is just carrying out a role, one that from the buyer's perspective nearly anyone could have carried out. But while friendships are star cases of intimate relationships, we do not count them as marriages; for while a person might count on a friend in a pinch to take her to the hospital, friendly relations do not usually manifest themselves through such necessities of life. Friendships are for the sake of fun, and tend to break down when put to other uses. Friendships do not count as marriages, for they do not develop in the medium of necessity's demand.

On the other hand, neither do we count roommates who regularly cook, clean, tend to household chores and share household finances as married, even though they "share the common necessities of life." This expression is the typical phrase used to define the threshold requirement for being considered "domestic partners" in towns that have registration programs for domestic partners.[26] Neither would we even consider as married two people who were roommates and even blended their finances if that is all their relationship comprised. Sharing the day-to-day is, at best, an ingredient of marriage.

Marriage requires the presence and blending of both necessity and intimacy. Life's necessities are a mixed fortune: on the one hand, they frequently are drag, dross, and cussedness, yet on the other hand, they can constitute opportunity, abidingness, and prospect for nurture. They are the field across which, the medium through which, and the ground from which the intimacies which we consider marital flourish, blossom, and come to fruition.

The Normative and Legal Consequence of Marriage

The Legal Rights and Benefits of Marriage

This required blend of intimacy and everyday living explains much of the legal content of marriage. For example, the required blend means that for the relationship to work, there must be a presumption of trust between partners; and, in turn, when the relationship *is* working, there will be a transparency in the flow of information between partners—they will know virtually everything about each other. This pairing of trust and transparency constitutes the moral ground for the common law right against compelled testimony between spouses, and explains why this same immunity is not extended to (mere) friends.[27]

The remaining vast array of legal rights and benefits of marriage equally well fit this matrix of love and necessity—chiefly by promoting the patient tendance that such life requires (by providing for privacy, nurture, support, persistence) and by protecting against the occasions when necessity is cussed rather than opportune, especially when life is marked by crisis, illness and destruction.[28]

First and foremost, state-recognized marriage changes strangers-at-law into next-of-kin with all the rights which this status entails. These rights include: the right to enter hospitals, jails and other places restricted to "immediate family"; the right to obtain "family" health insurance and bereavement leave; the right to live in neighborhoods zoned "single family only"; and the right to make medical decisions in the event a partner is injured or incapacitated.

Both from the partners themselves and from the state, marriage provides a variety of material supports which ameliorate, to a degree, necessity's unfriendly intervals. Marriage requires mutual support between spouses. It provides income tax advantages, including deductions, credits, improved rates, and exemptions. It provides for enhanced public assistance in times of need. It governs the equitable control, division, acquisition, and disposition of community property. At death, it guarantees rights of inheritance in the absence of wills—a right of special benefit to the poor, who frequently die intestate. For the wealthy, marriage virtually eliminates inheritance taxes between spouses, since spouses as of 1981 can make unlimited untaxed gifts to each other even at death.[29] For all, it exempts property from attachments resulting from one partner's debts. It confers a right to bring a wrongful death suit. And it confers the right to receive survivor's benefits.

Several marital benefits promote a couple's staying together in the face of changed circumstances. Included in the benefits are the right to collect unemployment benefits if one partner quits her job to move with her partner to a new location because the partner has obtained a new job there, and the right to obtain residency status for a noncitizen partner. Currently lesbians and gay men are denied all of these rights in consequence of being barred access to legal marriage, even though these rights and benefits are as relevant to committed gay relationships as to heterosexual marriages.

The Structuring of Lesbian and Gay Relationships

The portraits of gay and lesbian committed relationships that emerge from ethnographic studies suggest that in the way they typically arrange their lives, gay and lesbian couples fulfill in an exemplary manner the definition of marriage developed here.[30]

In gay relationships, the ways in which the day-to-day demands of necessity are typically fulfilled are themselves vehicles for the development of intimacy. It is true that gay and lesbian relationships generally divide duties between the partners—this is the efficient thing to do, the very first among the economies of scale that coupledom affords. But the division of duties is in the first instance a matter of personal preference and joint planning, in which decisions are made in part with an eye to who is better at doing any given task and who has free time—say, for ironing or coping with car dealerships. But adjustments are made in cases where one person is better at most things, or even everything. In these cases, the relation is made less efficient for the sake of equality between partners, who willingly end up doing things they would rather not do. Such joint decisions are made not from a sense of traditionally assigned duty and role, but from each partner's impulse to help out, a willingness to sacrifice, and a commitment to equality.[31] In these ways, both the development of intimacy through choice and the proper valuing of love are interwoven in the day-to-day activities of gay couples. Choice improves intimacy. Choice makes sacrifices meaningful. Choice gives love its proper weight.

Weddings and Licensing Considered

If this analysis of the nature of marriage is correct, then misguided is the requirement, found in most states, that beyond securing from government a marriage license, the couple, in order to be certifiably married, must also undergo a ceremony of solemnization, either in a church or before a justice of the peace.[32] For people are mistaken to think that the sacred valuing of love is something that can be imported from the outside, in public ceremonies invoking praise from God or community.[33] Even wedding vows can smack of cheap moral credit, since they are words, not actions. The sacred valuing of love must come from within and realize itself over time through little sacrifices in day-to-day existence. In this way, intimacy takes on weight and shine, the ordinary becomes the vehicle of the extraordinary, and the development of the marital relation becomes a mirror reflecting eternity. It is more proper to think of weddings with their ceremonial trappings

and invocations as *bon voyages* than as a social institution which, echoing the legal institution of marriage, defines and confers marital status. In a gay marriage, the sanctifications that descend instantly through custom and ritual in many heterosexual marriages descend gradually over and through time—and in a way they are better for it. For the sacred values and loyal intimacies contained in such a marriage are a product of the relation itself; they are truly the couple's own.

The model of marriage advanced here is highly compatible with, indeed recommends, what has been, until recently, by far the most usual form of marriage in Western Civilization, namely, common law marriage—in which there is no marriage license or solemnization. Currently only about one-fourth of the states legally acknowledge common law marriages, but over the largest stretches of Western Civilization, legally certifiable marriage was an arrangement limited almost exclusively to the wealthy, the noble—the few.[34]

In a common law arrangement, the marriage is at some point, as the need arises, culturally and legally acknowledged in retrospect as having existed all along. It is important to remember that as matter of law, the standard requirement of living together seven years is entirely evidentiary and not at all constitutive of the relation as a marriage.[35] So, for example, a child born in the third year of a common law marriage is legitimate from the moment of its birth and need not wait four years as mom and dad log seven years together. The marriage was there in substance all along. The social and legal custom of acknowledging common law marriage gives an adequately robust recognition to marriage as a lived arrangement and as a repository of values.

The securing of a marriage license is something the state may well want to encourage as a useful device in the administration of the legal benefits of marriage. But the licensing should not be seen as what legally constitutes the marriage when questions arise over whether the marriage in fact exists (say, in paternity, custody, or inheritance disputes). In turn, it is completely legitimate for the state to terminate marital benefits if in fact the couple gets a license but is not fulfilling the definition of marriage as a living arrangement. The state already investigates such cases of fraud when marriage licenses are secured simply to acquire an enhanced immigration status for one of the licensees.[36] Indeed, that immigration fraud through marriage licenses is even conceptually possible is a tacit recognition that marriage *simpliciter* is marriage as a lived arrangement, while legally certified marriage is and should be viewed as epiphenomenonal or derivative—and not vice versa.

The Relation between Love and Justice

If intimate or private relations of a certain quality provide the content of marriage, what can the law and public policy provide to marriage? Why do we need legal marriage at all? Folk wisdom has it that both love and justice are blind. But they are blind in different ways, ways which reveal possible conflicts and tensions between love and justice in practice.[37]

Justice is blind—blindfolded—so that it may be a system of neutral, impersonal, impartial rules, a governance by laws, not by idiosyncratic, biased, or self-interested persons. Principles of justice in the modern era have been confected chiefly with an eye to relations at arm's length and apply paradigmatically to competitions conducted between conflicting interests in the face of scarce resources. Equal respect is the central concern of justice.[38]

Love is blind—(as the song goes) blinded by the light—because the lover is stutteringly bedazzled by the beloved. In love, we overlook failings in those whom we cherish. And the beloved's happiness, not the beloved's respect, is love's central concern.

Within the family, we agree that the distribution of goods should be a matter of feeling, care, concern, and sacrifice rather than one conducted by appeal to impartial and impersonal principles of equity. Indeed, if the impersonal principles of justice are constantly in the foreground of familial relations, intimacy is destroyed. If every decision in a family requires a judicial-like determination that each member got an equal share, then the care, concern, and love that are a family's breath and spirit are dead. Justice should not be front and center in family life.

But love may lead to intolerable injustices, even as a spin-off effect of one of its main virtues. In the blindness of love, people will love even those who beat them and humiliate them. Conversely, aggressors in these cases will feel more free to aggress against a family member than a stranger exactly because the family is the realm of love rather than of civic respect. Some of these humiliations are even occasioned by the distinctive opportunities afforded by traditional family life—in particular, society's misguided notion that everything that occurs behind the family's four walls is private, and so beyond legitimate inquiry.

Conflicts between love and justice can be relieved if we view marriage as a legal institution that allows for appeals to justice when they are needed. Justice should not be the motivation for loving relations, but neither should love and family to exist beyond the reach of justice. Justice needs to be a reliable background and foundation for family life. Therefore legal marriage should be viewed as a nurturing ground for social marriage, and not (as now) as that which legally defines and creates marriage and so tends to preclude legal examination of it . . .

QUESTIONS FOR THOUGHT AND DISCUSSION

1. How are marital duties like other duties that arise from a contract? How are they unlike the duties that arise from the criminal law (for example, the duty not to injure others)?
2. What is the purpose of the marriage contract, according to Locke and Kant?
3. Both Locke and Mohr appear to argue that marriage is a moral relationship between persons that does not depend on a legal system for its

existence. But (according to Barbara Herman) Immanuel Kant says that marital relationships cannot exist independently of law and government. Why is this? Which position is correct?

4. According to A. John Simmons, why is it unfair to read Locke as saying that men enjoy a "natural dominion" over women in marriage, that is, that the equality of husband and wife is not something that can be made a part of the marital contract?

5. Why does Kant say that a man and a woman must marry each other if they want to enjoy each other sexually?

6. According to Andrea Dworkin, how does sexual intercourse turn women into mere objects or things? Why does she think that *only* women (not men) are objectified by sexual intercourse, even if it is consensual, and even if it is marital?

7. According to Herman, how does Kant distinguish between human love and sexual love? How is this distinction relevant to his general argument that sexual love is morally problematic?

8. Is there anything that is morally wrong with consensual premarital sexual relationships? If sexual relationships are morally problematic, then how does marriage make them morally permissible?

9. Should the state recognize marriage contracts that are intentionally of a short, definite duration (e.g., "five years, with an option to renew")?

10. In what ways (if any) does marriage protect the welfare of children?

11. In what ways (if any) does marriage promote interpersonal relationships?

12. What are some of the arguments that James Q. Wilson gives for restricting marriage to heterosexual, monogamous relationships? Are these arguments sound?

13. Why does Richard Mohr claim that the attempts to restrict marriage to heterosexual relationships "are conceptually disingenuous, unjust, and socially inefficient"?

14. What does Mohr mean when he writes that marriage is "a form of living and repository of norms independent of law"? Compare Mohr's definition with Richard Wasserstrom's account of marriage in Chapter 7.

FURTHER READING

Jeffrey Blustein, *Parents and Children: The Ethics of the Family,* 247–252. New York: Oxford University Press, 1982.

John Boswell, *Same-Sex Unions in Premodern Europe.* New York: Villard, 1994.

Andrea Dworkin, *Intercourse.* New York: Free Press, 1987.

Immanuel Kant, *Foundations of the Metaphysics of Morals.* Trans. L. W. Beck. Indianapolis: Bobbs-Merrill, 1976.

Immanuel Kant, *The Philosophy of Law.* Clifton, NY: Augustus M. Kelly, 1974.

John Locke, *Two Treatises of Government.* Ed. P. Laslett. New York: New American Library, 1965.

Catherine MacKinnon, *Towards a Feminist Theory of the State.* Cambridge, MA: Harvard University Press, 1989.

Lucy Mair, *Marriage.* Baltimore: Penguin Books, 1971.

Carol Pateman, *The Sexual Contract*. Stanford, CA: Stanford University Press, 1989.

Bertrand Russell, *Marriage and Morals*. Garden City, NY: Horace Livewright, 1929.

Andrew Sullivan, "Here Comes the Groom: A (Conservative) Case for Gay Marriage." *The New Republic,* August 28, 1989, 22ff.

NOTES

John Simmons

1. Kant, for instance, claims that while the natural end of marriage is producing and educating children, this is not *essential* to marriage, since people may have other ends (*Metaphysics of Morals,* part 1, section 24).

2. Again, see Kant, *Metaphysics of Morals,* part 1, section 26.

3. See the discussion of reciprocity between spouses in Becker, *Reciprocity,* 1985. I do not think that considerations of reciprocity can *override* the genuinely voluntary undertakings of spouses.

4. Contrary to what Hegel may have thought (*Philosophy of Right,* section 163).

5. Locke must receive mixed reviews on his liberality with regard to equality of the sexes. The passages I consider below (and Locke's views on paternal control of property) make it easy to simply dismiss his views as thoroughly permeated with the deep and casual sexism of his age. (See, e.g., Clark, "Women and John Locke," 721–24; Seliger, *Liberal Politics,* 211–12.) But while Dunn is certainly right that Locke's sexual egalitarianism fought a losing battle with his acceptance of the radically inegalitarian conventions of his age (*Political Thought,* 121–22n), there was at least a battle. Locke's insistence on equal parental authority and his very liberal views on the free determination of nonconventional marriage contracts deserve some notice. And, as I argue below, other aspects of Locke's views on the rights of women deserve more charitable readings than they usually receive. See Yolton, *Locke,* 58.

6. Locke's proof of this claim seems seriously confused (again involving a blurring of moral with physical "powers"). He argues that if the husband did have absolute power over his wife, "there could be no matrimony in any of those countries where the husband is allowed no such absolute authority" (II, 83). This seems to amount to the quite silly claim that if the state denies you exercise of a right to X, you cannot have a moral right to X (a claim, of course, which Locke emphatically and correctly rejects throughout the body of his work).

7. Clark, "Women and John Locke," 702–4, 708. See also Pateman, *Problem of Political Obligation,* 75.

8. Clark, "Women and John Locke, 709–11. On unconscionable contracts, see my "Consent, Free Choice," section 5.

9. Ibid., 721. See also Pateman, "Women and Consent," 152. While Locke never indicates any interest in considering,

for instance, female citizenship, these assessments of his views still seem unduly harsh (for reasons specified below).

10. The biblical text at issue merely "foretells what should be woman's lot" (I, 47); it does not *prescribe* it. Locke uses this same style of biblical interpretation on other occasions in the *First Treatise* (e.g., I, 118).

11. In the case of majority rule, of course, there is nothing straightforwardly more authoritative or fair about this procedure than many alternatives (e.g., lotteries, votes weighted by intensity of preference, etc.). Even the physical analogy (right must follow force) will not help here, since an intense minority might be a "greater force" than an apathetic majority. In the case of marriage contracts, even if greater ability were a ground for greater authority, a right of "last determination" is far from the only way to implement this authority. And again, the dispute need not fall on the side of the party possessing the greater physical strength.

12. Sidgwick, *Methods of Ethics,* 256.

13. Locke accepts the idea that unfair bargaining position can void an apparent contract (see, e.g., I, 42).

14. I leave untouched myriad difficulties concerning degrees of voluntariness, social conditioning, "false consciousness," and so on, as well as questions about the terms of the marriage contract (may they be renegotiated when one or both of the partners changes or grows in ways that make the initial specification unrewarding or inappropriate?).

Barbara Herman

1. Kant is almost always talking about sexual activity between consenting adult men and women. This aspect of his critique of sexuality would apply equally to same-sex sexual relations—although Kant has other sorts of "unnaturalness" objections to them.

2. It is this—and not sexual squeamishness—that is the basis for his claim that engaging in sexual relations without marriage is not morally possible.

3. Kant, *Lectures on Ethics,* trans. Louis Infield (New York: Harper Torchbooks, 1963), p. 164.

4. New York, Free Press: 1987. Quotations are from pp. 122–23, 140–141 and 142–143, respectively.

5. "Pornography is not imagery in some relation to a reality elsewhere constructed. It is not distortion, reflection, projection, expression, fantasy, representation, or symbol either. It is

sexual reality." Catharine MacKinnon, quoted in Christine Littleton, "Feminist Jurisprudence: The Difference Method Makes," *Stanford Law Review* 41 (February 1989): 772.

6. Dworkin, *Intercourse*, p. 136.

7. Transformations of the sexual appetite to having an object that is not the body of another can be ignored here.

8. There is some ambiguity in Kant's moral charge: Are we brought by the sexual appetite to regard our partners as objects, *as if* we had rights of disposal over them, or is it that in sexual relations we *are* objects for each other over which we do have rights of disposal?

9. "The sole condition on which we are free to make use of our sexual desire depends upon the right to dispose over the person as a whole—over the welfare and happiness and generally over all the circumstances of that person" (*Lectures on Ethics*, pp. 166–167).

10. As a law professor friend remarked, from the State's point of view, marriage is about divorce.

11. Stories such as this are the basis of Carol Pateman's critical analysis of the role of marriage in liberal political theory. See her *Sexual Contract* (Stanford, Calif.: Stanford University Press, 1989).

Richard D. Mohr

1. As one court put it, "Thus there has been for centuries a combination of scriptural and canonical teaching under which a 'marriage' between persons of the same sex was unthinkable and, by definition, impossible." *Adams v. Howerton,* 486 F.Supp. 1119, 1123 (1980) (upholding an Immigration and Naturalization Service ruling that a gay man could not be considered an "immediate relative" of another with whom he had lived for years and had had a marriage ceremony).

Similarly, in 1991, Hawaii's Director of the Department of Health argued before Hawaii's Supreme Court: "The right of persons of the same sex to marry one another does not exist because marriage, by definition and usage, means a special relationship between a man and a woman." Quoted in *Baehr* v. *Lewin,* 852 P.2d 44, 61 (Haw. 1993).

2. The *Oxford Concise Dictionary of Current English* (1969), for example, offers the following definitions:

> Marriage: relation between married persons, wedlock.
> Married: united in wedlock.
> Wedlock: the married state.
> Spouse: husband or wife.
> Husband: man joined to woman by marriage.
> Wife: married woman esp. in relation to her husband.

3. For example: "Kentucky statutes do not specifically prohibit marriage between persons of the same sex nor do they authorize the issuance of a marriage license to such persons." *Jones v. Hallahan,* 501 S.W. 2d 588, 589 (Kentucky 1973). One of the very first gay marriage cases—one from Minnesota—also dealt with a state statute that failed expressly to

prohibit same-sex marriages. *Baker* v. *Nelson,* 191 N.W. 2d 185 (1971).

4. *Baker* v. *Nelson,* 291 Minn. 310, 191 N.W.2d 185 (1971), appeal dismissed, 409 U.S. 810, 93 S.Ct. 37, 34 L.Ed.2d 65 (1972); *Jones v. Hallahan,* 501 S.W. 588 (Ky.Ct.App. 1973); *Singer v. Hara,* 11 Wash.App. 247, 522 P.2d 1187, review denied, 84 Wash.2d 1008 (1974); *De Santo v. Barnsley,* 328 Pa.Super. 181, 476 A.2d 952 (1984) (two persons of the same sex cannot contract a common law marriage notwithstanding the state's recognition of common law marriages between persons of different sexes).

5. Other cases that, in one way or another, have held that gays cannot marry are *Adams v. Howerton,* 486 F.Supp. 1119 (C.D. Cal. 1980); *Succession of Bascot,* 502 So.2d 1118, 1127–30 (La.Ct.App.) (holding that a man cannot be a "concubine" of another man); *Jennings v. Jennings,* 315 A.2d 816, 820 n.7 (Md.Spec.Ct.App. 1974) (explaining that "Maryland does not recognize a marriage between persons of the same sex"); *In re Estate of Cooper,* 654 N.Y.S.2d 684, 687 (N.Y. Sup.Ct. 1990) (refusing to "elevate homosexual unions to the same level achieved by the marriage of two people of the opposite sex"); *Anonymous v. Anonymous,* 325 N.Y.S.2d 499 (N.Y.Sup.Ct. 1971) (stating that "[m]arriage is and always has been a contract between a man and a woman); *Slayton v. Texas,* 633 S.W.2d 934, 937 (Tex.Ct.App. 1982) (stating that same-sex marriage is impossible in Texas); *Dean v. District of Columbia,* No. CA 90-13892, slip opinion 18-21 (D.C. Super.Ct. Dec. 30, 1991) (invoking passages from Genesis, Deuteronomy, Matthew, and Ephesians to hold that "societal recognition that it takes a man and a woman to form a marital relationship is older than Christianity itself").

6. *Singer v. Hara,* 522 P.2d 1187, 1193 (Wash.Ct.App. 1974).

7. *Black's Law Dictionary,* 6th ed. (1891; St. Paul: West, 1990) s.v. "Marriage."

8. Even the highly analytical historian John Boswell, in his recent book on the history of gay marriage, fares no better in coming up with a definition of marriage: "It is my understanding that most modern speakers of English understand the term 'marriage' to refer to what the partners expect to be a permanent and exclusive union between two people, which would produce legitimate children if they chose to have children, and which creates mutual rights and responsibilities, legal, economic, and moral . . ." (John Boswell, *Same-Sex Unions in Premodern Europe* [New York: Villard, 1994] p. 10, cf. p. 190). But if one asks "what partners?" "what union?" "what rights?" and "what responsibilities?", I fear the answer in each instance must be "marital ones," in which case the definition goes around in the same small circle as the law. And *legitimate* children just *are* children of a marriage, so, that component of the definition is circular as well.

9. Harry D. Krause, *Family Law in a Nutshell,* 2nd. ed. (St. Paul: West, 1986) 92 [hereinafter *Family Law*].

10. Id. at 96–103. See *Kirchberg v. Feenstra,* 450 U.S. 455, 101 S.Ct. 1195, 67 L.Ed.2d 428 (1981) (invalidated Louisiana's

community property statute that gave the husband, as the family's "head and master," the unilateral right to dispose of property jointly owned with his wife without her consent).

11. H. Krause, *Family Law* 127–29 (1986).

12. "However unpleasant, outmoded or unnecessary, whatever sex discrimination remains in family *law* is trivial in comparison with the inequality of spouses that result from family *facts,* from the traditional role division which places the husband into the money-earner role and the wife into the home where she acquires neither property nor marketable skills." H. Krause, *Family Law* 146 (1986).

13. See, for example, *Singer* v. *Hara,* 11 Wash.App. at 259–60, 522 P.2d at 1195.

14. Quoted in *Baehr* v. *Lewin,* 852 P.2d at 50 n.7 (Haw. 1993).

15. Id. at 48 n.1.

16. Id.

17. See "Polygamists Emerge from Secrecy, Seeking Not Just Peace, But Respect," *New York Times,* April 9, 1991, A22 (NYC edition).

18. H. Krause, *Family Law* 131 (1986).

19. See, for example, "Homosexuality Does Not Make Parent Unfit, Court Rules," *New York Times,* June 22, 1994, A8; "Gay and Lesbian Parents Grow More Visible," *New York Times,* September 30, 1993, A1; "Gay Parents Called No Disadvantage," *New York Times,* December 2, 1992, B7.

20. The Editors of the Harvard Law Review, *Sexual Orientation and the Law* (Cambridge, MA: Harvard University Press, 1990), p. 119.

21. Craig Dean, "Gay Marriage: A Civil Right," *New York Times,* September 28, 1991 (op-ed).

22. Andrew Sullivan, "Here Comes the Groom: A (Conservative) Case for Gay Marriage," *The New Republic,* August 28, 1989, 22.

23. *Michael H.* v. *Gerald D.,* 491 U.S. 110, 109 S.Ct. 2333, 105 L. Ed. 2d 91 (1989).

24. *Baehr* v. *Lewin,* 852 P.2d at 58 (Haw. 1993).

25. The Supreme Court's three "right to marry" cases implicitly acknowledge that marriage is a social reality and repository of norms, indeed of rights, independent of statutory law, since the right to marry is a substantive liberty right which overrides, trumps, and voids statutory marital law. *Loving* v. *Virginia,* 388 U.S. 1, 12 (1967) (voiding laws barring blacks and whites from marrying each other); *Zablocki* v. *Redhail,* 434 U.S. 374 (1978) (voiding law barring child support scofflaws from marrying); *Turner* v. *Safley,* 482 U.S. 78, 94–99 (1987) (voiding regulation barring prisoners from marrying).

26. See, for example, City of Berkeley, California, *Domestic Partnership Policy, Statement of General Policy,* December 4, 1984, quoted in Harry D. Krause, *Family Law: Cases, Comments and Questions,* 3rd ed. (St. Paul, Minn.: West, 1990), 159.

27. See H. Krause, *Family Law,* 131–132.

28. *Baehr* v. *Lewin,* 852 P.2d at 59 (Haw. 1993), catalogues the most salient rights and benefits that are contingent upon marital status. The benefits discussed in this section are drawn from this case and from a catalogue of marital privileges given in a 1993 Georgia Supreme Court case, *Van Dyck* v. *Van Dyck,* 1993 WL 30607 (February 8, 1993) (Sears-Collins, Justice concurring) (holding that a state law authorizing cutoff of alimony payments to a former spouse who enters into a voluntary cohabitation does not apply when the cohabitation in question is a lesbian one). See also H. Curry and D. Clifford, *A Legal Guide for Lesbian and Gay Couples* 1:2 (1991).

29. H. Krause, *Family Law,* 107 (1986).

30. See Alan P. Bell and Martin S. Weinberg, *Homosexualities: A Study of Diversity Among Men and Women* (New York: Simon and Schuster, 1978); Philip Blumstein and Pepper Schwartz, *American Couples: Money, Work, Sex* (New York: William Morrow, 1983); David P. McWhirter and Andrew M. Mattison, *The Male Couple: How Relationships Develop* (Englewood Cliffs, NJ: Prentice Hall, 1984); Kath Weston, *Families We Choose: Lesbians, Gays, Kinship* (New York: Columbia Univ. Press, 1991); Suzanne Sherman, ed., *Lesbian and Gay Marriages: Private Commitments, Public Ceremonies* (Philadelphia: Temple Univ. Press, 1992).

31. See, for example, K. Weston, *Families We Choose,* 149–50 (1991).

32. H. Krause, *Family Law,* 47–48.

33. On sacred values, see generally, Douglas MacLean, "Social Values and the Distribution of Risk," in Douglas MacLean, ed., *Values at Risk* (Totowa, N.J.: Rowman and Allanheld, 1986), 85–93.

34. H. Krause, *Family Law,* p. 50. For a review of the literature on the vagaries of marriage as an institution, see Lawrence Stone, "Sex in the West: The Strange History of Human Sexuality," *The New Republic,* July 8, 1985, pp. 25–37; see also John Boswell, *Same-Sex Marriage,* pp. 32–33, 35.

35. H. Krause, *Family Law,* p. 49.

36. H. Krause, *Family Law,* p. 47.

37. This section draws on some ideas in Claudia Mills and Douglas MacLean, *Love and Justice* 9:4 QQ: Report from the Institute for Philosophy and Public Policy 12–15 (Fall 1989).

38. For a classic statement of this position, see Ronald Dworkin, *Taking Rights Seriously,* (1977; Cambridge, MA: Harvard University Press, 1978), pp. 180–183, 272–278.

5

Criticisms of Traditional Marriage and Family

Introduction
Plato, A Proposal to Abolish the Private Family
Aristotle, On Plato's Proposal
Friedrich Engels, "The Origin of Monogamous Marriage
and the Patriarchal Family"
Susan Moller Okin, "Marriage and the Unjust Treatment of Women"

Early in the *Republic,* Plato's lengthy dialogue about the nature and defense of the just state, Socrates makes a number of recommendations about private property and the private family. He recommends not only that the members of the ruling ("guardian") class should be prohibited from possessing private property ("beyond what is wholly necessary"), but that they should not be allowed to have a spouse or children whom they can call their own. In the ruling class of the ideal state, none of the female rulers "are to live privately with any man . . . and . . . the children, too, are to be possessed in common, so that no parent will know his own offspring or any child his parent."

Plato's reasons for recommending the elimination of the private family are essentially the same as the reasons he gives earlier in the dialogue for abolishing private property in the ruling class. If the guardians are prohibited from having private families, there will be less dissension among them, because they will not be tempted to confer special favors or treatment on some members of the state (members of their families) to the exclusion of others.

Aristotle rejects Plato's proposal partly for the reason that if all wives and children belonged to everyone collectively, this is no guarantee that harmony would be achieved in the state. Second, collective ownership of children would inevitably produce child neglect: "Each citizen will have a thousand sons who will not be his sons individually, but anybody will be equally the son of anybody, and will therefore be neglected by all alike."

Engels' grounds for criticizing the private family are quite different than those given by Plato. First, he does not limit himself to a discussion of the family within the class of those who have political power. Second, he provides a history of the family, detailing the various forms that the family has taken during the stages of human development. Third, his main concern is to show a connection between the form of the family and the economic relationships that exist in a society at a particular historical period.

Under capitalism, Engels argues, the private and monogamous family is a necessary economic unit. Monogamy "was the first form of the family to be based, not on natural, but on economic conditions—on the victory of private property over primitive, natural communal property." Capitalism transforms relationships between family members into property relations in which the man is supreme, his wife is a domestic slave (or "head servant"), a "mere instrument for the production of children."

Engels has a few words to say about the ideal family. He mentions "the old, communistic household" composed of many couples and their children. In these households, all tasks (childrearing, procuring of food) are regarded as public and socially necessary. Men and women are legally equal. With the abolition of capitalism, when the means of production are transferred into common ownership, we will experience a return to this type of household. Since the single family will no longer be an economic unit of society, "the care and education of the children becomes a public affair," and women will be free from the constraints of a sexual ethic that requires that they refrain from intercourse prior to marriage. Marriages will be based on love, not on property relations, and women will achieve a new equality with men.

Other contributors to this anthology have also applauded the transition to a family that is founded on love, psychological intensity, and intimacy. John Demos (Chapter 2) and Michael Bayles (Chapter 4) have both argued that families based on love and related sentiments are of great psychological importance to the individuals who comprise them. It is also the type of family that other nineteenth-century philosophers (Rousseau, Kant, Hegel, Mill, and Bentham) applaud in their writings. And yet, as some feminists have recently argued, the "sentimental family" also became the vehicle for the oppression of women, inside and outside the family. Once the concept of the sentimental family became the ideal,

> this ideology acted, rather, as a reinforcement for . . . patriarchal relations between men and women. . . . First, women's spheres of dependence and domesticity are divided from the outside world more strictly than before. Second, women increasingly come to be characterized as creatures of sentiment and love rather than of the rationality that was perceived as necessary for citizenship. Finally, the legitimacy of male rule both within and outside the family is reinforced . . . on the grounds that the interests of the family are totally united, that family relations, unlike those outside, are based only on love, and that therefore husbands and fathers can be safely entrusted with power within the household and with the right of representing their families' interests in the political realm. While some women may have benefited in their personal lives from the increased emphasis on affect within marriage, the claims of the female sex to equal recognition as persons, to

freedom, and to political representation, can only be seen as having suffered from the newly idealized family type.[1]

There are other feminist critiques of the contemporary family. In "Marriage and the Unjust Treatment of Women," Susan Moller Okin argues that the distribution of both paid and unpaid work between husbands and wives within the family in most cases is unjust. Moreover, she says, the injustice of this distribution is usually overlooked by theorists of justice. There is, of course, no necessary connection between the concept of family and any particular distribution of paid and unpaid work, but the fact that husbands usually do more paid labor and wives do more unpaid labor in the family is an issue of justice that must be addressed by any serious theory of family ethics.

A Proposal to Abolish the Private Family

Plato

Plato (427–347 B.C.E.) is generally regarded as one of the greatest thinkers of the Western world. Deeply affected by the execution of his teacher Socrates, he began to reflect and write widely on many philosophical themes. He founded the Academy in Athens, a society or fellowship devoted to lectures, discussions, and guided research on a variety of topics.

Socrates: The law . . . is to the following effect,— "that the wives of our guardians are to be common, and their children are to be common, and no parent is to know his own child, nor any child his parent."

I do not think that there can be any dispute about the very great utility of having wives and children in common; the possibility is quite another matter, and will be very much disputed . . .

Glaucon: I think that a good many doubts may be raised about both.

Socrates: You imply that the two questions must be combined. Now I meant that you should admit the utility; and in this way, as I thought I should escape from one of them, and then there would remain only the possibility.

Glaucon: But that little attempt is detected, and therefore you will please to give a defense of both.

Socrates: . . . I should like, with your permission, to pass over the question of possibility at present. Assuming therefore the possibility of the proposal, I shall now proceed to enquire how the

rulers will carry out these arrangements, and I shall demonstrate that our plan, if executed, will be of the greatest benefit to the State and to the guardians. First of all, then, if you have no objection, I will endeavor with your help to consider the advantages of the measure; and hereafter the question of possibility.

Glaucon: I have no objection; proceed . . .

Socrates: You, who are their legislator, having selected the men, will now select the women and give them to them; and they must live in common houses and meet at common meals. None of them will have anything specially his or her own; they will be together, and will be brought up together, and will associate at gymnastic exercises. And so they will be drawn by a necessity of their natures to have intercourse with each other . . . and this, Glaucon, like all the rest, must proceed after an orderly fashion; in a city of the blessed, licentiousness is an unholy thing which the rulers will forbid. . . .

. . . [T]he principle has been already laid down that the best of either sex should be united with the best as often, and the inferior with the inferior, as seldom as possible; and that they should rear the offspring of the one sort of union, but not of the other, if the flock is to be main-

From Plato, *Dialogues of Plato,* Trans. B. Jowett (New York: Random House, 1937), *The Republic* 457d–460d. Used by permission of Oxford University Press.

tained in first-rate condition. . . . And I think that our better and braver youth, besides their other honors and rewards, might have greater facilities of intercourse with women given them; their bravery will be a reason, and such fathers ought to have as many sons as possible . . .

The proper officers will take the offspring of the good parents to the pen or fold, and there they will deposit them with certain nurses who dwell in a separate quarter; but the offspring of the inferior, or of the better when they chance to be deformed, will be put away in some mysterious, unknown place, as they should be.

Glaucon: Yes, he said, that must be done if the breed of the guardians is to be kept pure.

Socrates: They will provide for their nurture, and will bring the mothers to the fold when they are full of milk, taking the greatest possible care that no mother recognizes her own child; and other wet-nurses may be engaged if more are required. Care will also be taken that the process of suckling shall not be protracted too long; and the mothers will have no getting up at night or other trouble, but will hand over all this sort of thing to the nurses and attendants.

Glaucon: You suppose the wives of our guardians to have a fine easy time of it when they are having children.

Socrates: Why, and so they ought . . .

Glaucon: But how will they know who are fathers and daughters, and so on?

Socrates: They will never know. The way will be this:—dating from the day of the hymeneal, the bridegroom who was then married will call all the male children who are born in the seventh and tenth month afterwards his sons, and the female children his daughters, and they will call him father, and he will call their children his grandchildren, and they will call the elder generation grandfathers and grandmothers. All who were begotten at the time when their fathers and mothers came together will be called their brothers and sisters, and these . . . will be forbidden to intermarry. This, however, is not to be understood as an absolute prohibition of the marriage of brothers and sisters; if the lot favors them, and they receive the sanction of the Pythian oracle, the law will allow them.

Glaucon: Quite right.

Socrates: Such is the scheme, Glaucon, according to which the guardians of our State are to have their wives and families in common. And now you would have the argument show that this community is consistent with the rest of our polity, and also that nothing can be better—would not not?

Glaucon: Yes, certainly.

Socrates: . . . is not that the best ordered State in which the greatest number of persons apply the terms "mine" and "not mine" in the same way to the same thing? . . .

Glaucon: Quite true . . .

Socrates: . . . [W]ould any of your guardians think or speak of any other guardian as a stranger?

Glaucon: Certainly he would not; for every one whom they meet will be regarded by them either as a brother or sister, or father or mother, or son or daughter, or as the child or parent of those who are thus connected with him.

Socrates: . . . Shall they be a family in name only; or shall they in all their actions be true to the name? For example, in the use of the word "father," would the care of a father be implied and the filial reverence and duty and obedience to him which the law commands; and is the violator of these duties to be regarded as an impious and unrighteous person who is not likely to receive much good either at the hands of God or of man? Are these to be nor not to be the strains which the children will hear repeated in their ears by all the citizens about those who are intimated to them to be their parents and the rest of their kinsfolk?

Glaucon: These, and none other; for what can be more ridiculous than for them to utter the names of family ties with the lips only and not to act in the spirit of them?

Socrates: Then in our city the language of harmony and concord will be more often heard than in any other. . . . And the reason of this, over and above the general constitution of the State, will be that the guardians will have a community of women and children. . . .

Then the community of wives and children among our citizens is clearly the source of the greatest good to the State?

Glaucon: Certainly.

Socrates: And this agrees with the other principle which we were affirming,—that the guardians were not to have houses or lands or any other property; their pay was to be their food, which they were to receive from the other citizens, and they were to have no private expenses; for we intended them to preserve their true character of guardians. . . . Both the community of property and the community of families tend to make them more truly guardians; they will not tear the city in pieces by differing about "mine" and "not mine"; each man dragging any acquisition which he has made into a separate house of his own, where he has a separate wife and children and private pleasures and pains; but all will be affected as far as may be by the same pleasures and pains because they are all of one opinion about what is near and dear to them, and therefore they all tend towards a common end.

On Plato's Proposal

Aristotle

Aristotle (384–322 B.C.E.) was born in Stagira in northern Greece. At the age of seventeen, he moved to Athens and became a member of Plato's Academy, where he remained for twenty years. After leaving the Academy, he became the tutor to Alexander, the son of Philip, king of Macedonia. In 355, he returned to Athens to found the Lyceum, where he lectured, taught, and conducted research. Aristotle is generally regarded as one of the greatest contributors to Western intellectual culture.

Should a well-ordered state have all things, as far as may be, in common, or some only and not others? For the citizens might conceivably have wives and children and property in common, as Socrates proposes in the *Republic* of Plato. Which is better, our present condition, or one conforming to the law laid down in the *Republic?*

. . . [E]ven supposing that it were best for the community to have the greatest degree of unity, this unity is by no means proved to follow from the fact of all men saying "mine" and "not mine" at the same instant of time, which, according to Socrates [Plato], is the sign of perfect unity in a state. For the word "all" is ambiguous. If the meaning be that every individual says "mine" and "not mine" at the same time, then perhaps the result at which Socrates aims may be in some degree accomplished; each man will call the same person his own son and the same person his own wife, and so of his property and of all that falls to his lot. This, however, is not the way in which people would speak who had their wives and children in common; they would say "all" but not "each." In like manner their property would be described as belonging to them, not severally but collectively. There is an obvious fallacy in the term "all": like some other words, "both," "odd," "even," it is ambiguous, and even in abstract argument becomes a source of logical puzzles. That all persons call the same thing—mine in the sense in which each does so may be a fine thing, but it is impracticable; or if the words are taken in the other sense, such a unity in no way conduces to harmony.

And there is another objection to the proposal. For that which is common to the greatest number has the least care bestowed upon it. Every one thinks chiefly of his own, hardly at all of the common interest; and only when he is himself concerned as an individual. For besides other considerations, everybody is more inclined to neglect the duty which he expects another to fulfil; as in families many attendants are often less useful than a few. Each citizen will have a thousand sons who will not be his sons individually, but anybody will be equally the son of anybody, and will therefore be neglected by all alike. Further, upon this principle, everyone will use the word "mine" of one who is prospering or the reverse, however small a

From Aristotle, *Politics,* ed. Richard McKeon (Random House: New York, 1941), book II, chap.1,3. Used by permission of Oxford University Press.

fraction he may himself be of the whole number; the same boy will be "my son," "so and so's son," the son of each of the thousand, or whatever be the number of the citizens; and even about this he will not be positive; for it is impossible to know who chanced to have a child, or whether, if one came into existence, it has survived. But which is better—for each to say "mine" in this way, making a man the same relation to two thousand or ten thousand citizens, or to use the word "mine" in the ordinary and more restricted sense? For usually the same person is called by one man his own son whom another calls his own brother or cousin or kinsman—blood relation or connection by marriage either of himself or of some relation of his, and yet another his clansman or tribesman; and how much better is it to be the real cousin of somebody than to be a son after Plato's fashion! Nor is there any way of preventing brothers and children and fathers and mothers from sometimes recognizing one another; for children are born like their parents, and they will necessarily be finding indications of their relationship to one another. Geographers declare such to be the fact; they say that in part of Upper Libya, where the women are common, nevertheless the children who are born are assigned to their respective fathers on the ground of their likeness.

The Origin of Monogamous Marriage and the Patriarchal Family

Friedrich Engels

Friedrich Engels (1820–1895), a socialist philosopher, was the closest collaborator of Karl Marx in the foundation of modern communism. His first major joint work with Marx was *The German Ideology* (not fully published until 1932). Engels and Marx also drafted *The Communist Manifesto,* the first statement of communist principles, published in 1848.

The overthrow of Mother-right was the *world historical defeat of the female sex.* The man took command in the home also; the woman was degraded and reduced to servitude, she became the slave of his lust and a mere instrument for the production of children. This degraded position of the woman, especially conspicuous among the Greeks of the heroic and still more of the classical age, has gradually been palliated and glossed over, and sometimes clothed in a milder form; in no sense has it been abolished.

The establishment of the exclusive supremacy of the man shows its effects first in the patriarchal family, which now emerges as an intermediate form. Its essential characteristic is not polygyny, of which more later, but "the organization of a number of persons, bond and free, into a family, under paternal power, for the purpose of holding lands, and for the care of flocks and herds. . . . (in the Semitic form) the chiefs, at least, lived in polygamy. . . . Those held to servitude, and those employed as servants, lived in the marriage relation."[1]

Its essential features are the incorporation of unfree persons, and paternal power; hence the perfect type of this form of family is the Roman. The original meaning of the word "family" *(familia)* is not that compound of sentimentality and domestic strife which forms the ideal of the present-day philistine; among the Romans it did not at first even refer to the married pair and their children, but only to the slaves. *Famulus* means domestic slave, and *familia* is the total number of slaves belonging to one man. As late as the time of Gaius, the *familia, id est patrimonium* (family, that is, the patrimony, the inheritance) was bequeathed by will. The term was invented by the Romans to denote a new social organism, whose head ruled over wife and children and a number of slaves, and was invested under Roman paternal power with rights of life and death over them all.

This term, therefore, is no older than the iron-clad family system of the Latin tribes, which came in after

From Friedrich Engels, *The Origin of the Family, Private Property, and the State* (New York: International, 1975). Reprinted by permission.

field agriculture and after legalized servitude, as well as after the separation of the Greeks and Latins.[2]

Marx adds:

The modern family contains in germ not only slavery (servitus), but also serfdom, since from the beginning it is related to agricultural services. It contains in miniature *all the contradictions which later extend throughout society and its state.*[3]

Such a form of family shows the transition of the pairing family to monogamy. In order to make certain of the wife's fidelity and therefore of the paternity of the children, she is delivered over unconditionally into the power of the husband; if he kills her, he is only exercising his rights. . . . [The monogamous family] develops out of the pairing family, as previously shown, in the transitional period between the upper and middle stages of barbarism; its decisive victory is one of the signs that civilization is beginning. It is based on the supremacy of the man, the express purpose being to produce children of undisputed paternity; such paternity is demanded because these children *are* later to come into their father's property as *his* natural heirs. It is distinguished from pairing marriage by the much greater strength of the marriage tie, which can no longer be dissolved at either partner's wish. As a rule, it is now only the man who can dissolve it, and put away his wife. The right of conjugal infidelity also remains secured to him, at any rate by custom (the Code Napoleon explicitly accords it to the husband as long as he does not bring his concubine into the house), and as social life develops he exercises his right more and more; should the wife recall the old form of sexual life and attempt to revive it, she is punished more severely than ever.

We meet this new form of the family in all its severity among the Greeks. While the position of the goddesses in their mythology, as Marx points out, brings before us an earlier period when the position of women was freer and more respected, in the heroic age we find the woman already being humiliated by the domination of the man and by competition from girl slaves. Note how Telemachus in the *Odyssey* silences his mother. In Homer young women are booty and are handed over to the pleasure of the conquerors, the handsomest being picked by the commanders in order of rank; the entire *Iliad,* it will be remembered, turns on the quarrel of Achilles and Agamemnon over one of these slaves. If a hero is of any importance, Homer also mentions the captive girl with whom he shares his tent and his bed. These girls were also taken back to Greece and brought under the same roof as the wife, as Cassandra was brought by Agamemnon in Aeschylus; the sons begotten of them received a small share of the paternal inheritance and had the full status of freemen. Teucer, for instance, is a natural son of Telamon by one of these slaves and has the right to use his father's name. The legitimate wife was expected to put up with all this, but herself to remain strictly chaste and faithful. In the heroic age a Greek woman is, indeed, more respected than in the period of civilization, but to her husband she is after all nothing but the mother of his legitimate children and heirs, his chief housekeeper and the supervisor of his female slaves, whom he can and does take as concubines if he so fancies. It is the existence of slavery side by side with monogamy, the presence of young, beautiful slaves belonging unreservedly to the *man,* that stamps monogamy from the very beginning with its specific character of monogamy *for the woman only,* but not for the man. And that is the character it still has today. . . . [Monogamy] was not in any way the fruit of individual sex-love, with which it had nothing whatever to do; marriages remained as before marriages of convenience. It was the first form of the family to be based, not on natural, but on economic conditions—on the victory of private property over primitive, natural communal property. The Greeks themselves put the matter quite frankly: the sole exclusive aims of monogamous marriage were to make the man supreme in the family, and to propagate, as the future heirs to his wealth, children indisputably his own. Otherwise, marriage was a burden, a duty which had to be performed, whether one liked it or not, to gods, state, and one's ancestors. In Athens the law exacted from the man not only marriage but also the performance of a minimum of so-called conjugal duties.

Thus when monogamous marriage first makes its appearance in history, it is not as the reconciliation of man and woman, still less as the highest form of such a reconciliation. Quite the contrary. Monogamous marriage comes on the scene as the subjugation of the one sex by the other; it announces a struggle between the sexes unknown throughout the whole previous prehistoric period. In an old unpublished manuscript, written by Marx and myself in 1846, I find the words: "The first division of labor is that between man and woman for the propagation of children." And today I can add: The first class opposition that appears in history coincides with the development of the antagonism between man and woman in monogamous marriage, and the first class oppression coincides with that of the female sex by the male. Monogamous marriage was a great historical step forward; nevertheless, together with slavery and private wealth, it opens the period that has lasted until today in which every step forward is also relatively a step backward, in which prosperity and development for some is won through the misery and frustration of others. It is the cellular form of civilized society, in which the nature of the oppositions and contradictions fully active in that society can be already studied . . .

The legal inequality of [husband and wife in marriage], bequeathed to us from earlier social conditions, is not the cause but the effect of the economic oppression of the woman. In the old communistic household, which comprised many couples and their children, the task entrusted to the women of managing the household was as much a public and socially necessary industry as the procuring of food by the men. With the patriarchal family, and still more with the single monogamous family, a change came. Household management lost its public character. It no longer concerned society. It became a *private service;* the wife became the head servant, excluded from all participation in social production. Not until the coming of modern large-scale industry was the road to social production opened to her again— and then only to the proletarian wife. But it was opened in such a manner that, if she carries out her duties in the private service of her family, she remains excluded from public production and unable to earn; and if she wants to take part in public production and earn independently, she cannot

carry out family duties. And the wife's position in the factory is the position of women in all branches of business, right up to medicine and the law. The modern individual family is founded on the open or concealed domestic slavery of the wife, and modern society is a mass composed of these individual families as its molecules.

In the great majority of cases today, at least in the possessing classes, the husband is obliged to earn a living and support his family, and that in itself gives him a position of supremacy, without any need for special legal titles and privileges. Within the family he is the bourgeois and the wife represents the proletariat. In the industrial world, the specific character of the economic oppression burdening the proletariat is visible in all its sharpness only when all special legal privileges of the capitalist class have been abolished and complete legal equality of both classes established. The democratic republic does not do away with the opposition of the two classes; on the contrary, it provides the clear field on which the fight can be fought out. And in the same way, the peculiar character of the supremacy of the husband over the wife in the modern family, the necessity of creating real social equality between them, and the way to do it, will only be seen in the clear light of day when both possess legally complete equality of rights. Then it will be plain that the first condition for the liberation of the wife is to bring the whole female sex back into public industry, and that this in turn demands the abolition of the monogamous family as the economic unit of society.

We thus have three principal forms of marriage which correspond broadly to the three principal stages of human development. For the period of savagery, group marriage; for barbarism, pairing marriage; for civilization, monogamy, supplemented by adultery and prostitution. Between pairing marriage and monogamy intervenes a period in the upper stage of barbarism when men have female slaves at their command and polygamy is practiced.

As our whole presentation has shown, the progress which manifests itself in these successive forms is connected with the peculiarity that women, but not men, are increasingly deprived of the sexual freedom of group marriage. In fact, for men group marriage actually still exists even to this day. What for the woman is a crime, entailing grave legal and social consequences, is considered honorable in a man or, at the worse, a slight moral blemish which he cheerfully wears. But the more the hetaerism of the past is changed in our time by capitalist commodity production and brought into conformity with it, the more, that is to say, it is transformed into undisguised prostitution, the more demoralizing are its effects. And it demoralizes men far more than women. Among women, prostitution degrades only the unfortunate ones who become its victims, and even these by no means to the extent commonly believed. But it degrades the character of the whole male world. A long engagement, particularly, is in nine cases out of ten a regular preparatory school for conjugal infidelity.

We are now approaching a social revolution in which the economic foundations of monogamy as they have existed hitherto will disappear just as surely as those of its complement—prostitution. Monogamy arose from the concentration of considerable wealth in the hands of a single individual—a man—and from the need to bequeath this wealth to the children of that man and of no other. For this purpose, the monogamy of the woman was required, not that of the man, so this monogamy of the woman did not in any way interfere with open or concealed polygamy on the part of the man. But by transforming by far the greater portion, at any rate, of permanent, heritable wealth—the means of production—into social property, the coming social revolution will reduce to a minimum all this anxiety about bequeathing and inheriting. Having arisen from economic causes, will monogamy then disappear when these causes disappear?

One might answer, not without reason: far from disappearing, it will, on the contrary, be realized completely. For with the transformation of the means of production into social property there will disappear also wage-labor, the proletariat, and therefore the necessity for a certain—statistically calculable—number of women to surrender themselves for money. Prostitution disappears; monogamy, instead of collapsing, at last becomes a reality—also for men.

In any case, therefore, the position of men will be very much altered. But the position of women, of all women, also undergoes significant change. With the transfer of the means of production into common ownership, the single family ceases to be the economic unit of society. Private housekeeping is transformed into a social industry. The care and education of the children becomes a public affair: society looks after all children alike, whether they are legitimate or not. This removes all the anxiety about the "consequences," which today is the most essential social—moral as well as economic—factor that prevents a girl from giving herself completely to the man she loves. Will not that suffice to bring about the gradual growth of unconstrained sexual intercourse and with it a more tolerant public opinion in regard to a maiden's honor and a woman's shame? And, finally, have we not seen that in the modern world monogamy and prostitution are indeed contradictions, but inseparable contradictions, poles of the same state of society? Can prostitution disappear without dragging monogamy with it into the abyss? . . .

Full freedom of marriage can therefore only be generally established when the abolition of capitalist production and of the property relations created by it has removed all the accompanying economic considerations which still exert such a powerful influence on the choice of a marriage partner. For then there is no other motive left except mutual inclination.

And as sexual love is by its nature exclusive—although at present this exclusiveness is fully realized only in the woman—the marriage based on sexual love is by its nature individual marriage. We have seen how right Bachofen was in regarding the advance from group marriage to individual marriage as primarily due to the women. Only the step from pairing marriage to monogamy can be put down to the credit of the men, and historically the essence of this was to make the position of the women worse and the infidelities of the men easier. If now the economic considerations also disappear which made women put up with the habitual infidelity of their husbands—concern for their own means of existence and still more for their children's future—then, according to all previous experience, the equality of woman thereby achieved will tend infinitely more to make men really monogamous than to make women polyandrous.

But what will quite certainly disappear from monogamy are all the features stamped upon it through its origin in property relations; these are, in the first place, supremacy of the man, and, secondly, indissolubility. The supremacy of the man in marriage is the simple consequence of his economic supremacy, and with the abolition of the latter will disappear of itself. The indissolubility of marriage is partly a consequence of the economic situation in which monogamy arose, partly tradition from the period when the connection between this economic situation and monogamy was not yet fully understood and was carried to extremes under a religious form. Today it is already broken through at a thousand points. If only the marriage based on love is moral, then also only the marriage in which love continues. But the intense emotion of individual sex-love varies very much in duration from one individual to another, especially among men, and if affection definitely comes to an end or is supplanted by a new

passionate love, separation is a benefit for both partners as well as for society—only people will then be spared having to wade through the useless mire of a divorce case.

What we can now conjecture about the way in which sexual relations will be ordered after the impending overthrow of capitalist production is mainly of a negative character, limited for the most part to what will disappear. But what will there be new? That will be answered when a new generation has grown up: a generation of men who never in their lives have known what it is to buy a woman's surrender with money or any other social instrument of power; a generation of women who have never known what it is to give themselves to a man from any other considerations than real love, or to refuse to give themselves to their lover from fear of the economic consequences. When these people are in the world, they will care precious little what anybody today thinks they ought to do; they will make their own practice and their corresponding public opinion about the practice of each individual—and that will be the end of it. . . .

Marriage and the Unjust Treatment of Women
Susan Moller Okin

Susan Moller Okin is professor of political science at Stanford University. She is the author of *Women in Western Political Thought* (Princeton, NJ: Princeton University Press, 1979).

It is no secret that in almost all families women do far more housework and child care than men do. But the distribution of paid and unpaid work within the family has rarely—outside of feminist circles—been considered a significant issue by theorists of justice. Why should it be? If two friends divide a task so that each takes primary responsibility for a different aspect of it, we would be loath to cry "injustice" unless one were obviously coercing the other. But at least three factors make the division of labor within the household a very different situation, and a clear question of justice. First, the uneven distribution

of labor within the family is strongly correlated with an innate characteristic, which appears to make it the kind of issue with which theorists of justice have been most concerned. The virtually automatic allocation to one person of more of the paid labor and to the other of more of the unpaid labor would be regarded as decidedly odd in any relationship other than that of a married or cohabiting heterosexual couple.[1] One reason for this is that, as we shall see, it has distinct effects on the distribution of power. While the unequal distribution of paid and unpaid work has different repercussions in different types of marriages, it is always of significance. Second, though it is by no means always absolute, the division of labor in a traditional or quasi-traditional marriage is often

From Susan Moller Okin, *Justice, Gender, and the Family* (New York: Basic Books, 1989), 149–156.

quite complete and usually long-standing. It lasts in many cases at least through the lengthy years of child rearing, and is by no means confined to the preschool years. Third, partly as a result of this, and of the structure and demands of most paid work, the household division of labor has a lasting impact on the lives of married women, especially those who become mothers. It affects every sphere of their lives, from the dynamics of their marital relationship to their opportunities in the many spheres of life outside the household. The distribution of labor within the family by sex has deep ramifications for its respective members' material, psychological, physical, and intellectual well-being. One cannot even begin to address the issue of why so many women and children live in poverty in our society or why women are inadequately represented in the higher echelons of our political and economic institutions, without confronting the divisions of labor between the sexes within the family. Thus it is not only itself an issue of justice but it is also at the very root of other significant concerns of justice, including equality of opportunity for children of both sexes, but especially for girls, and political justice in the broadest sense.

The justice issues surrounding housework are not simply issues about who does more work. However, on average, wives living with their husbands do now work slightly more total hours than their husbands do. In addition, this averaging obscures a great variety of distributions of both quantity and type of work within marriages. For the purposes of this discussion, it will be helpful to separate couples into two major categories: those in which the wife is "predominantly houseworking" (either a full-time housewife or employed parttime) and those in which the wife is "predominantly wage-working" (employed full-time or virtually full-time). Within each category, I shall look at issues such as the distribution of work (paid and unpaid), income, power, opportunity to choose one's occupation, self-respect and esteem, and availability of exit. As we shall see, wives in each category experience a somewhat different pattern of injustice and vulnerability but, except in the case of some of the small numbers of elite couples who make considerable use of paid help,

the typical division of labor in the family cannot be regarded as just.

Predominantly Houseworking Wives

When a woman is a full-time housewife—as are about two-fifths of married women in the United States who live with their husbands—she does less total work, on average than her employed husband: 49.3 hours per week, compared with his 63.2. This is also true of couples in which the wife works part-time (defined as fewer than thirty hours per week, including commuting time), though the average difference per week is reduced to eight hours in this case. This is, of course, partly because housework is less burdensome than it was before the days of labor-saving devices and declining fertility. Not surprisingly however, during the early years of child rearing a nonemployed wife (or part-time employed wife) is likely to work about the same total number of hours as her employed husband. But the *quantity* of work performed is only one of a number of important variables that must be considered in order for us to assess the justice or injustice of the division of labor in the family, particularly in relation to the issue of the cycle of women's vulnerability.

In terms of the quality of work, there are considerable disadvantages to the role of housewife. One is that much of the work is boring and/or unpleasant. Surveys indicate that most people of both sexes do not like to clean, shop for food, or do laundry, which constitute a high proportion of housework. Cooking rates higher, and child care even higher, with both sexes, than other domestic work. In reality, this separation of tasks is strictly hypothetical, at least for mothers, who are usually cleaning, shopping, doing laundry, and cooking at the same time as taking care of children. Many wage workers, too, do largely tedious and repetitive work. But the housewife-mother's work has additional disadvantages. One is that her hours of work are highly unscheduled; unlike virtually any other worker except the holder of a high political office, she can be called on at any time of the day or night, seven days a week. Another is that she cannot, nearly as easily as most other workers, change jobs. Her family comes to depend on her to do all the things she does. Finding substitutes is difficult and expensive, even if the housewife is not discouraged or forbidden by her husband to seek paid work. The skills and experience she has gained are not valued by prospective employers. Also, once a woman has taken on the role of housewife, she finds it extremely difficult, for reasons that will be explored, to shift part of this burden back onto her husband. Being a housewife thus both impairs a woman's ability to support herself and constrains her future choices in life.

Many of the disadvantages of being a housewife spring directly or indirectly from the fact that all her work is unpaid work, whereas more than four-fifths of her husband's total work is paid work. This may at first seem a matter of little importance. If wives, so long as they stay married, usually share their husbands' standards of living for the most part, why should it matter who earns the income? It matters a great deal, for many reasons. In the highly money-oriented society we live in, the housewife's work is devalued. In fact, in spite of the fact that a major part of it consists of the nurturance and socialization of the next generation of citizens, it is frequently not even acknowledged as work or as productive, either at the personal or at the policy level. This both affects the predominantly houseworking wife's power and influence within the family and means that her social status depends largely upon her husband's, a situation that she may not consider objectionable so long as the marriage lasts, but that is likely to be very painful for her if it does not.

Also, although married couples usually share material well-being, a housewife's or even a part-time working wife's lack of access to much money of her own can create difficulties that range from the mildly irritating through the humiliating to the devastating, especially if she does not enjoy a good relationship with her husband. Money is the subject of most conflict for married couples, although the issue of housework may be overtaking it. Bergmann reports that in an informal survey, she discovered that about 20 percent of the housewife-mothers of her students were in the position of continually having to appeal to their husbands for money. The psychological effects on an adult of economic dependence can be

great. As Virginia Woolf pointed out fifty years ago, any man who has difficulty estimating them should simply imagine himself depending on his wife's income. The dark side of economic dependence is also indicated by the fact that, in the serious predivorce situation of having to fight for their future economic well-being, many wives even of well-to-do men do not have access to enough cash to pay for the uncovering and documentation of their husband's assets.

At its (not so uncommon) worst, the economic dependence of wives can seriously affect their day-to-day physical security. As Linda Gordon has recently concluded: "The basis of wife-beating is male dominance—not superior physical strength or violent temperament . . . but social, economic, political, and psychological power. . . . Wife-beating is the chronic battering of a person of inferior power who for that reason cannot effectively resist." Both wife abuse and child abuse are clearly exacerbated by the economic dependence of women on their husbands or cohabiting male partners. Many women, especially full-time housewives with dependent children, have no way of adequately supporting themselves, and are often in practice unable to leave a situation in which they and/or their children are being seriously abused. In addition to increasing the likelihood of the more obvious forms of abuse—physical and sexual assault—the fear of being abandoned, with its economic and other dire consequences, can lead a housewife to tolerate infidelity, to submit to sexual acts she does not enjoy, or experience psychological abuse including virtual desertion. The fact that a predominantly houseworking wife has no money of her own or a small paycheck is not necessarily significant, but it can be very significant, especially at crucial junctures in the marriage.

Finally, as I shall discuss, the earnings differential between husband and housewife can become devastating in its significance for her and for any dependent children in the event of divorce (which in most states can now occur without her consent). This fact, which significantly affects the relative potential of wives and husbands for exit from the marriage, is likely to influence the distribution of power, and in turn paid and unpaid work, during the marriage as well.

Predominantly Wage-Working Wives and Housework

Despite the increasing labor force participation of married women, including mothers, working wives still bear almost all the responsibility for housework. They do less of it than housewives, but they still do the vast bulk of what needs to be done, and the difference is largely to be accounted for not by the increased participation of men, but by lowered standards, the participation of children, purchased services such as restaurant or frozen meals, and, in elite groups, paid household help. Thus, while the distribution of paid labor between the sexes is shifting quite considerably onto women, that of unpaid labor is not shifting much at all, and the couple that shares household tasks equally remains rare. The differences in total time spent in all "family work" (housework and child care plus yard work, repairs, and so on) vary considerably from one study to another, but it seems that fully employed husbands do, at most, approximately half as much as their fully employed wives, and some studies show a much greater discrepancy.

Bergmann reports that "husbands of wives with full-time jobs averaged about two minutes more housework per day than did husbands in housewife-maintaining families," hardly enough additional time to prepare a soft-boiled egg. Even unemployed husbands do much less housework than wives who work a forty-hour week. Working-class husbands are particularly vocal about not being equal partners in the home, and do little housework. In general, however, a husband's income and job prestige are inversely related to his involvement in household chores, unless his wife is employed in a similarly high-paid and prestigious job. Many husbands who profess belief in sharing household tasks equally actually do far less than their wives, when time spent and chores done are assessed. In many cases, egalitarian attitudes make little or no difference to who actually does the work, and often the idea of shared responsibility turn[s] out to be a myth.

Some scholars are disinclined to perceive these facts as indicating unequal power or exploitation. They prefer to view them as merely embodying adherence to traditional patterns, or to justify them as efficient in terms of the total welfare of the family (the husband's time being too valuable to spend doing housework). There are clear indications, however, that the major reason that husbands and other heterosexual men living with wage-working women are not doing more housework is that *they do not want to, and are able, to a very large extent, to enforce their wills.* How do we know that the unequal allocation of housework is not equally women's choice? First, because most people do not like doing many of the major household chores. Second, because almost half of wage-working wives who do more than 60 percent of the housework say that they would prefer their husbands to do more of it. Third, because husbands with higher salaries and more prestigious jobs than their wives (the vast majority of two-job couples) are in a powerful position to resist their wives' appeal to them to do more at home, and it is husbands with the highest prestige who do the least housework of all. Even when there is little conflict, and husbands and wives seem to agree that the woman should do more of the housework, they are often influenced by the prevailing idea that whoever earns less or has the less prestigious job should do more unpaid labor at home. But since the maldistribution of wages and jobs between the sexes in our society is largely out of women's control, even seemingly nonconflictual decisions made on this basis cannot really be considered fully voluntary on the part of wives. Finally, the resistance of most husbands to housework is well documented, as is the fact that the more housework men do, the more it becomes a cause of fighting within couples. Examining factors that caused the breakup of some of the couples in their sample, Blumstein and Schwartz say:

> Among both married and cohabiting couples, housework is a source of conflict. . . . *[A] woman cannot be perceived as doing less housework than her partner wants her to do without jeopardizing the relationship.* However, a man, who is unlikely to be doing even half the work, can be perceived as doing less than his fair share without affecting the couple's dura-

bility. *It is difficult for women to achieve an equal division of housework and still preserve the relationship.* [emphasis added]2

As a result, in many of the households in which men and women both work full-time—those for which much paid household help or reliance on other purchased services is not a practical option—the unequal distribution of housework between husbands and wives leads to gross inequities in the amount and type of work done by each. "Drudge wives," as Bergmann has recently termed women in such households, do more total work than their husbands, averaging 71.1 hours a week to the husband's 64.9. But of greater overall significance is the fact that a vastly higher proportion of the wife's than of the husband's work is unpaid. She averages 28.1 hours of unpaid "family" work to 43 hours of paid work, whereas he averages only 9.2 hours of family work to 55.8 hours of paid work. One important effect of unequal sharing of housework and other family work within dual working couples is that the amount of time and energy the wife has left to commit to her wage work is considerably more limited than her husband's. It used to be assumed, in the days when the full traditional division of labor in the family prevailed, that any job requiring responsibility and commitment was incompatible with day-to-day responsibilities for home and children. This was why, or so it was argued, men could not, and should not be expected to, share in these tasks. But now many women, whether forced by economic need or refusing to accept the choice between parenthood and career that men have never had to make, are trying to do both. Their chances of success are significantly affected by the fact that, although they are likely to expend significant amounts of time on their homes and children, they must compete at work, not only with men from families like their own, who do significantly less family work than they do, but also with men whose wives are full-time housewives or work only part-time.

QUESTIONS FOR THOUGHT AND DISCUSSION

1. Why does Plato want to abolish the private family in the guardian or ruling class of his ideal state? With what kind of family does he propose to replace it? What doubts does Aristotle have about Plato's proposal?
2. Compare and contrast Plato's and Engels's critique of the private family. Why does Engels write that "the modern family contains in germ not only slavery, but also serfdom"?
3. Why does Engels claim that monogamy was "the first form of the family to be based, not on natural, but economic conditions—on the victory of private property over primitive, natural communal property"?
4. Will a transformation of the means of production (from private to social property) change the status of women in society? Explain.
5. The idea of the "sentimental family" is described in the introduction to this chapter. How does the sentimental family compare to the family type described by Beatrice Gottlieb (Chapter 2) that existed in western Europe prior to the eighteenth century?
6. Compare and contrast the "emotional significance" to individual family members of the sentimental and nonsentimental family. What other ethical

considerations are important in the moral evaluation of family types (e.g., sentimental and nonsentimental families)?

7. According to Susan Moller Okin, what three factors make the division of labor between husbands and wives within the household "a clear question of justice"?

8. Why does Okin think that "except in the case of some of the small numbers of elite couples who make considerable use of paid help, the typical division of labor in the family cannot be regarded as just"? Do you agree? Explain. Can the same criticism be made of the households of same-sex couples?

FURTHER READING

Jeffrey Blustein, *Parents and Children: The Ethics of the Family*, 31–38. New York: Oxford University Press, 1982.

Shulamith Firestone, *The Dialectic of Sex*. New York: William Morrow, 1970.

Joseph Margolis and Clorinda Margolis, "Separation of Marriage and Family." In M. Vetterling-Braggin, F. Elliston, and J. English, eds., *Feminism and Philosophy*. (Totowa, N.J.: Littlefield, Adams, 1977).

David McLean and Claudia Mills, "Love and Justice." *Report from the Institute for Philosophy and Public Policy* 9, 4 (Fall 1989): 12–15.

Francis Schrag, "Justice and the Family," *Inquiry* 19 (1976): 193–208.

NOTES

Friedrich Engels

1. Morgan, Lewis H., *Ancient Society* or *Researchers in the Lines of Human Progress from Savagery through Barbarism to Civilization* (London: MacMillan, 1877), p. 474.

2. Morgan, *op. cit.*, p. 511.

3. *German Ideology*, 1845–46.

Susan Moller Okin

1. Blumstein and Schwartz's comparisons of homosexual couples (male and female) with heterosexual couples (cohabiting and married) demonstrate vividly the extent to which the division of labor in the household is affected by sex difference. In all but about 1 percent of contemporary homosexual households, they found that the homemaker/provider division of roles is avoided. Even when one partner is not working, and is in fact doing more of the housework, the tendency is to think of him or her as "temporarily unemployed" or "a student." Lesbians take particular care to distribute household duties equitably. And yet, contrary to what one might expect on the basis of some arguments (including that of economist Gary Becker), such households seem to be managed with considerable efficiency. Blumstein and Schwartz, *American Couples*, pp. 116, 127–31, 148–51.

2. *Id.*

6

Nontraditional Families
and Family Values

Introduction
Alan Donagan, "The Permissible Variety of Family Structures"
David Popenoe, "Family Decline in America"
Shulamith Firestone, "An Alternative to the Family"
Patricia Smith, "Are Family Values Enduring Values?"

I n 1977, family sociologist Urie Bronfenbrenner published an essay called "The Calamitous Decline of the American Family."[1] Despite its alarming title, the piece got little attention because it first appeared in a small magazine published annually by the State University of New York.[2] A few weeks later it was noticed by the editors of the *Washington Post,* who ran it on the first page of the Sunday op-ed section. The article quickly became the focal point of national debate.

Bronfenbrenner was concerned to show that the American family had undergone radical and deleterious change between the years 1950 and 1975. She divided these changes into two categories: the number of parents and other adult relatives in the home and the amount of attention that parents devote to relationships with their children. There were fewer adults in the home in 1975 because there was a large drop in the number of other adults living in the home with the parents (for example, grandparents), there was a correspondingly large increase in the number of women in the workforce, and there was a dramatic rise in one-parent families.

Nearly twenty years later, the U.S. Census Bureau reported that only one-half of America's 32.3 million children lived in traditional nuclear two-parent families in which all the children were the biological offspring of their parents or had been adopted by them, and no other persons were present in the household. The other 16 million children lived with step-parents (blended families), single parents or other relatives (extended families). The words "single-parent family" cover a lot of territory. One has to distinguish the several different ways in which such families come about. Gregory Pence writes that "a marriage may be broken by death, divorce, separation, or desertion; an unmarried person may conceive and rear a child; an unmarried person may adopt a child." A single-parent family may not be the result of choice, and there may be numerous additional differences within each of the preceding types of single-parent families: "single parents differ in age, sex, education, occupation, etc.; families differ in size, race and ethnicity, socioeconomic status, community environment, etc."[3]

Approximately 8.4 million children in the U.S. grow up in single-parent families. Although there is no evidence that these children are worse off in terms of learning and behavior problems than children who live in blended families, most of those who deplore the "breakdown" of the family in the United States point to single-parent families as evidence, and especially to single-mother families created either by divorce or by births to unmarried women.

This chapter opens with a selection from a book on ethical theory published at about the same time that Bronfenbrenner was warning Americans about the decline of the family. Alan Donagan argues that if one assumes that "a child not brought up under the authority of its natural parents is at a disadvantage, the traditional doctrine that only monogamous marriage is permissible is well founded." However, Donagan is not prepared to grant this assumption. This is because he believes that a child is at a disadvantage while growing up only if the adults who rear her fail to respect her as a rational creature. Donagan argues that there may be many different types of family form which meet this minimum condition. One alternative family form that Donagan considers is a variation of Plato's communal family. A description of how a communal family might function in contemporary times is provided by Shulamith Firestone in this chapter. She uses the word "household" to signify a childrearing group of people living together for an unspecified time, with no specified set of interpersonal relations. They would be obligated to remain together only for the time necessary to raise their children. And responsibility for the early physical dependence of children would be evenly diffused among all members of the household. Firestone believes that the main advantage of households over the traditional family is that parent-child relationships in the family would be based on love alone and "women would be identical under the law with men."

Donagan does not discuss childrearing in single-parent households. But it would appear that there is no more reason to think that a single-parent family would violate Donagan's precept of parental responsibility than would a communal family.

Most single-parent families are headed by women. The main reason that single-mother families are said to be bad for children is that they are much more likely to be poor than families headed by men. Here is a summary of some of the recent statistics:

> The primary income for most of these children comes from their mothers. Court-ordered child support awards averaged only $2,100 per family in 1985, and many fathers failed to pay. The primary cause of the poverty of children in single-parent households is women's lack of earning power. In 1990, the median weekly earnings for women twenty-five years and over was $400, compared with $539 for men. . . .

. . . One-third of all single mothers do not participate in the official labor force. . . . Some reason that living on state subsidy will be better for their children, especially since as workers they must pay for clothes, transportation, child care, and other expenses they would not have if they did not have paid employment. Even so, less than 60 percent of poor children were subsidized by welfare in 1986, down from nearly 86 percent of poor children in 1973. Despite racist myths, only about 31 percent of welfare recipients are African American, a proportion that has remained constant in the last twenty years.[4]

In "Family Decline in America," David Popenoe is as alarmed about the current state of the American family as Urie Bronfenbrenner was twenty years earlier. He is concerned about the poverty of single-mother families, but he argues that there are several other reasons we should be concerned. He believes that current changes have destroyed the nucleus of the family (the bond between husband and wife) where earlier changes in the family did not have a similar effect. The decline of fertility, the sexual revolution, the new economic independence of women, and the availability of divorce are all changes that Popenoe says have undermined the traditional family as an ideal and have had an especially destructive effect on America's children.

There are three responses to Popenoe in this volume. First, in her description of the African-American family in Chapter 3, Patricia Hill Collins suggests that the model of family defended by David Popenoe has never applied to the black family in America. The cultural tradition of the black *extended* family in which "grandmothers, sisters, aunts, or cousins act as othermothers by taking on child-care responsibilities for one another's children"[5] requires Popenoe to explain why community-based child care in those African-American communities where it is still practiced has consequences for children that would be worse than traditional child care in intact two-parent families. Second, in this chapter, Shulamith Firestone underscores Collins's conclusions with a proposal for an alternative to the traditional nuclear family that she calls the "household."

Finally, Patricia Smith specifically responds to David Popenoe in her essay "Are Family Values Enduring Values?" She inquires about the values that are implied in the structure of the traditional family and points out that a commitment to family values is not necessarily a commitment to a particular family structure, such as the intact two-parent, heterosexual, childrearing family.

Second, Smith also challenges Popenoe to specify exactly what values he thinks have been lost in the past fifty years. She contends that what is gone is the traditional nuclear family and the values embodied by it—for example, full-time, lifetime childbearing, and the ideal of the economically dependent, full-time housewife who does not work outside the home. These values are being replaced by others, such as the value of sexual equality. But enduring through all these changes, Smith concludes, is the value of commitment to family living, and thus a commitment to the values of responsibility, cooperation, concern, loyalty, love, support, and identification with the interests of certain special others.

The Permissible Variety of Family Structures

Alan Donagan

Alan Donagan was professor of philosophy at California Institute of Technology. He was the author of *Choice: The Essential Element in Human Action* (London: Routledge and Kegan Paul, 1987), and many essays in philosophical ethics.

The family, as traditional morality understands it, is essentially a matter of relations having to do with parenthood.[1] It is a society instituted by an agreement between male and female human beings to enter into relations from which children may be expected to be born, and to join in bringing up any children who are born or adopted. However, since any natural or adopted children are members of the family that was instituted by the joint agreement of their parents, it is not a pure society; for it has members who belong to it whether they will or no. The family, so conceived, is not the family as it is now usually conceived in sociology: as a household, the members of which are not necessarily connected by the relation of potential or actual parenthood, real or adoptive.

The chief traditional moral precepts relating to the family derive from the respect due to children as human beings. Those who voluntarily enter into sexual relations from which a child is born are reasonably held to fail to respect the child as a rational creature if they refuse to provide for its upbringing. During childhood, nobody can live a genuinely human life unless he is protected, fed, and educated; but, although human beings at large have a duty to care for abandoned children as far as they can, if they cannot, they cannot be reproached with failing to care for a helpless human being whom they have brought into existence. If these considerations are sound, the fundamental principle of morality yields a precept of parental responsibility: *It is impermissible for human beings voluntarily to become parents of a child, and yet to refuse to rear it to a stage of development at which it can independently take part in social life.* This precept presupposes that *it is impermissible for human*

beings voluntarily to become parents of a child they cannot rear.

The traditional view of the permissible variety of family structures is largely derived from the precept of parental responsibility, by way of specificatory premises about what is necessary for rearing a child; until it can take its independent place in social life. The chief of these premises is that a child's upbringing is impaired unless the ultimate authorities in charge of it are its natural parents, joined in a stable marital union. For a child whose natural parents cannot assume this authority, for any reason from death to temperamental unfitness, other arrangements must be made, for example, adoption, but they are considered to be intrinsically inferior. This has implications both for the permissible varieties of marriage and their permissible duration.

Logically, there are four varieties of marital union: monogamy (one female with one male); and the various forms of polygamy—namely, polyandry (one female with more than one male), polygyny (one male with more than one female), and finally, a variety which exists only in primitive societies divided into exogamous clans and in experimental communes, more than one female with more than one male.

In the vast majority of civilized societies, the only varieties found are monogamy and polygyny. Polyandry is very rare; and the traditional moral objection to it is that, since in polyandrous families the natural father of a given child often cannot be known, polyandry makes it impossible for natural fathers to take the part they ought to take in the upbringing of their children.[2] This objection does not apply to polygyny, which was sanctioned by ancient Judaism and still is by modern Islam. The moral objection to polygyny is that it fails to respect, not the children, but the wives. In a polygynous family, as Aquinas pointed out, it is normal for wives to be reduced to a position of servitude. . . . Hence, even in societies which permit polygyny, growth of respect for women as human beings has gone with the supersession of polygynous marriage by monogamous. Both Jewish and Christian moralists now agree that only monogamous marriage is morally permissible.

Granting its assumption that a child not brought up under the authority of its natural parents is at a disadvantage, the traditional doctrine that only monogamous marriage is permissible is well founded. But, partly because the principal form of it they considered was the manipulative one devised by Plato in *Republic* V 457C–461E,[3] traditional moralists did not take sufficiently seriously the possible forms of marital union between more than one male and more than one female. Consider a possible form in which a group consisting more or less equally of males and females make a compact that they will have sexual relations exclusively with one another as they may agree, that when a female intends to have a child she will ensure that its natural father is known by cohabiting only with him in the period of conception, and that authority for bringing up any child born within the group shall be shared equally between those who agreed to form it. This libertarian variation upon Plato sufficiently resembles experiments in some communes and kibbutzim for there to be some reason to think it practicable. If it is, no doubt the psychological characteristics of children reared in such a family would differ in various ways from those brought up in monogamous families; but, although most Jewish and Christian moralists would consider those differences disadvantages, it is not obvious that they are right. It is at least thinkable that children brought up in such a communal family would not fail to be respected as rational creatures.

The possibility that there may be more than one permissible family structure is confirmed by considering structures which differ with regard to the duration of the marital union. A monogamous marriage endures as long as it is impermissible for either spouse to contract another. In both Judaism and Christianity, a marriage as a rule endures until the death of either husband or wife. But, as an institution, Jewish marriage differs from traditional Christian marriage in that it contains provisions for dissolution. Since most Jewish moralists agree that those provisions may be wrongly invoked, their nature is of less moral interest than the grounds on which it is held that they may be permissibly invoked; namely, the wilful refusal or the unfitness of either party to carry out the joint agreement both made in marrying. Quite evidently, these are serious grounds, and much undeserved suffering is avoided by permitting divorce upon them. In traditional Christian marriage, by contrast, if we except the view of the Eastern church that adultery is a valid ground of divorce, such grounds have been held sufficient only for separation, not for dissolution. And there is a serious reason for the Christian institution, although nowadays few except Roman Catholic moralists acknowledge it: namely, that in many cases, to dissolve a marriage will not make the party who seeks it any happier, but will make the other party, who opposes it, much less happy.

In most investigations of divorce by moral philosophers and theologians, it is assumed without examination that common morality must either permit the dissolution of marriage on certain grounds or forbid it. But that assumption is unfounded. The institution of dissoluble marriage (as in Judaism, Islam, and most modern pre-Christian societies) and that of indissoluble marriage (as in Roman Catholicism) each cause great and avoidable suffering which the other does not. And there is no way to find out which causes the greater suffering. Accordingly, it can be pleaded on behalf of each that for the suffering it causes there is proportionate reason. Hence, since the only objection to the permissibility of either is the suffering it causes, neither can be condemned as failing to respect every human being as a rational creature. As far as common morality goes, both are permissible.

Most moralists (Whewell was a happy exception) have failed to perceive that, while it is their business to criticize institutions, it is not their business to design them. Even when, as with the bringing up of children, common morality requires that a certain human activity be carried on only within an institution of a certain kind, there may be a variety of specific forms of that institution between which it does not pronounce.

Without attempting to ascertain what the variety of permissible forms of the family is, even this brief examination has given reason to think that there is a variety of them. It follows that on no ground on which any specific form of the family may reasonably be held to be mandatory can be moral—can, that is, be a ground upon which that form is mandatory for human beings merely as rational creatures. Those who accept the Jewish or the Christian religious revelation, and wish to have children, are obliged to find a partner with whom to found a Jewish or Christian family; but the obligation is religious, not moral.

Family Decline in America

David Popenoe

David Popenoe is professor of sociology at Rutgers University. His most recent book is *Life without Fathers* (New York: Martin Kessler Books, 1996).

As a social institution, the family has been "in decline" since the beginning of world history, gradually becoming weaker through losing social functions and power to other institutions such as church, government, and school. Yet during the past 25 years, family decline in the United States, as in other industrialized societies, has been both steeper and more alarming than during any other quarter century in our history. Although they may not use the term "decline," most family scholars now agree, with a growing tinge of pessimism, that the family during this period has undergone a social transformation. Some see "dramatic and unparalleled changes" while others call it "a veritable revolution."[1]

Agreement about the dramatic nature of family change over the past few decades, together with a pessimistic assessment of it, represent a recent shift of viewpoint on the part of many scholars. In the 1970s, in sharp contrast to the prevailing mood of the general public, the outlook of many family experts was one of complacency. For example, in their 1981 book *What's Happening to the American Family?*, economists Sar Levitan and Richard Belous noted that "currently fashionable gloom and doom scenarios miss the essential process of adjustment and change" and that "a critical analysis of the evidence does not paint such a dire picture, and thus a heartfelt 'hurrah' is in order."[2]

Yet after reviewing the events of the 1980s, their optimistic mood shifted strikingly. The second edition of this book, published in 1988, contains much apprehensive talk of "radical changes in family structure." The authors conclude, with some apologies for the "more sanguine scenario" of the earlier edition, that "American families are besieged from all sides" and "widespread family breakdown is bound to have a pervasive and debilitating impact not only on the quality of life but on the vitality of the body politic as well."[3]

The recent social transformation of the family has been so momentous that, in my opinion, we are witnessing the end of an epoch. Today's societal trends are bringing to a close the cultural dominance of what historians call the modern (I will use the term "traditional") nuclear family, a family situated apart from both the larger kin group and the workplace; focused on the procreation of children; and consisting of a legal, lifelong, sexually exclusive, heterosexual, monogamous marriage, based on affection and companionship, in which there is a sharp division of labor, with the female as full-time housewife, and the male as primary provider and ultimate authority. Lasting for only a little more than a century, this family form emphasized the male as "good provider," the female as "good wife and mother," and the paramount importance of the family for child rearing. (Of course, not all families

From David Popenoe, "Family Decline in America," in D. Blankenhorn, S. Bayne and J. Elshtain, eds., *Rebuilding the Nest: A New Commitment to the American Family* (Milwaukee: Family Service America, 1990), 1–20. Published by permission of Family Service America, Inc.

were able to live up to these cultural ideals.) During its cultural heyday, the terms "family," "home," and "mother" ranked extraordinarily high in the hierarchy of cultural values.[4]

In certain respects, this family form reached its apogee in the middle of the 20th century. By the 1950s—fueled in part by falling maternal and child mortality rates, greater longevity, and a high marriage rate—it is probably the case that a higher percentage of children than ever before were growing up in stable, two-parent families.[5] Similarly, this period witnessed the highest ever proportion of women who married, bore children, and lived jointly with their husbands until at least age 50.[6]

Flight from the Nuclear Family

In the 1960s, however, four major social trends emerged to signal a widespread "flight" from both the ideal and the reality of the traditional nuclear family: rapid fertility decline, the sexual revolution, the movement of mothers into the labor force, and the divorce revolution. None of these changes was new to the 1960s; each represented a tendency that was already evident in earlier years. However, a striking acceleration of these trends occurred in the 1960s, which was made more dramatic by the fact that during the 1950s these trends had leveled off and in some cases even reversed their directions.[7]

The Decline in Fertility

First (taking up these four trends without reference to their relative importance or causal priority), fertility declined in the United States by almost 50 percent between 1960 and 1989, from an average of 3.7 children per woman to only 1.9. Although fertility has been gradually diminishing for several centuries (the main exception being the two decades following World War II), the level of fertility during the past decade was the lowest in U.S. history and below that necessary for the replacement of the population. As a percentage of the total population, children over the past 25 years have dropped from more than a third to about one-fourth.[8]

Growing dissatisfaction with parenthood is now evident among adults in our culture, along with a dramatic decrease in the stigma associated

with childlessness.[9] Some demographers now predict that between 20 percent and 25 percent of today's young women will remain completely childless, and nearly 50 percent will be either childless or have only one child.[10]

The Sexual Revolution

Second, what is often called the sexual revolution has shattered the association of sex and reproduction.[11] The erotic has become a necessary ingredient of personal well-being and fulfillment, both in and outside marriage, as well as a highly marketable commodity. The greatest change has been in the area of premarital sex: from 1971 to 1982, the proportion of unmarried girls in the United States aged 15–19 who engaged in premarital sexual intercourse jumped from 28 percent to 44 percent.[12] This behavior reflects a widespread change in values: in 1967, 85 percent of Americans "condemned premarital sex as morally wrong," compared with only 37 percent in 1979.[13]

The sexual revolution has been a major contributor to the striking increase in unwed parenthood. Nonmarital births jumped from 5 percent of all births in 1960 (22 percent of births among blacks) to 22 percent in 1985 (60 percent of births among blacks). This is the highest rate of nonmarital births ever recorded in the United States.

Working Married Mothers

Third, although unmarried women have long been in the labor force, the past quarter century has witnessed a striking movement into the paid work force of married women with children.[14] In 1960, only 19 percent of married women with children younger than six were in the labor force (39 percent with children between 6 and 17); by 1986, this figure had climbed to 54 percent (68 percent of those with older children).[15]

Increased Divorce Rate

Fourth, the divorce rate in the United States over the past 25 years (as measured by the number of divorced persons per 1,000 married persons) has nearly quadrupled, increasing from 35 to 130. This increase has led many to refer to a divorce revolution.[16] A landmark of sorts was passed in 1974, when for the first time in American history more marriages ended in divorce than in death.[17] The probability that a marriage contracted today will end in divorce ranges from 44 percent to 66 percent, depending upon the method of calculations.[18]

Reshaped Family Experience

These four trends signal a widespread retreat from the traditional nuclear family in terms of a life-long, sexually exclusive unit, focused on children, with a separate-sphere division of labor between husband and wife. Unlike most previous family change, which reduced family functions and diminished the importance of the kin group, the family change of the past 25 years has tended to break up the "nucleus" of the family unit—the bond between husband and wife. Nuclear units, therefore, are losing ground to single-parent families, serial and step families, and unmarried and homosexual couples.[19]

The number of single-parent families, for example, has risen sharply as a result not only of marital breakup, but also of marriage decline (fewer persons who bear children are getting married) and widespread abandonment by males. In 1960, only 9 percent of children in the United States younger than 18 were living with one parent; by 1986, this figure had climbed to nearly one-fourth of all children. (The comparable figures for blacks are 22 percent and 53 percent, respectively.) Of children born between 1950 and 1954, only 19 percent of whites (48 percent of blacks) had lived in a single-parent family by the time they reached age 17. But for children born in 1980, the figure is projected to be 70 percent (94 percent for blacks).[20]

During the past quarter century there has also been a retreat from family living in general. For instance, the percentage of "nonfamily" households (households other than those containing two or more persons living together and related by blood, marriage, or adoption) has nearly doubled, from 15 percent to 28 percent of all households. Approximately 85 percent of these new households consist of a person living alone.[21]

To summarize the state of the family today compared with that of 25 years ago:

- fewer persons are marrying and they are marrying later in life.
- those marrying are having fewer children.
- more marriages end in divorce.

Trends such as these have dramatically reshaped people's lifetime family experiences, that is, their connectedness to the institution of the family. The proportion of an average person's adult life spent with spouse and children was 62 percent in 1960, the highest in our history. Today it has dropped to 43 percent, the lowest point in our history.[22]

In the United States, the changing family structure has helped to continue, and in some ways exacerbate, the tragedy of child poverty. Since 1974, the poverty rate among children has exceeded that among the elderly, and 40 percent of all poor people in this nation today are children.[23] According to a recent estimate, one out of every four American preschoolers in 1987 was living below the poverty line.[24]

In addition to family structural change, the psychological character of the marital relationship has also changed substantially over the years.[25] Traditionally, marriage has been understood as a social obligation—an institution designed mainly for economic security and procreation. Today, marriage is understood mainly as a path toward self-fulfillment: self-development is seen to require a significant other, and marital partners are picked primarily to be personal companions. Put another way, marriage is becoming deinstitutionalized. No longer comprising a set of norms and social obligations that are widely enforced, marriage today is a voluntary relationship that individuals can make and break at will. As one indicator of this shift, laws regulating marriage and divorce have become increasingly more lax.[26]

As psychological expectations for marriage grow ever higher, dashed expectations for personal fulfillment fuel our society's high divorce rate. Divorce also feeds upon itself. The higher the divorce rate, the more "normal" it becomes, with fewer negative sanctions to oppose it, and the more potential partners become available. In general, psychological need, in and of itself, has proved to be a weak basis for stable marriage.

These family trends are all interrelated. They are also evident, in varying degrees, in every industrialized Western Country, which suggests that their source lies not in particular political or economic systems but in the broad cultural shift that has accompanied industrialization and urbanization. Although scholars do not agree on all aspects of this shift, clearly an ethos of radical individualism has emerged in these societies, in which personal autonomy, individual rights, and social equality have gained supremacy as cultural ideals. In keeping with these ideals, the main goals of personal behavior have shifted from commitment to social units of all kinds (families, communities, religions, nations) to personal choices, lifestyle options, self-fulfillment, and personal pleasure.[27]

Family Change as Family Decline

Despite the dramatic nature of the recent social transformation of the family, many family experts are still reluctant to refer to the transformation as "family decline." This is unfortunate, because the concept of the family as a declining or weakening institution provides a "best fit" for many of the changes that have taken place. The concept also alerts us to examine the consequences of a rapidly changing institution.

During the past 25 years, the institution of the family has weakened substantially in a number of ways. Individual family members have become more autonomous and less bound by the family group, and the group has become less cohesive. Fewer of its traditional social functions are now carried out by the family; these have shifted to other institutions. The family has lost more power and authority to other institutions, especially to the state and its agencies. The family has grown smaller, less stable, and has a shorter life span; people are therefore family members for a smaller percentage of their life. The outcome of these trends is that people have become less willing to invest time, money, and energy in family life. It is the individual or herself, not the family unit, in whom the main investments are increasingly made.[28]

Why, then, are so many family scholars reluctant to speak of family decline? The short answer is that to speak of family decline within the intellectual community in recent years has been to be accused of opposing equality for women. The dominance of the traditional nuclear family in the 1950s helped to fuel the modern women's movement. Reacting strongly to the lingering patriarchy of this family form, as well as to its separate-sphere removal of women from the labor market, the women's movement came to view the traditional nuclear family in very negative terms.[29] Today, those who believe in greater equality for women—and that includes most academics and other intellectuals—favor an egalitarian family form, with substantial economic independence for wives. With respect to these characteristics, the flight from the traditional nuclear family is regarded as progress, not decline.

To speak of decline under these circumstances, therefore, is perceived as being implicitly in favor of a discredited family form, one that oppressed women. Indeed, the term "decline" has been used most forcefully by those conservatives who tend to view every recent family change as negative and who have issued a clarion call for a return to the traditional nuclear family.

But properly used, the term "decline" should not carry such ideological baggage. To empirically conclude that the family is declining should not automatically link one to a particular ideology of family or gender. Moreover, not all decline is negative in its effects; decline is not necessarily the opposite of progress. All sorts of institutional forms that were once fully accepted have declined: theocracies, hereditary monarchies, imperialism. The results of their decline have been by no means merely regressive. It is important to distinguish an empirical trend, such as the weakening of an institution, from both its positive and negative consequences.

The Social Consequences of Family Decline

How are we to evaluate the social consequences of recent family decline? At the outset, it must be stressed that the issue is extremely complex. Society has been ill-served by the simplistic, either/or terms used by both the political right and left in the national debate.

Certainly, one should not jump immediately to the conclusion that family decline is necessarily bad for our society. A great many positive aspects of the recent family changes stand out as noteworthy. During this same quarter century of family decline, women (and many minorities) have clearly improved their status and probably the overall quality of their lives. Much of women's gain in status has come through their release from family duties and increased participation in the labor force. In addition, given the great emphasis on psychological criteria for choosing and keeping marriage partners, it can be argued persuasively that those marriages today that endure are more likely than ever before to be emotionally rewarding companionships.[30]

This period has also seen improved health care and longevity as well as widespread economic affluence, all of which have produced, for most people, a material standard of living that is historically unprecedented. Some of this improvement is due to the fact that people are no longer so dependent on their families for healthcare and economic support; they no longer are so imprisoned by social class and family obligation. When in need, they can now rely more on public care and support, as well as self-initiative and self-development.

Despite these positive aspects, the negative consequences of family decline are real and profound. The greatest negative effect, in the opinion of nearly everyone, is on children. Because children represent the future of a society, any negative consequences for them are especially significant. Substantial, if not conclusive, evidence indicates that, partly due to family changes, the quality of life for children in the past 25 years has worsened.[31] Much of the problem is of a psychological nature and thus is difficult to measure quantitatively.

Perhaps the most serious problem is a weakening in many families of the fundamental assumption that children are to be loved and valued at the highest level of priority. The general disinvestment in family life that has occurred has commonly meant a disinvestment in children's welfare. Some refer to this as a national "parent deficit." Yet the deficit goes well beyond parents to encompass an increasingly less child-friendly society. The parent deficit is all too easily blamed on newly working women. But it is men who have left the parenting scene in large numbers, a phenomenon one scholar has called "a disappearing act by fathers."[32] More than ever before, fathers are denying paternity, avoiding their parental obligations, and absent from home (at the same time there has been a slow but not offsetting growth of the "house father" role).[33] Indeed, a persuasive case can be made that men began to abandon the "good provider" role at about the same time that many women started to relinquish the role of the full-time homemaker.[34] Thus, men and women may have been equally involved in triggering the recent flight from the traditional nuclear family.

The breakup of the nuclear unit has been the focus of much concern. Virtually every child desires two biological parents for life, and substantial evidence exists that child rearing is most successful when it involves two parents, both of whom are strongly motivated for the task.[35] This is not to say that other family forms cannot be successful, only that as a group they are not as likely to be successful. This is also not to say that the two strongly motivated parents must be organized in the patriarchal and separate-sphere terms of the traditional nuclear family.

Regardless of family form, a significant change has occurred over the past quarter century in what can be called the social ecology of childhood.[36] Advanced societies are moving ever farther from what many hold to be a highly desirable child-rearing environment consisting of the following characteristics: a relatively large family that does a lot of things together, has many routines and traditions, and provides a great deal of quality contact time between adults and children; regular contact with relatives, active friendships in a supportive neighborhood, and contact with the adult world of work; little concern on the part of children that their parents will break up; and the coming together of all these ingredients in the development of a rich family subculture that has lasting meaning and strongly promulgates family values such as cooperation and sharing.

As this brief sketch of the changing ecology of childhood suggests, not only the family has been transformed, but also the community environment in which families exist. Children are especially sensitive to their local environments; yet adults, too, have a big stake in the quality of their surroundings.

The family has always been a fundamental and probably essential unit of what some call "civil society"—the local society made up of kin and friendship networks, neighborhoods, religious institutions, and voluntary associations. Civil society provides meaning and attachment for people's lives and helps to protect them from the impersonal forces of market and state.[37] As the market and state "megastructures" grow ever more powerful, the need for the mediating structures of civil society becomes that much more compelling, both for psychic survival and political freedom.[38] Although reasonable doubt can be expressed about the empirical accuracy of the common phrase "as the family goes, so goes the nation," I am not so doubtful about the phrase "as the family goes, so goes civil society."

Family Decline and Today's Social Policy Debate

What should be done to counteract or remedy the negative effects of family decline? This is the most controversial question of all, and the most difficult to answer.

The problems of purposive social action are enormous. In remedying the negative effects, it is never easy to avoid canceling out the positive benefits. Also, if family decline in fact stems from a broad cultural shift, it will not be easy to modify. The underlying trend may simply have to play itself out. It could be, of course, that the problems we are seeing result not from the intrinsic character of the cultural shift, but rather from its extreme rapidity. From this perspective, as the changes become complete and society settles down, we may be able to adjust without great difficulty to the new conditions.

Let us assume, however, that purposive social action is both called for and can have a useful outcome. Among the broad proposals for change that have been put forth, two extremes stand out prominently in the national debate: (1) a return to the structure of the traditional nuclear family characteristic of the 1950s and (2) the development of extensive governmental family policies.

Aside from the fact that it is probably impossible to return to a situation of an earlier time, the first alternative has major drawbacks. Such a shift would require many women to leave the work force and to some extent become "de-liberated," an unlikely occurrence indeed. Economic conditions necessitate that even more women take jobs, and cultural conditions stress ever greater equality between the sexes.

In addition to such considerations, the traditional nuclear family form, in today's world, may be fundamentally flawed. As an indication of this, one should realize that the young people who led the transformation of the family during the 1960s and 1970s were brought up in 1950s families. If the 1950s families were so wonderful, why didn't their children seek to emulate them? In hindsight, the 1950s families seem to have been beset with problems that went well beyond patriarchy and separate-spheres. For many families the mother-child unit had become increasingly isolated from the kin group, the neighborhood, and community, and even from the father, who worked a long distance away. This was especially true for women who were fully educated and eager to take their place in work and public life. Maternal child rearing under these historically unprecedented circumstances became highly problematic.[39]

Despite such difficulties, the traditional nuclear family is still the family of choice for millions of Americans. They are comfortable with it, and for them it seems to work. It is reasonable, therefore, at least not to place roadblocks in the way of couples with children who wish to conduct their lives according to the traditional family's dictates. Women who freely desire to spend much of their lives as mothers and housewives, outside the labor force, should not be economically penalized by public policy for making that choice. Nor should they be denigrated by our culture as second-class citizens.

The second major proposal for change that has been stressed in national debate is the development of extensive governmental programs offering monetary support and social services for families, especially for the new "non-nuclear" families. In some cases these programs assist with functions that families are unable to perform adequately; in other cases, the functions are taken over, transforming them from family to public responsibilities.

This is the path followed by the European welfare states, but it has been less accepted by the United States than by any other industrialized nation. The European welfare states have been far more successful than the United States in minimizing the negative economic impact of family decline on family members, especially children. In addition, many European nations have established policies making it much easier for women (and increasingly men) to combine work with child rearing.[40] With these successes in mind, it seems inevitable that the United States will (and I believe should) move gradually in the direction of European countries with respect to family policies, just as we are now moving gradually in that direction with respect to medical care.

There are clear drawbacks, however, in moving too far down this road. If children are to be best served, we should seek to make the family stronger, not to replace it. At the same time that welfare states are minimizing some of the consequences of family decline, they may also be causing further decline of the family unit. This phenomenon can be witnessed today in Sweden, where the institution of the family has probably grown weaker than anywhere else in the world.[41] On a lesser scale, the phenomenon has been seen in the United States in connection with our welfare programs. Fundamental to the success of welfare-state programs, therefore, is keeping the legitimate goal of strengthening families uppermost in mind.

A New Social Movement

Although each of the above alternatives has some merit, I suggest a third alternative, which is premised on the fact that we cannot return to the 1950s family, nor can we depend on the welfare state for a solution. Instead, we should strike at the heart of the cultural shift that has occurred, point up its negative aspects, and seek to reinvigorate the cultural ideals of "family," "parents," and "children" within the changed circumstances of our time. We should stress that the individualistic ethos has gone too far, that children are being woefully shortchanged, and that, in the long run, strong families represent the best path toward self-fulfillment and personal happiness. We should bring again to the cultural forefront the old ideal of parents living together and sharing responsibility for their children and for each other.

What is needed is a new social movement whose purpose is the promotion of families and family values within the new constraints of modern life. It should point out the supreme importance of strong families to society, while at the same time suggesting ways that the family can better adapt to the modern conditions of individualism, equality, and the labor force participation of both women and men. Such a movement could build on the fact that the overwhelming majority of young people today still put forth as their major life goal a lasting, monogamous, heterosexual relationship that includes the procreation of children. It is reasonable to suppose that this goal is so pervasive because it is based on a deep-seated human need.

The reassertion of this personal goal as a highly ranked cultural value is not a legislative alternative; politics necessarily must respond to the obvious diversity in American life. But it is an alternative ideally suited to the leadership of broad-based citizens' groups. The history of recent social movements in America provides good reason for hope that such an initiative can make an impact. Witness the recent cultural shifts toward female and minority-group equality and the current move toward environmental protection, each of which has been led by popular movements focusing on fundamental social values. The time seems ripe to reassert that strong families concerned with the needs of children are, under modern conditions, not only possible but necessary.

An Alternative to the Family

Shulamith Firestone

Shulamith Firestone is a writer who lives in New York City. She is the author of *Notes from the Second Year: Women's Liberation* (New York: Radical Feminism, 1970).

I shall now outline a system that I believe will satisfy any remaining needs for children after ego concerns are no longer part of our motivations. Suppose a person or a couple at some point in their lives desires to live around children in a family-size unit. While we will no longer have reproduction as the life goal of the normal individual—we have seen how single and group nonreproductive life styles could be enlarged to become satisfactory for many people for their whole lifetimes and for others, for good portions of their lifetime—certain people may still prefer community-style group living permanently, and other people may want to experience it at some time in their lives, especially during early childhood.

Thus at any given time a proportion of the population will want to live in reproductive social structures. Correspondingly, the society in general will still need reproduction, though reduced, if only to create a new generation.

The proportion of the population will automatically select groups with a predictably higher rate of stability, because they will have had a freedom of choice now generally unavailable. Today those who do not marry and have children by a certain age are penalized: they find themselves alone, excluded, and miserable, on the margins of a society in which everyone else is compartmentalized into lifetime generational families, chauvinism and exclusiveness their chief characteristic. (Only in Manhattan is single living even tolerable, and that can be debated.) Most people are important: The word *family* implies biological reproduction and degree of division of labor by sex, and thus the traditional dependencies and resulting power relations, extended over generations; though the size of the family—in this case, the larger numbers of the "extended" family—may

From Shulamith Firestone, *The Dialectic of Sex* (New York: William Morrow, 1970), pp. 260–265. © 1970 by Shulamith Firestone. Used by permission of William Morrow and Company, Inc.

affect the strength of this hierarchy, it does not change its structural definition. "Household," however, connotes, only a large grouping of people living together for an unspecified time, and with no specified set of interpersonal relations. How would a "household" operate?

Limited Contract

If the household replaced marriage perhaps we would at first legalize it in the same way—if this is necessary at all. A group of ten or so consenting adults of varying ages could apply for a license as a group in much the same way as a young couple today applies for a marriage license, perhaps even undergoing some form of ritual ceremony, and then might proceed in the same way to set up house. The household license would, however, apply only for a given period, perhaps seven to ten years, or whatever was decided on as the minimal time in which children needed a stable structure in which to grow up—but probably a much shorter period than we now imagine. If at the end of this period the group decided to stay together, it could always get a renewal. However, no single individual would be contracted to stay after this period, and perhaps some members of the unit might transfer out, or new members come in. Or, the unit could disband altogether.

There are many advantages to short-term households, stable compositional units lasting for only ten-year periods: the end of family chauvinism, built up over generations, of prejudices passed down from one generation to the next, the inclusion of people of all ages in the childrearing process, the integration of many age groups into one social unit, the breadth of personality that comes from exposure to many rather than to (the idiosyncrasies of) a few, and so on.

Children

A regulated percentage of each household—say one-third—would be children. But whether, at first, genetic children created by couples within the household, or at some future time—after a few generations of household living had served the special connection of adults with "their" children—children were produced artificially, or adopted, would not matter: (minimal) responsibility for the early physical dependence of children would be evenly diffused among all members of the household.

But though it would still be structurally sound, we must be aware that as long as we use natural childbirth methods, the "household" could never be a totally liberating social form. A mother who undergoes a nine-month pregnancy is likely to feel that the product of all that pain and discomfort "belongs" to her ("To think of what I went through to have you!"). But we want to destroy this possessiveness along with its cultural reinforcements so that no one child will be *a priori* favored over another, so that children will be loved for their own sake.

But what if there is an instinct for pregnancy? I doubt it. Once we have sloughed off cultural superstructures, we may uncover a sex instinct, the normal consequences of which lead to pregnancy. And perhaps there is also an instinct to care for the young once they arrive. But an instinct for pregnancy itself would be superfluous—could nature anticipate man's mastery of reproduction? And what if, once the false motivations for pregnancy had been shed, women no longer wanted to "have" children at all? Might this not be a disaster, given that artificial reproduction is not yet perfected? But women have no special reproductive obligation to the species. If they are no longer willing, then artificial methods will have to be developed hurriedly, or, at the very least, satisfactory compensations other than destructive ego investments would have to be supplied to make it worth their while.

Adults and older children would take care of babies for as long as they needed it, but since there would be many adults and older children sharing the responsibility—as in the extended family—no one person would ever be involuntarily stuck with it.

Adult/child relationships would develop just as do the best relationships today: some adults might

prefer certain children over others, just as some children might prefer certain adults over others—these might become lifelong attachments in which the individuals concerned mutually agreed to stay together, perhaps to form some kind of nonreproductive unit. Thus all relationships would be based on love alone, uncorrupted by objective dependencies and the resulting class inequalities. Enduring relationships between people of widely divergent ages would become common.

Legal Rights and Transfers

With the weakening and severance of the blood ties, the power hierarchy of the family would break down. The legal structure—as long as it is still necessary—would reflect this democracy at the roots of our society. Women would be identical under the law with men. Children would no longer be "minors," under the patronage of "parents"—they would have full rights. Remaining physical inequalities could be legally compensated for: for example, if a child were beaten, perhaps he could report it to a special simplified "household" court where he would be granted instant legal redress.

Another special right of children would be the right of immediate transfer: if the child for any reason did not like the household into which he had been born so arbitrarily, he would be helped to transfer out. An adult on the other hand—one who had lived one span in a household (seven to ten years)—might have to present his case to the court, which would then decide, as do divorce courts today, whether he had adequate grounds for breaking his contract. A certain number of transfers within the seven-year period might be necessary for the smooth functioning of the household, and would not be injurious to its stability as a unit so long as a core remained. (in fact, new people now and then might be a refreshing change.) However, the unit, for its own best economy, might have to place a ceiling on the number of transfers in or out, to avoid depletion, excessive growth, and/or friction.

Chores

As for housework: The larger family-sized group (probably about fifteen people) would be more practical—the waste and repetition of the duplicate nuclear family unit would be avoided, e.g., as in shopping or cooking for a small family, without the loss of intimacy of the larger communal exper-iment. In the interim, any housework would have to be rotated equitably; but eventually cybernation could automate out almost all domestic chores.

Are Family Values Enduring Values?

Patricia Smith

Patricia Smith is professor of philosophy at the University of Kentucky. She is the author of *Liberalism and Affirmative Obligation* (New York: Oxford University Press, 1998). She recently completed *Omission: A Legal, Moral and Conceptual Analysis* (forthcoming) and is currently working on issues of family value and social change.

We live in anxious, unsettled times, and much of the chaos is centered around personal relation-ships that seem more tenuous and temporary, and family arrangements that seem more fragile and fragmented than they once were. In this era of so-cial upheaval it has become commonplace to lament the loss of family values and decry the ero-sion of the moral fiber of our society. Many of our worst social problems are blamed on the loss of family values and our consequent moral decline. In fact, it is sometimes ominously suggested that the destruction of our civilization is contained in the barbarous demise of the traditional family. Ex-amples abound. Rev. Jerry Falwell has expressed the fears of many in the face of personal upheaval:

> The American family is in revolution. It is not a revolution of guns, insurrections, and rioting in the streets, but its effects can be more devastating than any coup d'etat or bloody civil war. . . . A moral and emotional earthquake is rumbling across the land, col-lapsing homes, weakening values, shattering families, and threatening to crack open the very foundations of our culture.[1]

Nor is Falwell alone in this assessment. In his now famous "Murphy Brown" speech, former Vice President Dan Quayle articulated concerns that in fact reflected the attitudes of 85 percent of the American public according to several subse-quent polls. He said:

> Right now, the failure of our families is hurt-ing America deeply. When families fall, soci-ety falls. The anarchy and lack of structure in our inner cities are testament to how quickly civilization falls apart when the family foun-dation cracks.[2]

Many other examples could be supplied. "Family values" became the battle cry and catch phrase of the Republican party in 1992, but only because it captured a widespread feeling of uncertainty, as one writer put it "a quiet American obsession . . . the source of deep, vexing national anxiety."[3] Since that time expressing concern over the ero-sion of family values has become a national pre-occupation. Pat Robertson in 1992 and Patrick Buchanan in 1996 made these concerns the cen-terpiece of their presidential campaigns. President Clinton has decided that family values "matter most." Senator Bob Dole claims that he always thought so. Politicians and journalists, academics and movie makers, not to mention theologians and religious leaders of all persuasions are busily engaged in rescuing family values, or at least urg-ing the rest of us to do so.

The concern is very real. Unfortunately, all of this discussion has resulted more in anxiety and confusion than in understanding and direction. We seem to be scurrying in circles, maintaining sincerity but lacking control. Worrying about a problem doesn't solve it ordinarily, but maybe we think that in this case it will. If we worry about these values enough, will it mean that we have re-stored them? It might, in fact, given the way val-ues work, but only if we clarify what they are. The biggest problem with the popular phrase "family values" is that it could potentially mean almost anything. This, of course, undoubtedly accounts

---

for its popularity. This is why Dan Quayle can use the phrase on the one hand, and Bill Clinton can use it on the other, both with entire honesty. Who could be against family values then? It would be like being against "truth." But if family values can mean ten different things to ten different people, discussing them will never get us anywhere. I think it is time to attempt some clarification.

If we look at the quotations just cited (as representative of innumerable other similar ones) we find three general ideas embodied in them. The first is that the family as we know it is failing. The institution of the family is falling apart, or at least changing in a way that is seriously or fatally destructive. Second, it is supposed that this is happening because, or is in some way directly connected to a change in basic values. These basic values are what is represented vaguely but intuitively by the phrase "family values." Finally, it is projected that these basic values and the institution of the family that is based on them are crucial to the continued existence of civilized society. The loss of these values signals the descent of civilization into immorality and barbarism. The fear is that we are adrift in a morass of relativism that will ultimately destroy us, and the cause of this is our failure to transmit basic values to our children at an early age in the family. These are the feelings, right or wrong. They account for why the debate over family values has become so prominent, why it is felt to be important.

This debate raises interesting philosophical questions: What are family values? In what sense are they being weakened, eroded, or lost? Finally, in what sense are they fundamental to morality? Do fundamental moral values get lost? I don't expect to answer these questions here, but I would like to struggle with them a bit, in the hope of providing some direction for further study. Since the space here is short, I will focus these questions in terms of the model of the traditional nuclear family.

Is the Family in Decline?

To consider this question, (since we must start somewhere), I will begin with the quotations above and the assumptions embodied in them. While most Americans do not make the three assumptions so explicitly as those quoted, and some

deny them altogether, they do represent the inchoate anxieties of a broad range of people. There is a general feeling that something crucial is being lost, perhaps something necessary to morality itself. Perhaps, in our passion for freedom, we are going too far, becoming debased as a people, and will fall into decline like the Roman empire.

Of course such concerns and complaints are not new. As historians often point out, they are typical attitudes in any time of rapid social change, such as our own. Sanford Dornbusch, for example, has noted that "whenever social institutions shift their functions and structure, the usual perception is of decay."[4] It is widely known and easily documented (even if often forgotten) that family structures and functions have always varied greatly over time and place. Family organization and practice has always been both diverse and in a process of evolution since the beginning of recorded history, and yet no one now suggests that the basic idea of the family or basic commitment to it was undermined at any time until now.[5] Why wasn't the family undermined when tribal organization shifted to communal, or when the industrial revolution took fathers away from the home and put them in a separate work place? Why wasn't the family undermined early in this century when universal public education removed children from the home for the bulk of the day, or a century before that when the extended family was replaced with the nuclear family? Apparently all these historical transformations did not constitute the demise of the family. So, why worry now?

The claim must be that current changes are fundamentally different from earlier ones; and indeed, precisely that claim is made. David Popenoe, for example, has argued that while earlier changes narrowed family functions and weakened the connections between larger kin groups, current changes destroy the nucleus of the family, which is the bond between man and wife. Popenoe goes on to define the traditional nuclear family as (1) a family situated apart from kin and work place, (2) focused on procreation, and consisting of a (3) legal, (4) life-long, (5) sexually exclusive, heterosexual, monogamous marriage, (6) based on affection and companionship, (7) with a division of labor: the male as provider and ultimate authority and the female as housewife and care-giver. He ac-knowledges of course, that not everyone lived up to this norm; it was an ideal, and an ideal of short duration—about 100 years. Recent changes, how-ever, have undermined this norm as an ideal. Those recent changes are well known: the decline of fertility (families are now typically small—one or two children); the sexual revolution (sexual in-tercourse between unmarried consenting adults is now morally acceptable, although adultery is not); the economic independence of women (a majority of women now work sooner and longer in the work place whether married or not); and finally the availability of divorce. These are all social facts, easily verifiable by statistics. They signal, according to Popenoe, the end of an era—the decline from predominance of the twentieth century nuclear family.[6] So is the family in decline? If it is defined as Popenoe defines it, it most certainly is declining as a single predominant norm. The question is: Should that be a cause for alarm?

Popenoe, like many other social critics, con-nects these changes to a broad range of social problems and suggests that it is the loss of family values that accounts for much of the current un-rest. These are the same assumptions reflected in the quotations with which I began. So the next question is what values are implied in the struc-ture of the family as Popenoe defines it or other-wise, and in the change of that structure?

What Are Family Values?

There are many possible answers to that question. I will consider only three here with no presump-tion to comprehensive treatment. One thing that the phrase "family values" could stand for is the set of values necessary for maintaining a particular family form, such as that defined by Popenoe as the traditional nuclear family. Instead of listing those values here, let me point out what seems to be a fatal flaw in this approach. If we compare the traditional nuclear family to family forms from other times and places, many of the specific fea-tures are contradicted without undermining the commitment to the family as such. For example, all would admit, I suppose, that Mormons and Muslims are committed to their families, although not necessarily to monogamous ones. Historical

and current rural families may not situate the fam-ily apart from the work place, and extended fami-lies may not separate the nuclear family from broader kinship relations, but they are still com-mitted to the family. Even those who married by arrangement for economic, political and reproduc-tive reasons rather than for affection and compan-ionship were (or are) still committed to the family.

So, having introduced the possibility that fam-ily values could refer to commitment to a particu-lar family structure, I want to reject that possibility as incompatible with the diversity of historical and current family commitments in fact. We do not want to say that all those other family structures were not really families or that people were not re-ally committed to them. So we need not dwell on this approach any further. But it may be worth noting that many who use the term "family val-ues" have in mind precisely this definition.

Another approach might be to see if some val-ues, commitments, or structures run through all family forms despite their diversity in other re-gards. This would require empirical investigation that I cannot supply here. Nevertheless, let me venture a few purely speculative remarks. I suspect that we would find that families in general have the central functions of economic and reproduc-tive cooperation; they are legal (state sanctioned or publicly recognized), intended to be permanent (with default procedures also set out). They spec-ify acceptable sexual arrangements (whatever they may be), patterns of authority (usually patriarchal) and divisions of labor usually by gender and age. They provide the structure for raising children and thus for the transmission of values to the next gen-eration, and include higher levels of obligation, and entitlement to greater mutual security, love, trust and support than would be possible in the wider community. No doubt there will be excep-tions to all these points, but in general I suspect that we will find these themes running through all families in all times and places. Of course, whether they do or not is a separate question from whether they should or must.

In order to avoid the empirical pitfalls associ-ated with the speculations I just made, yet another approach might be taken to see if there are values that would be necessary to the flourishing or at least the existence of the family in any form. I take it that those values would depend on the purpose of the family. If the purpose of the family is to provide, as I suggested above, permanent economic and reproductive cooperation, standards of sexual restraint, patterns of authority and division of labor, all transmitted to the next generation in the form of child rearing, that provides a fairly traditional concept of the family that can still encompass most of the diverse patterns of family structure. (I am not proposing this set of purposes in fact, but only outlining one possible form that could accommodate a fairly diverse set of family arrangements.) If we use that model, what values would be implied in that complex purpose? The question can be interpreted at different levels.

At an abstract level, permanent reproductive and economic cooperation as well as the other purposes noted require commitment, concern for others, loyalty, responsibility, trustworthiness, unselfishness, self discipline, respect for authority, rules, and roles. Some of these may overlap; some might be reducible to one another. On the other hand, I may have omitted some crucial values, but I suspect that they will be largely covered by one of the terms listed here. At this level it is hard to see how there could be any disagreement over the importance of such values. Who would oppose them? The dispute then must be over whether a particular family form is necessary to instill them. The concern is over how these values are maintained or preserved and transferred to our children.

At a fairly concrete level the purposes set out above imply a permanent commitment to the value of bearing and/or raising children, to cooperative economic endeavor (a work ethic, perhaps), to a special (higher and more extensive) responsibility to support the group, to sexual fidelity (according to whatever standards are set by traditional expectations), to respect for patterns of authority and divisions of labor (also as set by community expectations), and to a willingness to do one's part, to fulfill one's role and view the interests of others as central to one's own. These may not be all the values necessary for the existence of the family, but they certainly represent the major requirements for the purposes set out above. If, in

general, these represent the values associated with the family, are they in fact being lost?

Are Family Values Being Lost?

Popenoe suggested that the traditional nuclear family has been undermined by four recent trends: the sexual revolution, the movement of mothers into the work force, the decline of fertility, and the availability of divorce. I think that he is right about that. But do these trends undermine the values necessary for any family or only for the particular form defined by Popenoe? None of them, I think, necessarily undermines family values as I just articulated them, although some do produce significant tensions.

Does the sexual revolution undermine family values? It would if family values necessarily include a prohibition of all extramarital sex. It is hard to see why that should be necessary, although it may be necessary to require sexual restraint (that is, a prohibition of adultery) within marriage. I am not suggesting that even this is logically necessary, but it is very basic to the idea of marriage and probably is humanly necessary. That is, human insecurity may require some sort of general standard of sexual fidelity within marriage. At least the absence of sexual fidelity as a standard of marital life would seem to change the institution quite drastically. But even if this change occurred, it is not clear that it would signal the end of family living so much as change the definition of what a family is. Furthermore, there is in fact little evidence that this part of family life has actually changed much at all. The incidence of marital infidelity may be no greater now than it ever was.[7] And there is no evidence that those who are sexually active, even promiscuous outside of marriage do not intend to get married or to enter a long-term committed and sexually exclusive relationship when they "find the right person." So sexual restraint within marriage apparently has not changed much, and sexual restraint outside of marriage may not be necessary to protect the family.

Does the sexual revolution, then, undermine family values? Teenage sexual promiscuity, pregnancy, and disease are social problems often attributed to the failure of parents to transmit values of sexual restraint to their children. That turns the issue on its head, of course. That is, it attributes an additional purpose to the family, rather than saying what values are necessary for the continued existence of the family. If that additional purpose is reasonable, the contemporary family has been unable to meet it. It is far from clear, however, that the social problem is attributable to family failure, or that family instruction alone can correct it. All this is a source of great debate, but none of it shows that the sexual revolution undermines family values if family values mean something like a commitment to family living.

Working mothers in no way undermine family values, unless, as in Popenoe's traditional definition, the family is defined to include a mother who does not work outside the home. That is a very narrow definition that excludes masses of family arrangements (most of the lower classes) throughout history and in the present, and is for that reason unacceptable.

It is often felt, however, that the exodus of women from the home leaves no one there to transfer crucial values to our children. The movement of mothers into the work place has created or exacerbated practical problems of how to raise and care for children. But these do not seem to be moral problems, much less the loss of family values. Working mothers are just as committed to reproductive and economic cooperation as other mothers are, and are just as committed to living and functioning within a family. So the increase of women in the work force is in itself no sign of family decline at all. It is, however, a significant change of role that probably affects authority structures, and certainly creates practical problems of child rearing. To construe that as a loss of family values, however, seems both inaccurate and counter productive.

The decline of fertility does signal a rather significant change of value. It suggests that reproduction is no longer the central value of families. If that were the case, then economic cooperation, love and companionship would become the predominant purposes of the family. Would that change the values necessary for the flourishing of long term committed, cooperative and sexually exclusive living arrangements that we call families? I don't see how it would. In any case, the trend should not be exaggerated. Even though demographers predict that 25 percent of young women today will have no children, it follows that three fourths will have at least one child. Thus, a very strong majority are still committed to having and raising children, although fewer of them. This may lead to a change in family organization and certainly to a change in the role of women, but hardly to a decline in family living or family values (other than high fertility.)

Finally, the increased divorce rate (a full 50%) suggests that people are not as committed to permanent relationships as they once were. There is a sense in which that is necessarily true. Indeed, the prevalence of divorce is troubling, since it destroys particular families and might lead to a weakened institution or sense of permanent commitment over time. But this position is also misleading. It seems to imply that people today lack loyalty, self-discipline, and commitment that they once had. But in fact, divorce was largely unavailable in the past, and even if they could show good cause, most women, being economically dependent, were not in a position to get a divorce even if they could meet the legal requirements. So the low divorce rate may well have been due to helplessness and lack of choice as much as to self-discipline and commitment. Very few people today enter a marriage without intending to make it permanent. Thus, the value of long-term commitment is still predominant, even though it is more often not met than it once was.

So, we can ask again, in what sense are family values being lost? Given a very specific definition of a particular family form—the twentieth century nuclear family as defined by Popenoe—some values implied in that family arrangement are indeed being lost; that is, they are not predominantly held to be values or ideals for emulation. Specifically, the value of full time, life-time childbearing (the value of high fertility) is no longer held; the ideal of the economically dependent, full-time housewife who does not work outside the home is not widely held; thus, the norm of divided labor between a male provider and a female caretaker has been seriously eroded. Do these value shifts undermine the family as more broadly defined? Apparently not. The commitment to family living or at least to long-term committed relationships is still predominant as an ideal. Thus, these changes seem more like shifts in social norms, than like shifts in fundamental values. Yet there are fundamental value changes implied in these; one of the biggest is the equalization of the sexes, the recognition of the moral and economic autonomy of women. That in turn undermines the ultimate authority of male spouses turning the spousal relationship into an equal partnership, or at least a relationship that is determined on individual characteristics rather than predetermined by gender. These are in fact significant value transformations, but fortunately they signal the reorganization of family structure and not the demise of the family as an institution. Nor are they incompatible with the broader conception of family values.

What family values then endure? First, and foremost, the commitment to family living itself endures, which is, after all, the central and fundamental family value. The commitment to family living itself implies the abstract values that I named earlier: responsibility, cooperation, concern, loyalty, love, support, and identification with the interests of certain special others as equal to your own. These values are still valued highly. They are associated with virtues and ideals. The social structures within which they function may vary and evolve, but the values apparently endure.

It might be asked, however, if these values so obviously endure and they are in fact the values necessary for the continuing institution of the family, then why are so many people worried about family decline? Why are so many anxious about the moral future of our society? Is all that concern and discussion misplaced? Not exactly.

Is the Future of Our Society at Risk?

It depends on what you think the foundations of society are. Let me address this question with a few remarks on the "moral and emotional earthquake [that] is rumbling across the land, collapsing homes, weakening values, shattering families, and threatening to crack open the very foundation of our culture." As an admitted liberal who is trying

hard to interpret sympathetically, honestly, and openly the conservative critique, I'd like to offer two interpretations of this "moral earthquake." There is no question that personal relations and especially the role and status of women have been dramatically transformed in the past 40 years or so. Cultural revolution of this basic sort is upsetting, disconcerting, even hurtful. It produces confusion, fear and anxiety until social standards become settled again. The conservative position is a clear articulation of that fear.

One way to interpret the position is as the manifestation of a religious view that freezes relationships into one particular form: a patriarchal hierarchy headed by an authoritative husband/father and supported by a dependent and deferential wife/mother. It is frequently expressed by religious leaders (although, of course, not all religious leaders) and reflected in religious practices (such as the banning of women from the clergy, or other leadership roles.) Falwell, for example, characterizes God's intended role for the man of the family as the moral and spiritual leader and authority, while the woman is characterized as the nurturer and supporter. This reflects a metaphysical view of the nature of men and women as dominators and subordinates or leaders and followers, respectively, as an act of God or a mandate of nature. To defy God and nature is not only futile, but self-destructive. Consequently, misguided progressives must be corrected, resisted, and overcome. This is why feminists are characterized as "enemies of the family" (e.g., by Falwell), as are secular humanists, among others. This view is reflected in vaguely inchoate and generally unarticulated feelings of many men and women, who "just feel uncomfortable with a woman boss," or who "just feel somehow that it's not right for a woman to work when she has children to take care of," or who just feel, as Pat Buchanan put it, that women are "simply not endowed by nature with the same measures of single-minded ambition and will to succeed."[8] Men and women are different in essence.

There is, in other words, a natural order that puts women in the home and makes them mothers first and foremost. It dictates the relations between men and women, and determines the structure of family organization. Violating that natural order defies God's will or the requirements of nature, and leads to the destruction of civilization. That is the strong metaphysical or religious interpretation of the perceived decline of family values. It should not be dismissed because it is in fact a view sincerely and firmly held by many people.

Unfortunately, if that is what is meant by family values, there is no way to reconcile liberals and conservatives with regard to it. It eliminates reform altogether, so it cannot be acceptable to reformers, and it is based on a religious view that a majority of people no longer hold. Furthermore, it is probably at this point in time a futile position. Social evolution has already progressed beyond the point of no return on these matters. Women are quite unlikely to give up their educations and professions to return to dependency at this point. In fact, given this social progress, conservatives of the absolutist ilk find themselves caught in the contradictions of their own position. If Pat Buchanan were consistent on his expressed view of women's capabilities, why would he hire his sister, a living counterexample to it, to run his presidential campaign? Right-wing women, boasting advanced university credentials, write lucrative books outlining the joys of traditional motherhood[9] or, like Phyllis Schlafley, amass political power by traveling the country to extol the virtues of staying home. Somehow these contradictions between word and deed are ignored or finessed, but the position itself is absolute and not negotiable. The position of women and their relationship to men is frozen in time and cannot be changed.

Fortunately, this is not the only interpretation of the conservative position, and not, I suspect, the position that most conservatives hold. A second interpretation is as follows. It has long been a central premise of conservative thought (too often ignored by optimistic liberals) that human nature has a dark side, a vicious immoral side that is always lurking in the background, waiting to get loose. Furthermore, virtue does not come naturally to most of us; it takes work, training, discipline. We are all susceptible to weakness, greed, selfishness, lust, depravity, and immorality that must always constantly be held in check by social institutions calculated to restrain vice and encourage virtue. One institution intended to do that is the family; another is tradition; a third is religion. How well they have succeeded is a separate question, and a highly speculative one. In any case, the constraints of law and government alone are not nearly enough to provide the moral reinforcement that human beings need for personal virtue and social cohesion. Communal standards such as tradition, religion, and family are needed to maintain morality.

So the conservatives watched in dismay as the bonds of tradition were trampled in the dirt by throngs of freed men in the nineteenth century and throngs of freed women in the twentieth. They watch with alarm as the bonds of religion dwindle to wispy threads of general disbelief and selective acceptance. And they wonder what will hold the dark side of human nature in check. If even the bonds of family are cast aside, then how will the values of responsibility, obedience, and restraint be transferred to our children? One reason to resist the rearrangement of authority in the family is that it might undermine respect for authority altogether. One reason for concern about the movement of mothers into the workforce is that, since they were the last adults left there, it seems to leave no one home with the children. One reason to oppose divorce is that it seems to make our permanent commitments into temporary ones. Family values are values of responsibility and restraint that clash with the liberal focus on freedom and rights, but may be crucial to a decent society. The conservative concern is that these values may be lost from lack of social reinforcement.

These are legitimate concerns. Liberals need to recognize that. But conservatives need to recognize that these legitimate concerns cannot be addressed by returning to the past. Nor should we pretend that the past didn't have significant problems of its own. We must find new solutions to our social problems. A step in that direction might be to develop a clearer discussion of how such values as responsibility, restraint (or self-discipline), commitment, loyalty, love, and cooperation fit into a liberal society based on freedom, individualism, and autonomy. Another step in the right direction would be to clarify the terms of the debate by explaining why, if at all, these values should be called family values. We need to understand better how, or even if, these values are connected to a commitment to family.

QUESTIONS FOR THOUGHT AND DISCUSSION

1. What are some of the reasons for thinking that the late twentieth-century American family is "in decline"?
2. What model or ideal of the family is assumed by those who say that the American family is in decline?
3. What are some alternative models of the family? Under which models of the family would one *not* conclude that the family is in decline?
4. What makes one model of the family better than other models? Defend your answer.
5. Describe the precept of parental responsibility advanced by Alan Donagan. According to this precept, would Donagan conclude that only the traditional two-parent, heterosexual family is permissible? Explain.
6. Describe the alternative to the family suggested by Shulamith Firestone. Does this model pass the test of "permissible varieties of the family" suggested by Alan Donagan? Would Firestone's "household" model be acceptable to Patricia Smith? To David Popenoe?
7. Why does David Popenoe believe that we should be concerned about the current state of the American family? Do Patricia Smith, Shulamith Firestone, or Patricia Hill Collins (Chapter 3) share his concerns? Explain.
8. According to Patricia Smith, what is meant by the phrase "family values"? What does it mean to be committed to family values?
9. Why does Patricia Smith think that there is no evidence that Americans are no longer committed to family values?

FURTHER READING

D. Blankenhorn, S. Bayne and J. Elshtain, eds., *Rebuilding the Nest: A New Commitment to the American Family.* Milwaukee: Family Service America, 1990.

Stephanie Coontz, *The Way We Never Were.* New York: Basic Books, 1992.

Norval Glenn, ed., "Change versus Continuity, Concern versus Sanguineness: Views of the American Family in the Late 1980s." *Journal of Family Issues* 8 (December 1987): 348–354.

Shirley M. H. Hanson et al., eds., *Single Parent Families: Diversity, Myth and Realities.* New York: The Haworth Press, 1995.

Sar A. Leviton and Richard S. Belous, *What's Happening to the American Family?* Baltimore: Johns Hopkins, 1981, 1988.

David Popenoe and Barbara DaFoe Whitehead, "The Vanishing Father." *The Wilson Quarterly* (Spring, 1996): 11–34.

Carol Stack, *All Our Kin: Strategies for Survival in a Black Community.* New York: Harper & Row, 1974.

NOTES

Introduction

1. *Washington Post,* January 2, 1977, C1.

2. *Search* 10 (November 1977): 1–5.

3. Gregory Pence, *Classic Cases in Medical Ethics,* 2nd ed. (New York: McGraw-Hill, 1995), 372.

4. Iris Marion Young, "Mothers, Citizenship and Independence," *Ethics* (April 1995): 541–542.

5. Compare the communal child-rearing model suggested by Plato in Chapter 5 and by Firestone in this chapter.

Alan Donagan

1. For the traditional Christian doctrine of the family, Catholic sources are the best. Aquinas's treatment of it is authoritative: see *Summa contra Gentiles,* III, 122–26, and *Summa Theologiae,* III, Supp. 41–68, esp. 41, 44–48, 51, 54, 65, 67. For a good summary account, see Vernon J. Bourke, *Ethics* (New York: Macmillan, 1951), pp. 419–23; and for a fuller account, Cronin, *Science of Ethics,* vol. 2, pp. 415–22. For the traditional Protestant view, Kant, *Metaphysik der Sitten,* pt. 2, 75–79 (pp. 424–26) is enlightening, although too ascetic to be representative; for a corrective, cf. Whewell, *Elements of Morality,* para. 524–29, 720–49 (pp. 279–82, 373–86). For the Jewish view, besides the standard encyclopaedias, I have found Feldman, *Birth Control in Jewish Law* (which, despite its title, is comprehensive) very useful. For the relations of the Christian view to the Jewish, see Caube, *The New Testament and Rabbinic Judaism,* pp. 71–86; for later Christian influence on Judaism, see Falk, *Jewish Matrimonial Law in the Middle Ages.*

2. Aquinas, *Summa contra Gentiles,* III, 124 (1–3).

[3. Reprinted in this volume, Ch. V—ED.]

David Popenoe

1. Norval Glenn, ed., "The State of the American Family," *Journal of Family Issues* 8 (No. 4, December 1987), Special Issue.

2. Sar A. Levitan and Richard S. Belous, *What's Happening to the American Family?* (Baltimore: Johns Hopkins, 1981), pp. 190, 15.

3. Sar A. Leviton and Richard S. Belous, *What's Happening to the American Family?* rev. ed. (Baltimore: Johns Hopkins, 1988), pp. vi, viii.

4. Carl N. Degler, *At Odds: Women and the Family in America from the Revolution to the Present* (Oxford, England: Oxford University Press, 1980); Lawrence Stone, *The Family, Sex, and Marriage in England 1500–1800* (New York: Harper and Row, 1977); Steven Mintz and Susan Kellogg, *Domestic Revolutions: A Social History of the American Family* (New York: Free Press, 1988).

5. Andrew Cherlin and Frank F. Furstenberg, Jr., "The Changing European Family: Lessons for the American Reader," *Journal of Family Issues* 9 (No. 3, 1988), p. 294; John Modell, Frank F. Furstenberg, Jr., and Douglas Strong, "The Timing of Marriage in the Transition to Adulthood: Continuity and Change, 1860–1975," *American Journal of Sociology* 84 (1978), pp. S120–S150.

6. Susan Cotts Watkins, Jane A. Menken and John Bongaarts, "Demographic Foundations of Family Change," *American Sociological Review* 52 (No. 3, 1987), pp. 346–358.

7. Andrew J. Cherlin, *Marriage, Divorce, Remarriage* (Cambridge, MA: Harvard University Press, 1981).

8. All data are from the U.S. Census Bureau, unless otherwise indicated.

9. Arthur G. Neal, Theodore Groat, and Jerry W. Wicks, "Attitudes about Having Children: A Study of 600 Couples in the Early Years of Marriage," *Journal of Marriage and the Family* 51 (No. 2, 1989), pp. 313–328; Joseph Veroff, Elizabeth Douvan, and Richard A. Kulka, *The Inner American: A Self-Portrait from 1957 to 1976* (New York: Basic Books, 1981); James A. Sweet and Larry L. Bumpass, *American Families and Households* (New York: Russell Sage Foundation, 1987), p. 400.

10. David E. Bloom and James Russell, "What Are the Determinants of Delayed Childbearing and Permanent Childlessness in the United States?" *Demography* 21 (No. 4, 1984), pp. 591–611; Charles F. Westoff, "Perspective on Nuptiality and Fertility," *Population and Development Review* Supplement (No. 12, 1986), pp. 155–170).

11. John D'Emilio and Estelle B. Freedman, *Intimate Matters: A History of Sexuality in America* (New York: Harper and Row, 1988).

12. From a 1987 study sponsored by the National Academy of Sciences, reported in the *New York Times,* February 27, 1989, p. B11.

13. Daniel Yankelovich, *New Rules: Searching for Self-Fulfillment in a World Turned Upside Down* (New York: Random House, 1981), p. 94.

14. Suzanne M. Bianchi and Daphne Spain, *American Women in Transition* (New York: Russell Sage Foundation, 1986); Victor R. Fuchs, *Women's Quest for Economic Equality* (Cambridge, MA: Harvard University Press, 1988).

15. Data assembled from U.S. Census reports by Maris A. Vinovskis, "The Unraveling of the Family Wage since World War II: Some Demographic, Economic, and Cultural Considerations," in Bryce Christensen, Allan Carlson, Maris Vinovskis, Richard Vedder, and Jean Bethke Elshtain, *The Family Wage: Work, Gender, and Children in the Modem Economy* (Rockford, IL: The Rockford Institute, 1988), pp. 33–58.

16. Lenore J. Weitzman, *The Divorce Revolution* (New York: Free Press, 1985).

17. Paul C. Glick, "Fifty Years of Family Demography: A Record of Social Change," *Journal of Marriage and Family* 50 (No. 4, 1988), p. 868.

18. Robert Schoen, "The Continuing Retreat from Marriage: Figures from the 1983 U.S. Marital Status Life Tables," *Social Science Research* 71 (No. 2, 1987), pp. 108–109; Teresa Castro Martin and Larry L. Bumpass, "Recent Trends in Marital Disruption," *Demography* 26 (No. 1, 1989), pp. 37–51.

19. Sanford M. Dombusch and Myra H. Strober, *Feminism, Children, and the New Family* (New York: Guilford Press, 1988).

20. Sandra L. Hofferth, "Updating Children's Life Course," *Journal of Marriage and the Family* 47 (No. 1, 1985), pp. 93–115.

21. The 20-year downward spiral of family households came to a (temporary?) halt in the 1986–87 period, when the percentage of family households increased slightly, as documented in Judith Waldrop, "The Fashionable Family," *American Demographics* (March 1988).

22. Susan Cotts Watkins, Jane A. Menken, and John Bongaarts, op. cit., 1987.

23. Eugene Smolensky, Sheldon Danziger, and Peter Gottschalk, "The Declining Significance of Age in the United States: Trends in the Well-being of Children and the Elderly since 1939," in John L. Palmer, Timothy Smeeding, and Barbara Boyle Torrey, eds., *The Vulnerable* (Washington, DC: Urban Institute, 1988), pp. 29–54.

24. Report of House Select Committee on Children, Youth and Families, *New York Times,* October 2, 1989, p. A12.

25. Kingsley Davis, ed., *Contemporary Marriage: Comparative Perspectives on a Changing Institution* (New York: Russell Sage Foundation, 1985).

26. Mary Ann Glendon, *The Transformation of Family Law* (Chicago: University of Chicago, 1989).

27. Robert N. Bellah, Richard Madsen, William M. Sullivan, Ann Swidler, and Steven M. Tipton, *Habits of the Heart: Individualism and Commitment in American Life* (Berkeley, CA: University of California Press, 1985).

28. Victor Fuchs, *How We Live* (Cambridge, MA: Harvard University Press, 1983).

29. Jean Bethke Elshtain, *Public Man, Private Women: Women in Social and Political Thought* (Princeton, NJ: Princeton University Press, 1981).

30. Francesca M. Cancian, *Love in America: Gender and Self-Development* (Cambridge, England, and New York: Cambridge University Press, 1987).

31. *U.S. Children and Their Families: Current Conditions and Recent Trends, 1989* (Washington, DC: U.S. Government Printing Office); Nicholas Zill and Carolyn C. Rogers, "Recent Trends in the Well-being of Children in the United States and Their Implications for Public Policy," in Andrew Cherlin, ed., *The Changing American Family and Public Policy* (Washington, DC: Urban Institute, 1988), pp. 31–115; Peter Uhlenberg and David Eggebeen, "The Declining Well-being of American Adolescents," *The Public Interest* (No. 82, 1986), pp. 25–38.

32. Samuel H. Preston, "Children and the Elderly: Divergent Paths for America's Dependents," *Demography* 21 (No. 4, 1984), p. 443.

33. Frank F. Furstenberg, Jr., "Good Dads–Bad Dads: Two Faces of Fatherhood," in Andrew Cherlin, ed., *The Changing American Family and Public Policy* (Washington, DC: Urban Institute, 1988), pp. 193–218.

34. Barbara Ehrenreich, *The Hearts of Men: American Dreams and the Flight from Commitment* (New York: Anchor, 1983).

35. E. Mavis Hetherington and Josephine D. Arasteh, eds., *Impact of Divorce, Single Parenting, and Stepparenting on Children* (Hillsdale, NJ: Lawrence Erlbaum Associates, 1988); Sara McLanahan and Karen Booth, "Mother-Only Families: Problems, Prospects, and Politics," *Journal of Marriage and the Family* 51 (No. 3, 1989), pp. 557–580.

36. Urie Bronfenbrenner, *The Ecology of Human Development* (Cambridge MA: Harvard University Press, 1979).

37. Alan Wolfe, *Whose Keeper? Social Science and Moral Obligation* (Berkeley, CA: University of California Press, 1989).

38. Peter L. Berger and Richard J. Neuhaus, *To Empower People: The Role of Mediating Structures in Public Policy* (Washington, DC: American Enterprise Institute, 1977).

39. Betty Friedan, *The Feminine Mystique* (New York: Laurel, 1983, 1963).

40. Sylvia Ann Hewlett, *A Lesser Life* (New York: William Morrow, 1986).

41. David Popenoe, *Disturbing the Nest: Family Change and Decline in Modern Societies* (New York: Aldine de Gruyter, 1988).

Patricia Smith

1. Falwell, Jerry, *The New American Family* (Word Pub: Dallas, 1992), p. 1.

2. Quayle, Dan, excerpt from speech delivered to the Commonwealth Club in San Francisco, May, 1992; reprinted in Falwell, 1992, p. 60.

3. Klein, Joe, "Whose Values?" *Newsweek,* June 8, 1992, 19.

4. Dornbusch, Sanford, *Family Affairs,* sum/fall; 1989.

5. Cf. Coontz, Stephanie, *The Way We Never Were,* Basic Books: NY; 1992.

6. Popenoe, David, "Family Decline in America," in *Rebuilding the Nest: A New Commitment to the American Family,* D. Blankenhorn, S. Bayne and J. Elshtain (eds.), Family Service America, Inc: Milwaukee, 1990. [Reprinted in this chapter.]

7. Fisher, Helen, *Anatomy of Love: The Natural History of Monogamy, Adultery, and Divorce* (Norton and Co: NY, 1992).

8. Buchanan, Pat, quoted from his syndicated column in "The Case Against Buchanan" by Richard Lacayo, *Time,* March 4, 1996, p. 26.

9. Hewlett, Sylvia, *When the Bough Breaks,* Basic Books: New York, 1991; see also Hewlett, *A Lesser Life: The Myth of Women's Liberation in America* (Warner Books: New York, 1986).

III

Marital Ethics

7

Adultery and Divorce

Introduction
Bertrand Russell, "Marriage, Adultery and Divorce"
Richard Wasserstrom, "Is Adultery Immoral?"
Mike W. Martin, "Love's Constancy"
Laurence D. Houlgate, "Children and the Ethics of Divorce"

Among the reasons given for the demise of the family in the latter part of the twentieth century is the rising incidence of adultery and divorce. Although a solid majority of Americans disapprove of extramarital sex (86 percent responding that it is "always wrong" or "almost always wrong"),[1] Kinsey reported (in 1953) that one-half of all men and one-fourth of all women in the United States had engaged in at least one extramarital affair.[2] More recent studies (1985) show that, after ten years of marriage, the gap between men and women is closing: 30 percent of all men and 22 percent of women have had at least one extramarital affair.[3]

Although there appears to be a considerable discrepancy between attitude and practice for extramarital sex, there is no such gap for divorce. There was a time when divorce between couples with children was believed to be wrong, but the rate at which this belief has changed has almost kept up with the recent rapid rise in the divorce rate. For example, in several surveys over the past twenty-five years, women have been asked whether they agree with the statement: "When there are children in the family, parents should stay together even if they don't get along." Between 1962 and 1980, the percentage who disagree with that statement rose from 51 to 82 percent.[4] During the same period, the divorce rate more than doubled, from 9 to 22 divorces per 1,000 married women.[5] The statistics do not reflect how many of these divorces involved couples with children, but the 1988 data indicate that 16.4 children per 1,000 under the age of 18 experienced the divorce of their parents.[6] It seems reasonable to conclude from these numbers that the divorce rate of parents with young children parallels the rising rate at which persons no longer disapprove of divorce.

It is a fallacy to conclude that an act is morally justifiable because a majority of people happens to believe so. We do not determine the morality of an act by taking a poll. Polls are interesting and relevant only if they indicate the reasons that people come to their particular moral conclusions. We can then look critically at their reasons in order to discover whether any of them are plausible.

We begin this critical process with a selection from Bertrand Russell's 1929 classic *Marriage and Morals*. Russell was writing at a time when divorce in the United States was granted only if certain "grounds" or conditions were satisfied—for example, that one's spouse had been cruel, was insane, or had committed adultery. Russell shocked most of his contemporaries by arguing that adultery should not be a grounds for divorce. His argument is that most people at some time in their life have "strong impulses to adultery" and that the presence of such impulses does not "necessarily imply that the marriage no longer serves its purpose." For Russell, marriage is not primarily a sexual partnership but "an undertaking to co-operate in the procreation and rearing of children." Therefore, one of the best ways to maintain a failing marriage is to *relax* the moral prohibitions on adultery. "A degree of mutual liberty" (i.e., the liberty to have extramarital sexual experiences), Russell writes, "makes marriage more endurable," and if the partners are happy, they will make better parents.

In his essay on adultery, Richard Wasserstrom critically examines two of the more popular reasons why adultery is regarded as seriously immoral. The first is that adultery is an instance of promise breaking (notably, the marital promise to be sexually exclusive) and the second is that adultery involves deception. Some of the deception is obvious: lying about the places where and the persons with whom one has been. Other forms of deception, Wasserstrom contends, are more subtle but pervasive. They arise from the close psychological connection that most of us make between sex and affection. If sexual intercourse is supposed to signal affection for one's partner, then adulterous spouses are either deceiving the persons with whom they are having extramarital sex, or they are deceiving their spouse about the presence of these feelings.

This argument leads Wasserstrom to explore the connection between sex and love, forcing us to think about questions such as: What if a marriage did not involve any promise of sexual fidelity, and there was no need for deception, because neither partner expected or wanted such fidelity? Is this conceptually possible? That is, can one really be married to someone with whom one does not expect to be sexually faithful? If it is possible, is it morally acceptable? Wasserstrom suggests that a prohibition on extramarital sex is a way to help maintain the institutions of marriage and the nuclear family. Does this position conflict in any way with Russell's claim that adultery may sometimes be necessary to help a failing marriage?

Wasserstrom and Russell both make us wonder whether the commitment to love faithfully that is part of traditional wedding vows can be regarded as morally desirable. Is faithfulness in marriage a virtue? It is not clear from his remarks whether Russell rejects the idea that faithfulness is a virtue or whether he thought that there was no connection between sexual fidelity and a commitment to love another faithfully. In "Love's Constancy," Mike W. Martin presents several reasons why marital faithfulness is a virtue. In the context of this discussion he refers to some events in Bertrand Russell's life to exemplify the point that faithfulness plays an important role in shaping good relationships.

One of the signs of a failing marriage is a weakening of the commitment to sexual fidelity. Marriages that lack such commitments often end up in divorce. But is divorce morally wrong? There is a difference between divorces between couples with young children at home and divorces between childless couples or couples whose children have grown and left home. Few would contend that the latter divorces present any moral problems other than the fact that a wedding vow to life-long marital union has been broken. Fewer still would contend that divorces between childless couples are immoral, especially when both partners consent to the divorce. But when a divorce involves young children, other morally relevant factors intrude.

According to Bertrand Russell, divorces are not justifiable "so long as the bi-parental family is the rule." He means that so long as there is a social expectation that the family shall have two adult parents, then there are "strong reasons why custom should be against divorce." Russell agrees with John Locke that marriage is "an undertaking to cooperate in the procreation and rearing of children." This undertaking "may involve, at times, very considerable self-repression." But parents must repress those feelings that might otherwise cause them to divorce because, as parents, they have a stronger duty to their children than they do to the pursuit "of their own romantic emotions." Hence, Russell concludes, at least until the time that the biparental family ceases to be the ideal, parents with young children who divorce, "except for grave cause," are behaving immorally.

In my contribution to this chapter ("Children and the Ethics of Divorce"), I support Russell's conclusion by presenting some recent research on the deleterious psychological effects of divorce on young children. Although I disagree with Russell's claim that it is only when the biparental family is held as a social ideal that divorce is morally wrong, I generally defend Russell against his critics. However, the assumption that both Russell and I make is that divorce is wrong only if it can be shown to have, on balance, more bad consequences than good. But the reader might also want to consider some nonconsequentialist objections to parental divorce. For example, can it be objected that in many (but not all) cases, parents with young children who divorce fail to give their children the respect due to them as human beings, treating them instead in the same way that they treat the house and furniture, as property to be divided between the divorcing parents? But the child is a rational creature. The child is a person, not a piece of property. This fact places on parents the duty to see that their child lives a genuinely human life and to rear the child to "a stage of development at which it can independently take part in social life."[7] Do (some) parents who divorce knowingly or recklessly place their child's development at risk and thereby fail to respect the child as a person?

Second, can it be objected that a child who is born into an intact marriage has a moral *right* that his parents maintain the marriage while he is young? The source of this right is not an agreement or contract: most parents do not promise their children that they will remain married. But rights do not only derive from voluntary agreements. A child's right against her parent to be sheltered, fed, clothed, and educated is an example of a *noncontractual* moral right. Another example of a noncontractual right is the right that arises from the fact that the child's parents *are responsible for the child's emotional dependency.* Let us call this a "dependency right." By bearing a child and raising it together, parents soon cause or bring about a state of affairs in which the young child becomes emotionally dependent on them; indeed, over time, the child becomes dependent on their *joint* participation in her care and nurture. It might be argued that this dependency creates a right in the child to the continuation of this state of affairs, at least until the time that we can say that he or she is no longer emotionally dependent on the presence of both parents for her daily care. Accordingly, it is argued that divorce violates this right of the child.

This is only an outline of some possible nonconsequentialist arguments. There are objections to these arguments that must be acknowledged and answered. But they present some alternatives to the usual consequentialist approaches to the discussion of the ethics of divorce.

Marriage, Adultery and Divorce

Bertrand Russell

Bertrand Russell (1872–1970), logician and philosopher, was one of the outstanding figures of twentieth-century British philosophy. Although his most important contributions were in mathematical logic, he wrote many popular essays and books on problems of social ethics. Russell was the recipient of the Nobel Prize for Literature in 1950.

Divorce as an institution has been permitted in most ages and countries for certain causes. It has never been intended to produce an alternative to the monogamic family, but merely to mitigate hardships where, for special reasons, the continuance of a marriage was felt to be intolerable. The law on the subject has been extraordinarily different in different ages and places. . . . The Mosaic law allows a husband to give a bill of divorcement; Chinese law allowed divorce provided the property which the wife had brought into the marriage was restored. The Catholic Church, on the ground that marriage is a sacrament, does not allow divorce for any purpose whatsoever, but in practice this severity is somewhat mitigated—especially where the great ones of the earth are concerned—by the fact that there are many grounds for nullity.[1]

. . . I think [the] distinction between law and custom is important, for while I favour a somewhat lenient law on the subject, there are to my mind, so long as the biparental family persists as the norm, strong reasons why custom should be against divorce, except in somewhat extreme cases. I take this view because I regard marriage not primarily as a sexual partnership, but above all as an undertaking to cooperate in the procreation and rearing of children. It is possible, and even probable . . . that marriage so understood may break down under the operation of various forces of which the economic are the chief; but if this should occur, divorce also would break down, since it is an institution dependent upon the existence of marriage, within which it affords a kind of safety valve. Our present discussion, therefore, will move entirely within the framework of the biparental family considered as the rule.

From Bertrand Russell, *Marriage and Morals* (New York: W. W. Norton, 1929), 221–239. Copyright © 1929 by Horace Liveright, Inc., renewed © 1957 by Bertrand Russell. Reprinted by permission of Liveright Publishing Company.

Both Protestants and Catholics have, in general, viewed divorce not from the point of view of the biological purpose of the family, but from the point of view of the theological conception of sin. Catholics, since they hold that marriage is indissoluble in the sight of God, necessarily maintain that when two persons have once married, neither of them can, during the lifetime of the other, have sinless intercourse with any other person, no matter what may happen in the marriage. Protestants, in so far as they have favoured divorce, have done so partly out of opposition to Catholic doctrine on the sacraments, partly also because they perceived that the indissolubility of marriage is a cause of adultery, and they believed that easier divorce would make the diminution of adultery less difficult . . .

Neither the Protestant nor the Catholic view in this matter can be upheld on moral grounds. Let us take the Catholic point of view first. Suppose that the husband or wife becomes insane after marriage; it is in this case not desirable that further children should spring from an insane stock, nor yet that any children who may already be born should be brought into contact with insanity. Complete separation of the parents, even supposing that the one who is insane has longer or shorter lucid intervals, is therefore desirable, in the interests of the children. To decree that in this case the sane partner shall never be permitted any legally recognized sex relations is a wanton cruelty which serves no public purpose whatever. The sane partner is left with a very painful choice. He or she may decide in favour of continence, which is what the law and public morals expect; or in favour of surreptitious relations, presumably childless; or in favour of what is called open sin, with or without children. To each of these courses there are grave objections . . .

It follows that in any country which refuses divorce for insanity . . . the man or woman whose wife or husband becomes insane is placed in an intolerable position, in favor of which there is no argument except theological superstition. And what is true of insanity is true also of venereal disease, habitual crime and habitual drunkenness. All these are things which destroy a marriage from every point of view. They make companionship

impossible, procreation undesirable, and association of the guilty parent with the child a thing to be avoided. In such cases, therefore, divorce can only be opposed on the ground that marriage is a trap by which the unwary are tricked into purification through sorrow . . .

Adultery in itself should not, to my mind, be a ground of divorce. Unless people are restrained by inhibitions or strong moral scruples, it is very unlikely that they will go through life without occasionally having any strong impulses to adultery. But such impulses do not by any means necessarily imply that the marriage no longer serves its purpose. There may still be ardent affection between husband and wife, and every desire that the marriage should continue. Suppose, for example, that a man has to be away from home on business for a number of months on end. If he is physically vigorous, he will find it difficult to remain continent throughout this time, however fond he may be of his wife. The same will apply to his wife, if she is not entirely convinced of the correctness of conventional morality. Infidelity in such circumstances ought to form no barrier whatever to subsequent happiness, and in fact it does not, where the husband and wife do not consider it necessary to indulge in melodramatic orgies of jealousy. We may go further, and say that each party should be able to put up with such temporary fancies as are always liable to occur, provided the underlying affection remains intact. The psychology of adultery has been falsified by conventional morals, which assume, in monogamous countries, that attraction to one person cannot coexist with a serious affection for another. Everybody knows that this is untrue, yet everybody is liable, under the influence of jealousy, to fall back upon this untrue theory, and make mountains out of molehills. Adultery, therefore, is no good ground for divorce, except when it involves a deliberate preference for another person, on the whole, to the husband or the wife as the case may be. In saying this I am, of course, assuming that adulterous intercourse will not be such as to lead to children. Where illegitimate children come in, the issue is much more complicated . . .

The grounds which may make divorce desirable are of two kinds. There are those due to the defects of one partner, such as insanity, dipsomania and crime; and there are those based upon the relations of the husband and wife. It may happen that, without blame to either party, it is impossible for a married couple to live together amicably, or without some very grave sacrifice. It may happen that each has important work to do, and that the work requires that they should live in different places. It may happen that one of them, without disliking the other, becomes deeply attached to some other person, so deeply as to feel the marriage an intolerable tie. In that case, if there is no legal redress, hatred is sure to spring up. Indeed, such cases, as every one knows, are quite capable of leading to murder. Where a marriage breaks down owing to incompatibility or to an overwhelming passion on the part of one partner for some other person there should not be a determination to attach blame. For this reason much the best ground of divorce in all cases is mutual consent. Grounds other than mutual consent ought only to be required only where the marriage has failed through some defect in one partner. . . . I should add that nullity, which is now decreed where sexual intercourse is impossible, should instead be granted on application whenever the marriage is childless. That is to say, if a husband and wife who have no children wish to part, they should be able to do so on production of a medical certificate to the effect that the wife is not pregnant. Children are the purpose of marriage, and to hold people to a childless marriage is a cruel cheat.

So much for the *law* of divorce; the *custom* is another matter. As we have already seen, it is possible for the law to make divorce easy while, nevertheless, custom makes it rare. The frequency of divorce in America comes, partly from the fact that what people seek in marriage is not what should be sought, and this in turn is due partly to the fact that adultery is not tolerated. Marriage should be a partnership intended by both parties to last at least as long as the youth of their children, and not regarded by either as at the mercy of temporary amours. If such temporary amours are not tolerated by public opinion or by the consciences of those concerned, each in its turn has to blossom into a marriage. This may easily go so far as completely to destroy the family, for if a woman has a fresh husband every two years, and a fresh child by each, the children in effect are deprived of their fathers, and marriage therefore loses its *raison d'etre* . . .

When marriage is conceived in relation to children, a quite different ethic comes into play. The husband and wife, if they have any love for their children, will so regulate their conduct as to give their children the best chance of a happy and healthy development. This may involve, at times, very considerable self-repression. And it certainly requires that both should realize the superiority of the claims of children to the claims of their own romantic emotions. But all this will happen of itself, and quite naturally, where parental affection is genuine and a false ethic does not inflame jealousy. There are some who say that if a husband and wife no longer love each other passionately, and do not prevent each other from sexual experiences outside marriage, it is impossible for them to cooperate adequately in the education of their children. . . . [But] to cooperate in rearing children, even after passionate love has decayed, is by no means a superhuman task for sensible people who are capable of the natural affections. To this I can testify from a large number of cases personally known to me. To say that parents will be "merely dutiful" is to ignore the emotion of parental affection—an emotion which, where it is genuine and strong, preserves an unbreakable tie between husband and wife long after physical passion has decayed. . . . Family feeling is extremely weak in America, and the frequency of divorce is a consequence of this fact. Where family feeling is strong divorce will be comparatively rare, even if it is legally easy. Easy divorce, as it exists in America, must be regarded as a transitional stage on the way from the biparental to the purely maternal family. It is, however, a stage involving considerable hardship for children, since in the world as it is, children expect to have two parents, and may become attached to their father before divorce takes place. So long as the biparental family continues to be the recognized rule, parents who divorce each other, except for grave cause, appear to me to be failing in their parental duty. I do not think that a legal compulsion to go on being married is likely to mend matters. What seems to me to be wanted is, first, a degree of mutual liberty which will make marriage more endurable, and, secondly, a realization of the importance of children which has been overlaid by the emphasis on sex which we owe to St. Paul and the romantic movement.

The conclusion seems to be that, while divorce is too difficult in many countries . . . easy divorce does not afford a genuine solution of the marriage problem. If marriage is to continue, stability in marriage is important in the interests of the children, but this stability will be best sought by distinguishing between marriage and merely sexual relations, and by emphasizing the biological as opposed to the romantic aspect of married love. I do not pretend that marriage can be freed from onerous duties. In the system that I commend, men are freed, it is true, from the duty of sexual conjugal fidelity, but they have in exchange the duty of controlling jealousy. The good life cannot be lived without self-control, but it is better to control a restrictive and hostile emotion such as jealousy, rather than a generous and expansive emotion such as love. Conventional morality has erred, not in demanding self-control, but in demanding it in the wrong place.

Is Adultery Immoral?

Richard Wasserstrom

Richard Wasserstrom is professor emeritus of philosophy at the University of California, Santa Cruz. He is the author of *The Judicial Decision* (Stanford: Stanford University Press, 1961) and *Philosophy and Social Issues: Five Studies.* (Notre Dame, IN: University of Notre Dame Press, 1980). He has written widely on topics in social ethics, including "Racism, Sexism and Preferential Treatment," and "The Relevance of Nuremberg."

Many discussions of the enforcement of morality by the law take as illustrative of the problem under consideration the regulation of various types of sexual behavior by the criminal law. It was, for example, the Wolfenden Report's recommendations concerning homosexuality and prostitution that led Lord Devlin to compose his now famous lecture "The Enforcement of Morals." And that lecture in turn provoked important philosophical responses from H. L. A. Hart, Ronald Dworkin, and others.

Much, if not all, of the recent philosophical literature on the enforcement of morals appears to take for granted the immorality of the sexual behavior in question. The focus of discussion, at least, is on whether such things as homosexuality, prostitution, and adultery ought to be made illegal even if they are immoral, and not on whether they are immoral. I propose in this essay to consider the latter, more neglected topic, that of sexual morality, and to do so in the following fashion. I shall consider just one kind of behavior that is often taken to be a case of sexual immorality—adultery. I am interested in pursuing at least two questions. First, I want to explore the question of in what respects adulterous behavior falls within the domain of morality at all, for this surely is one of the puzzles one encounters when considering the topic of sexual morality. It is often hard to see on what grounds much of the behavior is deemed to be either moral or immoral, for example, private homosexual behavior between consenting adults. I have purposely selected adultery because it seems a more plausible candidate for moral assessment than many other kinds of sexual behavior.

The second question I want to examine is that of what is to be said about adultery if we are not especially concerned to stay within the area of its morality. I shall endeavor, in other words, to identify and to assess a number of the major arguments that might be advanced against adultery. I believe that they are the chief arguments that would be given in support of the view that adultery is immoral, but I think they are worth considering even if some of them turn out to be nonmoral arguments and considerations.

A number of the issues involved seem to me to be complicated and difficult. In a number of places I have at best indicated where further philosophical exploration is required, without having successfully conducted the exploration myself. This essay may very well be more useful as an illustration of how one might begin to think about the subject of sexual morality than an elucidation of important truths about the topic.

Before I turn to the arguments themselves, there are two preliminary points that require some clarification. Throughout the essay I shall refer to the immorality of such things as breaking a promise, deceiving someone, and so on. In a very rough way I mean by this that there is something morally wrong in doing the action in question. I mean that the action is, in a strong sense of "prima facie," prima facie wrong or unjustified. I do not mean that it may never be right or justifiable to do the action—just that the fact that it is an action of this description always counts against the rightness of the action. I leave entirely open the question of what it is that makes actions of this kind immoral in this sense of "immoral."

The second preliminary point concerns what is meant or implied by the concept of adultery. I mean by "adultery" any case of extramarital sex, and I want to explore the arguments for and against extramarital sex, undertaken in a variety of morally relevant situations. Someone might claim that the concept of adultery is conceptually connected with the concept of immorality and that to characterize behavior as adulterous is already to characterize it as immoral or unjustified in the sense described above. There may be something to this. Hence the importance of making it clear that I want to discuss extramarital sexual relations. If they are always immoral, this is something that must be shown by argument. If the concept of adultery does in some sense entail or imply immorality, I want to ask whether that connection is a rationally based one. If not all cases of extramarital sex are immoral (again, in the sense described above), then the concept of adultery should either be weakened accordingly or restricted to those classes of extramarital sex for which the predication of immorality is warranted.

One argument for the immorality of adultery might go something like this: What makes adultery immoral is that it involves the breaking of a promise, and what makes adultery seriously wrong is that it involves the breaking of an important promise. For, so the argument might continue, one of the things the two parties promise each other when they get married is that they will abstain from sexual relationships with third parties. Because of this promise both spouses quite reasonably entertain the expectation that the other will behave in conformity with it. Hence, when one of them has sexual intercourse with a third party, he or she breaks that promise about sexual relationships that was made when the marriage was entered into and defeats the reasonable expectations of exclusivity entertained by the spouse.

In many cases the immorality involved in breaching the promise relating to extramarital sex may be a good deal more serious than that involved in the breach of other promises. This is so because adherence to this promise may be of much greater importance to them than is adherence to any of the other promises given or received by them in their lifetime. The breaking of this promise may be much more hurtful and painful than is typically the case.

Why is this so? To begin with, it may have been difficult for the nonadulterous spouse to have kept the promise. Hence that spouse may feel the unfairness of having restrained himself or herself in the absence of reciprocal restraint having been exercised by the adulterous spouse. In addition, the spouse may perceive the breaking of the promise as an indication of a kind of indifference on the part of the adulterous spouse. If you really cared about me and my feelings, the spouse might say, you would not have done this to me. And third, and related to the above, the spouse may see the act of sexual intercourse with another as a sign of affection for the other person and as an additional rejection of the nonadulterous spouse as the one who is loved by the adulterous spouse. It is not just that the adulterous spouse does not take the feelings of the nonadulterous spouse sufficiently into account, the adulterous spouse also indicates through the act of adultery affection for someone other than the nonadulterous spouse. I will return to these points later. For the present it is sufficient to note that a set of arguments can be developed in support of the proposition that certain kinds of adultery are wrong just because they involve the breach of a serious promise that, among other things, leads to the intentional infliction of substantial pain on one spouse by the other.

Another argument for the immorality of adultery focuses not on the existence of a promise of sexual exclusivity but on the connection between adultery and deception. According to this argument adultery involves deception. And because deception is wrong, so is adultery.

Although it is certainly not obviously so, I shall simply assume in this essay that deception is always immoral. Thus, the crucial issue for my purposes is the asserted connection between extramarital sex and deception. Is it plausible to maintain, as this argument does, that adultery always involves deception and is it, on that basis, to be condemned?

The most obvious person upon whom deceptions might be practiced is the nonparticipating spouse; and the most obvious thing about which the nonparticipating spouse can be deceived is the existence of the adulterous act. One clear case of deception is that of lying. Instead of saying that the afternoon was spent in bed with A, the adulterous spouse asserts that it was spent in the library with B or on the golf course with C.

There can also be deception even when no lies are told. Suppose, for instance, that a person has sexual intercourse with someone other than his or her spouse and just does not tell the spouse about it. Is that deception? It may not be a case of lying if, for example, he or she is never asked by the spouse about the situation. Still, we might say, it is surely deceptive because of the promises that were exchanged at marriage. As we saw earlier, these promises provide a foundation for the reasonable belief that neither spouse will engage in sexual relationships with any other person. Hence the failure to bring the fact of extramarital sex to the attention of the other spouse deceives

that spouse about the present state of the marital relationship.

Adultery, in other words, can involve both active and passive deception. An adulterous spouse may just keep silent or, as is often the case, the spouse may engage in an increasingly complex way of life devoted to the concealment of the facts from the nonparticipating spouse. Lies, half truths, clandestine meetings, and the like may become a central feature of the adulterous spouse's existence. These are things that can and do happen, and when they do they make the case against adultery an easy one. Still, neither active nor passive deception is inevitably a feature of an extramarital relationship.

It is possible, though, that a more subtle but pervasive kind of deceptiveness is a feature of adultery. It comes about because of the connection in our culture between sexual intimacy and certain feelings of love and affection. The point can be made indirectly by seeing that one way in which we can in our culture mark off our close friends from our mere acquaintances is through the kinds of intimacies that we are prepared to share with them. I may, for instance, be willing to reveal my very private thoughts and emotions to my closest friends or to my wife but to no one else. My sharing of these intimate facts about myself is, from one perspective, a way of making a gift to those who mean the most to me. Revealing these things and sharing them with those who mean the most to me is one means by which I create, maintain, and confirm those interpersonal relationships that are of most importance to me.

In our culture, it might be claimed, sexual intimacy is one of the chief currencies through which gifts of this sort are exchanged. One way to tell someone—particularly someone of the opposite sex—that you have feelings of affection and love for them is by allowing them, or sharing with them, sexual behaviors that one does not share with others. This way of measuring affection was certainly very much a part of the culture in which I matured. It worked something like this: If you were a girl, you showed how much you liked a boy by the degree of sexual intimacy you would allow. If you liked him only a little you never did more than kiss—and even the kiss was not very passionate. If you liked him a lot and if your feeling was reciprocated, necking and, possibly, petting were permissible. If the attachment was still stronger and you thought it might even become a permanent relationship, the sexual activity was correspondingly more intense and intimate, although whether it led to sexual intercourse depended on whether the parties (particularly the girl) accepted fully the prohibition on nonmarital sex. The situation for the boys was related but not exactly the same. The assumption was that males did not naturally link sex with affection in the way in which females did. However, since women did link sex with affection, males had to take that fact into account. That is to say, because a woman would permit sexual intimacies only if she had feelings of affection for the male and only if those feelings were reciprocated, the male had to have and express those feelings too, before sexual intimacies of any sort would occur.

The result was that the importance of a correlation between sexual intimacy and feelings of love and affection was taught by the culture and assimilated by those growing up in the culture. The scale of possible positive feelings toward persons of the other sex ran from casual liking, at one end, to the love that was deemed essential to, and characteristic of, marriage, at the other. The scale of possible sexual behavior ran from brief, passionless kissing or hand-holding, at one end, to sexual intercourse, at the other. And the correlation between the two scales was quite precise. As a result, any act of sexual intimacy carried substantial meaning with it, and no act of sexual intimacy was simply a pleasurable set of bodily sensations. Many such acts were, of course, more pleasurable to the participants because they were a way of saying what their feelings were. And sometimes they were less pleasurable for the same reason. The point is, however, that sexual activity was much more than mere bodily enjoyment. It was not like eating a good meal, listening to good music, lying in the sun, or getting a pleasant back rub. It was behavior that meant a great deal concerning one's feelings for persons of the opposite sex in whom one was most interested and with whom one was most involved. It was among the

most authoritative ways in which one could communicate to another the nature and degree of one's affection.

If this sketch is even roughly right, then several things become somewhat clearer. To begin with, a possible rationale for many of the rules of conventional sexual morality can be developed. If, for example, sexual intercourse is associated with the kind of affection and commitment to another that is regarded as characteristic of the marriage relationship, then it is natural that sexual intercourse should be thought properly to take place between persons who are married to each other. And if it is thought that this kind of affection and commitment is only to be found within the marriage relationship, then it is not surprising that sexual intercourse should only be thought to be proper within marriage.

Related to what has just been said is the idea that sexual intercourse ought to be restricted to those who are married to each other, as a means by which to confirm the very special feelings that the spouses have for each other. Because our culture teaches that sexual intercourse means that the strongest of all feelings for each other are shared by the lovers, it is natural that persons who are married to each other should be able to say this to each other in this way. Revealing and confirming verbally that these feelings are present is one thing that helps to sustain the relationship; engaging in sexual intercourse is another.

In addition, this account would help to provide a framework within which to make sense of the notion that some sex is better than other sex. As I indicated earlier, the fact that sexual intimacy can be meaningful in the sense described tends to make it also the case that sexual intercourse can sometimes be more enjoyable than at other times. On this view, sexual intercourse will typically be more enjoyable if strong feelings of affection are present than it will be if it is merely "mechanical." This is so in part because people enjoy being loved, especially by those whom they love. Just as we like to hear words of affection, so we like to receive affectionate behavior. And the meaning enhances the independently pleasurable behavior.

More to the point, an additional rationale for the prohibition on extramarital sex can now be developed. For given this way of viewing the sexual world, extramarital sex will almost always involve deception of a deeper sort. If the adulterous spouse does not in fact have the appropriate feelings of affection for the extramarital partner, then the adulterous spouse is deceiving that person about the presence of such feelings. If, on the other hand, the adulterous spouse does have the corresponding feelings for the extramarital partner but not toward the nonparticipating spouse, the adulterous spouse is very probably deceiving the nonparticipating spouse about the presence of such feelings toward that spouse. Indeed, it might be argued, whenever there is no longer love between the two persons who are married to each other, there is deception just because being married implies both to the participants and to the world that such a bond exists. Deception is inevitable, the argument might conclude, because the feelings of affection that ought to accompany any act of sexual intercourse can only be held toward one other person at any given time in one's life. And if this is so, then the adulterous spouse always deceives either the partner in adultery or the nonparticipating spouse about the existence of such feelings. Thus extramarital sex involves deception of this sort and is for that reason immoral even if no deception vis-à-vis the occurrence of the act of adultery takes place.

What might be said in response to the foregoing arguments? The first thing that might be said is that the account of the connection between sexual intimacy and feelings of affection is inaccurate—not in the sense that no one thinks of things that way but in the sense that there is substantially more divergence of opinion than the account suggests. For example, the view I have delineated may describe reasonably accurately the concepts of the sexual world in which I grew up, but it does not capture tile sexual *Weltanschauung* of today's youth at all. Thus, whether or not adultery implies deception in respect to feelings depends very much on the persons who are involved and the way they look at the "meaning" of sexual intimacy.

Second, the argument leaves unanswered the question of whether it is desirable for sexual intimacy to carry the sorts of messages described above. For those persons for whom sex does have

these implications there are special feelings and sensibilities that must be taken into account. But it is another question entirely whether any valuable end—moral or otherwise—is served by investing sexual behavior with such significance. That is something that must be shown and not just assumed. It might, for instance, be the case that substantially more good than harm would come from a kind of demystification of sexual behavior—one that would encourage the enjoyment of sex more for its own sake and one that would reject the centrality both of the association of sex with love and of love with only one other person.

I regard these as two of the more difficult unresolved issues that our culture faces today in respect of thinking sensibly about the attitudes toward sex and love that we should try to develop in ourselves and in our children.

Much of the contemporary literature that advocates sexual liberation of one sort or another embraces one or the other of two different views about the relationship between sex and love. One view holds that sex should be separated from love and affection. To be sure, sex is probably better when the partners genuinely like and enjoy being with each other. But sex is basically an intensive, exciting sensuous activity that can be enjoyed in a variety of suitable settings with a variety of suitable partners. The situation in respect to sexual pleasure is no different from that of the person who knows and appreciates fine food and who can have a satisfying meal in any number of good restaurants with any number of congenial companions. One question that must be settled here is whether sex can be thus demystified; another, more important, question is whether it would be desirable to do so. What might we gain and what might we lose if we all lived in a world in which an act of sexual intercourse was no more or less significant or enjoyable than having a delicious meal in a nice setting with a good friend? The answer to this question lies beyond the scope of this essay.

The second view of the relationship between sex and love seeks to drive the wedge in a different place. On this view it is not the link between sex and love that needs to be broken, but rather the connection between love and exclusivity. For a number of the reasons already given it is desirable, so this argument goes, that sexual intimacy continue to be reserved to and shared with only those for whom one has very great affection. The mistake lies in thinking that any "normal" adult will have those feelings toward only one other adult during his or her lifetime or even at any time in his or her life. It is the concept of adult love, not ideas about sex, that needs demystification. What are thought to be both unrealistic and unfortunate are the notions of exclusivity and possessiveness that attach to the dominant conception of love between adults in our culture and others. Parents of four, five, six, or even ten children can certainly claim, and sometimes claim correctly, that they love all of their children, that they love them all equally, and that it is simply untrue to their feelings to insist that the numbers involved diminish either the quantity or the quality of their love. If this is readily understandable in the case of parents and children, there is no necessary reason why it is an impossible or undesirable ideal in the case of adults. To be sure, there is probably a limit to the number of intimate, "primary" relationships that any person can maintain at any given time without affecting the quality of the relationship. But one adult ought surely to be able to love two, three, or even six other adults at any one time without that love being different in kind or degree from that of the traditional, monogamous, lifetime marriage. And between the individuals in these relationships, whether within a marriage or without, sexual intimacy is fitting and good.

The issues raised by a position such as the one described above are also surely worth exploring in detail and with care. Is there something to be called "sexual love" that is different from parental love or the nonsexual love of close friends? Is there something about love in general that links it naturally and appropriately with feelings of exclusivity and possession? Or is there something about sexual love, whatever that may be, that makes these feelings especially fitting? Once again, the issues are conceptual, empirical, and normative all at once: What is love? How could it be different? Would it be a good thing or a bad thing if it were different?

Suppose, though, that having delineated these problems we were now to pass them by. Suppose, moreover, that we were to be persuaded of the possibility and the desirability of weakening substantially either the links between sex and love or the links between sexual love and exclusivity. Would it not then be the case that adultery could be free from all of the morally objectionable features described thus far? To be more specific, let us imagine that a husband and wife have what is today sometimes characterized as an "open marriage." Suppose, that is, that they have agreed in advance that extramarital sex is—under certain circumstances—acceptable behavior for each to engage in. Suppose that as a result there is no impulse to deceive each other about the occurrence or nature of any such relationships and that no deception in fact occurs. Suppose, too, that there is no deception in respect to the feelings involved between the adulterous spouse and the extramarital partner. And suppose, finally, that one or the other or both of the spouses then has sexual intercourse in circumstances consistent with these understandings. Under this description, so the argument might conclude, adultery is simply not immoral. At a minimum adultery cannot very plausibly be condemned either on grounds that it involves deception or on grounds that it requires the breaking of a promise.

At least two responses are worth considering. One calls attention to the connection between marriage and adultery; the other looks to more instrumental arguments for the immorality of adultery. Both deserve further exploration.

One way to deal with the case of the "open marriage" is to question whether the two persons involved are still properly to be described as being married to each other. Part of the meaning of what it is for two persons to be married to each other, so this argument would go, is to have committed oneself to have sexual relationships only with one's spouse. Of course, it would be added, we know that that commitment is not always honored. We know that persons who are married to each other often do commit adultery. But there is a difference between being willing to make a commitment to marital fidelity, even though one may fail to honor that commitment, and not making the commitment at all. Whatever the relationship may be between the two individuals in the case just described, the absence of any commitment to sexual exclusivity requires the conclusion that their relationship is not a marital one. For a commitment to sexual exclusivity is a necessary but not a sufficient condition for the existence of a marriage.

Although there may be something to this suggestion, it is too strong as stated to be acceptable. To begin with it is doubtful that there are many, if any, necessary conditions for marriage; but even if there are, a commitment to sexual exclusivity is not such a condition.

To see that this is so, consider what might be taken to be some of the essential characteristics of a marriage. We might be tempted to propose that the concept of marriage requires the following: a formal ceremony of some sort in which mutual obligations are undertaken between two persons of the opposite sex; the capacity on the part of the persons involved to have sexual intercourse with each other; the willingness to have sexual intercourse only with each other; and feelings of love and affection between the two persons. The problem is that we can imagine relationships that are clearly marital and yet lack one or more of these features. For example, in our own society it is possible for two persons to be married without going through a formal ceremony, as in the common-law marriages recognized in some jurisdictions. It is also possible for two persons to get married even though one or both lacks the capacity to engage in sexual intercourse. Thus, two very elderly persons who have neither the desire nor the ability to have intercourse can nonetheless get married, as can persons whose sexual organs have been injured so that intercourse is not possible. And we certainly know of marriages in which love was not present at the time of the marriage, as, for instance, in marriages of state and marriages of convenience.

Counterexamples not satisfying the condition relating to the abstention from extramarital sex are even more easily produced. We certainly know of societies and cultures in which polygamy and polyandry are practiced, and we have no difficulty in recognizing these relationships as cases of marriages. It might be objected, though, that these are not counterexamples because they are plural marriages rather than marriages in which sex is permitted with someone other than one of the persons to whom one is married. But we also know of societies in which it is permissible for married persons to have sexual relationships with persons to whom they are not married, for example, temple prostitutes, concubines, and homosexual lovers. And even if we knew of no such societies, the conceptual claim would still, I submit, not be well taken. For suppose all of the other indicia of marriage were present: suppose the two persons were of the opposite sex; suppose they had the capacity and desire to have intercourse with each other; suppose they participated in a formal ceremony in which they understood themselves voluntarily to be entering into a relationship with each other in which substantial mutual commitments were assumed. If all these conditions were satisfied we would not be in any doubt as to whether or not the two persons were married, even though they had not taken on a commitment of sexual exclusivity and even though they had expressly agreed that extramarital sexual intercourse was a permissible behavior for each to engage in.

A commitment to sexual exclusivity is neither a necessary nor a sufficient condition for the existence of a marriage. It does, nonetheless, have this much to do with the nature of marriage—like the other indicia enumerated above, its presence tends to establish the existence of a marriage. Thus, in the absence of a formal ceremony of any sort an explicit commitment to sexual exclusivity would count in favor of regarding the two persons as married. The conceptual role of the commitment to sexual exclusivity can, perhaps, be brought out through the following example. Suppose we found a tribe that had a practice in which all the other indicia of marriage were present but in which the two parties were *prohibited* even from having sexual intercourse with each other. Moreover, suppose that sexual intercourse with others was clearly permitted. In such a case we would, I think, reject the idea that the two persons were married to each other, and we would describe their relationship in other terms, for example, as some kind of formalized, special friendship relation—a kind of heterosexual "blood-brother" bond.

Compare that case with the following one. Again suppose that the tribe had a practice in which all of the other indicia of marriage were present, but instead of a prohibition on sexual intercourse between the persons in the relationship there was no rule at all. Sexual intercourse was permissible with the person with whom one had this ceremonial relationship, but it was no more or less permissible than with a number of other persons to whom one was not so related (for instance, all consenting adults of the opposite sex). While we might be in doubt as to whether we ought to describe the persons as married to each other, we would probably conclude that they were married and that they simply were members of a tribe whose views about sex were quite different from our own.

What all of this shows is that a *prohibition* on sexual intercourse between the two persons involved in a relationship is conceptually incompatible with the claim that the two of them are married. The *permissibility* of intramarital sex is a necessary part of the idea of marriage. But no such incompatibility follows simply from the added permissibility of extramarital sex.

These arguments do not, of course, exhaust the arguments for the prohibition on extramarital sexual relations. The remaining argument that I wish to consider is—as I indicated earlier—a more instrumental one. It seeks to justify the prohibition by virtue of the role that it plays in the development and maintenance of nuclear families. The argument, or set of arguments, might, I believe, go something like this:

Consider first a far-fetched nonsexual example. Suppose a society were organized so that after some suitable age—say 18, 19, or 20—persons were forbidden to eat anything but bread and water with anyone but their spouse. Persons might still choose in such a society not to get married. Good food just might not be very important to them because they have underdeveloped taste buds. Or good food might be bad for them because there is something wrong with their digestive system. Or good food might be important to them, but they might decide that the enjoyment of good food would get in the way of the attainment of other things that were more important. But most persons would, I think, be led to favor marriage in part because they preferred a richer, more varied diet to one of bread and water. And they might remain married because the family was the only legitimate setting within which good food was obtainable. If it is important to have society organized so that persons will both get married and stay married, such an arrangement would be well suited to the preservation of the family, and the prohibitions relating to food consumption could be understood as fulfilling that function.

It is obvious that one of the more powerful human desires is the desire for sexual gratification. The desire is a natural one, like hunger and thirst, in the sense that it need not be learned in order to be present within us and operative on us. But there is in addition much that we do learn about what the act of sexual intercourse is like. Once we experience sexual intercourse ourselves—and, in particular, once we experience orgasm—we discover that it is among the most intensive short-term pleasures of the body.

Because this is so it is easy to see how the prohibition on extramarital sex helps to hold marriage together. At least during that period of life when the enjoyment of sexual intercourse is one of the desirable bodily pleasures, persons will wish to enjoy those pleasures. If one consequence of being married is that one is prohibited from having sexual intercourse with anyone but one's spouse, then the spouses in a marriage are in a position to provide an important source of pleasure for each other that is unavailable to them elsewhere in the society.

The point emerges still more clearly if this rule of sexual morality is seen as being of a piece with the other rules of sexual morality. When this prohibition is coupled, for example, with the prohibition on nonmarital sexual intercourse, we are presented with the inducement both to get married and to stay married. For if sexual intercourse is only legitimate within marriage, then persons seeking that gratification that is a feature of sexual intercourse are furnished explicit social directions for its attainment, namely, marriage.

Nor, to continue the argument, is it necessary to focus exclusively on the bodily enjoyment that is involved. Orgasm may be a significant part of what there is to sexual intercourse, but it is not the whole of it. We need only recall the earlier discussion of the meaning that sexual intimacy has in our own culture to begin to see some of the more intricate ways in which sexual exclusivity may be connected with the establishment and maintenance of marriage as the primary heterosexual love relationship. Adultery is wrong, in other words, because a prohibition on extramarital sex is a way to help maintain the institutions of marriage and the nuclear family.

I am frankly not sure what we are to say about an argument such as the preceding one. What I am convinced of is that, like the arguments discussed earlier, this one also reveals something of the difficulty and complexity of the issues that are involved. So what I want now to do in the final portion of this essay is to try to delineate with reasonable precision several of what I take to be the fundamental, unresolved issues.

The first is whether this last argument is an argument for the immorality of extramarital sexual intercourse. What does seem clear is that there are differences between this argument and the ones considered earlier. The earlier arguments condemned adulterous behavior because it was behavior that involved breaking a promise, taking unfair advantage of or deceiving another. To the degree to which the prohibition on extramarital sex can be supported by arguments that invoke considerations such as these, there is little question but that violations of the prohibition are properly regarded as immoral. And such a claim could be defended on one or both of two distinct grounds. The first is that actions such as promise-breaking and deception are simply wrong. The second is that adultery involving promise-breaking or deception is wrong because it involves the straightforward infliction of harm on another human being—typically the nonadulterous spouse who has a strong claim not to have that harm so inflicted.

The argument that connects the prohibition on extramarital sex with the maintenance and preservation of the institution of marriage is an argument for the instrumental value of the prohibition. To some degree this counts, I think, against regarding all violations of the prohibition as obvious cases of immorality. This is so partly because hypothetical imperatives are less clearly within the domain of morality than are categorical ones, and even more because instrumental prohibitions are within the domain of morality only if the end that they serve or the way that they serve it is itself within the domain of morality.

What this should help us see, I think, is the fact that the argument that connects the prohibition on adultery with the preservation of marriage is at best seriously incomplete. Before we ought to be convinced by it, we ought to have reasons for believing that marriage is a morally desirable and just social institution. And such reasons are not quite as easy to find or as obvious as it may seem. For the concept of marriage is, as we have seen, both a loosely structured and a complicated one. There may be all sorts of intimate, interpersonal relationships that will resemble but not be identical with the typical marriage relationship presupposed by the traditional sexual morality. There may be a number of distinguishable sexual and loving arrangements that can all legitimately claim to be called marriages. The prohibitions of the traditional sexual morality may be effective ways to maintain some marriages and ineffective ways to promote and preserve others. The prohibitions of the traditional sexual morality may make good psychological sense if certain psychological theories are true, and they may be purveyors of immense psychological mischief if other psychological theories are true. The prohibitions of traditional sexual morality may seem obviously correct if sexual intimacy carries the meaning that the dominant culture has often ascribed to it, and they may seem equally bizarre if sex is viewed through the perspective of the counterculture. Irrespective of whether instrumental arguments of this sort are properly deemed moral arguments, they ought not fully convince anyone until questions such as these are answered.

Love's Constancy

Mike W. Martin

Mike W. Martin is professor of philosophy at Chapman University. He is the author of *Self-Deception and Morality* (Lawrence, KS: University of Kansas Press, 1986) and *Love's Virtues* (Lawrence, KS: University of Kansas Press, 1996).

"Marital faithfulness" refers to faithful love for a spouse or lover to whom one is committed, rather than the narrower idea of sexual fidelity. The distinction is clearly marked in traditional wedding vows. A commitment to love faithfully is central: "to have and to hold from this day forward, for better for worse, for richer for poorer, in sickness and in health, to love and to cherish, till death us do part . . . and thereto I plight [pledge] thee my troth [faithfulness]."[1] Sexual fidelity is promised in a subordinate clause, symbolizing its supportive role in promoting love's constancy: "and, forsaking all other, keep thee only unto her/him."[2] . . .

Is marital faithfulness a virtue, that is, something morally desirable and admirable? Presumably virtues are intrinsically good. Marital constancy, however, is desirable in some cases but undesirable in others, depending on how well a marriage promotes the good of spouses and others (especially children). Faithfulness seems more a matter of self-interest, luck, and simple compatibility, rather than morality. Perhaps commitments to love should be understood in terms of intentions but not obligations. That would also free us to approach divorce without being preoccupied with betrayal and blame-mongering. In short, should not the entire topic of marriage be demoralized? Not if we value the goods made possible in long-term marriages. Here I will make six comments by way of clarifying faithfulness as a virtue.

First, we can acknowledge that when a marriage is disastrous and hopeless, constancy can be bad rather than virtuous in that it prolongs a bad thing. But it does not follow that faithfulness is not a virtue. Virtues are context-dependent. Michael Slote pointed out that "many virtues only count as such when they are attended by certain other virtues."[3] For example, conscientious-ness is a virtue, or at least a highly admirable virtue, only when it involves attention to duties that promote human good, as opposed for example to the conscientiousness of a Nazi. Similarly, Eva Braun's faithfulness in loving Hitler is not a virtue, nor is constancy in love for a wife-beating, child-abusing, sadistic husband. In general, faithfulness is desirable and admirable only in so far as there is something good about the love. That good centers on caring, mutual support, kindness, and joy—which is morally desirable in itself and which contributes to the fulfillment of persons.

Second, taking moral commitments seriously does carry with it the possibility of betrayal of one's spouse, of oneself, and of one's ideals of love. At the same time, not meeting an ideal does not automatically imply moral failure and blame-worthiness, given causes beyond our control. Marital betrayal is usually the result of not trying, or not trying hard enough. But all the effort in the world cannot by itself achieve marital success without luck.

Some loves are lucky; others are unfortunate, even tragic, due to circumstances that spouses can only partially influence.[4] Luck, as well as good judgment, plays a role in finding a promising partner whom one finds attractive physically, intellectually, morally, socially, and in terms of shared interests and values. Then, if a permanent relationship is to emerge, partners must be able to trust each other's commitments. During their shared history, the basis of love must remain sufficiently constant to overcome inevitable difficulties, such as money problems, major illness, temporary separations, and changing interests. Later, the relationship must survive the ravages of old age, and at any time the threat of death to one of the partners. In addition, there is luck in having the gifts of temperament conducive to monogamy, gifts that are in part genetic and in part the product of our up-

From "Love's Constancy," *Philosophy* vol. 68 (1993), pp. 63–71.
Reprinted by permission of Cambridge University Press.

bringing.[5] All these factors call for great reserve in judging people who are unable to meet their marital commitments.

Third, it is true that talk about faithfulness and betrayal should be set aside in some contexts. The therapist's office is one such context. In order to help couples or individuals deal with marital or divorce difficulties, counselors do well to keep matters focused on problem-solving skills, not blame-mongering and credit-grabbing. So do couples themselves, as they try to improve their relationship (rather than engage in exercises in self-righteousness). And observers who know little about the obstacles confronting a marriage should be wary of passing judgment. This does not, however, negate the appropriateness of moral language in other contexts, such as marriage ceremonies which publicly express solemn acts of acquiring responsibilities.

Fourth, acknowledging the role of luck does not remove the vital contribution of effort, responsibility, and moral virtue in shaping good relationships. Unless we are fatalists, who view human life as determined in ways that remove moral responsibility, we must recognize that faithfulness plays an important role. Precisely what role, in a given case, can be difficult to answer.

Thus, in examining individual cases, whether ourselves or others, we confront ambiguities that make it difficult to tell whether inconstancy is the result of temperament, luck, or irresponsibility of the sort that leads us to talk of betrayal and unfaithfulness. Consider Bertrand Russell, who reports that seven years into his marriage he suddenly fell out of love with his wife. "I went out bicycling one afternoon, and suddenly, as I was riding along a country road, I realized that I no longer loved Alys. I had had no idea until this moment that my love for her was even lessening."[6]

What does Russell mean by "love"? He goes on to record that he was no longer sexually attracted to Alys and that also he had become preoccupied with her character faults. In his autobiography, however, he admits the unfairness and self-righteousness in his criticisms of Alys, and in a passage omitted from the final draft of the book he explained the breakup by appeal to his temperament: "I now believe that it is not in my nature to remain physically fond of any woman for more than seven or eight years. As I view it now, this was the basis of the matter, and the rest was humbug."[7] We need not accept Russell's explanation as authoritative, any more than Russell had to accept his own earlier interpretation of events. Some might interpret the bicycle experience as a symptom of the "seven-year itch" which other couples deal with through marriage counseling or by taking a long vacation together. Possibly Russell was not only self-righteous but . . . guilty of bad faith in reducing his love to sexual desire and related feelings.[8] He prides himself on his honesty in promptly telling Alys that his love was gone, but perhaps full honesty would lead to a quite different conversation with Alys in which together they explored his troubled feelings with an eye to preserving an ideal-guided relationship.

As another possibility, perhaps Russell had undergone a fundamental change in his ideals since making his wedding vows. Perhaps he was rebelling against the Victorian ideals he had been raised with. Not temperament, but a new ideal of love was the reason he could so quickly conclude that his sexual relationship with Alys was over. In any case, some individuals do change their ideals, rejecting marital faithfulness after having earlier made lifelong commitments in good faith. Anais Nin, for example, arrived at this view of faithfulness after entering a fairly traditional marriage: "I really believe that if I were not a writer, not a creator, not an experimenter, I might have been a very faithful wife. I think highly of faithfulness. But my temperament belongs to the writer, not to the woman."[9] A year later, in the midst of her tumultuous affair with Henry Miller, her attitude changed again; "The ideal of faithfulness is a joke" and the essential value in love is "sincerity with one's self."[10]

Fifth, appreciating marital faithfulness as a virtue does not mean making it the supreme value. Marital obligations are not absolute in the sense of always overriding all other considerations. Consider Paul Gauguin, who after a decade into his marriage, and after fathering five children, quit his job as a successful stockbroker to become a full-time artist. For most of the remainder of his life he did not earn enough money to support his family.

It is difficult to avoid saying that he was unfaithful. It is also difficult to avoid admiring what he did—in one respect—if we value the art he produced and realize that it could not have been produced except at the expense of his family.[11] We, perhaps like him, may regret that the world did not make possible a happier accommodation of art and family, but we may also view aesthetic values and the moral value of self-fulfillment as providing some reasons for his conduct.

Sixth, we tend to think of faithfulness in terms of staying the same in the midst of changing circumstances, especially changes in our spouse. Shakespeare gave the classical expression of this idea: "love is not love/Which alters when it alteration finds . . ./it is an ever-fixed mark/That looks on tempests and is never shaken."[12]

Dorothy Day recounts how her common-law marriage with Forster Batterham ended because he could not adjust to her decision to have their child and herself baptized in the Catholic Church. Prior to her decision, the marriage had been joyous, and deeply rooted in a shared devotion to social justice—a devotion which Day sustained throughout her subsequent leadership in the Catholic Worker Movement. Yet Batterham was also adamantly anti-religious: "he was averse to any ceremony before officials of either Church or state. He was an anarchist and an atheist, and he did not intend to be a liar or a hypocrite. He was a creature of utter sincerity, and however illogical and bad-tempered about it all, I loved him."[13] In order for Batterham to remain faithful, his love would have had to adjust so as to accept, or at least tolerate, Day's new religious outlook.

The best marriages, like the best persons, are often seriously flawed. Faithfulness is a virtue when it supports good though imperfect relationships. The same is true of tolerance and humility. Nietzsche was no booster of marriages, but what he said of strong characters applies to strong marriages: "'Giving style' to one's character [and marriage]—a great and rare art! It is exercised by those who see all the strengths and weaknesses of their own natures [and marriage] and then comprehend them in an artistic plan until everything appears as art and reason and even weakness delights the eye . . . Here the ugly which could not be removed is hidden; there it has been reinterpreted and made sublime."[14]

Children and the Ethics of Divorce

Laurence D. Houlgate

Laurence Houlgate, the editor of this anthology, is professor of philosophy at California Polytechnic State University, San Luis Obispo. He is the author of *The Child and the State: A Normative Theory of Juvenile Rights* (Baltimore, MD: Johns Hopkins University Press, 1980) and *Family and State: The Philosophy of Family Law* (Totowa, NJ: Rowman & Littlefield, 1988). He is the cofounder, with Professor Nancy Jecker, of the Society for Philosophy and the Family.

In 1929 Bertrand Russell published *Marriage and Morals,* an extended critique of traditional sexual morality and prevailing moral views about marriage and divorce.[1] The book caused quite a sensation in Britain and the United States in part because of Russell's suggestion that adultery may not always be wrong and his recommendation that young people contemplating marriage might want to live together for one or two years before solemnizing their relationship. Russell referred to the latter as "trial marriage," and he argued that its encouragement might have the felicitous effect of reducing the chances of marital breakdown and divorce. For this and other mild suggestions Russell was vilified by much of the American press and public.[2] Forgotten in the commotion surrounding publication of the book was Russell's recommendation regarding divorce between couples who have young children. Russell was concerned about the high rate of divorce in America, which he attributed primarily to "extremely weak" family feeling. He regarded easy divorce "as a transitional stage on the way from the biparental to the purely maternal family," and he observed that this is "a stage involving considerable hardship for children, since, in the world as it is, children expect to have two parents, and may become attached to their father before divorce takes place." In characteristically strong language, Russell concluded that "parents who divorce each other, except for grave cause, appear to me to be failing in their parental duty."[3]

There have been significant changes in divorce law in the United States since Russell wrote these words. Every state but South Dakota has adopted some form of "no-fault" divorce rules, making it much easier for persons to divorce than it was when Russell wrote *Marriage and Morals.* Under no-fault laws there is no longer a need to establish grounds in order to obtain a divorce. For example, a woman who wishes to divorce her husband is not required to prove that he is guilty of adultery or cruelty or committed some other marital fault. It is sufficient to assert that "irreconcilable differences" caused the breakup of the marriage. Second, in many states only *one* of the spouses needs to claim that his or her differences with the other are irreconcilable. Mutual consent is no longer a necessary condition to the grant of a divorce.

Philosophers writing since Russell have had little to say about either the recent changes in divorce law or about the ethics of divorce, neither commenting on whether the new regulations represent moral progress, nor on the question whether it would ever be wrong for someone to seek a divorce.[4] The silence of philosophers about this and other matters related to marriage and family is unfortunate. Divorce is an act that has devastating personal and social consequences[5] for millions of adults and children.[6] If ethics is at least in part about conduct that affects the interests of others, then certainly the impact of divorce on the lives of so many people should qualify it as an act as deserving the careful attention of the moral philosopher as the acts of punishment, abortion, or euthanasia.

One year after the publication of *Marriage and Morals,* fiction writer and essayist Rebecca West echoed Russell's views about the divorce of couples with children in an article she wrote for the *London Daily Express.* West wrote that "the divorce of married people with children is nearly always an unspeakable calamity." She gave several reasons for this:

> It is only just being understood, in the light of modern psychological research, how much a child depends for its healthy growth on the presence in the home of both its parents . . . if a child is deprived of either its father or its mother it feels that it has been cheated out of a right. It cannot be reasoned out of this attitude, for children are illogical, especially where their affections are concerned, to an even greater degree than ourselves. A child who suffers from this resentment suffers much more than grief: he is liable to an obscuring of his vision, to a warping of his character. He may turn against the parent to whom the courts have given him, and regard him or her as responsible for the expulsion of the other from the home. He may try to compensate himself for what he misses by snatching everything else he can get out of life, and become selfish, and even thievish. He may, through yearning for the unattainable parent, get himself into a permanent mood of discontent, which will last his life long and make him waste every opportunity of love and happiness that comes to him later.[7]

This is a large catalog of psychological and behavioral ills to attribute to a single phenomenon, but Rebecca West thought that there was adequate research to support her claims.[8] Although there was a long period after World War II during which some psychologists argued that "children can survive any family crisis without permanent damage—and grow as human beings in the process,"[9] by the 1980s some thought that the earlier research referred to by West was being confirmed.

The Children of Divorce: Recent Studies

In a controversial, long-term study of 131 middle-class children from the San Francisco, California area, interviews conducted by clinicians at eighteen months, five years and ten years after their parents' divorce showed that many were doing worse at each of these periods than they were immediately after their parents' separation. (Only children who had no previous history of emotional problems were selected for the study.) At eighteen months after their parents' divorce, "an unexpectedly large number of children were on a downward course. Their symptoms were worse than before. Their behavior at school was worse. Their peer relationships were worse." At a five year follow-up, "some were better off than they had been during the failing marriage." But over a third of the whole group of these children "were significantly worse off than before. Clinically depressed, they were not doing well in school or with friends. They had deteriorated to the point that some early disturbances, such as sleep problems, poor learning, or acting out, had become chronic." At the tenth year interview, clinicians were astounded to discover that "almost half of the children entered adulthood as worried, underachieving, self-deprecating, and sometimes angry young men and women."[10]

Although children with previous histories of emotional problems were excluded from this study, this research was strongly criticized for using no control group: "So the entire study is predicated on the huge untested assumption that problems of adjustment don't occur as often in intact families."[11] However, a 1991 study remedied this defect in research design by employing a control group of several thousand intact families. This study of the effects of divorce on children in Great Britain and the United States found differences between the psychological health of the young people whose parents divorced and those whose parents remained married. In the British survey, for example, a subsample of children who were in two-parent families during an initial interview at age 7 were followed through the next interview at age 11. At both points in time, parents and teachers independently rated the children's behavior problems, and the children were given reading and mathematics achievement tests. 239 children whose parents divorced between these two age intervals were compared to over 11,000 children whose families remained intact. Boys whose parents divorced showed 19 percent more behavior problems and scored lower on the achievement tests at age 11. However, girls in both groups did not differ markedly in the kind and amount of behavior problems.[12]

The Divorce Child-Harm Argument

Although we should await the results of further research before drawing definite conclusions about the effects of divorce on children, let us assume for purposes of argument that there is some reason to believe that *boys* whose parents divorce while they are young are more at risk of suffering short-term and/or long-term psychological distress and social harm (for example, anxiety, depression, withdrawal, difficulties in school achievements, peer relationships, and handling of aggression) than are children in intact marriages.[13] If this is true, then the following simple argument for the immorality of the divorce of parents with young children seems to apply: (a) Parents have a duty to behave in ways that promote the best interests of their young children. In particular, they ought to refrain from behavior that causes or is likely to cause them harm. (b) Divorce is a type of behavior that psychologically harms some young children. Therefore, (c) It is morally wrong for the parents of some young children to divorce.

I call this the Divorce Child-Harm Argument or DCH. DCH is similar in structure to moral arguments used to condemn child abandonment and various forms of child abuse. When we think of child abuse, we usually think of cases in which children have suffered severe physical injury or death as a result of parental behavior. But some child abuse statutes recognize emotional or psychological harm. Thus, the New York Family

Court Act defines "impairment of emotional health" as

> a state of substantially limited psychological or intellectual functioning in relation to, but not limited to such factors as failure to thrive, control of aggressiveness or self-destructive impulses, ability to think and reason, or acting out or misbehavior, including incorrigibility, ungovernability or habitual truancy . . .[14]

If we think that parental behavior that causes or is likely to cause the kind of emotional or psychological harm specified in the preceding statute is morally wrong, and if we think that parents who divorce are likely to cause emotional harm to their children, then it would appear that divorce is wrong for the same reason that these parental behaviors are wrong.

Faced with the conclusion of DCH, there are a number of ways in which the divorced parents of young children might attempt to defend themselves against the charge that it was wrong for them to divorce.

1. First, it may be objected that the preceding analogy between divorce and child abuse is misplaced. Children of divorce may suffer, but their suffering never rises to the minimum level of suffering required by legal standards for determining emotional abuse.

The response to this objection is that DCH does not argue that divorce *is* child abuse. Legal definitions of child abuse and neglect are formulated solely to deal with the problem of the conditions under which the state may justifiably intervene in the family to protect the child. DCH says nothing about state intervention, nor does it recommend any change in the laws regulating divorce. Instead, DCH is an argument about the morality of divorce. It argues that some divorces are wrong *for the same reason* that child abuse is wrong. The reason that some divorces are wrong is that they cause or are likely to cause emotional harm to the children of the divorcing parents. Whether the emotional harm suffered by children whose parents divorce rises to the level of severity required by the child abuse standards of some

states is beside the point. The point is whether some children whose parents divorce suffer emotional harm, *not* whether they suffer the kind or amount required by the courts to recognize a child abuse petition for purposes of court-ordered intervention.

2. The second objection to DCH is that so long as parents aggressively treat any symptoms of emotional harm that their children may suffer post-divorce in order to minimize the deleterious effects of the divorce, then they have done nothing wrong by obtaining the divorce. What *would* be wrong would be to ignore the symptoms and to leave them untreated.

This argument has the following structure: It is not wrong to divorce; it is only wrong to divorce and do nothing to minimize its bad effects on children. But consider the following counterexample: so long as I secure medical treatment for my child after I have engaged in risky behavior that resulted in his leg getting broken, then I have done nothing wrong in putting my child at risk. The reason that we resist the conclusion "I have done nothing wrong in putting my child at risk" is that we do not think it justifiable to engage in behavior that puts the lives and health of our children at risk in the first place. This is why we think it morally incumbent on us not to smoke when children are in the house, to put them in restraining seats when we have them in the car with us, and do countless other things to minimize their chances of injury in and out of the home. It is simply not enough to announce that one is prepared to treat a child's injuries after they occur. We demand that parents take steps to prevent the harm *before* it occurs.

3. The third objection to DCH takes advantage of Russell's "loophole," or exception to his general claim (quoted above) that parents who divorce violate their parental duty. Russell's loophole is that the divorce might be justified if it was done for "grave cause." A grave cause exists when it is established that (a) the children will suffer less post-divorce emotional distress than they will suffer if the marriage of their parents remains intact; and (b) during the marriage, the parents could not control those behaviors that caused their children

emotional harm. For example, Russell mentions insanity or alcoholism as possible candidates for grave cause justifications for divorce because in both cases the affected parent may be unable to prevent himself from engaging in behavior detrimental to his child's welfare.

"Grave cause" is probably the most common of the rationales that parents will offer to justify their divorce. Some of the studies of the psychological effects of divorce show that the adverse effects observed in children were often seen prior to the divorce as a result of a hostile family environment.[15] One commentator has recently concluded from this that the transition, through divorce, from an intact two-parent family to a single-parent family can no longer be objected to on the grounds that divorce is bad for children.[16]

However, the preceding data only establishes the first of the two conditions that are together sufficient for a grave cause justification for divorce. That is, although a hostile family environment may cause a child to suffer as much or more than he or she would suffer from the divorce of her parents, it does not follow that the divorce is justifiable. In order to establish the existence of a grave cause, the parents must also prove that they could not control the "hostile family environment" that caused their children to suffer. Russell has the best rejoinder to those parents who claim that they were helpless to control the marital behavior that caused emotional distress in their children:

> The husband and wife, if they have any love for their children, will regulate their conduct so as to give their children the best chance of a happy and healthy development. . . . [T]o cooperate in rearing children, even after passionate love has decayed, is by no means a superhuman task for sensible people who are capable of natural affections. . . . [A]s soon as there are children it is the duty of both parties to a marriage to do everything that they can to preserve harmonious relations, even if this requires considerable self-control.[17]

In other words, to say that one had no choice but to obtain a divorce in order not to expose one's children to marital discord is to make the extraordinary assumption that one could not control one's behavior. It is analogous to the con-

tention of a cigarette smoker that he had to abandon his child in order to save her from the physical effects of his secondhand smoke. The point is that we are as capable of controlling the behavior toward our spouse that causes distress in our young children as we are capable of not smoking in their presence.

4. Finally, it may be objected that DCH puts far too much stress on the rights and interests of children, ignoring the legitimate needs of the parents. Surely, it might be said, the desires, projects, and commitments of each parent which give them reasons to divorce in the pursuit of ends that are their own may sometimes outweigh those reasons not to divorce that stem from the special noncontractual obligations that they have to nurture their young children.

To this I can only reply that if it is permissible for parents to divorce for such reasons, then I cannot imagine what it would mean to say that they have obligations to nurture their children. How can one be said to have an *obligation* to nurture her young child if it is permissible for her to perform an act that risks harming the child for no other reason than that she wants to pursue her own projects? This empties the concept of parental obligation of most of its content. Parents of young children who divorce for no other reason than that they find their marriage unfulfilling and believe that this is justifiable seem to me to be parents who lack an understanding of what it is to have an obligation to their children. They must believe that they can treat their own children as they would treat any other child. In the case of children other than our own, most of us would acknowledge that the effect on these children of what we do counts for something. But even if it is proved to me and my spouse that (e.g.) the children of our next door neighbor will suffer emotionally as result of our divorce, we would not think that this puts us under an obligation to cancel or delay our separation. If we did delay it, this would be an act of charity, not a perfect duty of obligation. But with our own children, things are otherwise. Our children exert an "ethical pull" on us not exerted by the children of others. Benevolent acts toward our children become perfect duties within the context of the family, and as such they outweigh parental desires to pursue their own projects when these come into conflict. This is surely part of what it means to become a parent.

Conclusion

I conclude that Russell is correct in contending that many of the divorces of parents who have young children are morally unjustifiable. Especially in the case of families with young boys, a divorce is not justifiable if the reason is similar to one or more of the reasons commonly given by parents who divorce: e.g., "We have grown apart," "We have become different persons than we were when we first married," "We are profoundly unhappy with one another," "We want to pursue a single lifestyle once again," or "I found someone else with whom I would much rather live." For those parents *who are capable of exercising self-control over their negative emotions* (e.g. spite, anger, jealousy), none of these reasons rises to the level of a grave cause. Hence, parents who divorce for such reasons are wrongfully violating their moral duty to their children.

QUESTIONS FOR THOUGHT AND DISCUSSION

1. Why did Bertrand Russell argue (in 1929) that adultery is neither morally wrong nor should it be a legal ground for divorce?
2. According to Richard Wasserstrom, what are some of the reasons that some people think that adultery is "seriously immoral"?
3. How would Wasserstrom respond to Russell's claim that we should relax the moral prohibitions on adultery?
4. Is it conceptually possible for two persons to be married and neither want nor expect one another to be sexually exclusive? If this is possible, is it desirable?
5. Why does Mike Martin argue that marital faithfulness is a virtue? How do these remarks apply to Russell's claim that we should relax the moral prohibitions on adultery?
6. If a couple is childless or their children are grown, is it ever wrong for one of them to divorce the other when the other refuses to consent to a divorce? Explain.
7. Is it ever morally permissible for parents to mutually consent to a divorce when their children are young? Explain.
8. Most of the moral arguments opposing divorce between parents with young children are *consequentialist,* that is, they are designed to prove that the consequences of such divorces are generally worse than the consequences of not divorcing. Are there any plausible *nonconsequentialist* arguments for opposing the divorce of parents with young children? Explain.

FURTHER READING

Reuven P. Bulka, "Jewish Divorce Ethics." *The Jewish Spectator,* 58, 3 (Winter 1993): 11–16.

R. J. Connelly, "Philosophy and Adultery." In Philip E. Lampe, ed., *Adultery in the United*

States, 131–164. Buffalo: Prometheus Books, 1987.

James B. Gould, "Discussing Divorce in Introductory Ethics." *Teaching Philosophy* 18, 2 (June 1995): 101–111.

Philip E. Lampe, "The Many Dimensions of Adultery." In Philip E. Lampe, ed., *Adultery in the United States,* 76–92. Buffalo: Prometheus Books, 1987.

Diane Medved, *The Case Against Divorce.* New York: Ballantine Books, 1989.

Susan Mendus, "Marital Faithfulness." *Philosophy: The Journal of the British Institute of Philosophical Studies* 59 (1984): 243–252.

Fred Moody, "Divorce: Sometimes a Bad Notion." *Utne Reader* (November/December 1990): 70–78.

Bonnie Steinbock, "Adultery." In Alan Soble, ed., *The Philosophy of Sex.* Savage, MD: Rowman and Littlefield, 1991.

Keith Thomas, "The Double Standard." *Journal of the History of Ideas* 20, 2 (April 1959): 195–216.

Brian T. Trainor, "The State, Marriage and Divorce." *Journal of Applied Philosophy,* 9, 2 (1992): 135–148.

Judith Wallerstein and Sandra Blakeslee, *Second Chances: Men and Women and Children a Decade After Divorce.* New York: Ticknor and Fields, 1989.

Michelle Weiner-Davis, *Divorce Busting.* New York: Summit Books, 1992.

Robert Weiss, *Marital Separation.* New York: Basic Books, 1975.

Lenore Weitzman, *The Divorce Revolution: The Unexpected Social and Economic Consequences for Women and Children in America.* New York: Free Press, 1985.

Barbara DaFoe Whitehead, "Dan Quayle Was Right." *Atlantic Monthly* (April 1993).

Michael J. Wreen, "What's Really Wrong With Adultery?" *Journal of Applied Philosophy* 3 (1986): 45–49.

NOTES

Introduction

1. August 1980, p. 38; National Opinion Research Corporation, 1982.

2. Alfred C. Kinsey and Paul H. Gebhard, *Sexual Behavior in the Human Female* (Philadelphia: Saunders, 1953).

3. Philip Blumstein and Pepper Schwartz, *American Couples* (New York: Dutton, 1974), 248.

4. Arland Thornton and Deborah Freedman, "The Changing American Family," *Bulletin of the Population Reference Bureau* 38, 4 (October 1983).

5. National Center for Health Statistics, *Divorce, Child Custody and Child Support,* series P-23, no. 84 (Washington, DC: U.S. Government Printing Office, 1985).

6. U.S. Bureau of the Census, 1993.

7. Alan Donagan, this volume, p. 109.

Bertrand Russell

1. It will be remembered that in the case of the Duke and Duchess of Marlborough it was held that the marriage was null because she had been forced into it, and this ground was considered valid in spite of the fact that they had lived together for years and had children.

Mike W. Martin

1. *Church of England Prayer Book* (1549). I will understand marriage as a moral relationship centered on lifelong commitments to love and significantly involving sexual desire at some time during the relationship, whether or not the marriage is formalized in legal or religious ceremonies, recognizing homosexual as well as heterosexual marriages, and independently of government intrusions. On the latter see David Palmer, "The Consolation of the Wedded," in *Philosophy and Sex,* 2nd edition, Robert Baker and Frederick Elliston (eds.) (Buffalo, NY: Prometheus Books, 1984), pp. 119–129.

2. Or its *presumed* supportive role. Some couples, of course, enter into (or transform their relationship into) "open marriages" in which they permit extramarital affairs while retaining lifetime commitments. For an early and especially interesting example, see Nigel Nicolson's portrayal of his parents in *Portrait of a Marriage* (New York: Atheneum, 1973).

Two illuminating (and contrasting) discussions of the rationale for traditional links between lifetime marital commitments and sexual fidelity are: Edmund Leites, *The Puritan Conscience and Modern Sexuality* (New Haven: Yale University Press, 1986), and Robert Scruton, *Sexual Desire* (New York: Free Press, 1986).

3. Michael Slote, *Goods and Virtues* (Oxford: Clarendon Press, 1983), p. 62ff.

4. Martha C. Nussbaum, *The Fragility of Goodness* (Cambridge University Press, 1986), pp. 359–361.

5. Bernard Williams, *Moral Luck* (New York: Cambridge University Press, 1981), p. 26ff.

6. Bertrand Russell, *The Autobiography of Bertrand Russell,* vol. 1 (New York: Bantam Books, 1968), pp. 195–196.

7. Quoted by Barbara Strachey in *Remarkable Relations* (London: Victor Gollianz, 1980), p. 216.

8. Mary Midgley, *Wisdom, Information and Wonder* (New York: Routledge, 1989), p. 157.

9. Anais Nin, *Henry and June* (New York: Harcourt Brace Jovanovich, 1986), p. 29.

10. Ibid., p. 229.

11. Michael Slote, *Goods and Virtue,* p. 77ff.

12. Sonnet 116.

13. Dorothy Day, *The Long Loneliness* (New York: Harper and Row, 1952), pp. 147–148.

14. Friedrich Nietzsche, *The Gay Science,* trans. Walter Kaufmann (New York: Vintage Books, 1974), p. 232.

Laurence Houlgate

1. Bertrand Russell, *Marriage and Morals* (Garden City, NY: Horace Liveright, Inc., 1929). See the relevant excerpts from Russell's book in the first essay of this chapter.

2. Nine years later, in 1938, Russell was denied a professorial appointment at the College of the City of New York for reasons remarkably similar to those used by the Athenians to justify their conviction of Socrates. In part because of the views expressed in *Marriage and Morals,* concerned New York citizens were afraid that Professor Russell would corrupt the morals of the young people who would attend his lectures.

3. Russell, p. 238.

4. There are some notable exceptions to this generalization. See, for example, Brian T. Trainor, "The State, Marriage and Divorce," *Journal of Applied Philosophy,* 9, 2 (1992): 135–148, for a defense of the claim that no-fault divorce laws are unjust; Christina Hoff Sommers, "Philosophers Against the Family," in George Graham and Hugh LaFollette, *Person to Person* (Philadelphia: Temple University Press, 1989), 99–103, for a brief argument suggesting that the divorce of couples with children is sometimes morally wrong; Iris Marion Young, "Mothers, Citizenship, and Independence: A Critique of Pure Family Values," *Ethics* 105 (April 1995): 535–

556, for a critical discussion of the claim that stable marriages are morally superior to single-parent families that either arise out of divorce or from births to unmarried women.

5. The adverse psychological effects of divorce on children are described below. Another deleterious consequence of divorce that some attribute to no-fault divorce laws is economic. Divorced women, and the minor children in their households—90 percent of whom live with their mothers—experience a sharp decline in their standard of living after divorce. See Lenore Weitzman, *The Divorce Revolution: The Unexplored Consequences* (New York: Free Press, 1985). Although 61 percent of women who divorced in the 1980s worked full time and another 17 percent worked part time, "the husband's average post divorce per capita income surpassed that of his wife and children overall and in every income group." McLindon, "Separate but Unequal: the Economic Disaster of Divorce for Women and Children," *Family Law Quarterly* 21, 3 (1987). (However, recent research indicates that the differences in income may not be as sharp as Weitzman originally reported.)

6. In 1988, for example, there were 1,167,000 divorces in the United States, involving 1,044,000 children, at a rate of 16.4 children per 1,000 under the age of 18 years. U.S. Bureau of the Census, *Statistical Abstract of the United States, 1993,* 113th ed. (Washington, DC: U.S. Government Printing Office, 1993).

7. Rebecca West, "Divorce," from *The London Daily Express,* 1930.

8. West was probably referring to the research in A. Skolnick and J. Skolnick, eds., *Family in Transition* (Boston: Little, Brown, 1929). In one early study of children of divorced parents between the ages of 6 and 12, half showed evidence of a "consolidation into troubled and conflicted depressive behavior patterns." Their behavior pattern included "continuing depression and low self-esteem, combined with frequent school and peer difficulties" (p. 452).

9. Mel Krantzler, *Creative Divorce: A New Opportunity for Personal Growth* (New York: M. Evans, 1974), 191.

10. Judith Wallerstein and Sandra Blakeslee, *Second Chances: Men, Women and Children a Decade after Divorce* (New York: Ticknor and Fields, 1989), xv, xvii, 299.

11. Patricia Hersch, "Take Note," *Psychology Today* 23, 6 (June 1989): 76–77.

12. Andrew Cherlin, Frank Furstenberg et al., "Longitudinal Studies of Effects of Divorce on Children in Great Britain and the United States," *Science* 252 (7 June 1991): 1386–1389.

13. In most cases of divorce it is fathers who leave the family home, and when they leave they have much less contact with their children than they had prior to the divorce. "One large survey in the late 1980s found that about one in five divorced fathers had not seen his children in the past year, and less than half of divorced fathers saw their children more than several times a year. A 1981 survey of adolescents who were

living apart from their fathers found that 52 percent had not seen them at all in more than a year; only 16 percent saw their fathers as often as once a week. Moreover, the survey showed fathers' contact with their children dropping off sharply with the passage of time after the marital breakup." (David Popenoe, "The Vanishing Father," *The Wilson Quarterly* [Spring 1996]: 14.)

Boys appear to suffer more than girls from the loss of their father. "Fathers are important to their sons as role models. They are important for maintaining authority and discipline. And they are important in helping their sons to develop both self-control and feelings of empathy toward others." Ibid., p. 22.

14. NY Fam CT Act 1012 (e).

15. Cherlin, et al., ibid.

16. Iris Marion Young, ibid.

17. *Marriage and Morals,* pp. 236–237.

8

Family Violence

Introduction

Linda Jackson, "Marital Rape: A Higher Standard Is in Order"

bell hooks, "Violence in Intimate Relationships"

Linda A. Bell, "Violence against Women Protected by 'Privacy' "

David Archard, "Child Abuse and Family Privacy"

Philip Fetzer, "Child Abuse: A Multicultural Perspective"

Moral problems arise out of moral conflict. We are pulled in two directions by opposing moral obligations, both of which cannot be satisfied
at once. But in thinking about the types of conduct that are the subjects
of the essayists in this chapter, it is difficult to imagine the nature of the moral
problem. Surely, we want to say, marital rape, child abuse and spousal violence are
all paradigm cases of moral wrongdoing. How could one possibly justify a case of
a man forcing his wife to have sexual intercourse or physically assaulting her and
their children?

Although the first essay by Linda Jackson is about the various legal justifications that have been offered for the rape of a woman by her husband, these justifications are also moral justifications that have been offered by individual men for
their behavior. Thus, a man might argue (and men have argued) that the rape of
his wife was justified because she gave her consent (at least implicitly) to sexual intercourse with him when they exchanged marital vows. Hence, the fact that she
did not want to engage in sexual intercourse at that particular time is irrelevant: a
promise is a promise. Alternatively, he might argue that he and his wife are "one
person," and as such, he cannot rape himself. Finally, he might argue that forced
sexual intercourse with his wife is either not harmful at all, or it is less harmful
than stranger rape. After all, he reasons, his wife has had voluntarily sexual intercourse with him on numerous past occasions. The only difference between this
act and those is that he had to use force. Since she knows him and knows what
sex with him is like, she can hardly complain on the grounds of emotional trauma
as a result of the sex act.

159

Linda Jackson has strong replies to each of these attempts at justification. But she is also interested in the reasons that judges and legislators have given to justify the nonintervention by the state in cases of marital rape, for example, the modern day justification that marriage is a private affair. This means that marriage is a private sphere of individual liberty with which government and law may not legitimately intervene. Hence (it has been argued), although a man's rape of his wife may be morally wrong, public authorities have no business attempting to regulate sexual behavior or any other kind of behavior in a marriage.

The essay by bell hooks draws our attention to a special case of violence against women: single incidences of assault. She writes that "while there is much material available discussing physical abuse of women by men, usually extreme physical abuse, there is not much discussion of the impact that one incident of hitting may have on a person in an intimate relationship." She finds it morally problematic that the label "battered woman" is to cover all of these cases. It is, hooks writes, "a label that appears to strip us of dignity, to deny that there has been any integrity in the relationships we are in."

A husband's battery of his wife was historically an exception to the crime of physical assault. A North Carolina court ruled in 1868 that it is legally permissible for a husband to strike his wife because "every household has and must have a government of its own . . . and we will not interfere or attempt to control it unless in cases where permanent or malicious injury is inflicted or threatened, or the condition of the party intolerable" (*State* v. *Rhodes* 61 N.C., 445, 448). Although the court announced that it will interfere in some of the most egregious cases of domestic violence, it left the door open to most of the battery that goes on in the home.

In her short essay on domestic violence, Linda A. Bell critically discusses some of the traditional reasons for promoting such a hands-off approach to domestic violence. Some of the reasons are utilitarian—that is, marital privacy is necessary to promote the greatest good. Some utilitarians might argue that no harm can be done in the home because everyone in the family can be presumed to consent to what goes on. Other utilitarians will claim that the harm of state intervention in the family will always outweigh any harm that family members cause one another. Finally, Bell considers the utilitarian argument that gives men and women unequal legal rights in order to promote "a stable social order." The implication of this discriminatory approach, Bell argues, is that men's privacy is protected by the legal system, not that of women, with the result that the public/private distinction harms women by protecting male violence in the home. Her main point is that what takes place within the "private" domain of the family is and should always be a matter of public and political concern.

David Archard continues Jackson and Bell's critique of the liberal distinction between public and private in his paper on "Child Abuse and Family Privacy." Archard agrees with Linda Bell that the judicial insistence on protecting a "private" sphere of the family from state interference has created far more harm than benefit to women and children in the home. His solution is to create "spaces" in which the health of children can be constantly monitored by public officials specially trained to do this. Second, he would not have them wait until a parent or guardian has committed an act of abuse: "I would rather that the State established affirmative duties of care which guaranteed the best possible conditions for the development of the child. "

In the final essay in this section, Philip Fetzer invites the reader to consider the various ways in which class and culture affect judgments made by family courts regarding child abuse and neglect. The standards used by the courts are sufficiently vague to allow judges to inject their own cultural preferences for what counts as "appropriate" methods of rearing children, with the result that a disproportionate number of children from black, Hispanic, Native American, and lower-income homes are removed from their homes than are children whose parents are white or in the middle and upper income groups. Fetzer questions the fairness of using the standards of the dominant class and culture to make allegations of abuse and neglect. He concludes by proposing an approach to family law that would balance our legitimate concern to protect children from harm with a desire to recognize both the constraints of poverty and the childrearing practices of minority cultures in a diverse society.

Marital Rape: A Higher Standard Is in Order

Linda Jackson

Linda Jackson received her B.A. in 1987 from Amherst College, and the Juris Doctor degree in 1994 from the College of William and Mary.

Marriage is the only actual bondage known to our law. There remain no legal slaves, except the mistress of every house. . . . [H]owever brutal a tyrant she may be unfortunately chained to. . . . [Her husband] can claim from her and enforce the lowest degradation of a human being, that of being made the instrument of an animal function contrary to her inclinations.[1]

John Stuart Mill

It is very little to me to have the right to vote, to own property, etc., if I may not keep my body, and its uses, in my absolute right. Not one wife in a thousand can do that now.[2]

Lucy Stone

Women, particularly married women, have advanced a great deal since the time of John Stuart

Mill and Lucy Stone. Mill and Stone's concerns regarding marital rape, however, are justified even today. Through the late 1970s, husbands enjoyed a virtually absolute right to rape their wives at will and without fear of legal recourse. Although our society is moving forward in this regard, it still has quite a road to travel.[3]

Marital rape, although not often discussed or confronted, is the most common form of rape. A recent poll found that 14 percent of women polled who have ever been married have been raped by their husbands, and of those women, 85 percent have been raped by their husbands on more than one occasion. Additionally, between 34 and 37 percent of women in physically abusive marriages are sexually assaulted by their husbands.

Public perception of marital rape lends some insight into why, in light of these statistics, most jurisdictions maintain some form of exemption for spousal rape. One 1982 survey indicated that only 35 percent of the population favors eliminating the marital rape exemption. In a separate survey conducted in 1986, when asked "What should happen

From Linda Jackson, "Marital Rape: A Higher Standard is in Order," *William & Mary Journal of Women and the Law* 1 (1994): 183–197. Used by permission of the William and Mary Journal of Women and the Law.

to men who force their wives to have sex?," only 20 percent of the respondents thought incarceration was appropriate whereas 26 percent believed the husband should not be treated criminally at all.

Consider, from this data, just what we expect from the women in our society and why. Consider also that just as our reasons for supporting or accepting marital exemptions have changed over time, so have our reasons for opposing a woman's right to reproductive freedom. Are these evolutions in legal and social reasoning concerning women related? That is, do we truly believe these rationales or are we searching for rationalizations in which we can anchor a fixed social goal or perhaps a preferred social order? . . .

Justifications for Marital Exemptions from Rape

Historical Justifications

The acceptance and development of marital rape exemptions are rooted in three theories: the theory of "implied consent," the "unity" and "women as marital property" theories, and the "narrow constructionist" theory. Although the implied consent theory was the initial rationale for American courts' recognition of marital exemptions, the unity/property and constructionist theories provided additional justification for the exemptions' widespread acceptance.

The "Implied Consent" Theory. The most frequently cited basis for marital rape exemptions, both legislatively and judicially, is the common law doctrine of irrevocable implied consent. The theory of implied consent originated with a seventeenth century statement by Sir Matthew Hale that a "husband cannot be guilty of a rape committed by himself upon his lawful wife, for by their mutual matrimonial consent and contract the wife hath given up herself in this kind to her husband, which she cannot retract."[4] A woman, upon entering marriage, impliedly and irrevocably consents to sex on command with her husband, at any time and under any circumstances.

Hale's legally unsubstantiated theory, previously offered only in treatise form and never in case law, was first adopted in the United States, without question or reservation, by the Massachusetts courts in 1857. Ironically, the English courts failed to adopt the theory of implied consent until 1949. In fact, several justices in the first recorded English opinion to discuss Hale's theory expressed reluctance to adopt the concept precisely because there was insufficient authority for the proposition. One justice stated that "[t]here may . . . be many cases in which a wife may lawfully refuse intercourse, and in which, if the husband posed it by violence, he might be held guilty of a crime."[5] Adding to the irony of continued reliance on English common law for marital exemptions is the 1991 unanimous House of Lords decision that marital rape exemptions "no longer form part of the law of England since a husband and wife are now regarded equal partners in marriage."[6]

Reasoning similar to that of the House of Lords is offered by modern American critics who suggest that even if implied consent was at one point a valid theory, that time has passed both socially and logically.[7] Additionally, the advent of no-fault divorce laws, and the inherent recognition that either spouse can unilaterally withdraw from the marriage contract, ensures that either spouse can unilaterally withdraw consent to marital sex. If the victim truly has "revoked" a term of the marriage contract by refusing sexual intercourse, the proper remedy for the harmed spouse is in the matrimonial courts, not in "violent or forceful self-help."[8]

The "Unity" and "Women as Marital Property" Theories. Blackstone best articulated the unity theory when he wrote that "[b]y marriage, the husband and wife are one person in law: that is, the very being or legal existence of the woman is suspended during the marriage, or at least is incorporated and consolidated into [her] husband."[9] Once the couple is married they become one, with the one being the man. The unity theory stands for the proposition that because the husband and wife are one, the husband is incapable of raping his wife because he is incapable of raping himself.

The unity doctrine is a basis for the historical view of women as the property of marriage.

Women are their husbands' chattels to be "deprived of all civil identity."[10] Early rape laws, which either explicitly exempted wives from the law's protection or were interpreted by their silence to include the English common law exemption, reflect this notion of women as property and were intended initially only to protect the property interests of the woman's husband, if married, or father, if single.

Courts have largely rejected the unity and "women as marital property" theories by invoking language from *Trammel v. United States,* which asserts that "nowhere in . . . modern society . . . is a woman regarded as chattel or demeaned by denial of a separate legal identity and the dignity associated with recognition as a whole human being."[11] Critics also challenge the unity theory on the basis that husbands can be charged with committing other crimes against their wives.

The "Narrow Constructionist" Theory. English common law defined rape as the unlawful carnal knowledge of a woman against her will. In the narrow constructionist theory, the term "unlawful," as it is used in rape statutes, means "not authorized by law." Because marriage sanctions, or authorizes, sexual relations between husband and wife, all carnal knowledge between husband and wife is lawful, and there are no sexual relations within a marriage that are unauthorized or unlawful. Thus, no sexual relations within a marriage fall within this definition of rape.[12]

Supporters of this theory find it superior to Hale's theory of implied consent not only because it is less likely to become outdated, but also because it alleviates the need to feign consent where there is none.[13] Modern legislatures have dismissed this argument by drafting statutes that no longer contain the "unlawful carnal knowledge" language.

Modern Justifications

Today, support for marital rape exemptions is grounded in four rationales that are as a group distinctly more modern, and thus more easily accepted, than their predecessors: marital privacy, marital reconciliation, fear of false allegations and difficult proof requirements, and the belief that rape within marriage is less severe than rape outside marriage.

Marital Privacy. Marital privacy is one of the foremost modern-day justifications for marital rape exemptions. Proponents of the marital privacy rationale suggest that the right to privacy within one's marriage is so fundamental that the public, and hence the legal system, should be precluded from defining or judging the activities therein. Professor Hilf analogizes marital privacy rights to "drawing a curtain" around the marriage so the "public stays out and the spouses stay in." Keeping the public out, Hilf argues, prevents voyeurism as well as the embarrassment of disclosing private lives.[14]

Courts have proposed numerous counterarguments to the marital privacy theory. The New York court of appeals in *People v. Liberta* rejected the marital privacy argument and stated clearly that the right recognized in *Griswold v. Connecticut* applies only to consensual acts, not to violent sexual assaults.[15] Nor is marital privacy an absolute right. States must balance their interest in protecting marital privacy against their interest in protecting individuals' bodily integrity. Some courts maintain that the exemption itself interferes with the marital relationship because it gives the husband legal control over his wife's bodily integrity that he otherwise would not have.[16]

Marital Reconciliation. The marital reconciliation rationale for marital rape exemptions is an extension of the "closed curtain" and marital privacy justifications. By keeping the spouse "in," and the law and the public "out," spouses are supposedly forced to resolve their differences independent of external interference. Reconciliation theorists maintain that this resolution process, as opposed to one which allows "access to the criminal justice system for every type of marital dispute," fosters greater mutual respect between the parties and eases their ultimate reconciliations. Inherent in this theory is the idea that if a victim of spousal rape is capable of bringing, and in fact does bring, criminal charges against her spouse, then the law will have fostered marital discord and prevented reconciliations.[17]

Although the court in *People v. Brown* accepted this reasoning, most courts and critics reject the reconciliation and marital harmony theory on the basis that little exists to reconcile if the relationship has deteriorated to the level of forcible rape.[18] Some courts and commentators have also noted that the relationship and potential for reconciliation is disrupted by the rape itself, not the rape charge.[19]

Evidentiary Concerns and the Fear of Women Lying. Evidentiary concerns are perhaps the most common basis for the partial or limited marital exemptions found in most current rape laws. One primary objective of the partial exemptions is to guard against false accusations made by deceitful or vindictive women.

Until recently, Lord Hale's infamous warning that rape "is an accusation easily to be made and hard to be proved, and harder to be defended by the party accused, tho [sic] never so innocent" was used as a cautionary jury instruction.[20] To guard against falsely convicting an innocent man, Wigmore advised that

> [n]o judge should ever let a sex offense . . . go to the jury unless the female complainant's social history and mental makeup have been examined and testified to by a qualified physician. . . . The psychic complexes [of women] are multifarious, distorted partly by inherent defects, partly by diseased derangements or abnormal instincts, partly by bad social environment, partly by temporary physiological or emotional conditions. *One form taken by these complexes is that of contriving false charges of sexual offenses by men.*[21]

Although these archaic procedural requirements no longer exist in the realm of stranger or non-stranger rape, the prejudicial notions supporting them do remain when victims are married to their assailants.

Opponents of this "fear based" justification offer three arguments. First, other crimes exist that are equally difficult to prove, yet they are not decriminalized. Our society instead relies on a criminal justice system that is sufficiently sophisticated to ensure that innocent individuals are not frivolously prosecuted or wrongly convicted.[22] Next is the jurisprudential view that convictions are not the sole reason for enacting laws. In addition to convicting criminals, laws serve as deterrents and educational tools, announcing to society what is morally right and morally wrong, what is socially acceptable behavior and what is not.[23] Finally, rape is recognized as a vastly underreported crime. Reasons offered for this phenomenon include the social stigma attached to victims of rape, fear of retaliation, and a reluctance to endure the double victimization of the judicial system. Fabrications of rape charges are unlikely not only for the reasons stated above, but also because "rape prosecutions are often more shameful for the victim than the defendant."[24]

Marital Rape Is Less Harmful than Nonmarital Rape. There is a perception that rape by a known individual, particularly an individual with whom the victim has had past voluntary sexual intercourse, is less severe than rape by an unknown individual.[25] This perception supports both broad marital rape exemptions and the treatment of marital rape as a lesser sexual offense.

Contrary to this "less harmful than" theory, victims of spousal rape suffer greater harm than victims of stranger rape. Data demonstrates that rape in marriage is actually more emotionally traumatic than any other kind of rape and carries with it longer lasting emotional effects.[26] Victims of marital rape also tend to suffer greater physical harm than victims of non-marital rape and are in fact often victims of the most brutal and life-threatening rapes.[27] Critics of the "less harmful than" theory also argue that the very existence of rape laws indicates a recognition that harm caused by rape, any rape, is more severe than harm caused by assault and should be treated as such. In the words of Dr. David Finkelhor, "[r]ape is traumatic not because it is with someone you don't know, but because it is with someone you don't want."[28]

Violence in Intimate Relationships

bell hooks

bell hooks is professor of English at City College in New York. She is the author of several books on racism and sexism in America.

We were on the freeway, going home from San Francisco. He was driving. We were arguing. He had told me repeatedly to shut up. I kept talking. He took his hand from the steering wheel and threw it back, hitting my mouth, my open mouth, blood gushed, and I felt an intense pain. I was no longer able to say any words, only to make whimpering, sobbing sounds as the blood dripped on my hands, on the handkerchief I held too tightly. He did not stop the car. He drove home. I watched him pack his suitcase. It was a holiday. He was going away to have fun. When he left I washed my mouth. My jaw was swollen and it was difficult for me to open it.

I called the dentist the next day and made an appointment. When the female voice asked what I needed to see the doctor about, I told her I had been hit in the mouth. Conscious of race, sex, and class issues, I wondered how I would be treated in this white doctor's office. My face was no longer swollen so there was nothing to identify me as a woman who had been hit, as a black woman with a bruised and swollen jaw. When the dentist asked me what had happened to my mouth, I described it calmly and succinctly. He made little *jokes* about, "Now we can't have someone doing *this* to us now, can we?" I said nothing. The damage was repaired. Through it all, he talked to me as if I were a child, someone he *had* to handle gingerly or otherwise I might become hysterical.

This is one way women who are hit by men and seek medical care are seen. People within patriarchal society imagine that women are hit because we are hysterical, because we are beyond reason. It is most often the person who is hitting that is beyond reason, who is hysterical, who has lost complete control over responses and actions.

Growing up, I had always thought that I would never allow any man to hit me and live. I would kill him. I had seen my father hit my mother once and I wanted to kill him. My mother said to me then, "You are too young to know, too young to understand." Being a mother in a culture that supports and promotes domination, a patriarchal, white-supremacist culture, she did not discuss how she felt or what she meant. Perhaps it would have been too difficult for her to speak about the confusion of being hit by someone you are intimate with, someone you love. In my case, I was hit by my companion at a time in life when a number of forces in the world outside our home had already "hit" me, so to speak, made me painfully aware of my powerlessness, my marginality. It seemed then that I was confronting being black and female and without money in the worst possible ways. My world was spinning. I had already lost a sense of grounding and security. The memory of this experience has stayed with me as I have grown as a feminist, as I have thought deeply and read much on male violence against women, on adult violence against children.

In this essay, I do not intend to concentrate attention solely on male physical abuse of females. It is crucial that feminists call attention to physical abuse in all its forms. In particular, I want to discuss being physically abused in singular incidents by someone you love. Few people who are hit once by someone they love respond in the way they might to a singular physical assault by a stranger. Many children raised in households where hitting has been a normal response by primary caretakers react ambivalently to physical assaults as adults, especially if they are being hit by someone who cares for them and whom they care for. Often female parents use physical abuse as a means of control. There is continued need for feminist research that examines such violence. Alice Miller has done insightful work on the impact of hitting even though

From bell hooks, *Talking Back: Thinking Feminist, Thinking Black* (Boston: South End Press, 1989). Reprinted by permission.

she is at times antifeminist in her perspective. (Often in her work, mothers are blamed, as if their responsibility in parenting is greater than that of fathers.) Feminist discussions of violence against women should be expanded to include a recognition of the ways in which women use abusive physical force toward children not only to challenge the assumptions that women are likely to be nonviolent, but also to add to our understanding of why children who were hit growing up are often hit as adults or hit others.

Hitting Children

Recently, I began a conversation with a group of black adults about hitting children. They all agreed that hitting was sometimes necessary. A professional black male in a southern family setting with two children commented on the way he punished his daughters. Sitting them down, he would first interrogate them about the situation or circumstance for which they were being punished. He said with great pride, "I want them to be able to understand fully why they are being punished." I responded by saying that "they will likely become women whom a lover will attack using the same procedure you who have loved them so well used and they will not know how to respond." He resisted the idea that his behavior would have any impact on their responses to violence as adult women. I pointed to case after case of women in intimate relationships with men (and sometimes women) who are subjected to the same form of interrogation and punishment they experienced as children, who accept their lover assuming an abusive, authoritarian role. Children who are the victims of physical abuse—whether one beating or repeated beatings, one violent push or several—whose wounds are inflicted by a loved one, experience an extreme sense of dislocation. The world one has most intimately known, in which one felt relatively safe and secure, has collapsed. Another world has come into being, one filled with terrors, where it is difficult to distinguish between a safe situation and a dangerous one, a gesture of love and a violent, uncaring gesture. There is a feeling of vulnerability, exposure, that never goes away, that lurks beneath the surface. I know. I was one of those children. Adults

hit by loved ones usually experience similar sensations of dislocation, of loss, of new found terrors.

Many children who are hit have never known what it feels like to be cared for, loved without physical aggression or abusive pain. Hitting is such a widespread practice that any of us are lucky if we can go through life without having this experience. One undiscussed aspect of the reality of children who are hit finding themselves as adults in similar circumstances is that we often share with friends and lovers the framework of our childhood pains and this may determine how they respond to us in difficult situations. We share the ways we are wounded and expose vulnerable areas. Often, these revelations provide a detailed model for anyone who wishes to wound or hurt us. While the literature about physical abuse often points to the fact that children who are abused are likely to become abusers or be abused, there is no attention given to sharing woundedness in such a way that we let intimate others know exactly what can be done to hurt us, to make us feel as though we are caught in the destructive patterns we have struggled to break. When partners create scenarios of abuse similar, if not exactly the same, to those we have experienced in childhood, the wounded person is hurt not only by the physical pain but by the feeling of calculated betrayal. Betrayal. When we are physically hurt by loved ones, we feel betrayed. We can no longer trust that care can be sustained. We are wounded, damaged— hurt to our hearts.

The Impact of Single Incidents of Hitting

Feminist work calling attention to male violence against women has helped create a climate where the issues of physical abuse by loved ones can be freely addressed, especially sexual abuse within families. Exploration of male violence against women by feminists and non-feminists shows a connection between childhood experience of being hit by loved ones and the later occurrence of violence in adult relationships. While there is much material available discussing physical abuse of women by men, usually extreme physical abuse, there is not much discussion of the impact that one incident of hitting may have on a person in an intimate relationship, or how the person who is hit recovers from that experience. Increasingly, in discussion with women about physical abuse in relationships, irrespective of sexual preference, I find that most of us have had the experience of being violently hit at least once. There is little discussion of how we are damaged by such experiences (especially if we have been hit as children), of the ways we cope and recover from this wounding. This is an important area for feminist research precisely because many cases of extreme physical abuse begin with an isolated incident of hitting. Attention must be given to understanding and stopping these isolated incidents if we are to eliminate the possibility that women will be at risk in intimate relationships.

The Stigma of the Phrase "Battered Woman"

Critically thinking about issues of physical abuse has led me to question the way our culture, the way we as feminist advocates focus on the issue of violence and physical abuse by loved ones. The focus has been on male violence against women and, in particular, male sexual abuse of children. Given the nature of patriarchy, it has been necessary for feminists to focus on extreme cases to make people confront the issue, and acknowledge it to be serious and relevant. Unfortunately, an exclusive focus on extreme cases can and does lead us to ignore the more frequent, more common, yet less extreme case of occasional hitting. Women are also less likely to acknowledge occasional hitting for fear that they will then be seen as someone who is in a bad relationship or someone whose life is out of control. Currently, the literature about male violence against women identifies the physically abused woman as a "battered woman." While it has been important to have an accessible terminology to draw attention to the issue of male violence against women, the terms used reflect biases because they call attention to only one type of violence in intimate relationships. The term "battered woman" is problematical. It is not a term that emerged from feminist work on male violence against women; it was already used by psychologists and sociologists in the literature on domestic violence. This label "battered woman" places primary emphasis on physical assaults that are continuous, repeated, and unrelenting. The focus is on extreme violence, with little effort to link these cases with the everyday acceptance within intimate relationships of physical abuse that is not extreme, that may not be repeated. Yet these lesser forms of physical abuse damage individuals psychologically and, if not properly addressed and recovered from, can set the stage for more extreme incidents.

Most importantly, the term "battered woman" is used as though it constitutes a separate and unique category of womanness, as though it is an identity, a mark that sets one apart rather than being simply a descriptive term. It is as though the experience of being repeatedly violently hit is the sole defining characteristic of a woman's identity and all other aspects of who she is and what her experience has been are submerged. When I was hit, I too used the popular phrases "batterer," "battered woman," "battering" even though I did not feel that these words adequately described being hit once. However, these were the terms that people would listen to, would see as important, significant (as if it is not really significant for an individual, and more importantly for a woman, to be hit once). My partner was angry to be labelled a batterer by me. He was reluctant to talk about the experience of hitting me precisely because he did not want to be labelled a batterer. I had hit him once (not as badly as he had hit me) and I did not think of myself as a batterer. For both of us, these terms were inadequate. Rather than enabling us to cope effectively and positively with a negative situation, they were part of all the mechanisms of denial; they made us want to avoid confronting what had happened. This is the case for many people who are hit and those who hit.

Women who are hit once by men in their lives, and women who are hit repeatedly, do not want to be placed in the category of "battered woman" because it is a label that appears to strip us of dignity, to deny that there has been any integrity in the relationships we are in. A person physically assaulted by a stranger or a casual friend with whom they are not intimate may be hit once or repeatedly but they do not have to be placed into a category before doctors, lawyers, family, counselors, etc. take their problem seriously. Again, it must be stated that establishing categories and terminology has been part of the effort to draw public attention to the seriousness of male violence against women in intimate relationships. Even though the use of convenient labels and categories has made it easier to identify problems of physical abuse, it does not mean the terminology should not be critiqued from a feminist perspective and changed if necessary.

Recently, I had an experience assisting a woman who had been brutally attacked by her husband (she never commented on whether this was the first incident or not), which caused me to reflect anew on the use of the term "battered woman." This young woman was not engaged in feminist thinking or aware that "battered woman" was a category. Her husband had tried to choke her to death. She managed to escape from him with only the clothes she was wearing. After she recovered from the trauma, she considered going back to this relationship. As a church-going woman, she believed that her marriage vows were sacred and that she should try to make the relationship work. In an effort to share my feeling that this could place her at great risk, I brought her Lenore Walker's *The Battered Woman* because it seemed to me that there was much that she was not revealing, that she felt alone, and that the experiences she would read about in the book would give her a sense that other women had experienced what she was going through. I hoped reading the book would give her the courage to confront the reality of her situation. Yet I found it difficult to share because I could see that her self-esteem had already been greatly attacked, that she had lost a sense of her worth and value, and that possibly this categorizing of her identity would add to the feeling that she should just forget, be silent (and certainly returning to a situation where one is likely to be abused is one way to mask the severity of the problem). Still I had to try. When I first gave her the book, it disappeared. An unidentified family member had thrown it away. They felt that she would be making a serious mistake if she began to see herself as an absolute victim which they felt the label "battered woman" implied. I stressed that she should ignore the labels

and read the content. I believed the experience shared in this book helped give her the courage to be critical of her situation, to take constructive action.

Her response to the label "battered woman," as well as the responses of other women who have been victims of violence in intimate relationships, compelled me to critically explore further the use of this term. In conversation with many women, I found that it was seen as a stigmatizing label, one which victimized women seeking help felt themselves in no condition to critique. As in, "who cares what anybody is calling it—I just want to stop this pain." Within patriarchal society, women who are victimized by male violence have had to pay a price for breaking the silence and naming the problem. They have had to be seen as fallen women, who have failed in their "feminine" role to sensitize and civilize the beast in the man. A category like "battered woman" risks reinforcing this notion that the hurt woman, not only the rape victim, becomes a social pariah, set apart, marked forever by this experience.

A distinction must be made between having a terminology that enables women, and all victims of violent acts, to name the problem and categories of labeling that may inhibit that naming. When individuals are wounded, we are indeed often scarred, often damaged in ways that do set us apart from those who have not experienced a similar wounding, but an essential aspect of the recovery process is the healing of the wound, the removal of the scar. This is an empowering process that should not be diminished by labels that imply this wounding experience is the most significant aspect of identity.

Difficulties of Recovering from Occasional Acts of Hitting

As I have already stated, overemphasis on extreme cases of violent abuse may lead us to ignore the problem of occasional hitting, and it may make it difficult for women to talk about this problem. A critical issue that is not fully examined and written about in great detail by researchers who study and work with victims is the recovery process. There is a dearth of material discussing the recovery process of individuals who have been physically abused. In those cases where an individual is hit only once in an intimate relationship, however violently, there may be no recognition at all of the negative impact of this experience. There may be no conscious attempt by the victimized person to work at restoring her or his well-being, even if the person seeks therapeutic help, because the one incident may not be seen as serious or damaging. Alone and in isolation, the person who has been hit must struggle to regain broken trust—to forge some strategy of recovery. Individuals are often able to process an experience of being hit mentally that may not be processed emotionally. Many women I talked with felt that even after the incident was long forgotten, their bodies remain troubled. Instinctively, the person who has been hit may respond fearfully to any body movement on the part of a loved one that is similar to the posture used when pain was inflicted.

Being hit once by a partner can forever diminish sexual relationships if there has been no recovery process. Again there is little written about ways folks recover physically in their sexualities as loved ones who continue to be sexual with those who have hurt them. In most cases, sexual relationships are dramatically altered when hitting has occurred. The sexual realm may be the one space where the person who has been hit experiences again the sense of vulnerability, which may also arouse fear. This can lead either to an attempt to avoid sex or to unacknowledged sexual withdrawal wherein the person participates but is passive. I talked with women who had been hit by lovers who described sex as an ordeal, the one space where they confront their inability to trust a partner who has broken trust. One woman emphasized that to her, being hit was a "violation of her body space" and that she felt from then on she had to protect that space. This response, though a survival strategy, does not lead to healthy recovery.

Often, women who are hit in intimate relationships with male or female lovers feel as though we have lost an innocence that cannot be regained. Yet this very notion of innocence is connected to passive acceptance of concepts of romantic love under patriarchy which have served to mask problematic realities in relationships. The process of recovery must include a critique of this notion of innocence which is often linked to an unrealistic and fantastic vision of love and romance. It is only in letting go of the perfect, no-work, happily-ever-after union idea, that we can rid our psyches of the sense that we have failed in some way by not having such relationships. Those of us who never focussed on the negative impact of being hit as children find it necessary to reexamine the past in a therapeutic manner as part of our recovery process. Strategies that helped us survive as children may be detrimental for us to use in adult relationships.

Talking about being hit by loved ones with other women, both as children and as adults, I found that many of us had never really thought very much about our own relationship to violence. Many of us took pride in never feeling violent, never hitting. We had not thought deeply about our relationship to inflicting physical pain.

Some of us expressed terror and awe when confronted with physical strength on the part of others. For us, the healing process included the need to learn how to use physical force constructively, to remove the terror—the dread. Despite the research that suggests children who are hit may become adults who hit—women hitting children, men hitting women and children—most of the women I talked with not only did not hit but were compulsive about not using physical force.

Overall the process by which women recover from the experience of being hit by loved ones is a complicated and multi-faceted one, an area where there must be much more feminist study and research. To many of us, feminists calling attention to the reality of violence in intimate relationships has not in and of itself compelled most people to take the issue seriously, and such violence seems to be daily on the increase. In this essay, I have raised issues that are not commonly talked about, even among folks who are particularly concerned about violence against women. I hope it will serve as a catalyst for further thought, that it will strengthen our efforts as feminist activists to create a world where domination and coercive abuse are never aspects of intimate relationships.

Violence against Women Protected by "Privacy"

Linda A. Bell

Linda A. Bell is professor of philosophy at California State University, Fresno. She is the editor (with David Blumenfeld) of *Overcoming Racism and Sexism* (Lanham, MD: Rowman & Littlefield, 1995).

Inasmuch as battering, rape, and child abuse, both sexual and non-sexual, are perpetrated by men in the vast majority of known cases, their treatment by the judicial system might be the result simply of unacceptable sexism, patriarchal attitudes, and male arrogance. Other explanations have been offered, though, including a rather Kantian concern for the intention of the perpetrator and the possibility that maintaining such a double standard in the law was deemed necessary to protect the "sanctity" of family and home.

In the name of fairness, judges and jurors might look at a perpetrator's intention, worrying about the injustice of punishing one who thought he was doing the right thing or, in the case of rape, really believed his victim was consenting. For the same reason, the abuser's love of his victims may be taken more seriously than the actual harm he inflicted. MacKinnon notes the way similar emphases on intention in rape laws and their enforcement jeopardize women, given that "men are systematically conditioned not even to notice what women want." She asks, "From whose standpoint, and in whose interest, is a law that allows one person's conditioned unconsciousness to contraindicate another's experienced violation?"[1]

A utilitarian, on the other hand, might try to argue that the double standard is necessary, to protect the intimacy and privacy of family and home. Utilitarians are likely to agree with Mill that the greatest good will be achieved only if human beings are allowed as much self-determination as possible. Thus, they will argue for minimal governmental interference in the so-called private affairs of citizens. Instead of prohibiting interference in cases where individuals' behavior affects only themselves or other consenting adults, though, too often they draw a curtain

over family and home, a curtain to be lifted only in cases of particularly egregious abuse and perhaps not even then. Too often this curtain protects virtually all that goes on beyond closed doors: *assent is presumed given because the activity occurred or normally occurs behind closed doors.* This means that individuals who are harmed by strangers and who are harmed in the so-called public sphere will be treated quite differently than those (mainly women and children) who are harmed in the home and by individuals with whom they are related or familiar. It even means that those who are harmed in ways deemed appropriate only to intimate relationships will be treated quite differently than individuals harmed in other ways.

Other utilitarian reasons have been offered for protecting the privacy and intimacy of family and home and thus distinguishing and treating so differently "public" and "private" harms. One line of reasoning has to do with the concern that efforts to prevent harm may only create additional harm. The argument goes something like this: If an individual (male) is not coping well with the competitive and demanding environment of the workplace, surely society adds one more layer of stress for him if it gives members of his own family rights against him, such as the right not to be abused. Moreover, if the law becomes involved in "protecting" those members from him, those very individuals are likely to suffer additional serious harm if the family is broken up and loses its chief means of financial support. Instead of examining ways protection could avoid such harm, this argument leaves the abused to fend for themselves and extends its primary solicitude to the abusers, who, we are told, frequently were abused when they were young.

A rather different but still utilitarian argument justifies denying men and women the same rights, particularly in the family, arguing that this denial

---

From Linda A. Bell, *Rethinking Ethics in the Midst of Violence* (Rowman and Littlefield, 1993). Reprinted by permission.

helps to secure a stable social order. As David L. Kirp, Mark G. Yudof, and Marlene Strong Franks more recently propose: "By denying an independent legal status to the married woman, this paternalism was meant to minimize family strife; in that sense, the law helped to secure a stable social order."[2]

William James attempts something like this when he challenges the equality of men and women for which Mill argues. James objects that the "representative American" dreams of home as a haven, a place of refuge from the struggle, the failure and humiliation, of the "outer world," a "tranquil spot where he shall be valid absolutely and once for all; where, having been accepted, he is secure from further criticism, and where his good aspirations may be respected no less than if they were accomplished realities." But, James continues, the security and repose essential to his ideal are not easily attainable "without some feeling of dependence on the woman's side—without her relying on him to be her mediator with the external world—without his activity overlapping hers and surrounding it on almost every side, so that he makes as it were the atmosphere in which she lives."[3] The requisite dependence would seem to entail minimal or no recognition of rights she could exercise against him.

While this argument supports legal respect for the privacy and sanctity of the home and family, it is deeply flawed. After all, what is James's argument but an expression of . . . arrogance . . . ? How else are we to understand his confusing of the "representative American," whose desires James voices, with the male? How else can we understand the way James so unabashedly either ignores the desires of women or subsumes them under the desires of men? What else can we make of his inability to recognize that what he says cannot even apply to many men who not only cannot afford such dependent wives but also have neither the time, energy, nor money to mediate between the world and wives whom they shelter in artificial cocoons? How else could he be so smugly satisfied with the status quo that he, unlike Virginia Woolf, would not even raise a question about whether "the public and the private worlds are inseparably connected; that the tyrannies and servil-ities of the one are the tyrannies and servilities of the other"?[4]

We are left to conclude that men's, not women's, privacy is protected by the legal system and by the public/private distinction itself. MacKinnon observes, in fact, that women are not allowed privacy under male domination: "The very place (home, body), relations (sexual), activities (intercourse and reproduction), and feelings (intimacy, self-hood) that feminism finds central to women's subjection form the core of the privacy doctrine. But when women are segregated in private, one at a time, a law of privacy will tend to protect the right of men 'to be let alone,' to oppress us one at a time."[5] This is in part, she believes, because the private is conceived as the realm of choice where "consent tends to be presumed." Although such a presumption is voided by coercion, it is nevertheless quite difficult for anything supposedly private to count as coercion. This conception of the private thus gives their urgency to questions like "Why would one allow force in private[?]—the 'why doesn't she leave[?]' question asked of battered women."[6]

This understanding of the private may lead theorists to misrepresent and misunderstand what happens both "in public" and "in private." For example, in their book *Gender Justice,* Kirp et al. present the private as a sphere of "sexual intimacy, procreation, and childrearing, informed by affection, trust, privacy, and responsibility." Not surprisingly, they then are unable to find anything "inherently oppressive" in the condition of the "American" housewife, certainly "nothing akin to such unambiguously imposed forms of association as slavery and apartheid."[7] They seem unaware of the fact that they are accepting at face value the *social meaning* of the one while looking critically at the *reality* of the other. If they were to consider only the social meanings of slavery and apartheid (as constructed by the societies institutionalizing these), they probably would not find much "inherently oppressive" about these institutions either. We know, *contra* the social rationale of what was going on, that slaves were indeed human beings and that they were held against their wills, raped, beaten, tortured, and killed under slavery, just as we know that women today are human beings, often held against their wills, raped, beaten, tortured, and killed by their husbands, lovers, fathers, brothers, and male "friends."

When Kirp et al. turn to the public "realm," they carry with them the optimistic social meaning of the private. Thus, they quickly rule out the hypothesis that men are "homosocial," "interested in working with other men, not women," and "have created segregated working conditions in order to associate with one another." Proclaiming this to be a "couple-oriented" society and citing the fact that hiring women would be in the self-interest of employers given the prevailing wage differential between men and women, they conclude: "Arguments based on employer's prejudices against women strain credulity." Though they acknowledge early in their book that a household with a sexist or racist bent may give a similar bent to the society,[8] they later seem unable to comprehend that the sexist hierarchy perpetuated in the home might explain the couples orientation of our society, the prevailing wage differential, *and* the homosocial nature of the distribution of power in the workplace and in politics. The resulting, somewhat confusing social order may indeed "strain credulity" for individuals who reject ambiguity and who expect rationality and particularly consistency in the realm of human affairs; but feminists must acknowledge the ambiguous and seemingly inconsistent situation so succinctly described by Letty Cottin Pogrebin: "That although we are a relentlessly *heterosexual* society, our nonromantic interactions are overwhelmingly '*homosocial.*'"[9]

Agreeing that the very way "woman" is conceived precludes privacy, Andrea Dworkin interprets the "privacy" of intimate relations a bit differently. For her, women are understood in terms of their sexuality, a sexuality perceived as a hole, a hole making a woman accessible to men: "a hole between her legs that men can, must, do enter"; this entry opens her up, splits her down the center, and occupies her "physically, internally, in her privacy." Unlike the hole men also have—the anus, which also can be entered—this hole, her hole, is synonymous with entry." This, in turn, supports the ideology that "men fuck women because the women attract, are sensual, are pretty, have some dimension of beauty or grace, however lowdown or elegant, that brings on desire," thus ignoring, as Dworkin observes, all the "ravaged junkie-prostitutes on our contemporary streets" and "toothless bawds of history who got fucked more than the elegant ladies by all accounts." It also protects men's boundaries and dominance by limiting male penetration to the hole only a woman has, it being regarded as an abomination, according to sodomy laws, to "fuck men as if they were women."[10]

For Dworkin, this conceptualizing of woman means a woman "is, in fact, human by a standard that precludes physical privacy, since to keep a man out altogether and for a lifetime is deviant in the extreme, a psychopathology, a repudiation of the way in which she is expected to manifest her humanity." This preclusion of privacy helps Dworkin understand why "*violation* is a synonym for sexual intercourse," explaining the "deep recognition in culture and in experience that intercourse is both the normal use of a woman, her human potentiality affirmed by it, and a violative abuse, her privacy irredeemably compromised, her selfhood changed in a way that is irrevocable, unrecoverable."[11]

In addition, Dworkin agrees with Catharine MacKinnon that sexual privacy functions as a shield for men. It means, Dworkin says, "a man has a right to shield himself when sexually using civil inferiors." Since laws have actually required sexual compliance from women (for example, the marital exemption in the rape laws of many states), she concludes, "Any act so controlled by the state, proscribed and prescribed in detail, cannot be private in the ordinary sense."[12]

While the private is thus not in actuality outside the purview of or even very different from and certainly not opposed to the public, the distinction itself is likely to obscure the similarities and exaggerate the differences, as Nancy Fraser suggests.[13] Of course, such obfuscation may be an essential rather than incidental feature of the distinction and may serve theoretical as well as practical interests. For example, as Andrea Nye argues, the public/private distinction is vital if democratic theory is to sustain the illusion that society is made up of competing individuals: noncompeting individuals whose existence would otherwise challenge the theory, can be in effect hidden in the privacy of the family and represented in society by the male head of the household. Moreover, since the family is necessary for the functioning of democratic society, the latter cannot recognize any rights the exercise of which would deflect women from marriage and motherhood.[14]

As Iris Young indicates, such ideological use of the public/private distinction may be consequent upon "defining privacy as what the public excludes." She urges feminists to preserve the public/private distinction but with a new understanding of privacy as "that aspect of his other life and activity that any individual has a right to exclude others from." No longer would any social

institutions or practices be excluded *a priori* from public discussion and expression. Moreover, such a revised notion of privacy places the onus for any such exclusion on individuals and thereby acknowledges the following principle: "no persons, actions or aspect . . . of a person's life should be forced into privacy."[15] Patricia Collins suggests that African-Americans communally constructed a recognition of privacy much along the lines advocated by Young: during slavery, for example, "[t]he line separating the Black community from whites served as a more accurate boundary delineating public and private spheres for African-Americans than that separating Black households from the surrounding Black community."[16]

Child Abuse and Family Privacy

David Archard

David Archard is senior lecturer in the Department of Philosophy and Politics, University of Ulster at Jordanstown, Newtownabbey, County Antrim, Northern Ireland. He is the author of *Children: Rights and Childhood* (London: Routledge, 1993).

A familiar defense of the right to privacy in respect of individuals . . . is that it permits the intimacy which is essential to relationships of love and friendship. Similarly, it has been argued that familial privacy is necessary for the healthy development of the normal, loving relationships between parent and parent, parent and child which characterize a healthy family. It may further be argued that such familial bonds are critical to every child's healthy growth and development.

My reply is two-fold. First, the kind of privacy to which the twentieth century Western family feels entitled and which it has come to expect is historically and culturally very specific. It is worth emphasizing the degree to which the private nuclear family, a self-contained household of kin only living within its own well-defined space, is a peculiarly late twentieth century Western phenomenon, a compound of various changes in so-

ciety—the separation of home and work activities, a decline in the number of children born per family, an end to apprenticeship and the "putting out" of children, the demise of servants as household members, the emergence in various architectural forms of the family house, and the development of entertainments which are or can be home-based.

Families in previous times and in other types of society have enjoyed a quite significantly smaller degree of privacy. Of course it can be shown that in all cultures and societies there is some line drawn to divide space, demarcate activities, specify roles in terms of a distinction between public and private. Thus, for example, a particular tribal culture may involve households comprising several kin groups preparing and eating food together, sleeping in the same unpartitioned building, but with some "private" spaces and times associated with sexual activity and enforced through rules of non-encroachment.

However, it is only in this century in the West that the line between private and public has been

Excerpted from David Archard, "Child Abuse: Parental Rights and the Interests of the Child," *Journal of Applied Philosophy*, 7, 2 (1990): 183–194. Reprinted by permission.

so clearly and sharply drawn around the nuclear family in so many of its aspects. Importantly, there is little or no evidence that these significant differences in the scope of familial privacy are correlatable with equally significant differences in the degree to which children develop into normal healthy adults.

Secondly, whilst privacy may serve as the precondition for a healthy and loving intimacy, it can equally function as a cloak for abuse and neglect. The ill-treatment of children takes place in a "private" space, the family home, and to the very extent that it is a private space, it may continue undetected and unsuspected. . . . The "privacy" of the family protects the abuser in a number of ways. The abuse is literally unobserved, and while physical abuse may display itself through the consequent bruises and bumps upon the child, sexual abuse has no obvious public face. Abused children may have no sense that what is "privately" happening to them is radically and terribly different from what would be "publicly" acceptable. So many victims of incest have subsequently reported that they did not think of their abuse as anything other than natural, as what happened within even "normal" families. Finally, the abused child within the "private" space of the family will probably be pressurized not to reveal the abuse, or to retract previous accusations of abuse. It is sometimes tragically ironic to read about accusations of social workers bullying confessions of abuse from children, when no mention is made at the same time of the brutal means by which abusing parents so frequently secure the silence of their victims.

All these are reasons why abused children will not—as our society sometimes seems to expect—step forward and publicly identify themselves as victims of abuse. They are also thus reasons why the disclosure of abuse will have to involve intrusions upon the privacy of the family prohibited by the liberal ideal. It is important—before I specify something of the intrusiveness upon the family which I favor—to emphasize the extent of the evil which it would help to prevent. The abuse of children—especially sexual abuse—ruins lives, and not just those of the victim. Abuse is deeply traumatizing, and its scarring effects last well into, if not throughout adulthood. There is increasing evidence of a cycle of abuse—abusers being themselves very frequently the victims of previous abuse. There is also evidence linking subsequent criminality, alcoholism, drug addiction and violent behavior to a history of childhood abuse.

So what intrusions upon family privacy would I favor? I would give those social workers who specialize and are trained in child abuse statutory powers of entry into family homes and access to children. It is of course significant that the biggest percentage of referrals to social services of suspected abuse in the United Kingdom comes from health workers who currently enjoy *de facto* rights of access into homes and to children. I would strive to redraw the line that separates the "private" family from the public domain by creating "spaces" in which the health of children can be reviewed and monitored with a view to possible abuse. By this, I mean that family doctors, consultants, emergency medical personnel, police and teachers—all those who for professional or statutory reasons may come into contact with children—must be specifically trained in the diagnosis of abuse, educated in the importance of detecting abuse and persuaded as to the need for their contact with the child to present opportunities for the diagnosis of possible abuse. The reporting of cases of suspected abuse to social services by such professionals must also be made mandatory.

It is clear that presently the vast majority of these professionals honor the liberal ideal of familial privacy, are loath to suspect parents of ill-doing, and favor interference only as a last resort. In their study of how the agencies concerned with child welfare operate within the U.K., *The Protection of Children* (1983), Robert Dingwall et al. conclude: "We have clearly shown that, at each and every stage, the structures of the organizations involved and the practical reasoning of their members have the effect of creating a preference for the least stigmatizing interpretation of available data and the least overtly coercive possible disposition. Officially-labelled cases of mistreatment are, quite literally, only those for which no excuse or justification can be found. Compulsory measures are employed only in those cases where parental recalcitrance or mental incompetence leave no room for voluntary action."

Closely related to my preference for a greater intrusiveness upon the family is a dislike for the liberal ideal's threshold for statutory action: the occasioning or risk of specific harms to the child. The criterion is essentially "negative." Parents are given the benefit of the doubt, and the onus is upon the State to establish neglect and abuse of a concrete form. I would rather that the State established affirmative duties of care which guaranteed the best possible conditions for the development of the child. This ideal is enshrined within the ancient prerogative of *patris patriae* whereby the State may assume, in the last analysis and last resort, the protective role of parent to its infant citizens. In turn, this doctrine justifies the jurisdiction of High Courts over minors in cases of wardship. Wardship has been defined as "essentially a parental jurisdiction" wherein the main consideration to be acted upon in its exercise is the benefit or welfare of the child . . . the Court must do what under the circumstances a wise parent acting for the true interest of the child would or ought to do." My point might be expressed rather baldly as follows: the liberal ideal requires that parents be shown to be palpably bad before the State will intervene. I would rather that the State requires its parents to be good, and act accordingly when they are not.

There is much talk nowadays of the emergence of children's rights, and the correlated fragmentation or disappearance of parental rights. As I have noted, the paramountcy of the child's best interests is, at least formally, insisted upon in the rhetoric of legal and social welfare provision. Interestingly, however, the doctrine of paramountcy derives principally from custody cases, in which the family *has already broken down*. Similarly, the liberal ideal of family policy presumes the benevolence of existing parental control and intervenes only when there is proven familial failure. If we are to take seriously the notion of the child's best interests, and the reality of children's rights, then we cannot continue uncritically to speak of competing rights to family privacy and parental autonomy. On the contrary, respect for these latter rights serves only to perpetuate the very conditions under which children, out of sight and too often out of the "public" mind, suffer the "private" hell of preventable abuse.

Child Abuse and Neglect: A Multicultural Perspective

Philip L. Fetzer

Philip L. Fetzer is associate professor of political science at California Polytechnic State University, San Luis Obispo. He is the author of several essays on civil rights law and the editor of a recent book of autobiographical essays by civil rights activists: *The Ethnic Moment: The Search for Equality in the American Experience* (Armonk, NY: M. E. Sharpe, 1997).

Introduction

In the summer of 1996, Isabel Gomez married her boyfriend, Juan Pineda. The Orange County Social Services Agency helped make it possible for Gomez and Pineda to marry. At the time of their marriage, Ms. Gomez was 13 and Mr. Pineda was 20. The head of the agency, Larry Leaman, acknowledged that in the last two years agency social workers with judicial approval had helped at least fifteen underage girls either to marry or to continue living with their adult male sex partners.

Many people who became aware of this practice were morally outraged. They felt that the girls were much too young to be married. Their adult male partners were simply taking advantage of their youth and inexperience for their own sexual gratification. The Orange County Social Services Agency, they argued, was helping the men commit sexual abuse. In response, it was pointed out that fourteen of the fifteen girls were Latinas and that sexual partnerships and marriages between teenage girls and adult males is an acceptable practice in some parts of the Hispanic subculture in Orange County. The implied general principle is that in a multi-cultural community we should take cultural information into account *before* we make moral and legal judgments about issues as serious as sexual abuse.

Allegations of child abuse or neglect raise serious issues that may lead to state intervention and termination of parental control of their children. In 1992, for example, over 140,000 children were brought into court on the ground that they had been neglected or abused.[1] If family law is based on a belief that "there is a preferred model for family structure," this perspective would naturally lead to the assumption that there is a "uniform methodology" that describes and defines doctrine appropriate for resolving family related issues.[2]

Surprisingly, there is no national consensus as to when a court should find a child abused or neglected.[3] Poverty is one of most common characteristics of families charged with abuse or neglect.[4] A disproportionate percentage of poor families is African American, Native American, or Hispanic. If an individual is a member of one of these ethnic groups he is *three times* as likely to be poor as someone who is white. Child abuse and neglect statistics indicate that while comprising 23 percent of the national population about 36 percent of all reported cases involve children who were part of a Black, Hispanic or Native American family.[5] A member of one of these ethnic groups is nearly *twice* as likely to be investigated for abuse or neglect compared with members of a white family. How might one account for this disparity?

The possibility of cultural or class bias in evaluating neglect and abuse cases appears to be significant. Current research in family law tends to support the argument that such bias is an important factor in abuse and neglect cases.[6] An important question then arises: Is it possible to write a child abuse standard that fairly and equitably applies to all regardless of culture, ethnicity, or class? If so, what would that standard look like? Furthermore, can one introduce evidence of cultural background *without* condoning violence against children?

Current Standards

What are some standards that might be used in evaluating allegations of abuse or neglect? In *Cases and Materials on Family Law* the authors present the following definition taken from the Model Child Protective Services Act of 1975:

> . . . an 'abused or maltreated child' means a child whose physical or mental health or welfare is harmed or threatened with harm when his parent or other person responsible for his welfare:
>
> (i) Inflicts or allows to be inflicted upon the child physical or *mental injury,* including *excessive* corporal punishment; or
>
> (ii) Creates or allows to be created a *substantial risk* of physical or *mental injury* to the child, including *excessive* corporal punishment; or
>
> (iii) Commits or allows to be committed, against the child, an act of sexual abuse as defined by state law; or
>
> (iv) Fails to supply the child with *adequate* food, clothing, shelter, education (as defined by state law), or medical care, though financially able to do so or offered financial or other reasonable means to do so . . .
>
> (v) Fails to provide the child with a *minimum degree of care* or *proper* supervision or guardianship because of his unwillingness or inability to do so by situations or conditions, such as, but not limited to, *social* or psychiatric problems or disorders, *mental incompetency,* or the use of a drug, drugs, or alcohol to the extent that the parent or other person responsible for the child's welfare loses his ability to properly care for the child . . .[7]

The Model Child Protective Services Act provides ample opportunity for the subjective value judgment of a family court judge to play a decisive role in determining abuse or neglect. This will occur when he or she must interpret such vague phrases as: (1) excessive corporal punishment, (2) substantial risk of physical or mental injury, (3) minimum degree of care, or (4) proper supervision. Cultural bias could lead to negative evaluations under this definition. For example, facial scarring may be viewed by a non–Native American judge as a violation of (2) above. But this practice may be a perfectly acceptable aspect of traditional behavior to certain Native Americans.

In *Family and State* Laurence Houlgate supplies the following alternative criteria for a family court to use in determining "serious harm":

1. Physical injury, illness, or condition that causes or creates a substantial risk of causing death, disfigurement, or impairment of bodily functioning.
2. Emotional damage evidenced by severe anxiety, depression or withdrawal or untoward aggressive behavior or hostility toward others.
3. Sexual abuse, that is, the use of a child by a parent or other family member for sexual purposes.
4. Delinquent behavior.[8]

But potential cultural bias applies to Houlgate's standard as well. For example, what does it mean to "use" a child for sexual purposes? The marriage of 13-year-old Isabel Gomez to 20-year-old Juan Pineda might constitute "sexual abuse" to a judge applying Houlgate's standard (3). But this might not be a reasonable interpretation given the norms of the Hispanic subculture in Orange County in the 1990s. And the members of some Native American tribes may not regard facial scarring as "disfigurement" under standard (1).

Rules that are open to a wide range of interpretations are difficult for any family involved in child abuse or neglect proceedings. Those who are less well educated or with fewer financial resources than their peers are also more vulnerable to arbitrary state intervention under such circumstances.

In *Alsager* v. *District Court of Polk County,*[9] Chief Judge Hanson found Iowa's termination statutes unconstitutionally vague. (Termination laws mandate the loss of custody and supervision by parents of their natural born children under certain conditions.) The Iowa laws included reference to "necessary parental care and protection" and parental conduct "detrimental to the physical or mental health or morals of the child." Because they afforded state officials with "so much discretion that arbitrary and discriminatory parental ter-

minations [would be] inevitable" the laws could not stand.[10] Commenting on the problem of vagueness in intrafamily relations, the *Alsager* court stated: "This danger is especially grave in the highly subjective context of determining an approved mode of child-rearing."[11]

In one of the leading Supreme Court rulings on family law, *Santosky* v. *Kramer,* Justice Blackmun held that prior to a state ruling favoring termination of parental rights the standard of proof must be the moderately high level of scrutiny: "clear and convincing evidence."[12] The Court also noted that in permanent neglect proceedings "imprecise substantive standards" may be employed "that leave determinations unusually open to the subjective values of the judge."[13] Furthermore, "[b]ecause parents subject to termination proceedings are often poor, uneducated, or members of minority groups . . . such proceedings are often vulnerable to judgments based on cultural or class bias."[14]

"Best Interests"

In abuse or neglect cases, a number of standards have been applied or suggested. One of the leading approaches is the "best interest of the child." Under this framework, abuse or neglect would be defined as the failure by parents or other responsible adults to act in the *child's best interest*. However, without a national consensus on what parenting or living arrangements fulfill children's "best interest," the standard "invites the same race, class and cultural bias upon judicial interpretation as child abuse and neglect statutes."[15]

For example, income level, floor space and plumbing may not meet the state health and welfare standards and lead to allegations of neglect. In noting the "almost fanatical pursuit of Indian children by county welfare officials," a member of the Devil's Lake Sioux said: "They use their own standards to judge us. What is the difference if an Indian home is poor but there is plenty of love?"[16]

"Minimal Needs"

Another criterion is to evaluate a child's treatment on the "minimal needs test." Under this guideline a child is considered harmed (and therefore, abused or neglected) if specified minimum needs are not met. The question that needs to be answered if this standard were to be adopted is: What needs does a child have? What would count as a *minimal* level of satisfaction of those needs?[17] While the first question implies an obvious answer (food, shelter, and attention, for example), the second is much more problematic: How much and what kind of food, shelter or attention does a child need to lead a healthy life? Whose standards apply? Why?

"Community Standards"

Under the "community standard" guideline, behavior that does not (a) meet the "norm" for a community and (b) results in a particular harm to a child would be considered abuse or neglect. A problem with this criterion, however, is this: Suppose the community norm includes facial scarring (a practice followed by some Native American nations) for purposes of cultural identification? While the practice does meet the "community norm" requirement, has the child been harmed? If so, does this practice "count" as abuse?

"Harmful Consequences"

Another closely related way to evaluate child abuse or neglect laws is to focus on possible harmful consequences to the child. The immediate harm in the facial scarring example is clear. Slashing of a child's cheeks is a violent and painful act. But it might be argued that one of the long-term effects is that the child is accepted into his cultural community. Circumcision is also violent and painful but is widely practiced on newborn babies. The practice is widely accepted because of the supposed long-term benefits.

Class and Ethnic Bias

Even though child abuse occurs in families of all ethnicities and income levels, the most common characteristic of families charged with neglect is poverty.[18] Additionally, there appears to be overreporting of levels of abuse and neglect among people of color. The possibility that class or cultural bias is a significant factor in deciding to label certain children "abused" or "neglected" must be addressed if laws are going to be applied in an equitable manner. In a 1994 article that appeared in the *Arizona Law Review,* the author commented:

> Child abuse and neglect happens to children of all races, in all kinds of communities, in all economic classes. But families of color, and poor families are more likely to be identified and coerced into accepting interventions by the child welfare system, and more likely to have their children removed and placed in foster care. Children of color are more likely to remain there for a long period of time, and to experience multiple placements before they are returned to their parents.[19]

Other studies reached similar conclusions:

> Because poor minority families receive many state social services, social workers evaluate these families more often than they evaluate middle class families to determine parental fitness, suitability to adopt, and other similar matters. Social workers are more likely to misreport child abuse and neglect in black and Native American communities because parental fitness evaluations are based on cultural indications, such as the number of people living under one roof.[20]

Finally, national studies have indicated that higher rates of child abuse occur among parents of low income, educational achievement, or who experience high rates of unemployment. Reporting biases, however, "enable much middle class family violence to go undetected."[21]

African Americans

Research published in the *American Journal of Public Health* indicated that reporting rates on child abuse are much higher for African Americans while rates for whites are underreported. In a study of health care professionals, African Americans represented 25.7 percent of the sample group but 74.3 percent of the cases reported by health care professionals. In the author's view, "the statistics *conclusively* prove that African Americans are disproportionately reported for child abuse."[22] Another report found that "[d]espite similar rates of substance abuse, black women were *ten times* more likely than whites to be reported to public health authorities for substance abuse during pregnancy."[23]

In *Physical Violence in American Families,* Straus and Cazenave reported that economic class appears to be a significant factor in black–white differences in family violence. They noted that blacks in the two highest income groups were less likely than whites at these income levels to report having engaged in child abuse within the previous year. Furthermore, they concluded: "Overall Black respondents are less likely to report slapping or spanking a child within the last year. This is directly contrary to much of the literature which suggests that Blacks, compared to Whites, are more likely to condone and use physical punishment of children." When income and husband's occupation are held constant, blacks are also *less* likely to engage in child abuse.[24]

Hispanics

Hispanic families also have many characteristics that may be negatively evaluated by health care or social workers responsible for reporting allegations of child abuse or neglect. These families tend to be larger than those of the general population. They are more than twice as likely to have three or more children in their households. Nearly one-fourth of Hispanic families are headed by women compared with only one-sixth among all American households. They are also less well educated and poorer than the white families. The poverty rate among Hispanic families in 1987 was about 26 percent compared with 10 percent among whites. Other characteristics of poverty are also more frequently associated with Hispanics than the general population: unemployment and receipt of welfare. For example, in 1986, 43 percent of Hispanics received welfare compared with 16 percent of whites.[25]

Hispanic children comprised 12 percent of all *reported* cases of physically abused children in 1984. At the same time, only 9.7 percent of all the children in the United States in 1985 were Hispanic. Therefore, Hispanic children were overrepresented by almost one-fifth in the official child abuse statistics. Among those earning less than twenty thousand dollars annually, however, Hispanic rates of parent-to-child violence were *similar* to that of whites.[26]

Nonetheless, overall reported rates of child abuse are higher for Hispanics even with statistical controls for poverty, urbanization and other demographic factors.[27] At the same time, a number of studies indicate that professionals are "more likely to recognize and report abuse involving ethnic minority and/or lower income families." For example, the conclusions of the NIS (National Incidence Study) on child abuse found that Hispanic cases comprised only 4.2 percent of all *substantiated* cases of child maltreatment.[28]

Native Americans

In 1977, William Byler reported that between 25 and 35 percent of Native American children were being placed in foster homes or other adoptive settings. In the state of Washington, adoption rates were nineteen times greater and foster care ten times the rate of that for non–Native Americans. Furthermore, "[i]n judging the fitness of a particular family, many social workers, ignorant of Indian cultural values and social norms, [were making] decisions . . . wholly inappropriate within the context of Indian family life and so they frequently discover[ed] neglect or abandonment where none exist[ed]."[29] An example may help to illustrate the problem. Native American extended families might be quite large. An Indian child may have as many as a hundred relatives in his community. While children are frequently left with some of these relatives, many social workers consider leaving a child outside the nuclear family as neglect and, therefore, grounds for terminating parental rights.[30]

A 1994 essay on the Indian Child Welfare Act refers to the "extraordinary high rate of placing Indian children with non-Indian families." The author believes that the reason for higher placement levels is that the standards are based on middle-class values such as the amount of floor space available in the home, plumbing, and income levels.[31]

Summary

Health care professionals and multidisciplinary child protection teams appear to overreport levels of abuse and neglect among the poor, African Americans, Hispanics, and Native Americans. The analogy with experiences in the criminal courts seems striking. Decision makers in American criminal courts are usually culturally different from those who are accused of crime. The differences work to the disadvantage of criminal defendants. Would not these differences apply with equal force to family law problems? The factors include: "the value system of the legal profession, the procedures by which juries are selected, the value system of the jurors, the lack of articulation in communication between the culturally different and the professionals composing the court, and the negative stereotypes of cultural minorities held by the professionals."[32] If the multicultural perspectives of health care professionals and legal officials were wider, poor families or those from nondominant ethnicities would have a greater opportunity to receive equitable treatment in abuse or neglect cases.

"Abuse" in a Multicultural Context: Some Problem Cases

> No culture or political community with which we are familiar gives its members good reasons for rejecting principles or practices that protect innocent people from being enslaved, tortured, murdered, malnourished, imprisoned, rendered homeless, or subject to abnormal physical pain and sickness.[33]

Certainly the most extreme example of child abuse is the taking of a child's life. The case of Fumiko Kimura, however, illustrates the difficulties faced in formulating a legal response to such an action in a cross-cultural context. Kimura was charged with first-degree murder in drowning her children in 1985. The Kimura defense argued that killing one's children was "required" by her culture's practice and would be treated as a misdemeanor in her country of origin.[34] The evidence that persuaded the prosecutor to reduce the charge to manslaughter was of a cultural nature. Kimura had presented evidence that the drownings (and her own attempted suicide) were "intended to purge the shame of her husband's infidelity." Ms. Kimura was found guilty of manslaughter and received a one-year sentence. The challenge for the legal system is how to respond appropriately to behavior that may be found acceptable in one culture while it is unacceptable in another.

A 1996 article in the *San Francisco Chronicle* raises additional questions about abuse in a cross-cultural environment. The article states that child abuse had been "grossly underreported for years because Pima traditions teach that such matters are to be kept quiet and handled by the family."[35] Most of the reported abuse is sexual—mainly fondling. Let us suppose, hypothetically, that sexual fondling is traditionally accepted by Pimas. What then would be the appropriate legal response from the majority culture?

Or, take the case of Jack Jones, an Inupiat, who was charged with sexual abuse in Fairbanks, Alaska. Jones was acquitted even though he had swatted "at the crotch area" and pulled down the pants of his son and grandson as a punishment. The defense brought in anthropologists and others who testified that his behavior was "part of a cultural tradition meant to teach boys to respond quickly to adversity."[36]

The *New York Times* recently reported the case of a 14-year-old Egyptian girl who died after genital mutilation.[37] Approximately 70 percent to 90 percent of girls in Egypt are subjected to what has been called "female circumcision" that may involve cutting away the tip of the clitoris and removing all exterior genitals. Reports of its occurrence are common in the United States.[38] How might family law principles be applied fairly to such cases?

Other examples raise similar problems. Is it "physical abuse" when a Nigerian immigrant punishes his nephew by hitting him and then putting pepper in the abrasions as was practiced in his village? Or when a Mexican woman beats her son with a wooden spoon and bites him in accordance with acceptable norms of her home country?[39]

Possible Modifications to Child Abuse and Neglect Laws

Alternative approaches that might provide for more equitable standards in cases alleging child abuse or neglect within a multicultural environment could include the following: (1) culturally specific parental fitness standards, (2) tribal jurisdiction for Native American families, or (3) considering cultural information as a relevant factor in evaluating proposed state intervention.

Culturally Specific Standards

A "culturally specific standard" might look like this:

> The standards to be applied . . . shall be the prevailing social and cultural standards in which the parent resides or maintains social and cultural ties.[40]

Many inner-city blacks, Hispanics and Native Americans live in overcrowded substandard housing, and may be unmarried or without a supporting spouse present. These characteristics do not conform to white, middle-class norms. Parents would be in a better position to retain custody of their children if such culturally specific standards were adopted. Children would also be more likely to be protected from inappropriate assignment to foster care if their situation was evaluated in this context.

Since poverty is a unifying characteristic of the families described above, it may be more appropriate to address the problem from a *class* rather than an ethnic perspective. After all, many white families are also subject to negative evaluations by health care professionals based on middle-class standards. If the child lives in a caring family but without the financial resources to "adequately" clothe or feed, or house that child, wouldn't it be more appropriate for the community to provide those resources than to destroy the family unit in order to "help" the child?

A deficiency of applying *culturally specific standards* is that doing so would permit such practices as genital mutilation. Health care workers and members of the legal system *should* take cultural information into consideration in making judgments about abuse or neglect. However, it would not be morally defensible simply to accept *without scrutiny* practices that may be questionable to members of the majority culture

Tribal Jurisdiction

The "tribal jurisdiction" approach resembles the "culturally specific standard" with the additional fact that Native Americans on reservations would be the judges within their own legal systems.

Granting Native Americans jurisdiction over local tribes in abuse and neglect cases could reduce state intervention that results in excessively high rates of removal and non-Indian placement of Indian children. As Calvin Isaacs, Chief of the Mississippi Band of Choctaw Indians, testified before a 1978 House Subcommittee: "Probably in no area is it more important that tribal sovereignty be respected than in an area as socially and culturally determinative as family relationships." An Oglala Sioux resolution reached a similar conclusion. If Native Americans are evaluated based on the values of their own culture, they could continue to maintain their culture by following its values.[41]

Cultural Information

Given the evidence that families who are not from the dominant culture or class appear to be disproportionately subject to its penalties in family law, excluding cultural evidence exacts a high price from those families. If family law standards for abuse and neglect were modified to take cultural information into account they would include a statement such as the following:

> Evaluation for abuse or neglect shall include *as one factor to be considered,* recognition of relevant cultural values of the family being evaluated.

Adoption of such a standard would *not* be dispositive. Much as with the decision in *Regents* v. *Bakke,* where race could be used as one factor in college admissions, so too, ethnicity, cultural background, or economic class would be relevant in making an equitable evaluation of allegations of abuse or neglect. However, because blanket acceptance of cultural or class information could lead to defense of violence against children it must be considered *only* as *one* factor in making an appropriate evaluation.

A cultural defense that mitigates *criminal responsibility* "where acts are committed under a reasonable, good-faith belief in their propriety," based upon the actor's "cultural heritage or tradition" was allowed in *People* v. *Croy* in 1990.[42] Such a cultural defense in the context of the family might be usefully compared with the "battered wife syndrome" or the Vietnam veteran defense.[43]

Inclusion of cultural information would generate a host of questions. For example, what definition of "culture" or "dominant culture" would be legally acceptable? On what basis would a court accept or reject use of cultural information in a family law case? Would recognition of cultural information violate international standards of human rights? How could one prevent the misuse of expert testimony by psychologists, sociologists, or anthropologists? What could be done to increase the level of knowledge of judges and health care professionals who make the decisions that so profoundly affect low income and ethnic minority families?

Exclusion of such evidence, however, will *certainly* continue to harm members of the non-dominant groups within American society. In recommending changes in *criminal* law procedures, the rationale from a recent law review article is clearly applicable to the problems of *family law* addressed in this essay:

> [T]he massive overrepresentation of people of color is the result, at least in part, of the inability or unwillingness of judges and juries from the dominant culture to understand, without information aimed at overcoming their ignorance, the perceptions or actions of people from minority cultures.[44]

QUESTIONS FOR THOUGHT AND DISCUSSION

1. Is the rape of a woman by her husband morally justifiable? What are some of the arguments that have been given for an affirmative answer to this question? Are these arguments persuasive? Explain.

2. Even if marital rape is not morally justifiable, it might be argued that the state has no business prohibiting such acts by law. What reasons have been or might be given for taking this position? According to Linda Jackson, are these reasons persuasive?

3. What are some of the reasons for the traditional reluctance of the legal system to intervene in cases of domestic violence? Are these reasons similar to those given for nonintervention in cases of marital rape? Explain.

4. What is the "public/private" distinction? Why do Linda Bell and David Archard both claim that the distinction has done more harm to women and children than it has done them any benefit?

5. Why does bell hooks believe that the term "battered woman" is not an appropriate phrase to characterize the woman who has been the victim of a single act of violence committed against her by someone with whom she has been intimate?

6. Linda Jackson indicates that in some cases of marital rape, the defense has been that a man's rape of his wife is not as harmful as the rape of a stranger. Compare Jackson's response to this defense with the remarks made by bell hooks about the damage that is done to a woman who is struck only once by a man with whom she is having an intimate relationship.

7. What are some differences between classes and cultures in childrearing standards and standards of appropriate behavior between husband and wife?

8. Should the standards of behavior of one class or culture be employed by the legal system to judge the behavior of other classes or culture? For ex-

ample, if it is the practice of a particular culture to scar the faces of their male children or to mutilate the genitals of their female children, should these practices be prohibited and prosecuted as child abuse under U.S. law?

9. What are the limits to what we should regard as morally or legally acceptable forms of childrearing practices? Compare Philip Fetzer's proposals with William Ruddick's "Life Prospects Principle" (Chapter 11).

FURTHER READING

David Archard, *Sexual Consent.* Oxford: Westview Press, 1998.

Natalie Abrams, "Problems in Defining Child Abuse and Neglect." In Onora O'Neill and William Ruddick, eds., *Having Children.* New York: Oxford University Press, 1979.

Ola W. Barnett, Cindy Miller-Perrin, and Robin Perrin, eds., *Family Violence Across the Lifespan.* Thousand Oaks, CA: Sage, 1997.

Catherine MacKinnon, *Feminism Unmodified: Discourses on Life and the Law.* Cambridge, MA: Harvard University Press, 1987.

Diana E. H. Russell, *Rape in Marriage,* 2nd ed. Bloomington: Indiana University Press, 1990.

Murray A. Strauss and Richard J. Gelles, *Physical Violence in American Families.* New Brunswick: Transaction, 1990.

NOTES

Linda Jackson

1. John Stuart Mill, *The Subjection of Women* (1869).

2. Letter from Lucy Stone to Antoinette Brown (1855), in Diana E. H. Russell, *Rape in Marriage* (2d. ed. 1990), p. 27.

3. Today 17 states have no marital rape exemption.

4. Sir Matthew Hale, *The History of the Pleas of the Crown* (P. R. Glazebrook ed., Biddles Ltd. 1971) (1736), p. 629.

5. *The Queen v. Clarence,* 22 Q.B. 23 (Cr. Cas. Res. 1888), at 57 (Field, J.).

6. R. v. R., 3 W.L.R. (H.L. 1991).

7. The New York Court of Appeals, in one of the most widely cited cases declaring marital rape exemptions unconstitutional, stated that "rape is not simply a sexual act in which one party does not consent. Rather, it is a degrading, violent act . . . To ever imply consent to such an act is irrational and absurd." *People v. Liberta,* 474 N.E. 2d 567, 573 (N.Y. 1984), *cert. denied,* 472 U.S. 1010 (1985).

8. *State v. Smith,* 426 A.2d 44 (N.J. 1981).

9. William Blackstone, *Commentaries* (Llayston Press, 1966) (1765), p. 430.

10. Note, "To Have and to Hold: The Marital Rape Exemption and the Fourteenth Amendment," *Harvard Law Review,* vol. 99 (1986), p. 1255.

11. 445 U.S. 40 (1980) . . .

12. Rollin M. Perkins, *Criminal Law* (2d ed. 1969), p. 156.

13. Perkins, ibid., p. 156.

14. Michael G. Hilf, "Marital Privacy and Spousal Rape," *New England Law Review,* vol. 16 (1980), p. 34.

15. *Liberta,* 474 N.E. 2d at 574.

16. *People v. DeStafano,* 467 N.Y.S. 2d 506, 517 (1983).

17. Note, p. 315.

18. See, e.g., *People v. Liberta,* at 567.

19. Ibid., at 574.

20. Cynthia A. Wicktom, "Focusing on the Offender's Forceful Conduct: A Proposal for the Redefinition of Rape Laws," *George Washington Law Review,* vol. 56 (1988), pp. 399, 401.

21. John H. Wigmore, *Evidence* (James H. Chadbourne ed., rev. ed. 1970) (1904), p. 737.

22. *People v. Liberta,* ibid., 567, 574.

23. Martin D. Schwartz, "The Spousal Exemption for Criminal Rape Prosecution," *Vermont Law Review,* vol. 7 (1982), pp. 50–51.

24. Note, ibid., p. 315.

25. Hilf reasons that because a married person maintains a lesser expectation of personal autonomy than an unmarried person, the affront to one's personal autonomy is by definition less in the case of marital rape than non-marital rape. Hilf, ibid., p. 41.

26. Russell refers to marital rape as "the most dreadful form of rape," as terrifying and life-threatening as stranger rape, yet carrying with it powerful senses of betrayal, disillusionment, isolation and self-blame. Ibid., p. 198.

27. Rape crisis centers report that victims of spousal rape are some of the most seriously injured women they encounter. Schwartz, ibid., p. 46.

28. David Finkelhor, Ph.D., Address to the New York County Lawyer's Association (May 3, 1984).

Linda Bell

1. Catherine MacKinnon, "Feminism, Marxism, Method, and the State: Toward Feminist Jurisprudence," in *Feminism and Methodology,* ed. Sandra Harding (Bloomington: Indiana University Press, 1987), p. 46.

2. David Kirp, Mark G. Yudof, and Marlene Strong Franks, *Gender Justice* (Chicago: The University of Chicago Press, 1986), p. 32.

3. William James. "A Review [of] 1. *Women's Suffrage, the Reform Against Nature,* by Horace Bushnell, New York, Scribner, 1869, [and] 2. *The Subjection of Women,* by John Stuart Mill, New York, Appleton, 1869." in *Visions of Women,* ed. Linda A. Bell, Clifton, NJ: Humana Press. 1983, p. 362.

4. Virginia Woolf, *Three Guineas* (New York: Harcourt Brace Jovanovich, 1938), p. 142.

5. MacKinnon, "Feminism, Marxism, Method, and the State," p. 148.

6. Catherine MacKinnon, *Feminism Unmodified: Discourses on Life and Law,* p. 100.

7. Kirp et al., pp. 17, 62, 72.

8. Ibid., pp. 149, 19.

9. Letty Cottin Pogrebin, *Among Friends: Who We Like, Why We Like Them, and What We Do with Them* (New York: McGraw-Hill, 1987), p. 251.

10. Andrea Dworkin, *Intercourse* (New York: Free Press, 1987), pp. 97, 122, 155–59.

11. Ibid., 59.

12. Ibid., pp. 147–48.

13. Nancy Fraser, "What's Critical about Critical Theory? The Case of Habermas and Gender," in *Feminism as Critique: On the Politics of Gender,* ed. by Seyla Benhabib and Drucilla Cornell (Minneapolis: University of Minnesota Press, 1987), p. 36.

14. Andrea Nye, *Feminist Theory and the Philosophies of Man* (New York: Croom Helm, 1988), p. 24.

15. Iris Young, "Impartiality and the Civil Public: Some Implications of Feminist Critiques of Moral and Political Theory," in Butler, p. 74.

16. Patricia Hill Collins, *Black Feminist Thought: Knowledge, Consciousness and the Politics of Empowerment* (New York: Routledge, 1990), p. 49.

Philip Fetzer

1. Judith Areen, *Cases and Materials on Family Law,* Westbury, N.Y.: Foundation Press, 1992, 1376.

2. Lundy Langstron, "Political and Social Construction of Families Through Pedagogy in Family Law Classroom," 73 *Denver University Law Review* 179 (1995).

3. Areen, op. cit.

4. Holly Maguigan, "Cultural Evidence and Male Violence: Are Feminist and Multiculturalist Reformers on a Collision Course in Criminal Courts?" 70 *New York Law Review* 36, 61 (1995).

5. *Statistical Abstract of the United States 1995,* Washington, D.C.: 1995, 19, 215.

6. Kristyn Walker, "Judicial Control of Reproductive Freedom: The Use of Norplant as a Condition of Probation," 78 *Iowa Law Review* 779, 808, n.286, 292–293 (1993), Murray A. Straus and Richard J. Gelles, *Physical Violence in American Families,* New Brunswick: Transaction Publishers, 1990, 323.

7. Caleb Foote, et al., *Cases and Materials on Family Law* 3d ed., Boston: Little Brown & Co. 1985, 433–434. Italics mine.

8. Laurence Houlgate, *Family and State,* Totowa, N. J., 1988, 147.

9. 406 Federal Supplement 10 (1975).

10. Id., 18.

11. Id.

12. 455 U.S. 745, 747–748 (1982).

13. Id., 762.

14. Id., 762–763.

15. Wendy Anton Fitzgerald, "Maturity, Difference, and Mystery: Children's Perspectives and the Law," 36 *Arizona Law Review* 11, 62 (1994).

16. Jeanne Louise Carriere, "Representing the Native American Culture, Jurisdiction, and the Indian Child Welfare Act," 79 *Iowa Law Review* 585, 604 (1994).

17. Natalie Abrams, "Problems in Defining Child Abuse and Neglect," in Onora O'Neill and William Ruddick, *Having*

Children, New York: Oxford University Press, 1979, 157.

18. Areen, op. cit. A 1991 Health and Human Services study indicated that of the reported victims of child abuse 55% were white, 26% were black and 9% were Hispanic. See: Costin, Lela, et al., *The Politics of Child Abuse,* New York: Oxford University Press, 1996, 145.

19. Fitzgerald, op. cit., 62.

20. Jacinda T. Townsend, "Reclaiming Self-Determination: A Call for Interracial Adoption," 2 *Duke Journal of Gender Law and Policy* 173, 183 (1995).

21. Straus and Gelles, op. cit., 322–323.

22. Walker, op. cit., 808–809.

23. Dorothy Roberts, "Punishing Drug Addicts Who Have Babies: Women of Color, Equality, and the Right of Privacy," 104 *Harvard Law Review* 14219, 1434 (1991). In cases where children have been removed from families and later returned, the average length of time for whites is two years but four years for African-Americans. Mary Pride, *The Child Abuse Industry,* Winchester, IL: Crossway Books, 1986, x.

24. Noel A. Cazenave and Murray A. Straus, in Straus and Gelles, op. cit., 326, 336.

25. Angela L. Carrasquillo, *Hispanic Children and Youth in the United States,* New York: Garland Publishing, 1991, 71–81.

26. Murray A. Straus and Christine Smith, in Straus and Murray, op. cit., 356.

27. Id., 364.

28. Id., 346. Research on Hispanic communities in California "demonstrates that the tendency for the poor to evidence higher incidences of problematic behavior [associated with reports of child abuse] may not be true for the Latino population." See: Costin, n. 19 supra, 148, citing the work of David Hayes-Baustista at UCLA.

29. William Byler, in Steven Unger, ed., *The Destruction of American Indian Families,* Association on American Indian Affairs: New York, 1977, 1–3.

30. Id., 3.

31. Carriere, op. cit., 604.

32. Daniel H. Swett, "Cultural Bias in the American Legal System," 4 *Law and Society Review,* 79, 101 (1969).

33. Amy Guttman, "The Challenge of Multiculturalism in Political Ethics," *Philosophy and Public Affairs,* Vol. 22 No. 3, 189 (1993).

34. Maguigan, op. cit., 63.

35. "Indian Tribe Beginning to Face Up to Child Abuse," *San Francisco Chronicle,* August 12, 1996, A10.

36. Maguigan, op. cit., 84. A Danish actress was arrested in New York after leaving her 14-month-old daughter in a stroller right outside a plate-glass window of a restaurant. The child's American father was also taken into custody. While viewed as "abuse" by many New Yorkers, this action would have been viewed as acceptable behavior in Denmark. Both were held in jail for two nights and later released. Harden Blaine, "Child Parked on New York Sidewalk Causes Stir," *Los Angeles Times,* May 14, 1997.

37. "Egyptian Girl Dies After Genital Mutilation," *New York Times,* August 25, 1996, 18.

38. Layli Miller Bashir, "Female Genital Mutilation in the United States: An Examination of Criminal Asylum Law," 4 *American University Journal of Gender and the Law* 415 (1996), 416. Parents who approve of female genital mutilation (FGM) believe that if the procedure is not performed their daughters would be viewed as immoral and that they would be unable to find a husband. Id. at 426. Bashir believes that "[e]ducation aimed at the cultural perceptions surrounding the benefits of FGM is regarded as the single most important factor in combating the practice." Id. at 434.

39. Myrna Oliver, "Immigrant Crimes; Cultural Defense—A Legal Tactic," *Los Angeles Times,* July 15, 1988, 1, 28.

40. Townsend, op. cit., 184.

41. Carriere, op. cit., 604–605.

42. Taryn F. Goldstein, Comment: Cultural Conflicts in Court: Should the American Criminal Justice System Formally Recognize a 'Cultural Defense'? 99 *Dickinson Law Review* 141 (1994). *People* v. *Croy* No. 5258 (Placer County Superior Court Apr. 1990). A cultural defense based on "anti-Indian sentiment" was permitted by the judge.

43. Id., 164. Both defenses address the actor's state of mind when the crime was committed. Successful applications of the defenses serve to mitigate criminal responsibility.

44. Maguigan, op. cit., 99.

IV

Parents and Children

9

The Ethics of Creating
a Family

Introduction

G. E. M. Anscombe, "Why Have Children?"

Bonnie Steinbock and Ron McClamrock,
"When Is Birth Unfair to the Child?"

Sherry L. Floyd and David Pomerantz,
"Is There a Natural Right to Have Children?"

Hugh LaFollette, "Licensing Parents"

Nancy Jecker, "Conceiving a Child to Save a Child:
Reproductive and Filial Ethics"

Why have a child? G. E. M. Anscombe regards this question as one that most persons would not have asked prior to the twentieth century. She compares it to the question: Why digest food? She asks us to imagine a future society in which people no longer had to digest food in order to be nourished by it. Her point is that the question "Why digest food?" is not asked today because we have no alternative; we must digest in order to be nourished. By analogy, contraception and abortion make it relatively easy for us not to have children; and this fact provides the condition for asking the question "Why have a child?"

Anscombe is writing from the Catholic tradition of natural law. Within this tradition human life is believed to have incommensurable value, that is, it has a value that cannot be measured, and thus cannot be weighed or balanced against any other value, such as autonomy or the free choice to do what one wants with one's body. Since the fetus is a human life, Catholics argue that it is always morally wrong to do something with the intent to kill it: the human fetus has incommensurable value. But the question "Why have a child?" presupposes that one has the option not to have a child. Of course, one may not intend to marry, and this may be all that one means when one says that one intends not to have a child. But if one marries, then Anscombe's point is that the intention not to have a child may itself be morally wrong since it presupposes that one might take steps to prevent conception or, if pregnant, to prevent the birth of the child, both of which are morally wrong because they are a violation of the natural law.

Anscombe's essay raises many questions. For example, one might question her analogy between deciding to refrain from digesting food and deciding to refrain from having a child by preventing pregnancy or having an abortion. And one might also wonder why a decision to prevent a natural process (such as digestion) from occurring should be faulted on moral grounds. If it should become physically possible at some future time to get nourishment without eating and digesting food, would it be morally wrong to do this? If not, then how could similar grounds be used to morally object to a decision to prevent or discontinue a pregnancy?

Another question that Anscombe gets us to think about is whether there are any morally unacceptable *motives* for having a child. At the conclusion of her essay, she writes that we should think of a child as "an occasion of love—to be embraced, not like those 'occasions' to be avoided—by destruction." Suppose, however, that a couple discovers that the fetus has a physical disorder so severe that it is highly probable that when born it will lead a brief, terrible life. They decide to have an abortion in order to prevent this outcome. Is this motive for abortion consistent with thinking of a child as "an occasion of love," or shall we conclude that even in tragic cases like this the couple sees their child as "an occasion for destruction"?

In their essay "When is Birth Unfair to the Child?" Bonnie Steinbock and Ron McClamrock argue that unless a decent minimum can be provided, then a decision to have a child can be criticized on moral grounds. They call this "the principle of parental responsibility," and they argue that it implies not only that persons who make "loving, concerned parents" will want their child to have a life that is worth living, but that it is unfair *to the child* to bring it into the world with "the deck stacked against it."

Steinbock and McClamrock would reject the idea that there is a natural right to have children. Anscombe, on the other hand, would probably regard the question "Is there a right to have a child?" to be as pointless as the question "Is there a right to digest food?" But what do we mean when we assert a natural right to have children? S. L. Floyd and David Pomerantz argue that it means "the natural liberty of all persons to introduce new beings into the world for whom they will care," where the word "natural" means "assertible by all persons equally and by virtue of the fact that they are persons."

Is there such a right? S. L. Floyd and D. Pomerantz argue that if there is, it does not follow from the right to autonomy, where this is understood either as the right to do with my body what I will or the right to self-determination. Their conclusion is that there is no theoretical basis for opposing a proposal to restrict childbearing—say, by requiring that persons obtain a license before they can bear a child. Hence, the only remaining grounds for opposition are practical.

In "Licensing Parents," Hugh LaFollette argues that since child rearing is a potentially harmful activity, the state has an interest in regulating it. LaFollette then rebuts several practical objections to a parent-licensing program. He isolates some "striking similarities" between the licensing program he proposes and current policies on the adoption of children. He argues that "if we retain these adoption policies—as we surely should—then, I argue, a general licensing program should also be established."

But this still leaves open the question "Why have a child?"—that is, "Why *exercise* this right?" This question would receive a variety of answers, for example:

"To have someone to care for me in my old age." "To have someone to love and who would love me in return." "To carry on the family name (blood line, etc.)." The answer given by Abe and Mary Ayala in Nancy Jecker's essay is rare: "To provide a potential donor of bone marrow for another family member."

Do some motives for having a child make this act morally wrong? Some philosophers have argued that motives are irrelevant to the evaluation of conduct—the only thing that counts are the consequences, good and bad, of the act itself. If the Ayalas' older daughter's life is saved by the bone marrow donated by her new sister, then this makes the act of giving birth to the new child morally permissible, so long as the infant does not suffer adverse consequences from the surgery. Other philosophers contend that motives are all that matters when conduct is evaluated. For example, Kant argued that in dealing with other persons we should always be motivated by a concern to treat them as ends in themselves, never merely as means to an end. Did the Ayalas violate this principle when they conceived and gave birth to their new child? If not, are there any other grounds for thinking that their behavior was morally suspect?

In attempting to answer this question, Nancy Jecker examines several arguments that might be used to support the claim that the Ayalas' act of conceiving a child in order to save their daughter's life was morally wrong. First, it is harmful to relationships within the family by treating the infant's body as a good to be manufactured and used. Second, the future relationship between the Ayalas and their new child might be harmed because their relationship was initiated with ulterior objectives. Third, if the Ayalas hide the reasons for her conception from their new child, this will harm their relationship with her. Fourth, conceiving a child to benefit another fails to accord proper respect to the child-to-be.

Why Have a Child?

G. E. M. Anscombe

Elizabeth Anscombe is professor of philosophy at Cambridge. She is generally regarded as one of the leading British philosophers of the twentieth century.

This very title tells of the times we live in. I would like you to imagine a title for a lecture eighty years hence: "Why digest food?" I leave it to the reader to imagine—or think of—the technology already with us; and the "scientific advance" and its practicalities, including the resultant apparatus ending in tubes with needles and switches in every house. Also the successful pro-

Excerpted from G. E. M. Anscombe, "Why Have a Child?" *American Catholic Philosophical Association, Proceedings* 63 (Washington, DC: 1990), pp. 48–53. Published by permission of the American Catholic Philosophical Association.

paganda denigrating the "merely biological" conception of eating and the hostility—known to have prevailed in the Catholic church for many centuries—towards its pleasure and thereby towards its spiritual meaningfulness and its civilized quality. As whole peoples in our time have regarded feeding their babies at the breast as something rather for savages, so might people of the future regard nourishment by digesting the lovely food we eat in the same way.

Don't think it inconceivable. The human race is a fallen race. It has fits of madness, sometimes merely local, sometimes nearly global. Let us imagine something rather nearer the spirit of our own time. Couldn't a government have a five-year plan—no more children this coming five years; there are enough of us for the present, and this is a solid population measure? . . .

Indeed, my suggestion of a plan to reduce the human race extensively does not sound likely to work. . . . But at most what has been effective has been so among what we call the advanced nations. But let us stretch our imaginations. A religion sweeps the world whose cardinal tenet is that the human race is too ghastly, too horrible in its ways of going on: it is a crime to perpetuate it. Everyone must be sterilized. This might be a sacrifice with a religious note in it, like that of the members of a Russian Christian sect who castrated themselves. But is it unreasonable to think of the human race as so evil? Think of the Aztecs cutting out the hearts of the captured among the peoples subject to them and piling them up as sacrifices before their frightful deities. Think of the many-armed statues of an Indian god or goddess, with as many means of killing as the many hands and a belt of human skulls. And think of us—encouraging lustful pretenses and confident of killing the resultant offspring. Either these things are good, and proofs that the destruction of human beings is desirable, or they are proofs that the human race is so thoroughly evil that it would be better to bring it to an end.

So you can see that if I ask this question in a general sort of way "Why have children?" the answer that the race will die out unless people do, is one that assumes that this would be a bad and regrettable thing—which may not be agreed.

The original natives of Tasmania, it is said, were a lot of them exterminated—white settlers not wanting them to be there. Indeed I have heard that at some stage the whites went in a line with a long rope across the whole island to make sure of no one escaping. It is also said that there were a remnant who were shipped off to some other but uninhabited island, and left to get on as they might. They were too depressed to reproduce themselves and so died out. Whether these stories are true, of course, I don't know. Certainly I have the impression that there aren't any aboriginal Tasmanians. True or not, this appears to us a

sad story. But by what means can we be confident that this might not happen to the human race that we know? Perhaps Neanderthal man died out like that. Several of the nations of Europe and North America look in a fair way to do so too.

Well, arguments about the continuation of the human race may have to confront replies expressing positive hostility or mere indifference to it.

What should we say to that? I don't know. I don't know how we can know—without prophetical revelation or a blind belief in the care of God in face of all the evidence, that our dreadful race is not better all damned (a proof of God's justice) or all abolished . . .

I have only imagined such policies, together with the thought that humans are mad enough to embrace them. Let me revert to my title: "Why have children?"—for my considerations so far have just concerned the attitudes which might make the world, or part of it, say "Why indeed?"

Luckily we don't seem to be faced with such attitudes in our time. On the other hand, the questions "Why have children?", "Shall we try to have children?" have become natural ones. . . . Formerly that now natural question would have been a natural one only in the minds of a pair who did not propose to marry or set up any very permanent relationship. Otherwise the question would have seemed absurd. You marry, you set up to live together or the like, and if not barren you expect to have children, they will come. But now the situation is greatly changed. Bernard Berenson took another man's wife, made her his, and got her pregnant. He insisted that she have the baby aborted. His life was not to be inconvenienced by babies.

An Indian woman was once reproached by some Westerner for having babies—India's population was too big and she was adding to it. The government didn't want there to be so many babies. She asked her interlocutor: "Will the government take care of me when I am old?" So she had a definite reason to reject the possibility offered her of seeing to it that she didn't have babies, or another baby. And because of this possibility, it is a perfectly familiar idea that a married couple should ask themselves "Shall we have children?" (Or an equivalent couple: marriage hasn't so much point now.)

There is, however, actually a desire to have children, or at least a child. You get married, you don't want a family straight away, you want a child some time. The time comes, and the woman conceives. And now we perceive the remarkable thing, that she has an abortion because tests suggest that the baby might be handicapped. It is odd indeed: kill the baby, just in case, and try to get a perfect one—one over whom there hangs no threat. The reason, suggested to me by a philosophical daughter, and which I found convincing, was: a baby is a luxury, an expensive one at that, a special thing to have. So, just as you'd not buy a car that you learned might be faulty in inconvenient ways, but go for the best you can afford, so you won't take the risk of an imperfect specimen if you can be forewarned. You'll get rid of it, if told the tests suggest it may be imperfect. You won't say "Well, if it's twins joined together in some awkward way, I'll take it the Lord's given me them to raise and he'll help me to raise them." That is something heard of sometimes—but not often . . .

It did not seem formerly that you had to be brave to exemplify those truths. (For the case I have sketched was a real one, and the mother was pressed to leave the babies in the "care" of the hospital.) It might be courage grimly to put up with what happened, once it had happened. But then you didn't know it was likely to happen. Now you have the choice: to kill (or leave to be killed) or to say: "If there's anything wrong with our baby, we are going to look after it and love it; no, we aren't going to kill our baby, or leave it for doctors and nurses to kill." This itself is different from that other attitude I sketched, that of saying "Well, we may have a grim time, having an imperfect child; but we'll put up with it as best we can—we'll have to, after all, won't we?" But it is even further from: "If there's even a small probability of its being handicapped, deformed, idiotic, we won't take the risk, we'll get rid of it."

This last attitude is an attitude of people who want a child—perhaps even want children—but what for? Not for loving except as one loves something that does one credit. Formerly there was not that often a choice, not for vast numbers of people. I have described the common attitude.

Why have children? Well, they come along, they happen, don't they? What a funny question "Why have children?" is. "Why want children?"—that's a different thing. Maybe you've been married for years and not managed to get one and you passionately want one, you look with envy and sorrow on those who are so lucky. But "Why have children?" was a question that simply didn't arise except for some who were wicked enough to not want them and think of ways of preventing them from ever being conceived, or destroying them if they were.

I suppose that very few who were unmarried wanted children, except as part of being married. Children to an unmarried woman were a disgrace to her, children without a known father earned the disreputable name of "bastard" (still a word of fighting talk in England). A bastard was not likely to have much of a good time. Another example of the wickedness of our race—this *fomes peccati,* tinder of sin, was not destroyed by Christianity, by baptism. Christians are capable of looking on a child as someone who ought not to exist—a bastard, the child of a priest unfaithful to his obligation perhaps. If we do so, we ought to reflect that by that standard none of us ought to exist, none can claim that there is no bastardy in their lines of descent from Adam—not our Lord himself. The race of men that he redeemed is a set of humans who would not have existed if Adam had not fallen.

Now, some people much want a child, but it's got to be a son. So they find out what it is, so as to kill it if it's a girl. Not an altogether new thing, though in other ages and places they waited for the birth.

It is distressing to live in a world where this question "Why have children?" so intelligibly presents itself—as "Why digest food?" does not. The purpose of my paper has been in the first place by that comparison, to show what a weird distorted question it is. The weirdness of the question forces our attention, however, on this: as we used to hear of "occasions of sin," we should now, because of this question, if we did not before, think of a child as an occasion of love—to be embraced, not like those "occasions" to be avoided—by destruction.

When Is Birth Unfair to the Child?

Bonnie Steinbock and Ron McClamrock

Bonnie Steinbock is professor of philosophy and Ron McClamrock associate professor of philosophy at the University at Albany, SUNY.

Consider the case of a teenager who wants a baby. Most people would agree that teenagers should not have babies. Teenagers who become mothers severely limit their own educational and job opportunities. They are more likely to be poor, and to raise families in poverty. In addition, teenage mothers tend to have babies whose birthweight is low, a condition associated both with a significantly higher mortality rate than that of normal-sized babies and with learning disabilities in the future. Children of teenagers are also unlikely to get adequate mothering, as their mothers are still children themselves. While there are no doubt exceptions, in general, young teenagers lack the maturity and stability necessary to be good parents. For all these reasons, it would be better if teenagers did not have babies.

Notice that many of these reasons appeal to the harmful physical and psychological effects on future children. A young girl who waits until she is older will give her child a better start in life; therefore, even if she herself does not mind having fewer opportunities and living in poverty, she ought to wait, we might say, for the sake of her child. However, this claim bears closer examination. [Derek] Parfit points out that a young girl who is contemplating having a child cannot make that child better off by waiting. If she delays childbirth, she will give birth not to that child, but to a different child, who will develop from a different egg and sperm. The child she will have if she becomes pregnant now cannot be born at a later time. It is either birth to a teenage mother, or no life at all.[1]

This simple fact has provocative implications. If we maintain that it is for the sake of the child she would bear that she should avoid pregnancy, we seem to be committed to the view that it

would be better never to be born at all than to be born to a very young mother. But this is surely implausible. Being born to a teenage mother isn't ideal, but neither can it be said to be so bad as to make nonexistence preferable. Despite the hardships they undergo, despite the fact that they might have preferred having an older mother, most children of very young mothers are probably glad they were born. If they were asked, "Would you prefer to have the life you have now, with a fourteen-year-old mother, or not to have been born at all?" they would choose life.

What conclusions should we draw from this? We might conclude—implausibly—that it is not wrong for fourteen-year-olds to decide to have children. Or we might conclude that the reasons why it is wrong all have to do with the deleterious effects on the young girls themselves, on their parents, and on society in general. But to say this is to leave out the idea that having children under very adverse conditions is unfair *to them*. Can we make clear and coherent the prima facie plausible idea that it is unfair for parents to bring children into being without some reasonable prospects at a nonmiserable life? . . .

The Principle of Parental Responsibility

A principle of parental responsibility should require of individuals that they attempt to refrain from having children unless certain minimal conditions can be satisfied. This principle maintains that in deciding whether to have children, people should not be concerned only with their own interests in reproducing. They must think also, and perhaps primarily, of the welfare of the children they will bear. They should ask themselves, "What kind of life is my child likely to have?" Individuals who will make good parents—that is, loving, concerned parents—will want their children to have lives well worth living and will strive

Reprinted from *Hastings Center Report*, vol. 24, no. 6 (1994), 15–21. Reprinted by permission.

to give them such lives. But what if the parents cannot give their children even a decent chance at a good life? The principle of parental responsibility maintains that under such conditions, it is better not to have children, and that it is in fact unfair to children to bring them into the world with "the deck stacked against them."

Although a principle of parental responsibility requires individuals to refrain, when possible, from having children if they cannot give them a decent chance of a happy life, this of course does not imply that responsible parents of born children should be willing to kill them if their lives fall below a certain standard. Given a child with severe handicaps, considerable pain, and a very limited life (but still a life the child finds worth living) parents should choose treatment that will allow their child to go on living as he or she wants, all things being equal—we're not assuming that issues about availability and cost of treatment or the like couldn't bear on the decision as well. Given a preference for life, it is not in general the parents' place to decide that the child would be better off dead.

When the child is too young to have preferences, the parents will have to judge whether continued life is in the child's best interest. Depending on the prognosis, a reasonable judgment might be made either way. A decision to stop life-prolonging treatment could be consistent with, or possibly even required by, the responsibility the parents have to the child.

But where there is no child at all, the question facing the prospective parents is not, What does my child want? nor, What is best for my child? It's rather a question of whether to create a child who is likely to have a life marked by pain and severe limitations. It seems to us that the answer to this question must be no. Anyone willing to subject a child to a miserable life when this could be avoided would seem to fail to live up to a minimal ideal of parenting.

We've claimed that a child's being tied to a miserable life may well count strongly against bringing the child into existence. However, the fact that a child would have a happy life if brought into existence does not obligate its putative parents to have the child. If one decides not to have

a child, one harms no one. It is not as if there are people in the wings, so to speak, hoping to get the gift of life. No one is injured or made unhappy or deprived by nonbirth.[2] By contrast, if one decides to have a child, then there will exist a real person, with needs and interests that must be considered. Mary Anne Warren expresses the point this way:

> Failing to have a child, even when you could have had a happy one, is neither right nor wrong. . . . But the same cannot be said of having a child, since in this case the action results in the existence of a new person whose interests must be taken into account. Having a child under conditions which should enable one to predict that it will be very unhappy is morally objectionable, not because it violates the rights of a presently existing potential person, but because it results in the frustration of the interests of an actual person in the future.[3]

How Bad Is Too Bad?

The principle of parental responsibility maintains that prospective parents are morally obligated to consider the kinds of lives their offspring are likely to have, and to refrain from having children if their lives will be sufficiently awful. But what is sufficiently awful? Laura Purdy considers the example of Huntington disease, a lethal genetic disorder.[4] Symptoms, which usually appear between ages thirty-five and fifty, include spasmodic, involuntary movements, as well as personality changes (moodiness, paranoia, violent behavior, manic activity), memory loss, and chronic depression. The disease lasts approximately fifteen to twenty years. At the end, the patient has degenerated to the point of being totally physically disabled and unable to communicate.[5] Huntington disease inflicts severe and prolonged suffering on its victims. It is a horrible way to die. Purdy maintains that individuals at high risk of transmitting a serious disease to their offspring are unable to provide them with "at least a normal opportunity for a good life" and therefore such individuals should not reproduce.

However, judgments about the value of life are inescapably subjective. They vary depending on the individual's experience, personality, and general approach to life. Purdy acknowledges that not everyone will concur with her conclusion that individuals at risk of transmitting Huntington disease should refrain from procreating, because not everyone will share her pessimistic assessment of life with the disease. She writes:

> Optimists argue that a child born into a family afflicted with Huntington's chorea has a reasonable chance of living a satisfactory life. . . . Even if it does have the illness, it will probably enjoy thirty years of healthy life before symptoms appear. . . . Optimists can list diseased or handicapped persons who have lived fruitful lives. They can also find individuals who seem genuinely glad to be alive. (p. 313)

Arlo Guthrie seems to have taken the optimistic point of view. His father, Woody Guthrie, died of Huntington disease, which means that Arlo has a 50 percent risk of developing it himself. Despite this, Arlo decided to have children, thereby imposing on each child a 25 percent chance of inheriting the disease. Of course, if Arlo did not have the disease, as now seems likely, then his children would not be affected. But he could not have known this at the time he decided to procreate. Therefore, he was taking a 50 percent chance that he would be passing on Huntington disease to his children. How could he justify this risk? Perhaps he reasoned as follows: "I haven't had a tragic life. I've had a very good life. The goodness of my life will not be destroyed if it turns out that I have Huntington. I won't regret having been born, or resent my parents for having had me. So why is it wrong for me to have kids? I can give them a decent chance for a good life— as good a life as I had." If this is a good argument, then even if we accept Purdy's principle regarding the wrongness of reproducing if one cannot give one's potential offspring a reasonable chance at a satisfactory life, we might not accept Huntington disease as coming under Purdy's principle.

A stronger case for the moral obligation not to reproduce exists in the case of HIV-infected women, who run the risk of transmitting AIDS to their offspring. John Arras asks, "Ought such women to forgo child-bearing for the sake of children who would have been born infected? If

already pregnant, should they abort 'for the sake of the fetus'?"[6] AIDS is a painful and, so far as we know, invariably fatal disease. The aggregate median survival time for infected children is about thirty-eight months from the time of diagnosis. The baby who develops AIDS does not get thirty (much less forty or fifty) healthy years, like the person with Huntington disease. Symptoms show up fairly early on, and for most afflicted children, their lives will be filled with considerable suffering. How, it may be asked, could someone aware of these facts even consider deliberately having a child?

The moral obligation of HIV-infected women to avoid conception is complicated by two factors. First, there is a pretty good chance that such women will not pass the virus on to their babies. Current studies indicate that the risk of actual perinatal HIV infection through any given pregnancy is somewhere between 20 and 30 percent. Second, the severity of the disease varies widely. The most severely afflicted children present with adult-style opportunistic infections, such as *Pneumocystis carinii* pneumonia, during the first year of life. These children face painful death within a month or two after diagnosis. Such children have lives that clearly qualify as "wrongful." However, other children develop far milder manifestations, are diagnosed at a later date, and live much longer. Arras says:

> Only a relatively small percentage (say, 10 to 20 percent) of those born HIV infected actually fit the worst-case scenario of early infection, chronic hospitalization, and death before the age of two. The rest will develop different and often less lethal manifestations of AIDS later on and will live longer, perhaps to the age of ten or beyond. The longer these children live with a tolerable quality of life, the more their lives will be worth living. A child who lives at home, goes to school, and attends summer camp does not fall into the same category as a Tay-Sachs baby. (p. 365)

Nevertheless, even the better-off AIDS babies have lives that are, in Arras's phrase, "decidedly grim." More than half will die before the age of seven, and the remainder must live under a cloud of impending death with progressively deteriorating immune systems. In addition, most infected babies are born to mothers (and fathers) who are themselves dying. Many of these parents are too sick to care for their own children, who are often abandoned in hospitals or put in foster care. When the medical and the social realities are considered, even an optimist should concede that it is very unlikely that an HIV-infected woman will be able to provide her baby with a reasonable (much less a normal) chance at a good life. Therefore, knowingly to conceive a child under such conditions is morally wrong.

The basic idea is that before embarking on so serious an enterprise as parenthood, people should think about the consequences for their offspring. Some circumstances may be so awful that birth is unfair to the child. However, the principle of parental responsibility says only that it is wrong to bring children into the world when there is good reason to think that their lives will be terrible. It does not suggest that people should not have children unless conditions are ideal, still less that only conventional childrearing circumstances are morally permissible. Consider, for example, the enormous fuss raised recently by the story of a fifty-nine-year-old British woman who gave birth to twins on Christmas Day 1993. The eggs, donated by a younger woman and fertilized in vitro by the older woman's husband, were implanted into her at a private fertility clinic in Rome. Doctors in London had earlier refused to perform the procedure because they believed she was too old to face the emotional stress of being a mother. Virginia Bottomley, the British Secretary of Health, told the BBC, "Women do not have the right to have a child. The child has a right to a suitable home." But as the *New York Times* put it in an editorial:

> What makes Ms. Bottomley believe the twins won't have a suitable home? Youth is no guarantee of parenting skills: all too often the contrary is the case. And how would Ms. Bottomley define the homes in which parentless children are raised by grandmothers? Are they, ipso facto, unsuitable?

Undoubtedly, pregnancy poses special risks for many postmenopausal women, but most IVT programs carefully screen out candidates who are not in excellent condition. If society is going to decide which women are physically unsuited for pregnancy, it might start with young teenagers, as pregnancy in children who are not yet full grown is risky for both the mother and the baby. And young teens are probably less well equipped emotionally to be good parents than women in their fifties or sixties.

Another worry is that post-menopausal women won't live long enough to rear their children. According to Gail Sheehy, author of *Passages* and *The Silent Passage: Menopause:* "It's not a very nice prospect for a child of 10 or 12 to go to sleep every night, praying that his or her mother will live as long as he needs her."[7] However, many women live into their eighties and nineties these days. The Italian doctor who helped the fifty-nine-year-old British woman give birth accepts only patients who have a life expectancy of at least twenty more years, based on their age and family history. They must be nonsmokers and pass psychological and physical tests. These are conditions we do not require of any other mothers. Nor are they conditions imposed on fathers. Telly Savalas, the television star of *Kojak,* recently died at the age of seventy. The fact that he left behind school-age children was not even a subject of comment, much less outrage. It seems likely that the opposition to older women having babies expresses a prejudice against what is new or unconventional, rather than a position that can be rationally justified. So long as a woman is emotionally and physically equipped to be a reasonably good mother, there is no reason why age should be an absolute barrier for women, any more than it is for men.

Life is always a mixture of good and bad, pleasure and pain. We know that our children will have their share of suffering and adversity; that is the price of the ticket. This fact should stop no one who wants children from having them. At the same time, the judgment that the child you will conceive is likely to have a life that falls below a decent minimum provides a strong reason to avoid procreation. In some cases, all that is necessary is to postpone parenthood, as in the example of the young teenager who wants to have a child. The principle of parental responsibility tells her to wait, because if she does, she will be a much better parent to the child she eventually has. In other cases, where the risk is transmitting a disease, whether a genetic condition, such as sickle-cell anemia or cystic fibrosis, or a viral illness, such as AIDS, postponing pregnancy will not help. Prospective parents will have to base their decision on such factors as the risk of transmission, the nature and seriousness of the disease, the availability of ameliorative therapies, the possibility of a cure, and their ability to provide the child with a good life despite the handicap. The principle of parental responsibility does not provide a formula for deciding such cases. Reasonable people can differ on what a decent chance at a happy life is, and what risks are worth taking.

Throughout this essay we have been assuming that parenthood is deliberately chosen, something that is not always—perhaps not even typically—true. In many parts of the world, fertility is not so easily controlled, and becoming a parent is more a question of what happens to one than a deliberate choice. The principle of parental responsibility is aimed only at those individuals who are capable of controlling their fertility, and of making a conscious decision whether to have children.

Is There a Natural Right to Have Children?

Sherry L. Floyd and David Pomerantz

Sherry Floyd is an attorney with the Department of Justice in Washington, D.C.
David Pomerantz is Minority Staff Director, Rules Committee, House of Representatives.

There is a tale told today about the history of having children that we have come to believe. It seems that for the first time raising a family is a matter of choice. With choice, however, comes responsibility, and so we consider it particularly appropriate to this era to discuss the morality of having children. Such a story only reveals our myopia.

In fact, people have long considered it their prerogative to have or to not have a family. The ancients, for example, considered it the right of parents to decide whether to bring up children, although they made their choice at a later stage than we now do. In Greece, if a couple elected not to raise a child, it was acceptable to throw it into a river or onto a dung heap, or expose it on a hill, "prey for birds or food for wild beasts to rend."[1] Roman essays entitled "How to Recognize the Newborn That is Worth Rearing" and "Should Every Child that Is Born Be Raised" manifest a similar attitude; unwanted children

could be disposed of after they were born because parents had the right to make this choice. Aristippus rehearses the argument for the rights of parents to dispose of their children: "for do we not cast away from us our spittle, lice and such like, as things unprofitable, which nevertheless are engendered and bred even out of our own selves?"[2]

Though we now condemn infanticide, we retain the assumption that people have the natural right to have children when they so choose. It is this assumption that our essay explores. . . . Ought we to recognize the natural liberty of all persons to introduce new beings into the world for whom they will care? We ask, are the wishes of potential parents owed special consideration over another person's, whose interests are affected by their choice to have children?

Autonomy and the Right to Have Children

In attempting to establish the existence of such a right, we note that a right to have children appears to reflect our autonomy. It seems that to deny me the liberty to have children is not to respect me as an autonomous agent. Perhaps, it is

Previously published in John Arthur, ed., *Morality and Moral Controversies* (Englewood Cliffs, NJ: Prentice-Hall, 1981), 131–138. Reprinted by permission of the authors.

on this basis that there is a natural right to have children. Now, we ask, why does the liberty to have children seem to be connected with autonomy? There are two answers. First, to recognize my liberty to have children, it may be argued, is to recognize my right to do with my body what I will. But it may not be simply autonomy with respect to my body which is at issue here. Being a parent is often an important part of one's self-conception; in this respect, the liberty to have children may be a part of one's right to self-determination. We will explore these suggestions in this section. There are intriguing consequences for the right to have children if it is based on our right to be respected as autonomous. But our most startling conclusion is that there is no sound moral argument that can show that the right to have children follows from the right to autonomy.

One way to understand bodily autonomy is to think of the body as an owned object. This body belongs to me, and thus it is up to me to decide how it shall be used and what shall be done to it. If I want my appendix or the hair under my arms removed, others ought to recognize my liberty to so decide. Of course, this right does not grant permission to use my body in ways that violate others' rights. The right to do with my body as I will no more permits me to strangle you than the right to use my baseball bat as I will permits me to bop you over the head.

What does this mean for the right to have children? The matter appears quite straightforward. The right to do with our bodies as we will yields a right to make love and bear the consequences. Bodily autonomy implies a right to have children. To deny the right to have children seems to require one to interfere with the right to have sex or to prevent the consequences by means of more direct intrusion on the bodies of participants. We will withhold evaluation of this argument, for the moment.

For now, let us consider what restrictions might apply to the right to have children if it is based on bodily autonomy. First of all, it is important to note that our right to use our bodies jointly toward a certain end requires that we both consent to the goal. In the usual way in which children are conceived, two people are needed. As a conse-

quence, no one can appeal to the right to have children to demand that another person bear a child. This is brought out clearly when we base the right to have children on the right to use one's body as one will; we cannot force others to use their bodies in ways that we wish. This line of argument, however, does permit people to agree to let their bodies be used in the production of children. On this view, the right to sell one's sperm or rent one's womb is akin to the punter's right to make contracts for his foot's services.

There is another restriction on the right to have children based on bodily autonomy. This right does not extend to having children by certain extraordinary means. One cannot, for example, claim a right to have a test-tube baby or to clone oneself on this basis. Doing either alternative is not simply doing with one's body what one will; such a person relies upon having access to the latest scientific research and method for reproduction.

The second restriction, in particular, suggests the problem with subsuming the right to have children under bodily autonomy. A child is not merely the physical product or extension of my body in the way that my hair is. Although it is convenient to speak of the baby as the product of a woman's labor, it is a misleading metaphor if we fail to recognize that the baby is a distinct being. Children become (or can become) full persons, our moral equals. A right to have children based on the potential parent's bodily autonomy neglects this other locus of moral rights, insofar as it treats the child as a mere appendage.

Can the right to self-determination fare any better as the basis for the right to have children? There is some reason for hope. The right to self-determination is the right to develop a self-conception and act on it. One determines for oneself what are the goals worth seeking and the vocational or cultural interests worth pursuing. After well-informed deliberation, one leads the kind of life one thinks one should. To think about oneself in certain ways or to lead a certain sort of life is beyond the scope of bodily autonomy. Another important feature is this: Some self-conceptions can be pursued in isolation and others cannot. If I wish to develop my muscles, for example, this does not require me to relate to others in any special ways. However, If I seek to share a long-term commitment with another, this essentially involves being related to another. It is a necessary condition for acting on some of my self-conceptions that I relate to others in special ways. The right to have children would fall under this rubric.

We can examine the right to be married as an instance of the relational right to self-determination and then see how it compares with the right to have children. Now, what does the right to be married entail? Does my right to be married imply that others ought not interfere with my being married? It would seem not. Surely you can refuse to marry me. Your refusal would interfere with my being married. By refusing to marry me, however, you do not violate my rights. If the right to self-determination includes the right to act on a self-conception that essentially involves being related with another person, it cannot require others to accede to my wishes.

But does self-determination generate an analogous right to have children? The right to be married is similar to the supposed right to have children in an important respect. Bearing and raising a child can be as significant to being the sort of person I wish to be as being married is. But there are some respects in which the right to be married and the presumed right to have children are disanalogous. These are both rights which require being related to another person in special ways. But while one can agree to be married, no one can consent to being born. There is no being to speak for itself on the matter. So our argument is: Since one can have a relational right based on self-determination only if all parties to the relation consent, and no one consents to be introduced into the world by someone else, it follows there is no relational right to be a parent.

One might object that we should retain the right to be a parent and speak of that right as coming into conflict with a right not to be born. For example, it is wrong for us to conceive a child that we know will lead a short but miserable life, not because the child fails to consent, but because it has a right not to be born which outweighs our right to be parents. While this description seems

plausible, here are our reasons for rejecting it. First, we have metaphysical qualms about attributing to nonexistent beings a right to remain nonexistent. Qualms aside, if we accept the conflict of rights description of this situation, must we not similarly describe other conflicts between relational rights? Suppose I want to be married and the person I want to marry detests me. A person who endorses the conflict of rights objection must suppose that in this case my right to be married is outweighed by the other's right not to be married. Surely, that's not correct. I have no right to marry someone unless that person agrees to marry me. Our objector might reply that we have failed to distinguish between a general right to be married and a right to be married to a particular person. The general right to be married stands whether or not anyone consents, whereas the right to marry a particular person requires the consent of another. Analogously, there may be a general right to have children. But, this reply can be easily countered. The right to be married does not dissipate when another chooses not to consent because someone else could consent. There are many fish in the sea. The alleged right to be a parent is not similar in that respect. It is not as if a particular being dissents from being a child where another can say yes; no being can consent or refuse to be born since there is no being to do it. So, the relational right of being a parent never arises because nothing can agree to be a child.

Some defend the relational right to be a parent on the ground that although no one does consent, some people would have consented to being born. What does it mean to say, "I would have consented to being born"? It does not make sense to say that if I were asked before I was conceived, I would agree to be born. There is no one to whom one might direct the question. The alternative is to understand hypothetical consent as: would I now give my consent to having been born?

There are two responses to this justification of the right to be a parent. First, if it is based on the hypothetical consent of the child, the right to have children seems severely restricted. No one has a right to produce children who would prefer not to have been born. It is this which potential parents must take into consideration and given the possibility of congenital defects, or the horrors of being raised by parents such as me, or even the woeful conditions of this world, the scope of the right to have children may be greatly diminished.

Let us clarify two points about hypothetical consent. First, such consent entails that I consider, in the present, what it would have been like had I not chosen to be born. That is certainly an odd consideration. In any event, hypothetical consent to being born is saying that I am content to have been born. But, saying this is possible only as a result of being born and raised in this manner by my parents. And, it is these parents who bear and raise me that need my consent in order to have the right to be parents. Consider this example: A spiritual leader brings me to believe I want to be a disciple. It is analogous in that my present consent to the relationship results from my having been in the relationship. The way in which I came to be content with the relationship is not specified. I might be brainwashed or, in some other way, de-

viously influenced. Insofar as my present consent to having been brought into this relationship can arise in these unacceptable ways, this sort of hypothetical consent should not have justificatory force. So the right to be a parent should not be based on hypothetical consent. For these reasons, there is no relational right to have children based on self-determination.

We have analyzed the right to have children based on the right to autonomy, specifically in terms of the right over one's body and the right to self-determination. My right to do with my body what I will cannot found the right to create and raise another autonomous being. If the right to have children were based on the right to self-determination it would be unlike all other relational rights insofar as it does not respect the autonomy of all the people engaged in the relationship. It does not take into account the impossibility of a being's actual or hypothetical consent to becoming a child. Thus, we conclude that the right to have children cannot be derived from respect for the autonomy of potential parents.

Licensing Parents

Hugh LaFollette

Hugh LaFollette is professor of philosophy at East Tennessee State University. He is the author of many articles and essays in social and political philosophy.

In this essay I shall argue that the state should require all parents to be licensed. . . . My strategy is simple. After developing the basic rationale for the licensing of parents, I shall consider several objections to the proposal and argue that these objections fail to undermine it. I shall then isolate some striking similarities between this licensing program and our present policies in the adoption of children. If we retain these adoption policies—as we surely should—then, I argue, a general licensing program should also be established. . . .

From Hugh LaFollette, "Licensing Parents," *Philosophy and Public Affairs* 9, 2 (1980): 183–197. Reprinted by permission of Princeton University Press. © 1980 Princeton University Press.

Regulating Potentially Harmful Activities

Our society normally regulates a certain range of activities; it is illegal to perform these activities unless one has received prior permission to do so. We require automobile operators to have licenses. We forbid people from practicing medicine, law, pharmacy, or psychiatry unless they have satisfied certain licensing requirements.

Society's decision to regulate just these activities is not ad hoc. The decision to restrict admission to certain vocations and to forbid some people from driving is based on an eminently plausible, though not often explicitly formulated, rationale. We require drivers to be licensed because driving an auto is an activity which is potentially harmful to others, safe performance of the activity requires a certain competence, and we have a moderately reliable procedure for determining that competence. The potential harm is obvious: incompetent drivers can and do maim and kill people. The best way we have of limiting this harm without sacrificing the benefits of automobile travel is to require that all drivers demonstrate at least minimal competence. We likewise license doctors, lawyers, and psychologists because they perform activities which can harm others. Obviously they must be proficient if they are to perform these activities properly, and we have moderately reliable procedures for determining proficiency. Imagine a world in which everyone could legally drive a car, in which everyone could legally perform surgery, prescribe medications, dispense drugs, or offer legal advice. Such a world would hardly be desirable.

Consequently, any activity that is potentially harmful to others and requires certain demonstrated competence for its safe performance is subject to regulation—that is, it is theoretically desirable that we regulate it. If we also have a reliable procedure for determining whether someone has the requisite competence, then the action is not only subject to regulation but ought, all things considered, to be regulated. It is particularly significant that we license these hazardous activities, even though denying a license to someone can severely inconvenience and even harm that person. Furthermore, available competency tests are not 100 percent accurate. Denying someone a driver's license in our society, for example, would inconvenience that person acutely. In effect that person would be prohibited from working, shopping, or visiting in places reachable only by car. Similarly, people denied vocational licenses are inconvenienced, even devastated. We have all heard of individuals who had the lifelong dream of becoming physicians or lawyers, yet were denied that dream. However, the realization that some people are disappointed or inconvenienced does not diminish our conviction that we must regulate occupations or activities that are potentially dangerous to others. Innocent people must be protected even if it means that others cannot pursue activities they deem highly desirable.

Furthermore, we maintain licensing procedures even though our competency tests are sometimes inaccurate. Some people competent to perform the licensed activity (for example, driving a car) will be unable to demonstrate competence (they freeze up on the driver's test). Others may be incompetent, yet pass the test (they are lucky or, certain aspects of competence—for example, the sense of responsibility—are not tested). We recognize clearly—or should recognize clearly—that no test will pick out all and only competent drivers, physicians, lawyers, and so on. Mistakes are inevitable. This does not mean we should forget that innocent people may be harmed by faulty regulatory procedures. In fact, if the procedures are sufficiently faulty, we should cease regulating that activity entirely until more reliable tests are available. I only want to emphasize here that tests need not be perfect. Where moderately reliable tests are available, licensing procedures should be used to protect innocent people from incompetents.

These general criteria for regulatory licensing can certainly be applied to parents. First, parenting is an activity potentially very harmful to children. The potential for harm is apparent: each year more than half a million children are physically abused or neglected by their parents. Many millions more are psychologically abused or neglected—not given love, respect, or a sense of self-worth. The results of this maltreatment are obvious. Abused children bear the physical and psychological scars of maltreatment throughout their lives. Far too often they turn to crime. They are far more likely than others to abuse their own children. Even if these maltreated children never harm anyone, they will probably never be well-adjusted, happy adults. Therefore, parenting clearly satisfies the first criterion of activities subject to regulation.

The second criterion is also incontestably satisfied. A parent must be competent if he is to avoid harming his children; even greater competence is required if he is to do the "job" well. But not everyone has this minimal competence. Many people lack the knowledge needed to rear children adequately. Many others lack the requisite energy, temperament, or stability. Therefore, childrearing manifestly satisfies both criteria of activities subject to regulation. In fact, I dare say that parenting is a paradigm of such activities since the potential for harm is so great (both in the extent of harm any one person can suffer and in the number of people potentially harmed) and the need for competence is so evident. Consequently, there is good reason to believe that all parents should be licensed. The only ways to avoid this conclusion are to deny the need for licensing *any* potentially harmful activity; to deny that I have identified the standard criteria of activities which should be regulated; to deny that parenting satisfies the standard criteria; to show that even though parenting satisfies the standard criteria there are special reasons why licensing parents is not theoretically desirable; or to show that there is no reliable and just procedure for implementing this program.

While developing my argument for licensing I have already identified the standard criteria for activities that should be regulated, and I have shown that they can properly be applied to parenting. One could deny the legitimacy of regulation by licensing, but in doing so, one would condemn not only the regulation of parenting, but also the regulation of drivers, physicians, druggists, and doctors. Furthermore, regulation of hazardous activities appears to be a fundamental task of any stable society.

. . . In the following section, I shall examine several practical objections designed to demonstrate that even if licensing were theoretically desirable, it could not be justly implemented.

Practical Objections
to Licensing

. . . The first objection is that there may not be, or we may not be able to discover, adequate criteria of a good parent. We simply do not have the knowledge, and it is unlikely that we could ever obtain the knowledge, that would enable us to distinguish adequate from inadequate parents.

Clearly there is some force to this objection. It is highly improbable that we can formulate criteria that would distinguish precisely between good and less than good parents. There is too much we do not know about child development and adult psy-

chology. My proposal, however, does not demand that we make these fine distinctions. It does not demand that we license only the best parents; rather it is designed to exclude only the very bad ones. This is not just a semantic difference, but a substantive one. Although we do not have infallible criteria for picking out good parents, we undoubtedly can identify bad ones—those who will abuse or neglect their children. Even though we could have a lively debate about the range of freedom a child should be given or the appropriateness of corporal punishment, we do not wonder if a parent who severely beats or neglects a child is adequate. We know that person isn't. Consequently, we do have reliable and usable criteria for determining who is a bad parent; we have the criteria necessary to make a licensing program work.

The second practical objection to licensing is that there is no reliable way to predict who will maltreat their children. Without an accurate predictive test, licensing would be not only unjust, but also a waste of time. Now I recognize that as a philosopher (and not a psychologist, sociologist, or social worker), I am on shaky ground if I make sweeping claims about the present or future abilities of professionals to produce such predictive tests. Nevertheless, there are some relevant observations I can offer.

Initially, we need to be certain that the demands on predictive tests are not unreasonable. For example, it would be improper to require that tests be 100 percent accurate. Procedures for licensing drivers, physicians, lawyers, druggists, etc., plainly are not 100 percent (or anywhere near 100 percent) accurate. Presumably we recognize these deficiencies yet embrace the procedures anyway. Consequently, it would be imprudent to demand considerably more exacting standards for the tests used in licensing parents.

In addition, from what I can piece together, the practical possibilities for constructing a reliable predictive test are not all that gloomy. Since my proposal does not require that we make fine line distinctions between good and less than good parents, but rather that we weed out those who are potentially very bad, we can use existing tests that claim to isolate relevant predictive characteristics—whether a person is violence-prone, easily frustrated, or unduly self-centered. In fact, researchers at Nashville General Hospital have developed a brief interview questionnaire which seems to have significant predictive value. Based on their data, the researchers identified 20 percent of the interviewees as a "risk group"—those having great potential for serious problems. After one year they found "the incidence of major breakdown in parent-child interaction in the risk group was approximately four to five times as great as in the low risk group."[1] We also know that parents who maltreat children often have certain identifiable experiences; for example, most of them were themselves maltreated as children. Consequently, if we combined our information about these parents with certain psychological test results, we would probably be able to predict—with reasonable accuracy—which people will maltreat their children.

However, my point is not to argue about the precise reliability of present tests. I cannot say emphatically that we now have accurate predictive tests. Nevertheless, even if such tests are not available, we could undoubtedly develop them. For example, we could begin a longitudinal study in which all potential parents would be required to take a specified battery of tests. Then these parents could be "followed" to discover which ones abused or neglected their children. By correlating test scores with information on maltreatment, a usable, accurate test could be fashioned. Therefore, I do not think that the present unavailability of such tests (if they are unavailable) would count against the legitimacy of licensing parents.

The third practical objection is that even if a reliable test for ascertaining who would be an acceptable parent were available, administrators would unintentionally abuse that test. These unintentional mistakes would clearly harm innocent individuals. Therefore, so the argument goes, this proposal ought to be scrapped. This objection can be dispensed with fairly easily unless one assumes there is some special reason to believe that more mistakes will be made in administering parenting licenses than in other regulatory activities. No matter how reliable our proceedings are, there will always be mistakes. We may license a physician who, through incompetence, would cause the

death of a patient, or we may mistakenly deny a physician's license to someone who would be competent. But the fact that mistakes are made does not and should not lead us to abandon attempts to determine competence. The harm done in these cases could be far worse than the harm of mistakenly denying a person a parenting license. As far as I can tell, there is no reason to believe that more mistakes will be made here than elsewhere.

The fourth proposed practical objection claims that any testing procedure will be intentionally abused. People administering the process will disqualify people they dislike, or people who espouse views they dislike, from rearing children.

The response to this objection is parallel to the response to the previous objection, namely, that there is no reason to believe that the licensing of parents is more likely to be abused than driver's license tests or other regulatory procedures. In addition, individuals can be protected from prejudicial treatment by pursuing appeals available to them. Since the licensing test can be taken on numerous occasions, the likelihood of the applicant's working with different administrative personnel increases and therefore the likelihood decreases that intentional abuse could ultimately stop a qualified person from rearing children. Consequently, since the probability of such abuse is not more than, and may even be less than, the intentional abuse of judicial and other regulatory authority, this objection does not give us any reason to reject the licensing of parents.

The fifth objection is that we could never adequately, reasonably and fairly enforce such a program. That is, even if we could establish a reasonable and fair way of determining which people would be inadequate parents, it would be difficult, if not impossible, to enforce the program. How would one deal with violators and what could we do with babies so conceived? There are difficult problems here, no doubt, but they are not insurmountable. We might not punish parents at all—we might just remove the children and put them up for adoption. However, even if we are presently uncertain about the precise way to establish a just and effective form of enforcement, I do not see why this should undermine my licensing proposal. If it is important enough to protect children from being maltreated by parents, then surely a reasonable enforcement procedure can be secured. At least we should assume one can be unless someone shows that it cannot.

An Analogy with Adoption

So far I have argued that parents should be licensed. Undoubtedly many readers find this claim extremely radical. It is revealing to notice, however, that this program is not as radical as it seems. Our moral and legal systems already recognize that not everyone is capable of rearing children well. In fact, well-entrenched laws require adoptive parents to be investigated—in much the same ways and for much the same reasons as in the general licensing program advocated here. For example, we do not allow just anyone to adopt a child; nor do we let someone adopt without first estimating the likelihood of the person's being a good parent. In fact, the adoptive process is far more rigorous than the general licensing procedures I envision. Prior to adoption the candidates must first formally apply to adopt a child. The applicants are then subjected to an exacting home study to determine whether they really want to have children and whether they are capable of caring for and rearing them adequately. No one is allowed to adopt a child until the administrators can reasonably predict that the person will be an adequate parent. The results of these procedures are impressive. Despite the trauma children often face before they are finally adopted, they are five times less likely to be abused than children reared by their biological parents.

Nevertheless we recognize, or should recognize, that these demanding procedures exclude some people who would be adequate parents. The selection criteria may be inadequate; the testing procedures may be somewhat unreliable. We may make mistakes. Probably there is some intentional abuse of the system. Adoption procedures intrude directly in the applicants' lives. Yet we continue the present adoption policies because we think it better to mistakenly deny some people the opportunity to adopt than to let just anyone adopt.

Once these features of our adoption policies are clearly identified, it becomes quite apparent that there are striking parallels between the general licensing program I have advocated and our present adoption system. Both programs have the same aim—protecting children. Both have the same drawbacks and are subject to the same abuses. The only obvious dissimilarity is that the adoption requirements are more rigorous than those proposed for the general licensing program. Consequently, if we think it is so important to protect adopted children, even though people who want to adopt are less likely than biological parents to maltreat their children, then we should likewise afford the same protection to children reared by their biological parents.

I suspect, though, that many people will think the cases are not analogous. The cases are relevantly different, someone might retort, because biological parents have a natural affection for their children and the strength of this affection makes it unlikely that parents would maltreat their biologically produced children.

Even if it were generally true that parents have special natural affections for their biological offspring, that does not mean that all parents have enough affection to keep them from maltreating their children. This should be apparent given the number of children abused each year by their biological parents. Therefore, even if there is generally such a bond, that does not explain why we should not have licensing procedures to protect children of parents who do not have a sufficiently strong bond. Consequently, if we continue our practice of regulating the adoption of children, and certainly we should, we are rationally compelled to establish a licensing program for all parents.

However, I am not wedded to a strict form of licensing. It may well be that there are alternative ways of regulating parents which would achieve the desired results—the protection of children—without strictly prohibiting nonlicensed people from rearing children. For example, a system of tax incentives for licensed parents, and protective services scrutiny of nonlicensed parents, might adequately protect children. If it would, I would endorse the less drastic measure. My principal concern is to protect children from maltreatment by parents. I begin by advocating the more strict form of licensing since that is the standard method of regulating hazardous activities.

Conceiving a Child to Save a Child: Reproductive and Filial Ethics

Nancy Jecker

Nancy Jecker, Ph.D., is associate professor at the University of Washington School of Medicine, Department of Medical History and Ethics in Seattle. She is the editor (with Albert Jonsen and Robert Pearlman) of *Bioethics: An Introduction to the History, Methods, and Practice* (Boston: Jones and Bartlett, 1997) and *Aging and Ethics: Philosophical Problems in Gerontology* (Clifton, NJ: Humana Press, 1991). She is the author (with Laurence Schneiderman) of *Wrong Medicine: Doctors, Patients and Futile Treatment* (Baltimore, MD: Johns Hopkins University Press, 1995).

Reproductive and filial ethics raise moral questions that touch our most intimate relationships with other persons. Often, relationships within the family are infused with strong emotions that seem to defy rational argument. Many philosophers even doubt that ethical concepts, such as justice, apply at all in the context of filial relationships. Aristotle, for example, wrote that justice does not pertain to relationships between parents and offspring, because young children are an extension or part of their parents and "the just and the unjust always involve more than one person."[1] More recently, Ferdinand Schoeman has argued that "traditional moral boundaries, which give rigid shape to the self," do not apply in the context of intimate relationships, and that "talk about rights of others, respect for others, and even welfare of others is to a certain extent irrelevant."[2] Other philosophers direct little attention to filial ethics because they regard the family itself as illegitimate. Plato reckoned that in a just state wives and children must be held in common by guardians in order to prevent "whatever tears [the city] apart into many communities instead of one."[3] In our own day, Rawls has characterized the family as violating a principle of fair equality of opportunity and considered the possibility that the family should be abolished.[4]

One reason that contemporary moral philosophy may lend little assistance to persons wrestling with questions about filial ethics is that it tends to frame ethical questions against a backdrop of impersonal relationships. Kant, for example, concentrates on the moral law that holds for rational beings as such, not for rational beings as members of special groups and alliances, such as a family. Likewise, utilitarian ethics originally was developed to justify reforms in the British legal system and to craft a more humane system of punishment. Contemporary versions of utilitarianism focus on the effect actions have on the welfare of society at large and treat individual members as replaceable by other persons.

Contemporary ethical theory itself reflects the modern age. As Bernard Williams notes, inhabitants of the modern world achieve an immense amount through impersonal relations: "We do a great deal by relying on egoistic micro-motivations, and it is a remarkable achievement of the modern world to have brought this about. Indeed, it is obvious beyond a certain level of social size and complexity that we must rely a lot on such motivations."[5] Yet the presence of personal relationships in our lives is highly valued, even if seldom acknowledged. These relationships shape the very persons we become, and a life wholly void of personal relationships would hardly be worth living. We cannot hold personal relationships immune from ethical reflection, then, nor can we afford to neglect thinking about our ethical responsibilities in personal relationships without paying a high price. Not considering personal relationships in ethical terms may make us less sensitive to close associates in situations where we find spontaneous support difficult to muster. It also may make it possible for the status quo to persist in personal relationships where it falls far short of ethical standards and ideals.

From Nancy S. Jecker, "Conceiving a Child to Save a Child: Reproductive and Filial Ethics," *The Journal of Clinical Ethics* 1, 2 (Summer, 1990): 99–103. Copyright © 1990 The Journal of Clinical Ethics. Reprinted by permission of the publishers.

How should we begin, then, to view personal relationships in an ethical light? Although impartial theories may define, in broad brush, the contours of an ethics for personal relationships,[6] they cannot begin to complete a rich and finished picture. In this essay, I will examine some of the broad ethical guides that govern personal relationships generally, and filial relationships in particular. I focus this task by describing a specific case that raises ethical questions about reproduction and parenting.

The Case

In July 1989, a middle-aged couple from a Los Angeles suburb conceived a child to save the life of their teenage daughter who was dying of cancer. The couple, Abe and Mary Ayala, had learned two years prior that their daughter, Anissa, was suffering from leukemia and needed a bone marrow transplant to survive. Neither Anissa's parents nor her brother, Aaron, have compatible bone marrow. A search for a non-related donor has been fruitless to date.

When the Ayalas first decided to conceive a child their chance of success was slim.[7] Abe, forty-four years old, had to undergo an operation to reverse a vasectomy performed sixteen years earlier. The chance of vasectomy reversal leading to pregnancy is 50 percent. Mary, at the age of forty-two, had a 73 percent chance of becoming pregnant. Finally, the likelihood that any offspring Abe and Mary conceived would qualify as a bone marrow match for Anissa was 25 percent. Overall, the odds of Anissa's being cured of leukemia by her parents' efforts to conceive a child to save her was 6.4 percent.

To date, many of these obstacles have been overcome. On April 3, 1990 Mary delivered a baby girl, Marissa, who is a suitable donor for her sister. While it was not possible to collect stem cells from Marissa's umbilical cord during delivery, doctors predict that once the baby grows enough bone marrow, surgery to obtain bone marrow from Marissa's hip will have a 70 to 80 percent chance of success. Family members apparently are delighted about their youngest member. "She's my baby sister," Anissa declares, "and we're going to love her for who she is not for what she can give me."[8] Abe reflects that even if Anissa didn't survive, "we'd have another child in the house to help us with our sense of loss."[9]

Outside the family, the Ayalas' success is greeted with mixed emotions. Some argue that conceiving persons to benefit others insinuates the norms of production and commodification into the parent-child relationship. For example, George Annas asserts that "children aren't medicine" manufactured for other people.[10] Alternatively, it could be claimed that conceiving children to benefit others violates a principle that should guide ethical decision making regarding becoming a parent; namely, doing what will be best from the potential child's point of view.[11] It also could be contended that Marissa is likely to suffer psychological harm as a result of being conceived for the purpose of benefiting her sister. For example, she might be prone in the future to regard her worth as conditional on the benefits she can provide others. She might harbor resentment toward her parents for choosing to conceive her for this purpose, or toward her sister for reaping benefits from her conception. These feelings could present formidable obstacles to loving relationships within the family, and thereby handicap Marissa in the future. Family relationships profoundly shape our relationships with persons outside the family circle, and they influence the kind of person we strive to become. Finally, some have voiced the concern that conceiving a child for the purpose of saving another violates the principle of respect for persons, because it involves using a child as a means to another's end. "One of the fundamental precepts of ethics," Alexander Capron states, "is that each person is an end in himself or herself and is never to be used solely as a means to another person's ends without the agreement of the person being used."[12]

Depersonalizing Personal Relationships

Let us first consider whether conceiving children to benefit another family member is harmful to persons or to relationships within the family. One way harm might occur is that conceiving a child in this way imputes the norms of production into the parent-child relationship. It might be said, on the one hand, that producing Marissa in order to make bone marrow for her sister degrades Marissa, because it implies treating her body as a good to be manufactured and used. On the other hand, it could be argued that Mary's and Abe's procreative labor is itself degraded, because its primary function becomes making an object for use, rather than a child to love. If either of these objections is valid, then Marissa's conception may violate an important principle governing personal relationships: actions should not depersonalize personal relationships, for doing so does violence to what these relationships are and to the intentions, desires, and hopes persons have in becoming involved in them.[13]   In response, it might be argued that prior to Marissa's conception, she did not stand in a personal relationship to her future parents; therefore, the decision to beget her does not depersonalize a personal relationship. After all, even if we may feel personally related to nonexistent persons (for example, dead family members), the parties in personal relationships must be particular and nonsubstitutable individuals. For example, if I stand in a personal relationship to someone, then I must be the object of that person's attention. Prospective parents cannot possibly be personally involved with still-to-be-conceived offspring, since there is no particular future person that could be the object of this involvement. Even after Marissa's conception and birth, it could be maintained that the parent-child relationship does not yet qualify as personal. To have a personal relationship with someone might be thought to imply "mutuality of meaning—either verbal or sign—because shared meanings are necessary for the mutual agreement on meaning that form the basis of the relationship."[14]

Initiating Personal Relationships

Yet perhaps the ethics that apply to personal relationships also govern relationships that are likely to be personal in the future. For example, initiating a personal relationship with ulterior objectives is ethically suspect, because this may harm a future personal relationship. One reason harm might

occur is that the touchstone of having a personal relationship is that the motive for being in it and continuing it is that we value it for its own sake. For example, friends simply want to give and receive from one another because of the joy and value inherent in doing so.[15] In the case of the Ayalas, the relationship between Marissa and her sister, Anissa, could be harmed because Anissa comes to it in dire need. As John Hardwig states,

> If I see myself primarily as a being in need, I will be too focused on myself and my needs. I will then tend to depersonalize you as someone who can meet my needs. And I will also be generally unable to freely and joyously give . . . Characteristically and normatively, the appropriate motive for action in personal relationships is simply that we want to do these things.[16]

Likewise, the future intimacy between Marissa and her parents could be endangered because Mary and Abe established this relationship to aid their other child. In some respects, this would be analogous to a person learning that a man had shown romantic attention or initiated a sexual relationship in order to benefit someone else; for example, to benefit himself by making a former girlfriend jealous. In this case, the desire to initiate a personal relationship is born of some motive other than the desire to be in a personal relationship. Similarly, Marissa is conceived not because she is wanted, but because she can be useful. Hence, upon learning the reason for her conception, Marissa might feel betrayed.

Although these points initially may appear troublesome, upon reflection they are much less so. First, it is reasonable to suppose that intimacy and harmony already will have developed by the time Marissa is able to comprehend the circumstances of her conception. This intimate basis will make it more likely that harmony and good relationships can be restored if they are suspended or strained, because in once intimate associations the pain of disaffection and the desire for union offer strong motives for reconciliation.[17] Similarly, if the woman betrayed by the man who displays affection finds out about his initial motives after many years of intimacy, there would be good reason to think that intimacy between the two would not wither. Of course, reparations may not restore harmony automatically, or entirely eliminate bad feelings. For example, these feelings can continue to operate at an unconscious level. But even if there can be no guarantee that strong family relationships can be sustained, intimate associations always involve the risk of dissolution.

A second redeeming point is that, unlike other actions that can render personal relationships hurtful, the decision to conceive Marissa is not intended to hurt Marissa. For example, neither Abe, Mary, nor Anissa is motivated by spite or by a desire to harm Marissa. Quite the contrary, they say that they intend to love her. By contrast, someone who bestows romantic attention or sexual favors to make a former partner jealous does not intend to love the object of his favors (even if he later does).

In addition, it is far from clear that the act of conceiving Marissa for the purpose of benefiting Anissa could cause any tangible harm to Marissa. The argument here is that Marissa is better off having been conceived and living the life that she does, despite its added tensions, than she would be if she had never been conceived at all.[18] Presumably, Marissa will prefer to endure certain hardships so long as the hardships in question are necessary for her coming into existence.

Honesty in Personal Relationships

One way that her conception could impose a clear harm to Marissa is if she were not told about the surrounding facts. Once an intimate relationship is formed, parties to it should establish honest and open relations. This is partly owing to the fact that the more time people spend together, the less likely it is that they can keep up a dishonest front.[19] Each can maintain an artificial posture for only so long. Another consideration about honesty that applies in the context of close relationships is that intimates have more reason to reveal important details of their lives because such revelations create and sustain their intimacy. By contrast, withholding important facts can bar intimacy or

create the false appearance of intimacy where genuine intimacy is absent. False intimacy exists to varying degrees in personal relationships. It develops, for example, when we encourage distortions in another's view of us, or when we deny another's shortcomings. Shakespeare called these processes "love's best habit,"[20] and noted the costs associated with lovers' efforts to know each other. In the case of parent-child relationships, false intimacy would be created if, for example, Marissa's parents and sister concealed, altered, or denied the facts surrounding her conception. Yet there is no reason to expect that this will occur. Marissa's family does not express shame about their decision or view it as something to hide. As one commentator puts it, "By all appearances the Ayalas are not an exploitive family. To them the ethical questions that swirl around them are airy abstractions, not the terrifying reality they daily confront."[21]

Privacy in Personal Relationships

In addition, the Ayalas' decision can be defended on the grounds that a sphere of privacy surrounds families and protects their decisions about whether and when to procreate. Family privacy might be elaborated in terms of a "family privacy right," which is a right to be free from surveillance and interference within the internal workings of the family.[22] This right implies that Mary and Abe should be left alone in making decisions about whether to conceive a child. It implies more generally that we should reject the position that the state is the proper authority to making reproductive choices, a position which Plato states in stark terms: "If a man still of begetting years unites with a woman of child-bearing age without the sanction of the rulers . . . we shall say that he brings into the city an unauthorized and unhallowed bastard . . . born in darkness."[23]

Even if the state's interests did override a family's privacy right, it is unlikely that the state could bar couples from conceiving children where they are able to conceive on their own. Unlike conception that is carried out through new reproductive technologies and relies upon the assistance of others, reproductive acts between two consenting persons are far more difficult to control. Mary and Abe's sexual and procreative acts are as antithetical to regulation as are present efforts to prohibit consensual sodomy or homosexuality.

Respect for Individuals in Personal Relationships

Let us next turn to examine the question of whether conceiving a child to benefit another fails to accord proper respect to the child-to-be. One objection to Mary and Abe's decision was that respecting persons calls for treating persons as ends in themselves. According to this objection, by conceiving and bearing Marissa as a means to save their daughter's life, Mary and Abe treat Marissa as a means to their own end.

Yet this way of stating the objection glosses over important distinctions. First, parents have multiple reasons for conceiving, and it is not unethical if some of these involve using their child. For example, it is not unethical if a royal couple conceives to have an heir, or if a couple produces a second offspring to give their first a sibling, or if two people have a child to enrich their own lives. Second, reasons for reproducing reveal a lack of respect only if prospective parents do not also want and love their children. The point here is that there is nothing blatantly unethical about treating persons as means to our own ends. Using persons as means is unethical only when we regard persons as nothing but means. Respect for offspring requires recognizing, as Kant said, "that man, and in general every rational being exists as an end-in-himself, not merely as a means for arbitrary use by this or that will," and that a person "must, in all his actions, whether they are directed to himself or to other rational beings, always be viewed at the same time as an end."[24]

Understood in this way, Abe and Mary's decision to conceive Marissa fails to show respect toward her only if their sole reason for conceiving is to use Marissa, for example, as a means to save their other daughter's life, or to keep the house from feeling empty if their other daughter dies. But their statements and actions indicate that they intend to love Marissa for who she is, quite apart from what she can give. Thus, the Ayalas' action is morally different from a situation where a couple intends to conceive a child to serve as a bone marrow donor and abort the child if it is not medically useful. It also is morally distinct from a situation where a woman becomes pregnant with the sole intention of providing fetal tissue to a parent with Parkinson's disease, and then terminates her pregnancy. In these cases the desire to create a child is disassociated from any intention to raise a child and value it for its own sake. Thus in these instances prospective parents truly fail to respect the individual they call to life.

Now it might be argued that the injunction to treat rational beings always as ends does not even apply to Marissa, because she is not even minimally rational. Arguably, she will not be rational for some time to come. Her cerebral cortex did not form until late in the second trimester, and even well after birth she will not have developed her full rational powers. Kant states in *The Groundwork* that "every rational being exists as an end-in-himself." This suggests that being rational is sufficient for being valuable as an end in oneself. He also states that "nothing but the idea of the law in itself, which . . . is present only in rational beings . . . can constitute that preeminent good which we call moral." This last passage suggests that being rational is necessary for possessing moral value within oneself. Are Abe and Mary absolved of the responsibility to treat Marissa as an end on the grounds that Marissa is not yet a person?

To answer this question, let us consider next what form respect should take in the context of personal relationships. One way of elaborating the requirement of respect in close relationships is that Marissa should be treated always as an end by persons who stand in a special relationship to her, regardless of whether she possesses the intrinsic moral qualities that confer strict moral status. Unlike animals of similar cognitive functioning, Marissa is Mary and Abe's daughter, and she is Anissa and Aaron's sibling. Thus Mary, Abe, Anissa, and Aaron are not entitled to treat Marissa as they would treat any being of similar cognitive functioning. Even if Marissa were never to develop rationality or consciousness, she merits respect by virtue of her position in a family.[25] Regardless of whether Marissa is a person in the

Kantian sense, she is nonetheless a person in the social sense.[26]

Sacrifices in Personal Relationships

Should the above remarks quiet the concern that Marissa is not being fully or adequately respected, and that she deserves to be? One answer to this question is that treating persons as ends implies obtaining their consent before making them the subject of medical procedures. Since Marissa obviously cannot give consent, perhaps it is disrespectful to harvest her marrow for transplant. Ordinarily, Mary and Abe would be vested with the ethical authority to make this decision,[27] but it could be argued that their obvious stake in the situation biases their ability to dispassionately weigh the pros and cons of the decision.

However, the ethical requirement of respect takes different shape when placed against a backdrop of personal relationships. Where an antecedent tie or bond exists between the person who makes some sacrifice and the person who benefits, the requirements of respect subtly shift. Relationships vary in the degree to which they are personal, and the closer and more personal a relationship is, the stronger the claims it can make ethically on our allegiance. This is not to say that persons can legitimately exploit those with whom they are most intimate. Rather, it establishes that family members are governed by stronger ethical responsibilities than strangers, and we expect them to serve each other's welfare to a greater extent.

The ethical quandary with which Mary and Abe are left is where to draw the line. How much can they ask of one daughter on behalf of another? The operation Marissa may undergo to extract marrow from her hipbone involves slight pain and minimal risks. Thus, it is considerably less than asking Marissa to give a kidney or other organ. It would have involved still less sacrifice if Marissa's marrow could have been taken from her umbilical cord at birth. In either case, I would argue that the demands placed upon Marissa do not exceed the ordinary sacrifices family members make and expect from one another. Marissa's sacrifice differs only in that it requires her to give a tangible product. Ordinarily, the benefits we bestow upon family members are more intangible, such as time and energy, or love and affection. What we give up is often less tangible as well; for example, other ways of using that time and attention.

It might be said, in response, that parents are required to do far more for offspring than offspring are required to do for siblings. After all, we choose whether to conceive, bear, and rear children, but children do not choose to be siblings. Yet, even so, we still owe far more to siblings than to strangers because of the presence of a close relationship. However, it might be argued that families are not always a locus of intimacy and closeness. Thus, if filial duties are founded on intimacy, then merely being someone's sibling does not show that one is required to make special sacrifices. In reply, it should be noted that families in fact are a common locus of intimacy, because we live in a family for an extended period during early, formative years. The Ayala family's rallying around Anissa to save her life attests to the strength of their love. There is no reason to think that this love will not permeate Marissa's relationship with her sister.

Summary and Conclusion

I conclude that Mary and Abe's decision to conceive a child to save a child does not impose harm on persons or on relationships in the family. Nor does it evince a lack of respect for the child they have conceived. The ethical guidelines that support this conclusion can now be summarized. First, actions should not depersonalize or otherwise endanger personal relationships. Second, although ideally personal relationships are initiated and continued for their own sake, after a personal relationship has been established and sustained the motives for establishing it recede in importance. Third, the requirement of honesty looms especially large in the context of personal relationships. Fourth, privacy protects personal relationships in the family from intrusion by the state. Fifth, even if those with whom we stand in personal relationships are not fully rational or self-conscious, we should treat them with respect. Finally, persons often are called upon to make greater sacrifices in personal relationships.

These principles represent only the barest beginnings of an ethics for filial relationships.

Nonetheless, they mark progress in the direction of developing a more complete account. We should not suppose that ethics in the family always will be spontaneous or "natural."[28] Over a century ago, Mill warned that nature and natural are "one of the most copious sources of false taste, false philosophy, false morality, and even bad law."[29] Especially in the wake of medical advances, such as recombinant DNA and new reproductive technologies, the complexity of filial ethics will only increase. The demographics of an aging society will add further complexity to filial contexts.[30] We can hardly afford to cling tenaciously to the idea that ethical conduct in the family will issue forth in a spontaneous fashion.

QUESTIONS FOR THOUGHT AND DISCUSSION

1. Why does G. E. M. Anscombe compare the question "Why have a child?" to the question "Why digest food?" What point is she attempting to make with this comparison? Is the analogy a good one?

2. From the fact that it is technically possible to prevent pregnancy and childbirth, does it follow that it is morally permissible to do these things? Why would someone argue that it is not (always) morally permissible to prevent pregnancy or childbirth?

3. Anscombe suggests that when a woman has an abortion she thereby indicates that she did not think of her future child as "an occasion for love." Is this true?

4. According to Steinbock and McClamrock, it is not acceptable to bring children into the world when they are destined to have terrible lives. Can this claim be made consistent with Anscombe's suggestion that the only morally acceptable motive for having a child is that it is to be an occasion for love?

5. What is the "principle of parental responsibility"? What are the implications of this principle for the moral problem of abortion?

6. Under what conditions, if any, does a woman have a moral obligation not to reproduce? Are these conditions different than the conditions under which a man has a moral obligation not to reproduce?

7. What does one presuppose by the question "Is there a right to have a child?"

8. According to Floyd and Pomerantz, what do we mean when we assert a *natural* right to have a child?

9. If the right to have a child is derivative, then can it be derived from the right to autonomy? From the right to self-determination?

10. Is the right to have a child a basic right? Is it "self-evident"?

11. Are there any strong practical objections to a state program that would require potential parents to acquire a license as a condition for having a child?

12. If it is appropriate to require licensing for adoption, then why shouldn't we also require licenses in order to become a biological parent of a child?

13. Is it ever morally wrong to conceive a child? What would make it wrong? The motive for conceiving the child or the consequences of having the child?

14. What are some of the arguments (reviewed by Nancy Jecker) for claiming that it was morally wrong for Abe and Mary Ayala to conceive a child? Are these arguments sound?

15. Is it morally wrong for an infertile couple to use a "surrogate" to have a child? Suppose that the surrogate mother was the sister of a woman who could not conceive. The sister agrees to be artificially inseminated with the sperm of the infertile woman's husband. Compare this case with a situation in which the surrogate is an unrelated woman who is paid $10,000 to gestate and give birth to the child.

FURTHER READING

Lori B. Andrews, *Between Strangers: Surrogate Mothers, Expectant Fathers, and Brave New Babies.* New York: Harper and Row, 1989.

Lawrence E. Frisch, "Licentious Licensing: A Reply to Hugh LaFollette." *Philosophy and Public Affairs* 11, 2 (Spring 1982): 173–180.

Philip J. Greven, Jr., *Child-Rearing Concepts, 1628–1861.* Itasca, IL: Peacock Publishers, 1973.

Anthony Graybosch, "Parenting as a Profession: Children's Rights and Parental Responsibility." *Cogito* 2, 3 (September 1984): 95–107.

R. McIntire, "Parenthood Training or Mandatory Birth Control: Take Your Choice." *Psychology Today* (October 1973): 34–40.

Hugh LaFollette, "A Reply to Frisch," *Philosophy and Public Affairs* 11, 2 (Spring 1982): 181–183.

R. L. Perkins, ed., *Abortion: Pro and Con.* Cambridge, MA: Schenkman, 1974.

Scott B. Rae, *The Ethics of Commercial Surrogate Motherhood.* Westport, CT: Praeger, 1994.

John A. Robertson, *Children of Choice: Freedom and the New Reproductive Technologies.* Princeton: Princeton University Press, 1994.

Sharon E. Rush, "Surrogacy and Gay Fathers." In Robert C. L. Moffat, Joseph Grcic, and Michael D. Bayles, eds., *Perspectives on the Family,* 102–142. Lewiston, NY: Mellen Press, 1990.

William B. Weil, Jr., and Martin Benjamin, eds., *Ethical Issues at the Outset of Life.* Boston: Blackwell Scientific Publications, 1987.

NOTES

Bonnie Steinbock and Ron McClamrock

1. Derek Parfit, *Reasons and Persons* (Oxford: Clarendon Press, 1984), pp. 357–61.

2. Richard Brandt, "Morality of Abortion," in *Abortion: Pro and Con,* ed. R. L. Perkins (Cambridge, Mass.: Schenkman Publishing Company, 1974), pp. 151–69, at 163.

3. Mary Anne Warren, "Do Potential People Have Moral Rights?" in *Obligations to Future Generations,* ed. R. I. Sikora and Brian Barry (Philadelphia: Temple University Press, 1978), p. 25.

4. Laura M. Purdy, "Genetic Diseases: Can Having Children Be Immoral?" in *Ethical Issues in Modern Medicine,* ed. John Arras and Nancy K. Rhoden, 3rd ed. (Mountain View, Calif.: Mayfield Publishing Company, 1989), pp. 311–17.

5. C. L. Becker, "Legal Implications of the G-8 Huntington's Disease Genetic Marker," *Case Western Law Review* 39 (1988–89): 273.

6. John D. Arras, "AIDS and Reproductive Decisions: Having Children in Fear and Trembling," *Milbank Quarterly* 68, 3 (1990): 353–82, at 353.

7. Quoted in "How Far Should We Push Mother Nature?" *Newsweek,* 17 January 1994, p. 56.

S. L. Floyd and D. Pomerantz

1. Euripides, *Ion,* 504.

2. See Lloyd deMause, "The Evolution of Childhood" in Lloyd deMause, *The History of Childhood,* New York: Harper & Row, 1974. The Roman essays are by Musonius Rufus, "the Roman Socrates."

Hugh LaFollette

1. The research was reported by Ray Helfer in "Review of the Concepts and a Sampling of the Research Relating to Screening for the Potential to Abuse and/or Neglect One's Child," presented at a workshop sponsored by the National Committee for the Prevention of Child Abuse, 3–6 December 1978.

Nancy Jecker

1. Aristotle (1966). *Nichomachean Ethics,* trans. W. D. Ross (Oxford: Clarendon Press, 1966). See esp. 1138a19.

2. F. Schoeman, "Rights of Children, Rights of Parents and the Moral Basis of the Family" *Ethics,* 91 (1990), pp. 6–19. [Reprinted in this volume]

3. Plato (1974). *Republic,* trans. GMA Grube. (Indianapolis: Hackett Pub. Company, 1974), p. 123. [The Jowett translation of this passage is reprinted in this volume. –Ed.]

4. John Rawls, *A Theory of Justice* (Cambridge: Harvard University Press, 1971), p. 511.

5. B. Williams, "Formal Structure and Social Reality." In D. Gambetta (Ed.), *Trust: Making and Breaking Cooperative Relations* (Oxford: Basil Blackwell Press, 1989), pp. 3–13.

6. N. S. Jecker, "Impartiality and Special Relations." In D. T. Meyers, C. Murphy, & K. Kipnis (Eds.), *Kindred Matters: Rethinking the Philosophy of the Family* (Lewiston, NY: Edwin Mellen Press, 1993).

7. A. Toufexis, "Creating a Child to Save Another," *Time,* March 15, 1990, p. 56.

8. Ibid.

9. "Having a Baby to Save a Daughter," *New York Times,* February 17, 1990.

10. Quoted in Toufexis, "Creating a Child to Save Another."

11. Although this principle is stated in another context, it pertains in obvious ways to the case at hand. S. Callahan, "An Ethical Analysis of Responsible Parenthood," in A. M. Capron (Ed.), *Genetic Counseling: Facts, Values and Norms* (New York: Alan R. Liss, Inc., 1970), pp. 218–38.

12. "Having a Baby to Save a Daughter."

13. J. Hardwig, "In Search of an Ethics of Personal Relationships," in G. Graham & H. LaFollette (Eds.), *Person to Person* (Philadelphia: Temple University Press, 1989), pp. 63–81.

14. S. J. Mills, "Conceptualizing Personal Relationships," *Generations,* 10 (1986), pp. 6–9.

15. Ibid.

16. Ibid.

17. J. Deigh, " Morality and Personal Relations," in G. Graham & H. LaFollette (Eds.), *Person to Person* (Philadelphia: Temple University Press, 1989), pp. 106–123.

18. N. S. Jecker, "Reproductive Risk Taking and the Non-identity Problem," *Social Theory and Practice,* 13 (1987), pp. 219–35; Parfit, D. *Reasons and Persons* (Oxford: Clarendon Press, 1984), Ch. 16.

19. G. Graham & H. LaFollette, "Honesty and Intimacy." In G. Graham & H. LaFollette (Eds.), *Person to Person* (Philadelphia: Temple University Press, 1989), pp. 167–181.

20. William Shakespeare, Sonnet 138. In W. J. Craig (Ed.), *Complete Works* (London: Oxford University Press, 1980).

21. "Creating a Child to Save Another."

22. F. Schoeman, "Adolescent Confidentiality and Family Privacy." In G. Graham & H. LaFollette (Eds.), *Person to Person* (Philadelphia: Temple University Press, 1989).

23. Plato, *Republic,* 122.

24. Emmanuel Kant, trans. H. J. Paton, *Groundwork of the Metaphysics of Morals* (New York: Harper & Row, 1964).

25. N. S. Jecker, "Anencephalic Infants and Special Relationships," *Theoretical Medicine II* (1990), pp. 333–342.

26. N. S. Jecker, "The Moral Status of Patients Who are not Strict Persons," *The Journal of Clinical Ethics,* 1 (1990), pp. 35–38.

27. N. S. Jecker, "The Role of Intimate Others in Medical Decision making," *The Gerontologist,* 30 (1990), pp. 65–71.

28. S. M. Okin, *Justice, Gender, and the Family* (New York: Basic Books, 1989), p. 33ff.

29. J. S. Mill, "Nature." In M. Lerner (Ed.), *Essential Works of John Stuart Mill* (New York: Bantam Books, 1961), pp. 367–401.

30. N. S. Jecker, "Are Filial Duties Unfounded?" *American Philosophical Quarterly,* 26 (1989), pp. 73–80.

10

Parental Power and the Rights of Children

Introduction

Howard Cohen, "Children's Rights and Borrowed Capacities"

Ferdinand Schoeman, "Rights of Children,
Rights of Parents, and the Moral Basis of the Family"

Samantha Brennan and Robert Noggle,
"The Moral Status of Children: Children's Rights,
Parents' Rights, and Family Justice"

On the fourth day of July of every year since 1776, Americans have cele-
brated their independence. They do this with speeches, parades, beach
parties, and especially with spectacular nighttime fireworks displays. The
best of these displays are conducted by licensed professionals for public entertainment. But in thousands of communities where private sales of pyrotechnics are
legally permitted, parents will purchase fireworks for backyard display on the
Fourth of July. Although the vast majority of these private events are harmless,
fireworks injure about 6,000 children and 6,000 adults every year.[1] The injuries
range from burns, skin punctures, cuts, and bruises to permanent partial or total
loss of vision and death.

Some organizations have called for a total ban on all fireworks except those
used by licensed professionals.[2] Others have defended the status quo, arguing that
such a ban would sweep too broadly, prohibiting not only children but all adults
from access to fireworks. Although they agree that children should not be allowed
to purchase fireworks, they believe that there should be no prohibition on sales to
adults. Moreover, they say, although it is permissible for parents to prevent their
children from playing with fireworks, it would be an unacceptable use of state
power to prohibit adults from engaging in private pyrotechnical activities so long
as they do not risk harm to others.

But shouldn't the same freedoms extend to children as well? Is it permissible for
a young child's parents to prevent her from engaging in activities that the parent is
free to do? This is the general question raised by authors in this chapter: What is
the extent of the power (rights) that parents should have over their children?

Correlatively, is there a sphere of liberty a child should be able to enjoy that should be kept immune from parental control?

The seventeenth-century philosopher Thomas Hobbes would have been astonished at the suggestion that children have liberty rights. According to Hobbes, children have only duties of obedience to their parents and no liberty rights at all.[3] The child, from the time of its birth, has consented to obey her parent's command. And if it is objected that an infant is incapable of giving her consent, Hobbes replied (incredibly) that she can be "supposed" to have consented from the fact that her parents, having it in their power to either "save or destroy" the child, have chosen to save her.

Another seventeenth-century philosopher, John Locke, placed the relationship between parent and child on a footing that was much different than the Hobbesian foundation of fear and obedience. Unlike Hobbes, Locke argued that parental power derives from the natural duty of the parents to preserve, nurture, and educate their children.[4] That is, parents have the right to control their children's behavior, not because the children have consented to this control out of fear of death, but because parents need it in order to carry out their duty to protect their children from harm. It would be much more difficult than it now is to meet my obligation to protect my ten-year-old child from injury if he has the right to decide on his own whether to set off a bottle rocket during a Fourth of July celebration. Moreover, he cannot protect himself because he has not reached the age of reason.

Locke is part of a long tradition in ethics that ties the ascription of liberty rights to possession of the capacity for reason. According to this tradition, children are denied the liberty rights that we normally give to adults because children, unlike adults, are incapable of guiding their conduct by "the law of nature." In the first essay in this chapter, "Children's Rights and Borrowed Capacities," Howard Cohen challenges an important assumption made by both Locke and Hobbes as well as many other philosophers. Since a right requires the use of a certain capacity if it is to be successfully exercised, it is assumed that the person who has the right must also possess the relevant capacity. But, Cohen argues, this assumption is false. For example, the right to remove a skin cancer from my face requires the capacity of a skilled surgeon, a capacity that I lack. I must "borrow" (or "purchase") this capacity from a skilled surgeon in order to have the cancer removed. But from the fact that I must borrow the capacity required to exercise my liberty right, it certainly does not follow that I have no right to have the cancer removed!

Cohen argues that children are in a position identical to an adult who must borrow the capacity of another in order to exercise a liberty right. The only difference between adults and children is that a child might find it necessary to borrow more capacities and borrow them more frequently than an adult. But this is not sufficient ground for denying children the relevant right. It follows that "any rights currently enjoyed by adults which children could exercise with the aid of agents are rights which children should have."[5]

In 1990, the American philosopher Ferdinand Schoeman published an essay, reprinted in this chapter, which attempted to undermine another assumption made by all previous philosophers of the family, including Howard Cohen. Schoeman contended that the traditional categories employed by philosophers "misrepresent moral features of intimate relationships," including relationships between parents and young children. Second, he argued that the significance of intimate relationships is such as to morally insulate persons in such relationships from state intervention. Third, "it is the significance of intimacy, and not just a concern for the best interest of the child, that is essential to understanding the basis of the parents' moral claim to raise their biological offspring in a context of privacy, autonomy, and responsibility."

In "The Moral Status of Children," Samantha Brennan and Robert Noggle try to forge a compromise among Locke, Hobbes, and Cohen on one hand, and Schoeman on the other, by distinguishing between *basic rights* to which all persons are entitled (e.g., the right not to be killed) and *constructed rights,* which depend on other factors than being a person (e.g., driving an automobile). In the latter case, possessing the right depends on the role one has (e.g., automobile operator). Hence, children are denied the right to drive an automobile not because they are children but because they do not possess the qualifications necessary to occupy the *role* of driver. And in response to Howard Cohen, they would argue that this is not to treat children unequally at all. It is to deny them a role that we would deny to *anyone* who does not fulfill the qualifications necessary for that particular role. Moreover, from the fact that we deny someone, such as a child, from occupying a particular role, it does not follow that they are not being given equal moral consideration as persons. Finally, they respond to the concerns of Ferdinand Schoeman that talk about children's rights will "depress the sense of security" that children ordinarily have in the intimate relationship they enjoy with their parents.

Children's Rights and Borrowed Capacities
Howard Cohen

Howard Cohen is Provost of the University of Wisconsin, Green Bay. He was previously associate professor of philosophy at the University of Massachusetts, Boston.

Let us assume that some rights, anyhow, require the use of certain capacities if they are to be exercised in a meaningful way. Does that mean that the person who has the right must also have the relevant capacities? At first glance, it may seem obvious that the person must have these capacities. But on reconsideration, it is far from obvious; in fact, I would say that it is simply false. What makes it seem so obvious is that we typically think of rights in terms of noninterference: If a person

From Howard Cohen, *Equal Rights for Children* (Totowa, NJ: Littlefield Adams, 1980), 56–61. Published by permission of Rowman and Littlefield.

has a right to something, then everyone else has an obligation not to interfere with that person's having or doing that thing. A person is pretty much left alone with rights understood in this way. Lacking the capacities, the person lacks what is needed to exercise the right. But not all rights are understood in this way. Some rights are better expressed in terms of a principle of performance: If a person has a right to something, then someone has an obligation to help that person have or do that thing. When we think of rights in this way, we can see that a person without the relevant capacities may still have certain rights as long as someone who has the capacities can be obligated to help the person with the right. In other words, the principle of performance allows us to borrow the capacities of others in order to secure whatever it is we are entitled to.

I want to explain the idea of borrowed capacities more fully, but it is important, first, to be aware of its significance. . . . [T]hose who would say that [the double standard of rights for children and adults] is not unjust must show a relevant difference between children and adults—relevant to granting rights to one group which are denied to the other. The difference most commonly cited is the difference in capacities. Although this difference does not correspond very precisely to the difference between children and adults, we concede that the imprecision was not of overwhelming theoretical importance. However . . . the differences in capacities seemed so relevant to the granting of rights primarily because of the assumption that a person must be able to initiate the exercise of a right on her or his own in order to have it. But this did not seem to me to be so. What is true is that a person who is incapable of initiating certain kinds of actions misses out on the joys of doing those things for herself. While there is undeniably joy in self-reliance, it does not provide life's only satisfactions. And a person who misses out on it should not also have to forfeit her rights, for she can still have those rights as long as she is in a position of demanding performance from others who do have the relevant capacities. So if children can borrow the capacities of those who have them, then the fact that some children do not have full capacities is not a relevant reason to impose a double standard of rights.

Borrowing the capacities of others is not at all unusual; we all do it at one time or another. None of us is so multitalented that we can shape our lives without relying on the abilities and skills of others. I would not defend myself in court or remove a growth from my leg. And it is not just that I do not have the time or the interest in doing so; I could not do either job because I am incapable. I do not have the training of a lawyer or a doctor; I do not have their experience or their skills. I have these capacities as potentials, I suppose, but it would take time and effort to develop them. In this respect, my position is quite analogous to the child's. And I certainly do not

forfeit my rights to a lawyer or to medical attention because of my incapacity to attend to these things myself.

For some of our rights, the relative incapacities of children and adults are basically a matter of degree. Adults have the right to information about themselves which they may be incapable of understanding. Medical or psychiatric reports are most likely to fit into this category, but some financial information could be of this sort as well. When we cannot understand this information, we have the right to seek out someone—a doctor, a psychologist, an accountant, a knowledgeable friend—who can interpret it for us. Children have a similar problem—or they would if they had the right to access to information about themselves. They may well be incapable of understanding medical reports that find their way into a child's school file. But if this difference is one of degree, then the lack of capacity should not be used as an excuse to deny them the right to information, for children, too, could find someone who had the capacity to understand these things and make them accessible.

Another right in which the incapacities of children differ only in degree from those of adults is the right to vote. One commentator has suggested that the capacity required for that right is the capacity to "decide whether the candidates of one or the other major party are most likely to pursue the general policies which serve his interest." What is necessary here is, on the one hand, a clear perception of your own interests. This would be your actual interests, and not what you may think your interests to be in some intuitive or uncritical way. On the other hand, in order to have this capacity you would have to have a pretty good sense of what the impact of various general policies would be if they were actually implemented. If we took this requirement seriously, I do not think anyone could honestly be said to possess this capacity. Leaving aside the fact that nobody seems to have the capacity to tell which candidates are likely to keep their campaign promises, we must still admit to precious little knowledge about how policies will work when put into practice. And what knowledge there is belongs to the "experts" in economics and government. These experts are more often than not in disagreement over technical points which the average and even the superior voter is incapable of understanding. Again, the problem is not simply a lack of information, or a lack of motivation to take the time to find out what is at issue. We do not have the intellectual tools to settle these debates—even to our own satisfaction. In this sense we are incapable of making an accurate judgment. What many of us end up doing at voting time is to take the word of some "expert" or another, second hand, from news analysts or political commentators. In short, we borrow their capacities to judge which candidates are pursuing which policies to what social ends. We are left on our own to decide which pursuits are in our own interests although, if the truth be known, that is a separate, highly abstract political question. So, although children understand relatively less than we adults of these matters, it is not quite so that we have a capacity which they lack when it comes to voting. We only rely a bit less on the capacities of others.

To be sure, with some other rights children would need to borrow capacities which most adults actually have. The rights related to running one's own financial affairs are rights which most adults are capable of exercising on their own. What I have in mind here are the rights to hold property, enter contracts, have an independent source of income (the right to work or receive welfare payments), receive credit, and have a bank account. In light of the economic organization of our society, this constellation of rights is necessary in order to maintain an independent financial existence. Such an existence is well within reach of most adults. The fact that they manage—for better or for worse—shows that they have the relevant capacities.

Many children are pretty clearly incapable of doing some of these things. A five-year-old could not manage a checkbook alone; a seven-year-old could probably not keep a budget or buy or sell a car without assistance. But this does not mean that these children could not make financial decisions. It means that they could not make them and carry them out on their own. There is no reason to think that they could not make these decisions with the help of a financial advisor. Such an advisor would have to be sufficiently adept at running the economic life of another and at doing so in such a way as to leave the major decisions in the

client's hands. As a matter of fact, people of great wealth rely on such advisors all the time, and they do not forego their economic rights. There is no reason why children with financial advisors should have to forego theirs, either.

The point here is that by relying on the capacities of agents children could exercise their rights without doing harm to themselves or to others, without interfering with the obligations their parents or guardians might have to society at large, and without doing much damage to the system of rights and liberties. The role of the child's agent would be to supply information in terms which the child could understand, to make the consequences of the various courses of action a child might take clear to the child, and to do what is necessary to see that the right in question is actually exercised. A sensitive agent would try to do these things in such a way that the child could build on the experience and eventually act on her or his own. Any rights currently enjoyed by adults which children could exercise with the aid of agents are rights which children should have.

When I say that children should have these rights, I mean that all children should have them. I am not attempting to draw a new line fixing some lower age as the age of majority. . . . [D]rawing lines according to age is arbitrary, and drawing lines according to individual capacity is unwise at best and dangerous at worst. Strictly speaking, of course, children (and adults) who do not have the capacities even to use an agent do exhibit relevant differences from right holders. We might justifiably deny them rights on these grounds, but it is easier and safer not to do so. Very little is lost by granting children rights which they rarely claim. Nobody is obliged to claim their rights, and as a practical matter young children might rarely do so. In the typical cases we would expect that children below the age of six might well lack the combined skills and understanding necessary to recognize violations of right and to seek aid. ("Six" is only a rough guess here, figured from the age that children begin to learn and act on information from their peers.) But if children below this age are in a position to use an agent, there is no good reason to place barriers in their way. People should have their rights from birth.

Rights of Children, Rights of Parents, and the Moral Basis of the Family

Ferdinand Schoeman

Ferdinand Schoeman (1945–1992) was professor of philosophy at the University of South Carolina. He wrote many influential essays and books on the philosophy of family law, social ethics, and family ethics, including *Privacy and Social Freedom* (Cambridge: Cambridge University Press, 1992).

> He lets it [the state] dictate to him what is possible or permissible, instead of stipulating, as an unruffled partner, what is to be stipulated to the state of every time, namely, what space and what form it is bound to concede to creaturely existence.
>
> *Martin Buber*

Because moral and social philosophy have concentrated almost exclusively on abstract relationships among people, emphasizing either individual autonomy or general social well-being, certain key aspects of our moral experience—those aspects which deal with intimate relationships—have been virtually ignored. It is with this relatively untitled terrain of intimate relationships that the following analysis is concerned. Specifically, I try to show (1) why traditional categories employed by philosophers misrepresent moral features of intimate relationships; (2) that the significance of intimate relationships is such as to morally insulate persons in such relationships from state obtrusions; and (3) that it is the significance of intimacy, and not just a concern for the best interest of the child, that is essential to understanding the basis of the parents' moral claim to raise their biological offspring in a context of privacy, autonomy, and responsibility.

The discussion focuses first on the notion of children's rights and child welfare, then critically reviews certain proposals for regarding parents as having rights to rear their children, and finally suggests that the right to a private and autonomous relationship with one's biological children

stems from the importance of intimate relationships in general.

Children's Rights and Child Welfare

Philosophers debate whether children, especially infants, are the kinds of beings who can have moral rights; whether rights talk in general has any point unless the being to whom rights are ascribed is in a position to exercise choice (which infants are not); and whether ascribing some rights to beings commits us to ascribing others (i.e., must one have a whole packet of general rights or none at all, or may one ascribe rights to one kind of being and other rights to other kinds of beings?). Not only have many of these abstract philosophical issues about rights been argued inconclusively, but for the most part we can do without talk about children's rights and can express ourselves instead in terms of the needs and welfare of (small) children and the duties of their parents. I shall regard it as given that parents have a duty to protect their children from abuse and neglect, both physical and emotional, recognizing that what should count as abuse or neglect for legal purposes is difficult to determine and may even change from context to context. Also I shall assume that, if a parent or guardian fails to promote the child's interest at some threshold level of adequacy, a form of intervention, ranging from counseling to imprisonment of the parent as well as loss of parental rights to the child, may be legitimate.

There is a different and more practical reason for hesitating to stress the rights of infants vis-à-vis their parents. We typically pay attention to the rights of individuals in order to stress their moral independence—the fact that one individual constitutes a limit on what others, whether well intentioned or not, may legitimately do. In other words, the language of rights typically helps us to sharpen our appreciation of the moral boundaries which separate people, emphasizing the appropriateness of seeing other persons as independent and autonomous agents. While such emphasis constitutes an important point when it comes to structuring relationships between older children and their parents, it may obscure the real point of moral criticism intended in the case of parent-infant relationships. When we are tempted to admonish parents for morally failing in their relationship to their young children, it is presumably and usually because we find them not furnishing the love, attention, and security we think it every parent's duty to provide. We find them short on caring and intimacy and insensitive to the state of dependency and vulnerability into which children are born and remain for several years.

Ideally the relationship between parent and infant involves an awareness of a kind of union between people which is perhaps more suitably described in poetic-spiritual language than in analytic moral terminology. We *share our selves* with those with whom we are intimate and are aware that they do the same with us. Traditional moral boundaries, which give rigid shape to the self, are transparent to this kind of sharing. This makes for nonabstract moral relationships in which talk about rights of others, respect for others, and even welfare of others is to a certain extent irrelevant. It is worth mentioning that the etymology of "intimate" relates it to a verb meaning "to bring within," and that the primary meanings of "intimate" focus on this character of being innermost for a person. It is also worth mentioning that establishing such relationships tends to be the primary reason adults in our culture give for wanting and having children.

The danger of talk about rights of children is that it may encourage people to think that the proper relationship between themselves and their children is the abstract one that the language of rights is forged to suit. So, rather than encouraging abusive parents to feel more intimate with their children, it may cause parents in intimate relationships with their infants to reassess the appropriateness of their blurring the boundaries of individual identity and to question their consciousness of a profound sense of identification with, and commitment toward, their families. Emphasis on the rights of children might foster thinking about the relationship between parent and child as quasicontractual, limited, and directed toward the promotion of an abstract public good. Such emphasis unambiguously suggests that the relationship is a one-way relationship aimed almost solely at promoting the best interest of the child.

There are many circumstances when the independence of children, primarily older ones, ought to be stressed; for these circumstances, stress on children's rights makes sense. But when it is the dependence and vulnerability of the child that we want to emphasize, as we unfortunately must at times do, some different moral strategy would be more appropriate. And when we become conscious of the possibilities that intimacy here, as in other relations, is a two-way sharing of benefits, primary emphasis on the rights perspective becomes even more distorting. To avoid misunderstanding, however, I wish to reiterate that in recommending a different moral strategy I am not to be taken as denying that infants have rights, either in relation to their parents or in relation to abstract others. Rather, I am questioning the moral advantages of extolling the rights of infants in our consciousness of their most important relationships.

Let me try now to articulate briefly the principles at which we have arrived and then proceed to describe and execute the objective of this essay. As persons, children ought to be thought of as possessing rights; but as infants in relationship to their parents, they are to be thought of primarily as having needs, the satisfaction of which involves intimate and intense relationships with others. As against society, we might yet think of infants and parents as having rights to conditions which permit or encourage, or at least do not discourage, the social and material conditions conducive to parent-child intimacy—a point we will return to in the discussion of intimacy later. What I want to discuss primarily is the moral basis for thinking that biological parents have a presumptive right to keep their children under their care in the setting of privacy, autonomy, and responsibility which is usually accorded the family.

For purposes of this essay, I shall mean by "family" an intense continuing and intimate organization of at least one adult and child, wherein the child is extensively and profoundly dependent on the adult, in which the adult supplies the child with its emotional and material needs, and in which the parent is dependent on the child for a certain kind of intimacy. This relationship is to be understood as moral, not biological. Furthermore, the family is to be understood as entitled to certain rights of privacy and autonomy. The right of privacy entitles the adults of the family to exclude others from scrutinizing obtrusions into family occurrences. The right to autonomy entitles the adults of the family to make important decisions about the kinds of influences they want the children to experience and entitles them to wide latitude in remedying what they regard as faults in the children's behavior. Neither the right to privacy nor the right to autonomy associated with the family is absolute. These rights are to be conceived as rights against society at large. In relation to the children, they impose upon parents the duty to employ considered judgments in taking into account each child's needs, and eventually his rights. But in large part, such duties are unenforceable by the state because of the rights of privacy and autonomy already mentioned.

Just how much discretion should be left to the parents—how wide should their latitude be in structuring the environment of their children? For theoretical reasons to be advanced in the discussion of intimacy later, I follow Michael Wald and others in setting strict threshold conditions (amounting to a clear-and-present-danger criterion) which must be met before coercive state intervention is permitted. Wald argues that coercive intervention should be authorized only if (1) serious physical or emotional harm to the child is imminent and (2) the intervention is likely to be less detrimental than the status quo.[1] Wald cites several practical factors in justifying his recommended policy of restraint. (1) Typically, good alternatives to unfortunate family circumstances are not available. (2) It is difficult to predict which circumstances will have harmful long-range effects. (3) There is a lack of consensus about proper methods of child rearing and the ideal end product of child rearing. (4) Our social commitment to diversity of life-styles requires a great deal of tolerance in what should be permitted.

While such factors reflect important desiderata, it is notable that concern for the parent appears to be irrelevant in Wald's article, as in much of the legal literature of recent vintage. Though I find this exclusion of the parents' perspective peculiar, very widespread, and in need of remedy, it is to a certain extent understandable. For the infant, the family as here defined involves an intimate relationship with at least one adult. Since the psychological evidence suggests that children need this type of relationship for their cognitive and emotional well-being, we may conclude that children must be provided with such an arrangement (or, if you prefer, that they have a right to it). But from the child's perspective it does not matter whether the adult who will become its psychological parent is also its biological parent.

In what follows, I shall focus on the parents' perspective and attempt to address this question: Why should the biological parents be thought to have a right to raise their child in an intimate setting even before it is determined that their child will fare best under their care and guidance (however "faring best" is defined)? Ultimately, what I shall want to emphasize is that the functional, efficiency-oriented approach to the family found in much of the literature defending family autonomy represents neither the only nor the best assessment of the moral basis of the family.

It should, however, be noted that not all social theorists see the family as an institution worth preserving. For not only does it provide a context for abuse and brutality in which the law has traditionally declined to take an interest, it also interferes with what might be called "equality of opportunity" because it makes children depend on the spiritual and material resources of the family they happen to be born into. Though these points do constitute genuine moral worries which are theoretically inseparable from family institutions, pursuing such worries is not part of my present interest, though they will be touched on in the final portion of the essay.

Why Should Biological Parents Have the Right to Raise Their Children?

Since surprisingly little philosophical attention has been devoted to the moral meaning of intimate relationships such as arise in family settings, it should prove a useful exercise to see just what can be said in behalf of the biological parents' rights to raise their offspring, obvious though it may appear. The right of biological parents (hereinafter referred to as just "parents") with which I am concerned is not a right to certain services from their children, but a right against all the rest of society to be indulged, within wide limits, to share life with each child and thus inevitably to fashion the child's environment as they see fit, immune from the scrutiny of and direction from others.

It might be impatiently suggested that parents' rights to raise their children stem from an evolutionary phenomenon: parents' natural affections for their offspring and their infants' needs make for something like a preestablished harmony of interests. Since everyone, or almost everyone, benefits from this arrangement, and since provisions can be made for those few biological anomalies in which natural passions and natural needs do not correlate, what better basis could there be for our traditional arrangement? The suggestion might be given added weight by calling to mind the reported deleterious effects of impersonal, institutional efforts at raising children.

Three comments are in order in response. First, it has been observed that parental attachments may be more the result of enculturation than we naively suppose. Second, there is sufficient evidence to suggest that not all alternative modes of distributing children involve impersonal institutions in which children languish emotionally and intellectually. Third, and philosophically most significant, I wish to consider what we would think parents' rights would amount to if means equal or superior to those parents can typically supply could be found for benefiting the child outside the biological parents' domain. Would parents still have a claim on their children, as against society? And if so, what would its basis be? Is the parents' right to their children contingent on the biological family's being the most efficient arrangement for benefiting children? Or is there some less incidental account of parental prerogative? (As indicated above, most recent proponents of family autonomy and state restraint have argued that promoting the child's interest is the

primary or sole basis of their advocacy. Though I am in agreement with these policy recommendations, I find that more needs to be said about their justification.)

One not very plausible account for the parents' right, despite the fact that the account can be traced back to Aristotle, involves looking at the child as the property of the parent, analogous to teeth and hair which have fallen. Since the child is the product of material and labor supplied prenatally by the mother, the child would seem to be the natural possession par excellence but for the fact that this product is a person. (I suppose that those who think that the newborn infant is not yet a person would have an easy time thinking of the parent as entitled to the infant in Aristotelian fashion.)

Another justification for our current arrangements might follow these lines: as long as children are adequately cared for under our present practices, we can take into account parental preferences. True, these preferences as such do not constitute rights, but in our way of allocating benefits, once children's needs are satisfied—a precondition we have set into our scheme—preferences should count in our determination of which claims will be recognized as entitlements.

This account of the basis of parental rights is not contingent solely on the fact of benefiting children but also makes essential reference to parents as persons with preferences which must be considered as long as the child's basic needs are met. But ultimately this justification of parental right is not satisfying, for all that would be necessary to override it would be a showing of some increased benefit to children in nonparental settings. True, the needs of the children and the preferences of the parents go some way toward showing that it is the parents, and not someone else, that should be accorded rights over their children. But if marginally more good resulted for children from alternative setups, this-fact could immediately outweigh parental preferences and militate against according parents' rights. I take it as a given that a parent's stake in her relationship to her children is based on something more profound than parental preferences, even when we add to such preferences a realistic skepticism about the state's competence to distribute children in a manner more advantageous to them.

In discussing sources of authority, Elizabeth Anscombe has recently proposed that institutionalized practices which carry out important tasks thereby gain legitimization or authority.[2] Anscombe suggests that the parent's rights to obedience from her child and respect for her exercise of discretion from others outside the family evolve from the manifestly crucial functions parental authority performs. So long as families maintain their position of being necessary conditions for the performance of such functions, Anscombe's argument captures common sense and preserves family entitlements. But the emergence of alternative, possibly superior (relative to the child), means of rearing children would deprive the family of its position of being necessary and hence undermine its claim to rightful autonomy, except on a customary basis.

We must note that these last two theories are by no means clearly false or even clearly wanting. Whether they are fully adequate must be judged in light of alternative dimensions we can manage to elaborate.

Intimacy Is the Moral Foundation of Parental Rights

We have yet to supply the justification of three institutions which we, for the most part, take for granted. Why should the family be accorded rights to privacy and autonomy? Why should the family be given extensive responsibilities for the development of children? Why should the *biological* parent be thought entitled to be in charge of a family? I believe that the notion of intimacy supplies the basis for these presumptions and would like now to elaborate an account more successful than those mentioned in the preceding section. But I shall try to show first why intimacy requires privacy and autonomy as its setting, and second why we should recognize a right to intimate relationships. I shall then argue that the parent's right to raise her children in a family stems naturally from the right to engage in intimate relationships, even when recognition of this right involves some comparative cost to the child.

At an earlier point in this essay, I described an intimate relationship as one in which one shares one's self with one or more others. It was suggested that, via intimate relationships, one transcends abstract and rather impersonal associations with others and enters personal and meaningful relationships or unions. Such relationships are meaningful because of the personal commitments to others which are constitutive of such relationships. For most people, not only are such unions central to defining who one is, but human existence would have little or no meaning if cut off from all possibility of maintaining or reestablishing such relationships. Though such relationships are undoubtedly culturally dependent in the form they take, they constitute one's roots in life or attachment to living, even when the concerns of the relationship are independent of, or hostile to, the values of the culture and the welfare of others.

Practically speaking, the strength or very possibility of intimate relationships varies inversely with the degree of social intrusion into such relationships generally tolerated. The prospect of state intervention into a relationship depresses the sense of security of the relationship. It makes people hesitant to see their interests fused with those of another. The intimate sharing described as part of these close unions presupposes limited sovereignty on the part of those reaching out to and sharing with others to determine the conditions of the relationship. Without privacy and autonomy, the relationship would be neither secure nor on the parties' own terms.

Privacy and autonomy provide the moral space within which concrete personal relationships can be formed independently of general social concerns. To give the state authority to regulate such relationships would inevitably result in a redirection or "socialization" of these relationships. We see evidence of this shift in doctor-patient relationships, wherein doctors are seen increasingly to have direct responsibilities for the health of the population and not for the comfort of specific patients. While it would be presumptuous of me to declare, without marshaling evidence, that such shifts in loyalties ought on balance to be forestalled, it should be recognized and made part of our reckoning that systems of meaning can be uprooted in the process of re-aligning commitments.

Lon Fuller has devoted considerable attention to understanding principles of human association and the law's varying capacities to regulate diverse kinds of relationships.[3] He distinguishes two different principles of association, the relative mix of which in any particular relationship determines what the relationship is. One principle is shared commitment, the other is the legalistic. The legalistic aspect is that which makes explicit rules of duty, and entitlements. While the former principle, shared commitment, is concerned with conditions of mind and degrees of inner resolution, the latter is concerned with overt, clearly definable acts. As the legalistic principle comes to dominate the parties' image of their relationship with one another, the element of shared commitment tends to sink out of sight. State intervention into a relationship, Fuller argues, tends to shift the emphasis of the relationship in the direction of formality and abstractness. The very act of precisely sorting things out in conformity with the legalistic paradigm tends to wring out aspects of inner commitment.

Fuller's analysis helps to indicate why intimate relationships must be accorded privacy and autonomy and why they deserve social and legal respect. Friendship, love, and family represent institutions in which intimacy is central to the relationships. Because of the importance of these relationships to the self-image and meaningful existence of most people, the state, before intruding, should impose high standards like the clear-and-present-danger test suggested above. The state should be very chary in trying to alter the terms of such relationships to serve social ends. As has been noted by others, while the state is quite limited in its ability to promote relationships, it can do much to destroy them. The state threatens relationships by requiring the parties to think of themselves as primarily serving public ends and as having public duties. This intrusion beclouds the integrity of the trust and devotion that can arise between people. Though it may be that important ends are served by such intrusion, as, for example, ends are served by such intrusion, as, for example, when doctors are required to report suspected cases of child abuse, we should be willing at the very least to acknowledge the cost of such intrusions. Parenthetically, it is worthwhile noting that the state does find certain relationships privileged, like the lawyer-client relationship, even at some possible cost to public welfare.

Yet to show the importance of intimate relationships, even family relationships, as characterized in this essay, is not yet to show that parents have any rights to their children. After all, adults can establish intimate relationships with other consenting adults. Insuring that children become part of an intimate and secure setting is not the same as assuring the biological parents of these children that they (the parents) will be part of this same setting.

The alternative to the natural and customary distribution of children to their parents is some kind of social decision determining who goes with whom. Such distribution schemes are not necessarily, from the perspective of the infant, inimical to intimacy, as the institution of early adoption establishes. But it does or may preclude such kinds of intimacy for those who are determined by popular social criteria to be not maximally fit or not maximally competent to really provide children with all that they need or can use. But such a preclusion would, I believe, represent an interference with a practice from which intimacy and with it life meaning typically emerge.

Once this is acknowledged, I am not sure what else would have to be added before we could come to speak of such structures of meaning as investing individuals with a moral right to be free from intentional interferences. Presumably, part of what would be required would include a moral comparison of various elaborated social structures. Because I am not equipped to articulate such comparisons, I shall speak of moral claims as distinct from moral rights, claims being justified on the basis of their importance to our present conditions. So, rather than arguing that we have a moral right to family autonomy or that we should have a positive legal right to such autonomy, I will be content in encouraging a kind of appreciation for the meaning of the family over and above the recognition of its accomplishments as an institution dedicated to the production of future citizens.

Though the infant is nonconsenting, it does not represent a denial of its rights for it to be entrusted to its parents even if better surroundings are available, since we are assuming that minimal conditions for adequate upbringing will be met. (We are, after all, utilizing something like the clear-and-present-danger test to protect children from abuse and neglect, though of course such standards raise problems of their own.) To set terms for emotional parenting more stringent than required for the protection of children from abuse and neglect constitutes an interference in a person's claim to establish intimate relations except on the society's terms. We have already indicated reasons for thinking that such regulation transforms relationships into less intimate ones. Such allocation schemes could redefine the parenting role as one in which the objective is abstract social well-being, not intimacy and the kind of meaning found in commitment to particular others.

The practice of entrusting children to their parents ultimately limits the control of society to determine the life-style and beliefs of persons because it means there would be one important relationship a person could be in without the requirement of prior social approval. Since society cannot determine and should not try to determine who may have intimate relationships with whom, if a person chooses to have his relationships in a family setting, society should not interfere, since that kind of choice is essential to intimate relationships in general.

Thus, as a way of transcending oneself and the boundaries of abstract others, as a way of finding meaning in life, and as a means of maintaining some kind of social and moral autonomy, the claim to freedom from scrutiny and control in one's relations with others should be thought of as a moral claim as important as any other that can be envisioned. It must not be up to society in general, without there being some special cause, to decide whom one can relate to and on what terms. Other things being equal, parents consequently are entitled to maintain their off-spring and seek meaning with and through them.

Though there are many questions which plague the account of family privacy advanced here, there is one in particular I would like to raise and address because of the direction it suggests for further reflection. The problem is: Given the subjective basis of the importance of intimate relationships, how can it be used to defend privacy and autonomy within families in general, since the members of many families manifestly fail to invest their relationships with the requisite kind of personal meaning? And looked at the other way, there are surely many relationships in which personal meaning is sought and found but to which the law is and, as things stand, ought to remain oblivious. If we distinguish the substance from the structure of an intimate relationship, we can see the question as requiring that we justify our practice of according privacy and autonomy to people who comply only in form to meaningful relationships while denying them to other people who may be far more committed to one another but who fail to establish the formal, institutional accouterments of close relationships.

In responding, we need to note that the state cannot employ the subjective or substantial criterion when judging whether privacy and autonomy are appropriate for a particular relationship. The state is unequipped to investigate souls, and even were it so equipped it could set its standards and make its particular findings only at the expense of just the kind of intrusions which shatter the very relationships it would be seeking to protect. Consequently, it is essential that there be formal or ritualized means of "privatizing" a relationship, on the basis of overt acts or habits, even though inevitably there will result two tragic consequences: abuses of privileged privacy and intrusions into some morally deserving relationships. Ultimately, what is being suggested here is that it is important for states to respect relationships the very point of which is to insulate the people so related from ordinary forms of social and legal control. The state needs to be cognizant of those means—culture specific and conventional, though not necessarily popular—that people have for finding meaning; and it must do so by means of clearly structured and easily recognizable institutions of relating. It can do neither more nor less without changing the nature or possibility of such relationships. Any effort to gauge the meaning of a particular relationship that goes beyond superficially based presumptions will involve distorting intrusions. Consequently, what is important about the biological relationship between parents and children is the *conventional meaning* given to it within our culture. Since people do in fact vest the biological relationship with meanings of intimacy, the state must not interfere with that relationship unless the danger is serious, clear, and immanent.

Most justifications of family autonomy that one finds in the literature have concentrated on the child's perspective and stressed the point that families, as we know them, represent the least-detrimental means we have of child rearing. In contrast, my arguments on behalf of the family, though concerned with the well-being of children, have had as their chief focus an idea of human relationships. Consequently, even if someone could demonstrate that there were some more efficient and effective institution for promoting the interests of children than the traditional family, I would still think that the family would have a strong, though rebuttable, moral presumption in its favor. The implications of such a presumption extend beyond requiring high threshold conditions before the state intervenes coercively into family affairs. The presumption would seem to imply that the state should not, to the extent possible, make the family and parental responsibility otiose through the provision directly to children of services which parents are in a position to supply.

One final point. Some people have argued recently that, while the family deserves the privacy and autonomy suggested above, in case the state is presented with a claim of rights violation by a child, the state is in a situation in which it must either find for the child or find for the parent, and that accordingly it should make its decision by regarding the interests and rights of the parents and child as being on a par. However plausible this picture of restricted options appears, it ignores one crucial alternative. Parents can be seen as representing the interests of the family as an integrated whole in addition to representing their own particular interests. Though entrusting individuals with the responsibility of making judgments for the common good when their own interests are involved does not accord well with modern constitutionalist conceptions, we should not discount on a priori grounds the prospects for such an arrangement being feasible in certain contexts. The context in which such kinds of representation can work are those in which people in fact conceive their roles and their very identity as requiring such an attitude. Informal custom rather than formal institutional means of resolving conflict of interest generally sufficed in ancient and medieval government, imbued with notions of virtue and right as they typically were.

Given social expectations and governmental noninterference, important ends are served by relegating to parents the right to decide important issues for the family, even when what is at issue is a conflict in interests between the parent as individual and the child as individual. I have been suggesting that if the state takes the attitude that conflicts within families are the same as conflicts anywhere, the state will be adding considerable impetus to the evolution of the family as a nonintimate structure.

The Moral Status of Children: Children's Rights, Parents' Rights, and Family Justice

Samantha Brennan and Robert Noggle

Samantha Brennan is assistant professor of philosophy at the University of Western Ontario, London, Ontario, Canada. She is the coeditor, with Tracy Isaacs and Michael Milde, of *A Question of Values: New Canadian Perspectives in Ethics and Political Philosophy* (*Value Inquiry* book series, Rodopi Press, 1997), and author of articles on rights in *The Canadian Journal of Philosophy* (September 1994), and *The Southern Journal of Philosophy* (Summer 1995).

Robert Noggle is assistant professor of philosophy at Florida International University. His articles on personal autonomy, manipulation, and moral motivation have appeared in *American Philosophical Quarterly* and *Philosophical Studies*.

Mainstream ethical philosophy has had little to say about issues of family justice.[1] Even feminist moral theories often focus more on questions of justice for families than on questions of justice within them.[2] In contrast, there is a large body of literature on children's rights in sociology and legal theory. But little of this theorizing rests on a foundation in moral philosophy any stronger than a vague appeal to the notion of the best interests of the child.

This essay is an attempt to provide a philosophical foundation for thinking about the moral status of children. It is driven by what we think are widespread convictions about how we ought to treat children—convictions which we share.[3] In part, we hope to develop a theory that accords with and justifies our moral convictions and the public policies we favor. However, we intend to do more than merely clarify our own intuitions. Not only will we begin to construct philosophical foundations for the approach to children's issues that we advocate, but we will also stake out various possible ways of arguing for those foundations.

The essay, then, has two parts. In the first, we propose several plausible claims. These claims constitute an attractive common sense understanding of children's moral status. However, the three claims appear to be inconsistent. And if the three claims do capture a commonsense picture of the moral status of children, then that picture would seem to be inconsistent as well. In the second part of the essay we offer a rights-based theory of the moral status of children which, we claim, both meets the constraints that define the common sense position and resolves its internal conflicts.

The Commonsense Understanding of Children's Moral Status

We think that any acceptable theory of the moral status of children must be compatible with three claims: that children deserve the same moral consideration as adults, that they can nevertheless be treated differently from adults, and that parents have limited authority to direct their upbringing. These claims embody a position which we think is quite plausible and attractive. In fact, they define a position which seems to be the subject of a large and growing consensus about the moral status of children in contemporary liberal democracies. Though this consensus is of some evidential value in itself, there are independent considerations to support the three claims. While they do not conclusively *prove* that the claims are true, they do show that the claims are very plausible. Indeed, the considerations we will discuss seem sufficient to shift the burden of proof onto those who would reject the three claims.

But while each claim seems independently plausible, the set seems prima facie inconsistent. This apparent inconsistency is evidence of certain tensions in our commonsense thinking about children. The philosophical challenge here is to develop a theory which embodies and makes

A longer version of this paper appears in *Social Theory and Practice* 23, 1 (Spring 1997): 1–26. Published here by permission of the authors and the editors of *Social Theory and Practice*.

sense of all three claims in a way that resolves the tensions between them.

The first claim is simply that the moral status of children is on par with that of adults. Call it the Equal Consideration Thesis.

> **The Equal Consideration Thesis:** Children are entitled to the same moral consideration as adults.

Notice that this thesis demands moral *consideration* for children which is equal to that of adults. This means that children are to be taken seriously as moral agents, and that their moral claims are not to be discounted merely because they are children. As we will argue later, this thesis does not necessarily imply that children always have exactly the same duties and rights as adults. It seems to us that two people can receive equal moral *consideration* without having exactly the same package of moral rights and duties. But the Equal Consideration Thesis does mean that the moral status of children does not depend merely on their age. The mere fact that they are children does not give them an inferior moral status.

The basis for the Equal Consideration Thesis is the fact that children are persons.[4] Because they are persons, they are entitled to the same moral consideration to which *anyone* is entitled merely in virtue of being a person. In other words, a certain moral status attaches generally to all persons, including children. To deny this would be to claim either that persons do not derive moral status from their status as persons, or that children are not persons. Because neither of these claims is particularly plausible, it does not seem plausible to deny the Equal Consideration Thesis.

The second thesis that makes up the commonsense view of the moral status of children concerns the legitimacy of treating children differently from adults. Call this the Unequal Treatment Thesis.

> **The Unequal Treatment Thesis:** Children—at least at certain ages—can be legitimately prevented from doing certain things that it would be illegitimate to prevent adults from doing.

Most of us accept this thesis. Well-known and plausible examples of things we allow adults but not children to do are voting, driving cars, owning firearms, signing contracts, and drinking alcohol. The Unequal Treatment Thesis is so widely held and so central to most people's understanding of the moral status of children that it would be difficult to accept a theory that denied it.

Other considerations besides the appeal to intuition and current practice support the Unequal Treatment Thesis. One is public policy. No matter what we decide about children's moral status, as a practical matter, few of us are ready to endorse letting children—especially young children—vote, sign important contracts, or have unrestricted access to firearms, alcohol, tobacco, automobiles, and so on. While it is probably an overstatement to say that this would lead to utter chaos, we do take it to be an empirical fact that the results of such a radical shift in public policy would be pretty undesirable both for the children and for us. Thus there seem to be strong practical reasons for favoring the Unequal Treatment Thesis.

The Unequal Treatment Thesis also seems plausible on contractarian grounds. Most of us are glad that our parents did not hand us a shotgun, a six-pack, and the keys to the car on our sixth birthday. The Unequal Treatment Thesis seems plausible partly because grown children would recognize that they themselves needed to have their actions restricted when they were young children. Most of us would give a sort of "retroactive consent" to having had various sorts of restrictions placed on us when we were children—even if we did not agree with them at the time.[5]

The third commonsense thesis concerns the legitimacy of the role parents play in raising children. We'll call it the Limited Parental Rights Thesis.

> **The Limited Parental Rights Thesis:** Parents can legitimately exercise limited but significant discretion in raising children.

It is difficult to see how one could deny this thesis. Children are immature in a number of ways. Their limited cognitive powers and experience make them prone to mistakes in judging their own interests and how to further them. The healthy mental, physical, and emotional development of children seems to require that someone have the responsibility to nurture and protect the child, and the authority to exercise her own judgment in doing so on a day-to-day basis. Given that someone must do these things, and that children are often too immature to do so, it seems natural to assign parents the right to do so. For this reason, parents are typically thought to be free to make choices for their children that range from seemingly trivial ones like how to dress their children, to very serious ones like how to discipline them, and how and where they should be educated.

Are the Three Claims Consistent?

The Equal Consideration Thesis, the Unequal Treatment Thesis and the Limited Parental Rights Thesis capture what seems to be the common sense position about the moral status of children. This commonsense position contrasts with extreme views which deny one or more of the claims. It contrasts on one side with the children-as-property view which denies the Equal Consideration Thesis and takes children, especially young ones, to be owned by their parents.[6] On the other side, the position staked out by the three claims contrasts with the extreme child-libertarian view which regards children as having exactly the same package of rights and freedoms as adults. That view denies the Unequal Treatment Thesis and the Limited Parental Rights Thesis. It claims that parents have no rights qua parents and that children should be treated in exactly the same way as adults.[7] Our position treads the middle ground between these two extremes.

The philosophical challenge is to see whether there *is* any middle ground here to tread. For the Equal Consideration Thesis seems to conflict with the Unequal Treatment Thesis and the Limited Parental Rights Thesis. It is puzzling how unequal treatment and even very limited parental rights could be consistent with a thoroughgoing acceptance of the claim that children have the same moral status as other persons.

Reconciling the Three Claims

Is the Equal Consideration Thesis Compatible with the Unequal Treatment Thesis?

Much of the moral status a person has comes simply from the fact that she is a person. Since children are persons, they have this same basic moral status. This moral status is an important source of rights (often called "human rights"). Whatever rights adults have simply in virtue of being persons, those same rights belong to children as well. We won't try to give and defend a list of human rights here, but we take them to include the rights to life, liberty, property, and freedom from deliberate harm.

The question, then, is whether giving equal moral consideration in the form of recognizing the basic human rights of children precludes treating children and adults differently. Notice that we said above that *much* of a person's moral status derives directly from her status as a person. But personhood is not the only source of moral status. A person's moral rights and duties typically depend on many other things in addition to her status as a person. Roles, for example, often confer moral status. A doctor or a lawyer, for instance, has duties in virtue of her role over and above those that she has merely in virtue of being a person. Roles also sometimes confer rights: one's role as a student confers certain rights against her teachers, for instance. Promises are another obvious source of moral status: the promisor has duties and the promisee has rights that neither has merely in virtue of their status as persons. The fact that I may have such a right and you don't is not evidence of my superior innate moral status, but rather is a result of other facts, namely the fact that the promise was made to me and not to you. Similarly, property produces a complex network of rights and duties that result not merely from anyone's status as a person. Need and differences in political power also would seem to affect one's moral status: those who are in need or oppressed would seem to have a moral claim on us that others do not.

It appears then, that granting equal moral consideration does not imply that each person has the same package of rights and duties. Rather, to accord someone equal moral consideration is to do two things. First, it is to respect the moral status she has merely in virtue of being a person. Second, it is to be willing to consider any other moral claims she might make due to other factors which affect her moral status. So whether unequal *treatment* is consistent with equal moral *consideration* will depend on the nature of the differential treatment at issue. That is, equal moral consideration is compatible with some sorts of inequalities in treatment but not others. It requires the recognition of the basic moral status each person has, but does not require equal treatment in every way. For this reason, we claim that the Unequal Treatment Thesis is compatible with the Equal Consideration Thesis. Children can have a *total* package of rights and duties that differs from that of an adult; yet this is compatible with children having the same moral status, and thus the same basic rights, as any other persons.

This point is crucial, and so it is worth elaborating. The reason that unequal treatment is consistent with equal consideration lies in an important difference between two kinds of rights. On the one hand, there are *basic* rights (often called "human rights") which everyone has; they attach to persons simply in virtue of their being persons. The rights not to be harmed or killed fall into this category. On the other hand, some rights are *constructed* from basic moral rights plus other factors. They depend in part on facts about the persons who bear them, facts about the relationships of which they are a part, facts about previous commitments they have made, and facts about the societies in which they live. Often these constructed rights are attached to roles. Doctors, for example, have the right to prescribe medications, lawyers have the right to partake in certain legal proceedings, teachers have the right to conduct classes, judges have the right to rule on cases, referees have the right to make binding decisions, and so on. A person can have a role-dependent right only if she can fill the role in question. When rights depend on roles, if you can't play the role, then you don't get the right. So whether one has a role-dependent right is partly a function of the capacities and abilities of the person to play the role associated with that right. Many political rights derive partly from certain roles one has, such as the role of citizen, or voter, or automobile operator. If a person does not fulfill the qualifications necessary for the role with which these rights are associated, then she need not be accorded those rights. Thus the relative lack of maturity of children counts against their having certain role-dependent rights; since they are not mature enough to play those roles, they cannot

have the rights attached to them. And this is the reason that they can be denied the right to drive, to vote, and so forth. But it is a mistake to conclude from their lack of these constructed, role-dependent rights that they are not being given equal moral consideration.

Consider the right to drive an automobile. This right derives from and protects a certain way of exercising a basic right to freedom of movement. It depends on more than just one's status as a person. It is also dependent on a person's occupying a certain role, what we might call the role of "driver." Like other roles, the role of driver is a complex of rights and duties. And like other roles (such as those of doctor and lawyer and teacher), it requires certain qualifications consisting of skill, judgement, training, and so on. Because children lack these qualifications, they can be legitimately denied the rights associated with this role. We do not deny this right to children simply because they are children, but because they lack the relevant abilities. But to deny a child's right to drive an automobile is not to deny them the basic human rights due to them in virtue of their status as persons. Indeed, we deny the right to drive to anyone—regardless of age—who lacks the abilities associated with the role to which the right to drive is attached.

Is the Equal Consideration Thesis Compatible with the Limited Parental Rights Thesis?

The Nature of Parental Rights. How can we reconcile equal treatment of children with the parental right to make decisions for them? An answer to this question will depend on the nature of and the basis for parental rights. In this section we will sketch the formal nature of parental rights. In the next, we will offer a theory about the basis of parental rights.

We claim that the Limited Parental Rights Thesis is best interpreted as the claim that parental rights are rights with *thresholds*.[8] A right with a threshold is a right which can be permissibly infringed, that is overridden, when at least one of two conditions is met. First, a right may be overridden when it conflicts with a stronger right. For example, if my car will either run over Susan's foot or Fred's entire body, then Susan's right not to be harmed in this way gives out in the face of Fred's stronger claim. Second, a right may be overridden if doing so will bring about a large enough benefit to others. Consider a common property right to the ownership of one's car. While in general we take this right seriously, there are conditions under which the right may be permissibly infringed. Suppose that the car was needed to transport a dying person to the hospital, or that the police required it to apprehend a felon who presents a clear and grave danger to the community. Most people think it is permissible for the right to be infringed and the car used—even without the consent of the owner—to transport the dying person or apprehend the criminal. One natural kind of account of what has happened to the property right in such cases is that it has been overridden by what is at stake for others.

Both of the conditions for overriding a right are often satisfied in interactions between parents and children, when parental rights conflict with children's rights and children's needs. An application of the first overriding condition to the realm of parental rights is the common sense judgment that a parent's right to make choices involving the child generally gives out at the point at which the child's right not to be harmed is violated. The alternative to claiming that parental rights have thresholds after which they give out would be to posit parental rights so strong that they could not be overridden by the child's right not to be harmed. This seems equivalent to granting parents a property right in the child.

The second overriding condition is often satisfied when the child's needs are not being met. These unmet needs sometimes will justify overriding a parental rights claim. We won't give a full account of exactly when a child's unmet needs will justify the infringement of a parental right, but some preliminary remarks are certainly in order. First, the fact that parents do have rights means that so long as the child is not being harmed, parental rights are generally not to be infringed merely to provide some marginal benefit for the child. This is one value of describing the situation in terms of parental rights rather than in terms of competing interests. Thus, for example, if a set of parents is doing an adequate job of nur-

turing their child, then one cannot justify terminating their parental rights simply because some other set of parents have more money to clothe and educate the first parents' child.

Second, the rights of parents may be overridden if the parents are not meeting the child's needs, or if they are violating the child's rights (or allowing others to do so). For example, parents might lose their parental rights if the child is severely neglected or abused. But so long as the parents are not harming their child—either directly as in the case of outright abuse, or indirectly as in the case of neglect—their rights cannot be justifiably infringed.

An interesting third application of the overriding conditions is one we will mention for the sake of completeness but not discuss in any detail here. Some might think that parental rights can be overridden by potential substantial benefit to people *other than the parents or the children involved.* One might think that the interests others have in how we raise our children count towards overriding parental rights. Jan Narveson argues that parental rights are limited in just this way. He claims that children do not have rights since, in his view, all rights are contract based and children cannot engage in contracts. According to Narveson, parents have property rights in their children. Narveson thinks that these property rights are limited, though, because of the effects that children can have on people besides their parents. Writes Narveson: "In view of humans' enormous potential for third-party effects, there is certainly a large public interest factor in the construction of these rights. We can reasonably restrict what parents may do in light of this potential."[9] Narveson is forced to the position that other adults' interests in our children limit our rights because he believes both that we cannot do whatever we want to our children—for example, we may not kill them—and that children do not have the right sort of status (as rational contractors) which would allow their rights or needs to override parental rights. Of course we disagree sharply with Narveson's claim that children are the property of parents. It is interesting, though, that even a libertarian such as Narveson accepts limits on the rights of parents.

In summary, we claim that parents do have rights, but because those rights have thresholds, they can be infringed if this is necessary for preserving the rights of the child or for making sure that her needs are met. If the parents fail to meet their child's needs at all, then even if they do not actively harm the child, their parental rights can be overridden. Viewing parental rights as rights with thresholds is part of the explanation of how parental rights can exist even though we grant equal moral consideration to children. The rest of the explanation will depend on claims about the basis for parental rights.

The Basis for Parental Rights. Our view of the basis for parental rights can be seen as a development of John Locke's claim that parental rights are based neither on parental ownership of children nor on the rational consent of children to be governed by their parents. According to Locke parental power is "that which parents have over their children, to govern them *for the child's good.*"[10] Locke argues that parents must govern children until children develop the use of reason and come to be able to govern themselves. Yet there is an important difference between our view and Locke's. While we share with Locke the belief that the basis of parental rights is the parents' responsibility for the welfare of children—as Locke puts it, "for the help, instruction, and preservation of their offspring"[11]—we also believe that children's rights also impose limits on the rights of parents.[12] If parental rights were something like property rights over the child, then reconciling equal consideration with parental rights would be difficult, if not impossible. Counting a person as the property of another person is clearly inconsistent with granting her equal moral consideration. Of course, we claim that parental rights are nothing like property rights. Instead, they derive from the fact that children are often incapable of effectively exercising their rights and making rational decisions about their interests.

Parental rights are necessary to allow the parents the freedom to effectively protect and nurture children. Parental rights, then, are what we will call "stewardship rights." A stewardship right is a right someone has in virtue of being the steward—as opposed to an owner—of someone or something. This conception of parental rights explains both why children's rights take priority over most other considerations and why parents still have much freedom to raise their children. In this way, it reconciles the Limited Parental Rights Thesis with the Equal Consideration Thesis.

The stewardship conception of parental rights gives the parent a complex moral status. That status involves two main factors. The most important is the rights of the children themselves, together with the fact that children are typically incapable of fully exercising and protecting these rights. Children need help in asserting their rights, and it is the role of the parent-as-steward to give them this help. A second factor from which the moral status of parents derives is the needs of the child. These needs are many—a need to be nurtured, a need to be educated, a need to be fed, and the need to develop the capacities to satisfy her own needs and exercise her own rights, to mention just a few. Because children are not yet mature, they often do not possess the capabilities necessary to effectively satisfy all of their own needs. The role of the parent is to both see that these needs are met, and to help the child develop the capabilities for satisfying her own needs in the future.

An important implication of this way of thinking about the moral status of parents is that, morally speaking, parenthood is not primarily a biological relation. Rather, it is a relation of care, advocacy, and protection. Now in most cases the person best suited and most motivated to take on this role of care-giver, advocate, and protector will in fact be the biological parent. But it is not biology that makes someone a parent, rather it is a fulfilling of a complex and demanding role in the life of a child. Stewards typically take on their duties voluntarily, and ideally the role of parent-as-steward will also be undertaken voluntarily. In cultures where contraception, abortion, and adoption are all genuine options, the role of parent often is in fact undertaken voluntarily. But just as the parent-as-steward model implies that children are not property of their parents, it also suggests that adults should have a choice as to whether to become parents.

The role of parent-as-steward gives the parent a set of duties toward the child. These duties are threefold. First, there is the duty not to violate the rights of the child. Second, there is the duty to prevent others from violating the rights of the child. Third, there is the duty to promote the interests of the child.[13] While the first and second duties are, in the Kantian sense, more or less perfect duties, the third is and must be an imperfect duty. Thus the parent has a great deal of leeway in deciding how to promote the interests of the child, and to a large extent it is up to her to decide what fulfilling this duty will amount to. It is difficult to see how it could be otherwise.

Because the duty to advance the interests of the child is an imperfect duty, it gives the parent the right to exercise considerable discretion in raising children. In other words, the fact that she has this imperfect duty to advance the child's interest means that she has the right to exercise her own judgement in carrying it out. But—and this is crucial—the rights of the parent to make decisions for the child are only rights to exercise discretion in fulfilling the duty to promote the interests of the child. Thus in this stewardship conception of parenthood, parental rights only extend to deciding how to promote the child's interests. They do not constitute anything like property rights over the child. And they exist only insofar as the parent is indeed promoting the interests of the child.

The stewardship conception of parental rights allows us to posit parental rights—and thus keep the state from meddling too much in family affairs—without treating the child as property of the parent. In this way, we can explain why parents have the right to exercise considerable discretion in raising their children without owning them. That is, it explains both the fact that parents have the right to exercise considerable discretion in limiting the freedom of their children, and the fact that the parents' rights to do so do not outweigh the basic rights of their children. It explains, in effect, why parental rights have the thresholds that they do.

So it appears that by distinguishing basic rights to which all persons are entitled from constructed rights which depend on factors besides one's status

as a person, and by thinking of parental rights as stewardship rights and thus as right with thresholds, we can reconcile the three claims that make up the common sense position with regard to the moral status of children.

Rights, Conflict, and the Moral Nature of Parenting

Some will claim that conceptualizing the parent-child relationship in terms of rights introduces an element of conflict between parents and children.[14] While this line of thought is implicit in the anti-rights position of many feminists, it has been most explicitly developed by Ferdinand Schoeman. While Schoeman does not deny that children have rights, he does think that "talk about rights of children . . . may encourage people to think that the proper relationship between themselves and their children is the abstract one that the language of rights is forged to suit."[15] He worries that talk of children's rights "might foster thinking about the relationship between parent and child as quasi-contractual, limited, and directed toward the promotion of an abstract public good."

Schoeman's worries about the "dangers" of talking about the rights of children are based on two main claims. First, he notes that "via intimate relationships, one transcends abstract and rather impersonal associations with others and enters personal and meaningful relationships and unions." These relationships, he continues, are so important that "not only are [they] central to defining who one is, but human existence would have little or no meaning if cut off from . . . such relationships."[16] Second, Schoeman claims that according rights is detrimental to relationships because rights emphasize the separateness of persons while relationships emphasize the union of persons: "the language of rights typically helps us to sharpen our appreciation of the moral boundaries which separate people, emphasizing the appropriateness of seeing other persons as independent and autonomous agents."[17] He also thinks that talk of rights introduces the "the prospect of state intervention into a relationship" which "depresses the sense of security of the relationship" and "makes people hesitant to see their interests fused with those of another."

We do not deny that deep committed personal relationships are constitutive of a full, meaningful life. Nor do we deny that according rights to children makes the family a more public institution by introducing the possibility that society might intervene on behalf of those whose rights are violated. But unlike Schoeman, we think this is an advantage of rights—they often make claims on all of us that we can ignore only at our moral peril; they move children into the public realm, so to speak, so that they are not at the mercy of parents. Our most central disagreement with the anti-rights position of Schoeman and others is over the claim that talk of rights is somehow incompatible with deep personal relationships. While this topic is too large to deal with fully here, a couple of points are in order.

Rights and relationships both enshrine and respect the same thing: the unique value of persons. Because rights and relationships share this goal, recognizing rights is perfectly compatible with being in a relationship. For genuine relationships with others exist partly on the basis of respect for the other as a person, and so they already involve the same attitude toward persons that rights embody. Certainly relationships involve more than just respect, but they do involve respect. Someone who fails to respect another as a person can only engage in pathological relationships with her. According someone rights and engaging in a genuine relationship both involve (but are not exhausted by) respect for the other.[18] So in good relationships people will respect each other's rights as a matter of course, with no need to become obsessed with "legalistic" thinking that emphasizes distinctions between persons at the expense of relationships.

Yet it is often difficult to tell from the outside what sort of relationship (if any) is in place. It is typically much easier to tell whether rights are being violated. So while we certainly favor strong and healthy relationships between parents and children, we do not think that this is incompatible with talking about rights. Indeed, we think rights are necessary in part because we need a way to tell whether a relationship is healthy or not. Rights are one tool of doing this: a pattern of systematic rights violation by one partner in the relationship is certainly a sign that the relationship is pathological. (And surely those who extol the virtues of relationships do not want to defend relationships of that sort.)

Because children have the same moral status as other persons, we are morally obligated to take their rights seriously. In addition to basic rights, children have various needs, and these needs create (imperfect) duties for parents. One kind of injustice to children occurs when parents ignore children's rights in an effort to fulfill their duties to provide for the children's well-being. Of course the two kinds of duties will sometimes be in conflict, and part of the role of parents as stewards is to strike some sort of balance between them, or as a last resort, to subordinate one to the other. Since the perfect duty to respect rights is always more stringent than the imperfect duty to promote interests, there will in general have to be a lot of utility at stake for the child—or perhaps her future ability to exercise her rights—before the child's rights should be infringed. But since children's rights do have thresholds, there will be cases where this is permissible.[19]

But even in cases where the rights of the child must be infringed, the parent must not do so by completely ignoring the rights that get subordinated. This is part of what it is to take a right seriously: that in cases where a right must be infringed or limited, one should try to infringe or limit it as little as possible. Thus the moral nature of parenting is in large part a balancing of the duty to nurture with the duty to respect the rights of the child. And taking her job seriously requires that the parent minimize—both in number and in scope—whatever infringements or limitations are necessary, and that she look for other ways for the child to meaningfully exercise whatever rights must be infringed or limited.

This task is particularly difficult when the need for nurturing collides with the basic right of self-determination. The right to self-determination is not, of course, the right simply to follow any whim that arises. Rather, it is something like a right to choose a life-plan and to control how it is implemented. The eight-year-old deciding she wants to be a firefighter is not choosing a life plan, though she is learning some of the skills she will need to do so later on. So while her choice need not be accorded the same status as that same choice when she is twenty-three, it is not to be completely dismissed either. Creative compromises can enable parents to respect the rights of children even when some specific exercise of them must be overruled. Thus a parent ought not to give in to her eight-year-old child's demand that she be excused from math class on the grounds that she wants to be a firefighter when she grows up. Yet the right to self-determination plus the right to nurturing together create a duty to the parent to educate the child in what it takes to choose and implement a life-plan. Part of that education no doubt involves playing games of "what do I want to be when I grow up." One way a parent can respect the aspiring firefighter's right to self-determination, while still overruling the decision to forgo math classes, would be to encourage her to explore what it is to be a firefighter while still requiring the math classes. Thus the parent might require her to do her math but also take her to visit fire stations and talk with firefighters. Of course, when a child begins to exhibit a stable preference for a certain life-plan, it may be the sign that the child is now beginning to make a more earnest decision, and that the "real" life-choice might well end up being for this very form of life, or one closely related to it. When this occurs, the choice will, of course, need to be granted a higher status than before.

This is but one example of how parenting involves the duty to balance the rights and interests of the child, and how those rights and interests might be balanced creatively. Our point is twofold. First, the rights of the child are not mere prima facie rights. Even if some of them must be overridden in a particular case, they do not vanish completely.[20] The moral nature of parenting involves more than simply deciding whether the need for nurturing should take precedence over a right in a given situation. It also involves seeing to it that any rights subordinated are still respected as much as possible. Second, the parent is uniquely placed to do this sort of balancing, both because she knows the child—and thus is able to devise the sort of creative solutions such dilemmas require—and because she identifies with her—and thus can take an interest in making sure that *all* of the child's rights are respected, even when certain exercises of some of them must be disallowed. Presumably in cases like this, where much of the right is left intact, the threshold is lower. That is, if the parent can find a way to only partially infringe a right—by some creative compromise of the sort mentioned above—then she may do so in conditions in which a more extreme infringement of the right would be impermissible. Thus for the parent who respects the spirit of the basic rights of the child, and who is willing to infringe them only when necessary and only to the degree necessary, the rights of the child will generally not interfere with the effective nurturing of the child.

QUESTIONS FOR THOUGHT AND DISCUSSION

1. What are the differences between Thomas Hobbes and John Locke on the justifications that they provide for the right of parents to restrict the liberty of their children?

2. Are there any limits to the power that parents should have over their children? What is the justification for setting limits to parental power?

3. According to Howard Cohen, what is a "borrowed capacity"? Does a person who must borrow a capacity from someone else to perform a particular task (for example, to defend herself in court) lose the right to do

that task? Do we unfairly discriminate against children when we deny them the right to do something (for example, vote in an election) if they must borrow the capacity of another person in order to do it?

4. What support does Schoeman give for the claim that the traditional categories employed by philosophers "misrepresent moral features of intimate relationships," including relationships between parents and young children?

5. Why does Schoeman argue that the significance of intimate relationships is such as to morally insulate persons in such relationships from state interventions? How would David Archard (Chapter 8) respond to Schoeman's recommendation?

6. Why does Schoeman contend that "it is the significance of intimacy, and not just a concern for the best interest of the child, that is essential to understanding the basis of the parents' moral claim to raise their biological offspring in a context of privacy, autonomy, and responsibility"?

7. Explain Brennan and Noggle's distinction between *basic* and *constructed* rights. What kind of right is the right to vote? The right to drink alcoholic beverages? The right to have sexual intercourse?

8. Why do Noggle and Brennan claim that denying a child a constructed right is not to treat children unequally? Would Cohen agree? Would Schoeman agree?

9. How do Brennan and Noggle respond to the concerns of Ferdinand Schoeman that talk about children's rights will "depress the sense of security" that children ordinarily have in the intimate relationship that they have with their parents?

FURTHER READING

William Aiken and Hugh LaFollette, eds., *Whose Child? Children's Rights, Parental Authority, and State Power.* Totowa, NJ: Littlefield, Adams, 1980.

David Archard, *Children: Rights and Childhood.* New York: Routledge, 1993.

Laurence D. Houlgate, "Children and Ethical Theory." In L. Becker and C. Becker, eds., *Encyclopedia of Ethics,* 136–139. New York: Garland, 1992.

———, "Children, Paternalism, and the Right to Liberty." In Onora O'Neil and William Ruddick, *Having Children: Philosophical and Legal Reflections on Parenthood,* 266–278. New York: Oxford University Press, 1979.

———, *The Child and the State: A Normative Theory of Juvenile Rights.* Baltimore: The Johns Hopkins University Press, 1980.

Rosalind Ladd, ed., *Children's Rights Revisioned.* Belmont, CA: Wadsworth, 1996.

John Kleinig, "Mill, Children and Rights." *Education, Philosophy and Theory* 8, 1 (1976): 1–16.

Ferdinand Schoeman, "Childhood Competence and Autonomy." *Journal of Legal Studies* 12 (June 1983): 267–287.

Francis Schrag, "The Child in the Moral Order." *Philosophy* 52 (1977): 167–177.

NOTES

Introduction

1. U.S. Consumer Products Safety Commission.

2. For example, the National Fire Protection Association, a private nonprofit policy group based in Quincy, Massachusetts.

3. Thomas Hobbes, *Leviathan* (1651), part II, chap. 20, 4–9.

4. John Locke, *Second Treatise of Government* (1690), 54–63, 170.

Ferdinand Schoeman

1. Michael Wald, "State Invervention on Behalf of 'Neglected' Children: A Search for Realistic Standards," *Stanford Law Review* 27 (1974–75): 985–1040.

2. Elizabeth Anscombe, "On the Source of Authority of the State," *Ratio* 20 (1978): 1–28.

3. Lon Fuller, "Two Principles of Human Association," in *Nomos XI: Voluntary Associations,* ed. J. R. Pennock and J. W. Chapman (New York: Atheron Press, 1969): 1–36.

Samantha Brennan and Robert Noggle

1. See Susan Moller Okin's *Justice, Gender and the Family* (New York: Basic Books, 1989). Okin argues that both historical and contemporary theorists of justice leave out the family either by assuming it to be just, or assuming that the family is outside the scope of justice.

2. Will Kymlicka pursues this line of criticism of Okin in his "Rethinking the Family," *Philosophy and Public Affairs* 20 (1991): 77–97. Kymlicka faults Okin for remaining silent on crucial questions of family justice such as who has the right to form a family and what the rights of parents, especially fathers, are.

3. We do not think that it is illegitimate. After all, in the more activist incarnations of political philosophy, practice often precedes theory. Even in such mainstream theories as that of Rawls, legitimate political theories are thought to be the outcome of an interplay of theory and pre-theoretic moral convictions. What we are doing is no different, though it takes place at the level of applied political philosophy rather than political philosophy proper.

4. We ignore here the issue of whether a neonate counts as a person. Anyone who has been around infants knows that they begin at a very early age to develop into beings with enough features of personhood that they must be counted as persons. Whatever the metaphysical status of neonates with regard to personhood, public policy must count them as full-fledged persons because by the time decisions concerning

them are put into effect, they will usually end up being decisions about persons.

5. Note that the kind of contractarian argument we offer here, based on retroactive consent, is different from the contractarian argument Thomas Hobbes uses to establish unlimited parental rights. According to Hobbes, the child's consent while she is a child, "either expressed or by other sufficient arguments declared," establishes parental dominion over children. On Hobbes's view children are the subjects of their parents when their parents preserve the children's lives and "every man is supposed to promise obedience, to him, in whose power it is to save, or destroy him." Needless to say, we disagree with Hobbes that threats of death—both in general and in the more specific case of the parent's threat to "expose" an infant—is a legitimate basis for authority. See Thomas Hobbes, *Leviathan,* Part II, Chapter 20, pp. 253–254. London, England: Penguin, 1985.

6. Jan Narveson has endorsed this position, claiming that young children are "eligible for ownership" by their parents (personal communication, spring, 1995). See also the chapter on children in Narveson's *The Libertarian Idea* (Philadelphia: Temple University Press, 1988).

7. For a classic statement of the child libertarian view, see Howard Cohen, *Equal Rights for Children,* Totowa, NJ: Littlefield, Adams and Co., 1980. [See the preceding selection from Cohen in this chapter.—Ed.]

8. For accounts of thresholds for rights, see Judith Thomson, *The Realm of Rights* (Cambridge, Mass.: Harvard University Press, 1990) and Samantha Brennan, "Thresholds for Rights," *Southern Journal of Philosophy* 33 (Summer 1995), pp. 143–168. Although significantly different in detail, both agree that rights can be overridden when enough is at stake for those who will benefit from the right's infringement.

9. Jan Narveson, *The Libertarian Idea,* p. 273.

10. John Locke, *Second Treatise of Government,* sect. 170, emphasis added.

11. *Id.*

12. Locke's views of the moral status of children are controversial. While he is clearly an important early spokesperson for the view that parents do not have absolute authority over their children, it is also the case that the limits on parental power he proposes are not generated by a belief in children's rights. For some discussion of this issue, examine Laura Purdy's use of Locke in her book *In Their Best Interest?: The Case Against Equal Rights for Children,* Cornell University Press, 1992 and David Archard's chapter "John Locke's Children" in his book *Children: Rights and Childhood,* Routledge, 1993. We have benefitted from Susan Turner's useful examination and critique of Locke's view of children which is contained in "Li'l Savages: Locke and a Sort of Parental Dominion" (unpublished manuscript, University of Leth-

Dominion" (unpublished manuscript, University of Lethbridge, Alberta, 1996).

13. Here our approach differs from that of Onora O'Neill, who argues that children do not have rights but instead are merely the objects of imperfect duties. "Children's Rights and Children's Lives" in her *Constructions of Reason: Explorations of Kant's Practical Philosophy* (Cambridge: Cambridge University Press, 1989), pages 187–207. Kant's views on the moral status of children and parents' duties towards them can be found in his *The Philosophy of Law: An Exposition of the Fundamental Principles of Jurisprudence as the Science of Right* (T&T Clark Law Publishers, Edinburgh, 1887), Chapters 28 and 29, pp.114–118.

14. Such a claim would be much in the spirit of recent feminist criticisms of the role of rights in moral theory. For an example see John Hardwig's "Should Women Think in Terms of Rights?" in *Feminism and Political Theory,* Cass Sunstein, ed., University of Chicago Press, 1990, pp. 53–68. For a response to feminist criticisms of rights see Samantha Brennan's "What's Wrong With Rights?: A Response to Some Feminist Criticisms" (paper presented at the American Philosophical Association, Central Division, April 1996). Similar criticisms of rights have been made by communitarians. For a response see John Tomasi, "Individual Rights and Community Virtues," *Ethics,* 1991, 101: 521–536.

15. Ferdinand Schoeman, "Rights of Children, Rights of Parents, and the Moral Basis of the Family." *Ethics* 91 (October 1980): 6–19, page 11 [Reprinted in this chapter.—Ed.].

16. Ibid., p. 14.

17. Ibid., p. 8. We will treat the "incompatibility thesis" as a conceptual claim. At times Schoeman and others write as though the thesis asserts an empirical fact. If the "incompatibility thesis" is supposed to be empirical, then we think it is pretty fair to say that Schoeman and those who hold similar anti-rights positions offer little in the way of empirical evidence to support it. Certainly it seems plausible to think that a preoccupation with rights might lead to a breakdown of relationships. But there is no reason to suppose that merely postulating and respecting rights is tantamount to, or necessarily leads to, a preoccupation with rights.

18. Compare a relationship with another person with the relationship one has with a pet. Both may involve care, but only one can involve relating to the other as another infinitely valuable, irreplaceable, unique person. To engage in a relationship with another person that is more than the relationship one has with a pet involves (among other things) having this attitude of respect for the other person as a person. While the best relationship may be genuine unions, they are still unions of persons. Indeed, much of what makes a relationship meaningful and valuable is the fact that another person is involved. Yet this attitude of respect for the other as a person is the same attitude that is embodied in according rights to persons.

19. See Samantha Brennan, "Paternalism and Rights," *Canadian Journal of Philosophy* 24 (September 1994), pp. 419–440.

20. For a useful discussion of the distinction between prima facie obligations and obligations that do not go away even when they must be subordinated to other obligations, see Alan Donagan, "Moral Dilemmas, Genuine and Spurious: A Comparative Analysis," *Ethics* 104 (1993): 7–21; esp. pp. 16–21.

11

The Ethics
of Childrearing

Introduction

William Ruddick, "Parenthood: Three Concepts and a Principle"

R. Paul Churchill, "The Obligation of Parents
to Raise Their Children as Altruists"

David Hoekema, "Trust and Punishment in the Family"

I n the summer of 1996, Gary and Tealisa Downes were accused in the state of
Michigan of forcing their six-year-old twins to fight each other while they were
being videotaped. Prosecutors showed 11 minutes of the videotape during the
preliminary hearing. It showed the boy and girl kicking, hitting and pulling each
other's hair. The voice of Mrs. Downes could be heard urging the girl to punch
her brother: "I told you what to do, now do it. If he kicks your ass, I'm kicking
yours."

At the time of their arrest, the Downeses told police that they made the tape
as a teaching device to remind the children what could happen if they fight. The
judge responded by ordering the Downeses to stand trial on charges of child abuse
and extortion. He said: "Clearly, it's blatantly obvious that this is going to cause
serious mental damage to two kids."

Most persons who heard about this case were horrified. They certainly would
not accept the parent's attempt to justify their behavior. Even if the Downeses
were telling the truth, we do not think that parents should force their children
into violent confrontations with each other or with other children. We believe
that there are limits to morally permissible childrearing activities, and the Downeses
exceeded these limits.

But what exactly are the moral limits to what a parent can do in the name of
rearing her children to adulthood? The judge indicates in his remarks that some of
the limits are specified by emotional harm to one's children. Parents cannot require their children to act in ways that might cause them "mental damage." Are
there other limits to childrearing? In general, are there any limits to the *kind of per-*

son that parents are morally required to raise their children to be (or not to be)? Are there *kinds of lives* that we think that we, as parents, should teach our children to want to pursue?

In the opening essay of this chapter, William Ruddick is concerned with the last of these two questions. He notices that disputes about pediatric, educational, and other child-related matters may reflect more general concepts of parenthood, including parental rights and responsibilities. These concepts may be child centered, focusing either on a child's needs or on a child's development. Needs and development are not wholly distinct or in competition, but some parents may emphasize one or the other and, in case of conflict, favor one over the other. Such emphasis and preference tends to distinguish parents as child carers and parents as child raisers (in most cases, adult raisers). So distinguished, these kinds of parental focus involve different temporal perspectives (present and future), as well of different categories of assessment and analogies (associated with nursing and teaching).

A third concept of parenthood mentioned by Ruddick widens the focus to include family members, present and future, as well as past or departed members. He observes that parents who think of parenthood as family making and maintaining are very like political rulers and are appraised in quasipolitical terms.

When these concepts come into conflict, Ruddick argues that at least three principles may be invoked to resolve matters: the Amish Parent-Perpetuating principle, the liberal Option-Maximizing principle, and the Life-Prospect principle. The last is a principle that allows parents to foster life prospects that may eliminate a number of alternatives, as well as blocking life prospects that, on reflection, they think could never lead to lives for their children that they, the parents, could accept. This Life-Prospect principle draws on notions of a life ("biographical," or, better "psychosocial") that is distinct from biological existence, and (Ruddick claims) helps formulate parent-child relationships better than the usual notions of autonomy, best interests, and rights—all of which presuppose fully distinct individuals.

The examples that Ruddick uses to illustrate his principle are of life possibilities that are self-regarding for the child, that is, they are about lives that a child might lead that might be difficult for him as an adult and even make him unhappy but do not involve doing deliberate harm to others. But suppose that a child's parents set out to rear their children so that they will grow up to be adults who are prone to and enjoy hurting others. Does Ruddick's Life-Prospect principle commit us to endorsing this morally questionable project in childrearing?

Paul Churchill's essay is directly relevant to this question. Churchill asks whether parents have a moral obligation to raise their children as altruists. In raising this question, he joins a long line of philosophers since Plato to write about the duty of parents to shape the character of their children. Both Plato and Aristotle were convinced that the cultivation of virtuous traits of character is one of the primary functions of parenting. Plato advocated the Socratic thesis that virtue is knowledge—that is, that acquiring moral knowledge is sufficient to compel morally right conduct. Aristotle, on the other hand, argued that children must acquire not only the right moral beliefs, but the desire and the will to put these beliefs into practice.

But what exactly are the "right moral beliefs" that we should instill in our children? If one of them is that there is an obligation to promote the good of others (the duty of beneficence), do we as parents have a secondary obligation to raise our children to want to do things for others, and to get satisfaction out of doing them? In the words of Paul Churchill, do we have a specific duty to raise our children to be altruists?

If we do have a duty, what are the morally appropriate methods to use in the difficult task of raising our children to be good people? In "Trust and Punishment in the Family," David Hoekema argues that punishment is a morally indispensable method of rearing children, not because of its value as a deterrent to future wrongdoing, nor because of a violation of rights. Instead, Hoekema argues, parental punishment is the imposition of a penalty for the betrayal of trust. Parents extend trust to their children in stages, as the child grows older and becomes more competent. When children violate parental rules, they betray that trust. When punishment is imposed on the children, it "not only reflects the violation of trust but also makes possible its restoration." Without the possibility for restoration, the children would have been left with "the burden of having betrayed their parents' expectations."

Hoekema does not indicate whether his theory of justifiable parental punishment extends to *corporal* punishment; that is, whether we are justified in hitting our children as a form of punishment. In thinking about this question, the reader should consider bell hooks's claim in Chapter 8 that violence in the parent-child relationship is itself an act of betrayal of the child's trust.

Parenthood: Three Concepts and a Principle
William Ruddick

William Ruddick is professor of philosophy and adjunct professor of psychiatry at New York University, where he codirects the Philosophy and Medicine Program. He has written on a variety of issues in family ethics and medical ethics and has edited *Philosophy in Medical Centers* (Society for Philosophy and Public Affairs, 1980) and coedited *Having Children: Philosophical and Legal Reflections on Parenthood* (New York: Oxford University Press, 1979).

In parental practices and disputes, there are often three distinct governing thoughts at work, namely,

1. Parents tend, or care for their children.
2. Parents raise their children.
3. Parents make and maintain a family.

Although normally compatible and intertwined, these distinct notions may come into conflict, especially in disputes between parents and doctors or teachers, or between parents themselves. After sketching these notions, I'll consider examples of these disputes and underlying parent conceptions, as well as three principles for resolving them. Of the three, I'll argue for the Life-Prospect principle (LPP) that falls between two extremes, namely, the Parent-Perpetuating principle (PPP) that gives parents too much power over their children's future lives and the Option-Maximizing principle (OMP) that gives them too little.

Parenthood as Child-Caring

Caring for children involves various activities—attending to them, feeding them, protecting them.

Published by permission of the author.

Perhaps "child-tending" is the better term, for it focuses on parental activities, not the sentiments that "caring for" may suggest. Of course, parental activities *are* often prompted by affection, but much effective child-caring involves little affection—contrary to the usual sentimental accounts of mothering. Nonetheless, I'll use the more familiar "child-care," but mean "child-tending."

These child-caring activities are in part defined by law, religion, and analogies with other work. The law regards parents as their children's *guardians* from birth (or earlier) until maturity—the age at which young people officially no longer need parental protection or support.[1] As child-carers, parents are traditionally compared to gardeners planting and tending saplings and offshoots,[2] or to shepherds tending their flocks, or to nurses caring for the ill and helpless. ("Nurse" and "nurture" are cognates.) On certain religious views, God the Creator appoints parents to protect the innocent souls and spiritual welfare of the children whom He entrusts to them.

One striking feature of child-caring is its temporal focus on a child's present needs, especially those that require continuous or frequent satisfaction. This explains the distinctive appraisals we make of parents as child-carers. So conceived, they are praised for being *attentive, responsive, patient, devoted,* and generally *responsible.* Likewise, they are blamed for being deficient in these respects, as most teenage or drug-abusing parents are supposed to be. Or, alternatively, parents are blamed for "smothering" their children with too much attention or being too patient, hence too permissive or indulgent of their children's misconduct.

Mothers are especially subject to such criticisms. Still regarded as the primary care-takers, they are held to a strict standard often pictured by doting mothers serenely cradling a nursing child or securely holding the hand of a toddler. Fathers are held to a lesser standard of care, perhaps because of stereotypes of masculinity that make them less suited for attentiveness, responsiveness, and patient care of the helpless or dependent.

Although focused on present needs, the care even of very young children may have some future aspect. Parents worry about inculcating bad habits through the ways they feed their children

or respond to their crying. These short-term concerns lend themselves to more long-range parental concerns about a child's developing character, trustfulness, expression of feelings, and the like. For many parents, whatever the immediate satisfactions of caring for a young child, this work is motivated primarily by their larger child-raising project.

Parenthood as Raising Children

Sooner or later, most parents come to form and guide their parental activities by ideas of what they want their children to become in adulthood. At the outset they may think of themselves as artists with large creative powers. But just as artists work within often narrow constraints of materials, genres, and taste, just so parents must take account of children's biology, temperament, peers, and culture. Nonetheless, most parents try to shape their growing child's character, values, and tastes to favor or exclude certain adult outcomes. Raising a child, in short, is raising an adult.

In their child-raising parents are subject to various distinctive appraisals. They are judged to be *realistic* or *unrealistic* in their hopes for a child; *open-* or *narrow-minded* in the interests they allow or foster, or the lessons they instill; *supportive* or *retarding* of a child's development; *deftly guiding* or *relentlessly pushing* a child in certain directions.

It is striking how many of these same assessments apply to teachers, but this should not be surprising. Parents are their children's earliest and often their most influential teachers in a variety of matters—language, emotional expression, domestic skills, moral matters. How much and how long parents may control their children's education is, of course, a complex legal and moral issue in many locations. Some parents battle public school teachers over books and topics they think morally subversive (*Heather Has Two Mommies*; techniques of safer sex, Socialism), or they seek to supplement the standard "one-sided" curriculum (with Creation Science, ROTC, Wall Street investing techniques). Or, against children's wishes, parents may shift their children from public to private school to prepare them for life in a special social class, or remove them from school altogether so that they can begin to assume their allotted roles in a religious community. Again, such parental efforts at educating their children may persist through a lifetime, prompted especially by emerging or persisting political and religious differences.

Parenthood as Family-Making

These first two parental concepts are child-centered, the first focused on the current needs of a child, the second on the adult prospects of a child. But for many people parental thoughts have a wider, longer family-focus on the family. Some children are conceived in order to start, or enlarge a family, to commemorate a family member lost through death, or to satisfy parents' desire for grandchildren. Likewise, contraceptive or abortive efforts often have familial motives, for example, not to shame or burden one's parents, or to postpone one's own family-making or family-enlarging to a better time.

Such familial thoughts about parenthood reflect the fact that all births are familial events: Most children are born or adopted into a family of parents and siblings, and even first children have a larger family of grandparents, aunts and uncles, and cousins. And if death or separation deprives a child of immediate relatives, children will nonetheless feel their presence through the tales they are told or invent and the prayers they are taught.

Parenthood conceived as family-making or enlarging has itself distinctive temporal features. Starting a family has a point in time, but the family one starts or enlarges may have no intended or foreseen end. Indeed, having children may be a way of creating or continuing a family with no end—for some people, a reassuring kind of immortality in the face of death, or, at least, a possible perpetual continuity with subsequent generations (subject of course to the fortunes of fertility, disease, war—and children's continuing procreative desires).

In addition to these temporal features, parenthood as family-making carries distinguishing spatial, or topological features. Child-tending may require fences and shelter that protect children from the elements, animals, kidnappers, while child-rearing requires rooms and other places for instruction, practice, study, and playful time-off. But for family-making and maintaining, what matters most is a *home*. Parents may make a home for their family in various places—trailers, caves,

tree-houses, or even welfare hotel rooms (but not welfare shelters, aptly named), so long as it remains a place of relative security and easy return.[3]

In addition to these distinctive features of time and place, there are special assessments of parents as makers and maintainers of a family.[4] They are judged to be *fair* or *unfair, restrained* or *overbearing, beneficent* or *exploitative* and *dictatorial* in the use of their power. Relatedly, parents may create a *secure* or *fearful* home, a *hospitable* or *clannish* home, a *cooperative* or *competitive* homelife, a *loyal* or *disloyal* family feeling.

These are the very terms in which political rulers are assessed. Like rulers, parents wield economic and psychological power, as well as the threat of physical force, over their children, aging parents, and other family dependents. Not surprisingly, philosophers have found political analogies the most illuminating of parental roles. Aristotle likened fathers to their children's sovereigns. Locke assigned regal powers to both mothers and fathers, for the purpose of raising children to neither need nor desire monarchs in adulthood.

The dangers of such parental power is obvious from exercises of political powers. As in political communities, some family members have the power to define those common values and hence dissent, as well as the power to silence dissent so defined through shame or the threat of expulsion. Bernard Shaw aptly noted that a man's home may be his castle but a prison for his wife and daughters.

Despots aside, traditional families are still liable to various political faults, including subversion of civic values and communal life.[5] Plato made family ties impossible for the Guardian class by making conception communal and paternity untraceable. Families, he thought, were acquisitive and hence corrupting of civil servants.[6] More seriously, families like nations tend to be clannish, defining themselves by contrast with "inferior outsiders." This identity so defined often set limits to the kinds of acceptable outsiders who may enter or marry in. Such family clannishness is a society's racism or xenophobia writ small—small enough for children to readily read and enact in school.[7]

On the other hand, families may foster civic virtues by preserving (and embellishing) tales of virtuous ancestors who were Abolitionists, political opponents of corrupt officeholders, volunteers in the Lincoln Brigade in the Spanish Civil War. The desire to emulate family saints or carry on a family tradition of political courage may be more influential that the moral admonitions of school teachers and clergy. Like parental maxims, family stories may have directive influence throughout life.

Conflicts of Parental Notions

Despite differences in analogies, appraisals, spatial requirements, and temporal perspectives, these three concepts of parenthood are often harmoniously combined, for better or for worse. As I noted, the ways parents define and respond to a young child's needs may reflect their concerns with character formation, as well as the child's intended family rank and role. In many families, young girls may be fed less and later than their brothers, thereby being trained to contribute more to daily family life and preparing them for adult roles as wives and mothers.

Yet conflict between the three parental concerns and concepts is always possible and is often invoked in parental disputes. A mother may insist that a young daughter's need for corrective eye surgery, a matter of tending, should take precedence over the father's insistence on private school for an older son, an expense integral to his child-raising ambitions. The father may argue that the son's education will eventually bestow rewards on all the family, including better suitors and a larger dowry for the daughter.

Sometimes physicians and probate judges will be drawn into such disputes, or themselves become disputants. Physicians often seek temporary guardianship of children whose parents refuse clearly beneficial treatment, such as chemotherapy for leukemia, as in the publicized case of Chad Greene.[8] For court intervention, however, a condition need not be life-threatening. Kevin Sampson's mother kept him home from school, protecting him from the ridicule occasioned by his disfiguring, but operable tumor of the head and neck. Again protectively, she refused consent for surgery out of fear for her son's life, a fear the surgeons dismissed as excessive.[9] The court sided with the surgeons, regarding them as having the proper parental regard for the child's educational and social development.

On occasion, it may be the physicians who take the role of child-tending protectors against parents who are focusing, as zealous child-raisers, solely on long-range consequences. Growth hormones provide an example. Appealing to the social and occupational advantages of height, parents concerned with raising a child might insist on hormonal treatment for a child whose predicted full height would otherwise fall in the lowest percentile of his society's normal range. Pediatricians might well refuse, wishing to protect the child from a long, arduous treatment with uncertain promise—a refusal parents would find short-sighted and overprotective. In the pediatricians' view, by contrast, the parents will seem negligent of the child's current welfare, focused too narrowly and distantly on the child's adult condition.

Growth hormones for a child who has inherited his parents' achondroplastic dwarfism may provide a conflict of a different sort. Rather than a dispute between a child-protecting physician and a child-raising parent, the dispute may between a child-raising physician and a family-making and maintaining parent. Suppose that parents with achondroplastic dwarfism refuse to have their second child treated with growth hormones on the following *familial* grounds:

> Our first son was treated with success: several years of treatment with growth hormone put him into the low end of the normal height range by the age of 7. But, as he grew, it became difficult for us to restrain or protect him, physically. Moreover, he became increasingly embarrassed by our height and refused to bring his friends home, even for birthday parties. If pressed, he would admit that we worked in the circus, but he said we were musicians, not clowns. His intention is to leave home as soon as possible and support himself by whatever work he can find, preferably far away. We don't want to raise another child like that!

Admittedly, a small person has fewer job options than other people, but a small son would not have to stay in the circus, even if that is what they might hope and help him prepare for. Employers in other fields are becoming more accommodating, thanks to anti-discrimination law, TV exposure, and efforts of Little People of America to foster both self-pride and public acceptance. But regardless of the work he does, they and he will have the rewards of continuing family ties that his brother has foregone.

Clearly, it is not the burden of treatment on the child, but the burden of his normal growth on the family that is at the heart of the parents' refusal of treatment. How might physicians or judges respond? How should they? Are there any principles which address this case and argument?

Principles

One such principle is that proposed by Joel Feinberg in criticizing a U.S. Supreme Court decision that permitted the Amish to end their children's public schooling at 14, two years short of the legal limit.[10] The Court majority accepted the Amish argument that the continued existence of their nineteenth century religious farming community was at stake: if their children attended public high school, they would be less likely and less able to take up their roles in the community. Feinberg argued that the Amish violate their children's "right to an open future," namely, the right to be "permitted to reach maturity with as many open options, opportunities, and advantages as possible."[11] This complex right has as its general basis the right to autonomy or self-determination, that is, "the sovereign authority to govern oneself, which is absolute within one's own moral boundaries (one's "territory," "realm," "sphere," or "business")."[12] Of course, like other adult rights, the child's right to autonomy is a right-in-trust, to be fully granted when a child has developed the capacities necessary for its exercise. On this view, it is a principal parental duty to help a child to develop the capacity for autonomy.

Do the dwarf parents violate this liberal, Option-Maximizing principle (OMP)? Yes, although perhaps not to the extent that the Amish, Hasidim, and some local social elite (Boston Brahmins?) do. Admittedly, the dwarf parents are not trying to reproduce their own lives through their children, but they are reducing the son's adult options by keeping him small in the hope that this physical likeness will favor continuing

family ties. To that extent his future is less "open" than it would be with medical treatment.

But should we accept Feinberg's Option-Maximizing principle and so condemn them for this violation? At first glance, his principle seems far superior to the principle of parental self-perpetuation (PPP) of the Amish, Hasidic, or Boston Brahmin parents, for it is more realistic in the assumptions it makes about the future and less coercive of children's interests and activities. (Being realistic and uncoercive, recall, were positive assessments of parental child-raisers.) The greater realism lies in allowing for a wider range of future contingencies in social circumstances and in a child's aptitudes and interests. Amish parents must count on the stability of their nineteenth century rural community, despite the increasing encroachment of late twentieth century culture, as well as on their children's continuing acceptance of their mothers' and fathers' strict division of labor and recreation for their own lives. To insure that compliance, the Amish must be more coercive than Hasidim and Boston Brahmins whose worlds are far less isolated, even if still rigidly defining. And, of course, all these parental self-perpetuators need to be more coercive than the Feinberg liberal fostering a variety of options for a child's eventual choice.

Even so, Feinberg's Option-Maximizing principle may itself require parents to make some unrealistic assumptions, especially about their own capacities for parental self-denial. If their children are to "reach maturity with as many open options, opportunities, and advantages as possible," they may have to give up or at least reduce the importance of their own ideals for their children's lives. A number of adult occupations require early and steady preparation (for careers in music, athletics, Talmudic scholarship, acrobatics). Such early specialization will almost certainly leave a child quite unprepared for a whole range of occupations which jointly are more promising, financially and otherwise. Does the OMP allow such specialization? It would seem not.

If OMP does rule out such specializations, however, then it requires that these parents forego to abandon their fondest parental hopes and goals in favor of more likely, but less rewarding lines of work and kinds of life for their children. Such restrictions are, I think, unrealistic: How can we expect parents to raise children whole-heartedly for a whole range of lives they regard as all inferior to the life they are able and eager to foster for their children? (Think here of a cook having every day to set out a vast smorgasbord. What incentive does she have to cook, if her specialties are bound to be lost or ignored among the vast array of other dishes, many of which she herself has little taste for?)

Moreover, even if far less coercive than PPP, the OMP may still require coercive methods to get children to cooperate with the parents' optimizing program. Suppose the parents' informed assessment of future societal demands and opportunities prescribes not only the computing, literacy, and Spanish skills taught in school, but also social skills like public speaking, Mandarin, and golf that are not. Few children will accept such heavy bookings without resistance, nor can the parental pressures required be easily construed as autonomy-training. (Again, think of a child being forced to sample too many dishes from a smorgasbord.)

To steer between the parental extremes of parental self-perpetuation and parental self-denial, we need a principle that requires parents to allow for deviations of their children's circumstances and interests from their own, but nonetheless allows them to raise their children to reflect parental ideals and to maintain family ties. One such possible guide is a "Life Prospects Principle" (LPP). It requires that parents provide life-prospects, or possibilities for a child

1. that jointly encompass a range of likely societal changes, and
2. each of which would be acceptable sooner or later to both parents and child.[13]

The first condition is meant to rule out narrow parental ambitions for a child that make unrealistic assumptions about the child's future life circumstances—whether conservative Amish assumptions of social stability or radical Marxist assumptions of revolutionary change. The greater the uncertainty about those long-range circumstances, the greater the range of life-prospects parents should foster or allow. But, as the second

condition makes clear, in this provision for the future, parents need not include life possibilities likely to cause them or their child deep distress if the child were to realize any of them.

Before applying this principle to the dwarf parents, let us examine the meaning and epistemic demands of this proposed principle. The "life" of "life-prospects" refers to the patterns of aims, activities, and relationships that characterize most human existence, not to the biological matters they depend upon. It is this sense of "life" in which we talk of leading, shaping, or judging our lives—what some philosophers have called the "biographical" sense of "life."[14] As for "prospects," they are the opportunities defined by social and psychological categories in a culture, as well as the even more general conditions of human existence. As such, they include the forms of love and work a culture approves, or at least accepts. (In late twentieth century, North Atlantic societies, almost all kinds of computer work are approved, while gay and lesbian domestic partnership and child-rearing are increasingly accepted, even if not endorsed.)

In the second condition, I speak of *realizing,* not choosing a life-prospect. Choice plays a far smaller part in patterns of love and work than liberal or autonomy theorists presuppose. Much about the lives we lead are the result of chance, temperament, the influence of others. Even if we have several life-prospects in our youth or later, there may be no moments or deliberative decisions that mark the realizing of one or the other. Hence, the occasional shock when on reflection people see clearly the course of their life, much as a sailor without a compass, chart, or visible destination suddenly realizes the course she is on across a bay with few landmarks or buoys.

Our concern is with the parental attempts to influence that course, however, inconstant or ill-defined or unchosen it is. To continue the analogy, to what extent may they try to set the course and the kind of boat and sail a child will have? And how much do they have to know or predict about weather, currents, water depth, and sandbars to responsibly and safely influence course and conveyance?

LPP may seem to impose an impossible epistemic burden. The first condition requires parents to make informed predictions, for example, about social and economic circumstances that will define a child's occupational and other social possibilities and rewards many years hence. The second condition requires them to make similar long-range assessments of what they and their child will find an acceptable life for the child, then an adult. The Utility Principle and other consequentialist principles also require long-range predictions, but there is something especially problematic about predicting one's own future attitudes about deeply felt matters. It would seem either too easy or too hard—too easy, because if I hold them strongly, I must feel that they are, as firm convictions, very unlikely to change—or too hard, because in order to assess the likelihood of my strong convictions changing, I will have to imagine becoming a very different person.

Let's see how these epistemic matters play out in two cases, one of parental opposition to a child's dreams, one of parental dreams for a child. Suppose a daughter wants nothing more than a classical ballet career, but her mother refuses to let her take ballet class for the variety of reasons our three parental concepts identify. The mother fears that ballet training will be physically harmful, foster eating disorders, seriously limit her daughter's intellectual and social development, and make a stable marriage and family almost impossible. Her daughter, of course, thinks her mother exaggerates the dangers and underestimates her own chances of success and family life.

If the mother's fears are to satisfy the LPP's first realism demand, they will need to be grounded in evidence wider than anecdote—a difficult task insofar as ballet directors, like surgeons, are not eager to record or share such data.[15] Would LPP's second mutual acceptability demand be less of a challenge for the mother's objections to meet? In addition to her fears about her daughter's physical, intellectual, and social well-being, the mother has moral and political objections to the whole ethos of classical ballet, especially its celebration of sylphlike, regal, or prince-worshipping women. She could take no pride in her daughter, however successful, serving these oppressive ideals of femininity.

But how sure can she be that her attitudes won't change? Even strong attitudes wax and wane, especially under pressure from children's passions and attachments. She may have already, for example, come to appreciate, or at least tolerate, her daughter's passions for certain popular music, or clothes, or spiritualism just because they were her daughter's passions. And if she allowed her daughter to dance, wouldn't a mother's pride in her achievements be all the more likely to change her assessment of classical ballet, even of *Sleeping Beauty*?

Perhaps, but given her strong moral and political critique of classical ballet, the mother would have to think of herself undergoing a sea-change in her attitudes. But to imagine such a change might require imagining herself becoming a person she can no longer identify with or recognize. Such radical conversions do occur. Parents who renounce a child who marries outside the faith, or makes a public commitment to a partner of the same sex, have been known to becoming reconciled to their child when she gave birth to their first grandchild. But even though such radical conversions are known to occur, they are necessarily unpredictable in one's own case. Like a religious or political conversion, they result from the impact of unique personal experiences, "bolts from the blue," and as such are unexpected.

Admitting the possibility of radical change, the mother could still appeal to self-image or self-conception to justify her certainty that she would continue to disapprove even if her daughter were to become a star. There is, however, one more possible source of change she must consider, namely, the possibility of deeply and permanently alienating her daughter by her adamant, disparaging opposition to ballet. Vividly imagining that possibility, the mother might find her animus somewhat lessening, at least enough for her to foresee that she could tolerate or accept her daughter's life in ballet, even if she could not endorse or approve of it.

I have formulated LPP in terms of "life prospects *acceptable* to both parents and children" in order to allow for just such modification of principled opposition into grudging acceptance. Foreseeing the need for such accommodation to maintain connection with her daughter, she might begin now to make concessions. ("Well, so long as you maintain your weight, your school grades, and interest in some contemporary dance companies, I'll let you take two classical classes a week.") In so doing, she would act as if she did have some doubts about the convictions she holds, without the self-denying thought that they are really not convictions after all. She can, thereby, meet the epistemic demand without imaginative self-denial.

A converse case of a child's grudging acceptance of his parents' dreams will bring out other facets of the LPP's conditions. Consider academic parents who push their son to excel in school, but not just to improve his college and career options: they want him to have an academic career, repeating their successes or compensating for their disappointments (in the universities they did or did not get into, and even in the scholarly fields they pursued or wished they had pursued). What cautions, or limits, might LPP set on such parental projects?

Like many self-referring parental projects (of professional golfers, musicians, real estate investors, Mafiosi), this runs several risks even when children cooperate. Self-deceptively overestimating their son's ability or ambition, parents may well expect him to have greater success than he achieves. Ironically, he may find his prospects acceptable, but they do not when they realize that those prospects are less than they had hoped. For them, there has been no appreciable difference between what is acceptable, or tolerable, and what is worthy of approval: any life of his they can accept must be a source of pride for them. But aware of the risk their disappointment and disapproval poses to continuing close ties with their son (and his wife), they may have to draw that distinction, or alter their criteria of what is praiseworthy.

Their son's fulfillment of their ambitions may, ironically, force the same reflections and revisions of original ambitions for him. Suppose he does excel as they had hoped, but at the cost of two divorces and loss of his children's custody—and, for them, close ties to grandchildren. Supposing (like the Amish) they assumed that the academic world they had known would remain stable, and they made no allowance for the strains on family life new conditions of academic competition imposed (fewer tenure-track lines, more and earlier publication, more trips for consulting and conferences, visiting appointments abroad). Belatedly, they may come to revise deep-seated, self-identifying values in the light of their regrets about costs their son was in fact willing to pay for success, but as it turned out they were not. Had they been able in advance to take such costs into account, they would have been able earlier to modify the goals toward which they drove him.

In these two academic cases, as with the ballet scenario, LPP's second condition of "eventual mutual acceptability" proves more difficult to assess in advance than it seemed, largely because of what in the various circumstances the parents would eventually find acceptable. This is not a problem for adherents of the Option-Maximizing principle: the options which parents must maximize need not take account of the parents' own desires for a child. In each case, the question is, Would fostering or discouraging this life-prospect seriously reduce the range of prospects the child would otherwise have? (Probably, ballet more so than academic training, but both are significantly reductive.) But, as I have argued, disallowing strong parental preferences and ambitions threatens to make parenthood a kind of self-denying servitude for anyone whose parental aims are more selective than that of a life-prospects smorgasbord.

After these explorations of how LPP might guide deliberation and judgment, let us return to the dwarf parents who refuse consent for growth hormone therapy for their child. Do the dwarf parents violate LPP, as I have been developing it? Arguably, not. In their family-maintaining efforts, they do not try to make their son replicate their lives, or stay within their own hermetic world. They do not restrict his education to circus arts, but rather argue that he will have many options in the larger world, despite his small size. But they are willing to sacrifice the greater options normal height would provide in order to keep him closely related to them. So long as they are aware of the risk they are taking of angering and alienating him by their refusal, they would seem to be satisfying the conditions of LPP.

Let's consider a final case that extends LPP into life and death issues and shows both the utility of LPP and its limits. Consider a familiar case of an infant born with Down's syndrome and a life-threatening constriction of the gastro-intestinal tract. Does LPP allow a parent to withhold consent for life-saving surgery? Suppose, with the LPP in mind, she insists that the child will have no life-prospects that she deems acceptable. Even if she did not already have other children to care for, she could not devote herself to the care of a child with such limited prospects, whatever the special care and education others might provide, and if he did survive to adulthood, she could not tolerate the thought of him living in a sheltered community of people with similar or worse disabilities. Her conclusion: Since he could not have a life she could foster and accept, it is better that he not live.

"Better for whom—her or the child?" we might ask. The LPP does not take up the lives of parents and children separately assessed, but rather a child's life-prospects as assessed by the parents whose efforts provide and develop them. The more appropriate challenge under LPP is to ask, "Are her assessments of life-possibilities fully informed?" Probably not. Despite much favorable publicity about Down's children, the public no doubt still overestimates the special care they need and underestimates their developmental capacity and the special rewards they provide their parents and siblings, at least in many, if not all cases. But, granting all that, she may still refuse consent on the ground that one cannot tell at birth how severe the Down's disabilities may be and that she will not gamble on her child being one of the less disabled, dependent, and educable ones.

Such reasoning cannot, I think, be faulted on grounds of LPP properly applied. Of course, she would face objections based on more familiar principles from religion and law. Many physicians would invoke a child's right to life, on religious or other metaphysical grounds. Hospital lawyers would invoke laws that forbid discrimination against handicapped persons in medical treatment, arguing that the operation is routinely performed on infants without disabilities. I will, however, not try here to weigh LPP against these general rights to life or non-discriminatory medical treatment. These rights are too complex to discuss briefly, and so too is the meta-issue of how rights or principles are to be weighed or ranked when they conflict.[16]

Backing for LPP

The liberal Option-Maximizing principle is founded on the alleged general right to Autonomy. Is there a general right or some other wide

moral considerations that would justify LPP? The right to Liberty will serve here if properly distinguished from the right to Autonomy with which it is often conflated. Unlike Autonomy, Liberty is not a notion of self-governance, but of freedom from governance by those in power, especially governmental authorities. More specifically, Liberty is constituted by a variety of specific freedoms such as freedom of movement and association, especially in matters or work and family life. In family matters, many women in recent years have gained the freedom to choose, refuse, or leave a marriage partner, and to use various means or assistants in avoiding or producing pregnancy and childbirth. Such liberties are clearly crucial for leading a life not subject to control by authorities, political, religious or domestic. But since such liberties are equally important to children when they become adults, parents are not morally free to extend their early authority over children into a child's adult years. Accordingly, parents cannot so limit a child's life-prospects that the child will have to lead a life he or she does not want. Both conditions of the LPP are meant to rule out such parental restriction of a child's future liberty, while at the same time allowing parents the freedom to raise children in ways that give their own lives purpose and hope.

In exercising their limited parental freedom, parents clearly cannot do anything that would deny their children the same degree of parental liberty in their maturity. Hence, LPP as liberty-preserving over generations rules out the kinds of arranged marriage parents often make to insure that their grandchildren will be of their own class, race, or religion. Even in inheritance tax law allows "generation skipping," the LPP does not, at least in matters of parental liberty.

I do not mean to suggest that a principle of liberty, or the value of liberty is a *foundation* for LPP. Liberty derives its value from the value of lives, not vice versa.[17] Therefore, the value of life-prospects does not derive from the value of liberty, any more than it does from the value of autonomy.

I may have drawn the contrast between Liberty and Autonomy too sharply. They are clearly close relatives. Witness the role of rationality and maturity in each. For Autonomy, these are defining properties; for Liberty, they are moral and legal preconditions. But even this contrast is dropped by theorists who use rationality and maturity to distinguish Liberty from "license." Nonetheless, Liberty's greater scope and specificity make it better suited than Autonomy for moral analysis of familial and other personal ties.

Liberty and Autonomy aside, further support for LPP can be found in feminist work under the rubric, "the ethics of care." Although not always explicit, much of this writing assumes that preserving of human relationships is a basic good underived from other values.[18] As we have seen from several cases, LPP's "mutually acceptable" condition serves this good, as well as the goods of Liberty and of a psychosocial life of one's own. Recall that it was the dwarf parents' desire to preserve their parent-child relationship through childhood and beyond that prompted their refusal, and, likewise, it was the same desire that might prompt the mother to try to moderate her opposition to ballet, when no other consideration would.

In closing, I should make clear that I do not think of the Life-Prospect principle as having the authority or clarity of application to serve as a moral decision procedure. (Recall its inconclusive role in the Down's syndrome case.) The most we can ask of any moral principle, however, is that it formulate an important moral factor that we might neglect or distort without its help. In so doing, it can enrich moral deliberations that are oversimplified, or occasionally tip the balance in a moral stalemate. The notion of life-prospects that parents foster or foreclose is, I suggest, just such an important moral factor. In invoking this notion, the Life-Prospect principle defines the scope and limits of parental selection of those prospects, with due respect for each of the parental concerns that distinguish the three common concepts of parenthood I have identified. When those concerns of child-caring, child-raising, and family-making conflict with regard to pedagogic or pediatric decisions, the Life-Prospect principle can help clarify the conflict, and on occasion help resolve it (as in the academic and sectarian cases). Accordingly, the principle would seem to deserve a place in our moral repertory, even if it is not as clear and user-friendly as I might wish.

The Obligation of Parents to Raise Their Children as Altruists

R. Paul Churchill

Robert Paul Churchill is professor of philosophy and director of the Peace Studies Program at George Washington University. He is the editor of *The Ethics of Liberal Democracy* (Oxford: Berg, 1994), and the author of "On the Difference between Non-Moral and Moral Conceptions of Toleration: The Case for Toleration as a Moral Virtue," in M. A. Ravazi and D. Ambuel, *Philosophy, Religion and the Question of Intolerance* (Albany: State University of New York Press, 1997).

> The purpose of life is undoubtedly to know oneself. We cannot do it unless we learn to identify ourselves with all that lives.
>
> *Mahatma Gandhi*

For the purposes of this essay, I take it as noncontroversial that, given their access to necessary resources, persons choosing parenthood have a manifest moral obligation to raise human beings who will be as healthy, happy and autonomous as circumstances will allow. Now suppose it were possible for parents to choose, from among alternative strategies, child-rearing practices that would predispose their children to become other-regarding and altruistic adults? Ought parents then to recognize a moral obligation to raise their children as budding altruists?

Both affirmative and negative responses to this question readily spring to mind. For the affirmative it can be argued that every member of society presumably would benefit from enhanced social cooperation and other-regarding care and concern brought about by increased altruism. In addition, significant, or "heroic" altruistic actions,

Published by permission of the author.

although presently regarded as wholly supererogatory, often dramatically promote welfare. Finally, insofar as altruistic attitudes and behavior are positively correlated with virtuous dispositions and behavior, training children to be behave altruistically should contribute significantly to their development of virtuous character, and hence, if Aristotle was correct, to their greater happiness. Such considerations suggest at least a *prima facie* moral obligation to raise one's children in such a manner as to become altruistic adults.

On the other hand, common and presumptively true assumptions about the dangers posed (especially for "self-sacrificing" individuals) by our shared social world, the uncertainty that altruistic acts will produce meritorious consequences, and the apparent rewards attached to selfish, egoistic behavior all suggest a *prima facie* case for not selecting parenting strategies that will result in altruism. It might be argued, therefore, that parenting strategies that over-emphasize the development of altruistic traits would result in the deformation of persons who would have diminished capacities for happiness and autonomy and, most troubling, whose psychological health would be impaired by dispositions and attitudes (related to excessive caring or helping behaviors) that are "dysfunctional" in a social world characterized by the aggressiveness, individualism, narrow (means-ends) rationality, preference satisfaction, and narcissism characteristic of liberal democratic societies.

The project of this essay is to argue against the negative, pessimistic response reviewed above. Contrary to popular expectations, there is no conceptual inconsistency between altruism and affirmative self-centeredness, nor are there grounds for supposing that altruism necessitates suffering or necessarily limits personal autonomy. On the contrary, by drawing on a body of empirical research as well as on theories in the psychology of moral development, I argue that altruistic child-rearing strategies would actually enhance capacities for experiencing happiness, even in our unregenerate and hazardous social world; and furthermore, that they extend rather than diminish capacities for autonomous choice.

Thus, paradoxically, those capable of freely choosing to behave altruistically are not those who have a weak sense of selfworth or too little healthy self-regard. On the contrary, egotistical or narcissistic individualists who are injured in their capacities to be caring and giving are also most likely to be diminished in their capacities for happiness and autonomous agency. Thus I argue that we shall continue to discover that persons inclined to be altruistic are most full of life and most confident in their self-identity. Hence, an altruistic childrearing practice, carefully chosen and monitored, would appear to greatly enhance parents' chances of fulfilling their moral obligations to assist their children to grow into happy, healthy and autonomous adults.

To be fully complete, the argument sketched above would require that I establish four theses, or at least, make a strong case—pending further research in psychology—for the plausibility of each. One thesis concerns the definition and coherence of the concept of altruism. Obviously, a second thesis concerns the real availability of an altruistic child-rearing strategy as one that can be selected by parents as a matter of deliberate choice. A third thesis would establish causal connections between child-rearing practices and altruism, by demonstrating that the latter has its origins in family patterns of interaction and especially those involving early childhood experiences. It is with a fourth thesis that I am primarily concerned in this short essay; that is, with the moral grounds, or argument, for selecting an altruistic child-rearing strategy. For this reason, I comment only briefly on the first two theses—with the confidence, however, that they each could be given adequate defense—and focus on the last two: with the causal connections between child-rearing practices and altruism and parents' moral obligations to select such practices.

What Is Altruism?

Turning then briefly to the first issue, what is altruism? In 1988, Samuel P. Oliner and Pearl S. Oliner published *The Altruistic Personality,*[1] the results of the Altruistic Personality Project. This large-scale study is an in depth analysis of hundreds of "rescuers of Jews": people who, despite grave risk and terrible hardship, rescued Jews during the Holocaust. The Oliners' study further inspired a major international and interdisciplinary conference that resulted in the publication in 1992 of the collection of essays called *Embracing the Other.*[2] These combined research efforts now make it possible to specify with greater confidence what altruism is and to identify the distinguishing characteristics of the altruistic personality.

Combining the Oliners' research with that of other contributors, and especially Lawrence A. Blum,[3] we may define altruism as behavior that meets the following conditions: (1) it is voluntarily undertaken; (2) it is motivated by concern for others or by conscience or moral principle (or some combination of these); (3) it is done in the absence of expectation of gain—of receiving "external" rewards; (4) it manifests an absence of concern for the self, or more accurately, the subjection of concerns of safety for the self or advantage to the self to concerns for the other, and (5) it manifests care marked by a significant degree of "inclusiveness" that renders irrelevant such characteristics as the gender, race, ethnicity, religion, or nationality of the others toward whom concern is shown. The question thus ineluctably arises: what "produces" altruism, or more accurately, what are the necessary *prerequisites* for the ability persons have to "construct themselves" as altruists? Among researchers there is an overwhelming consensus on the answer to this question: childhood experiences. As psychologist Ervin Staub says, "[t]he challenge of raising children is to help them evolve strong, well-developed but at the same time connected identities that embody caring about others' welfare and the experience of deep feelings of satisfaction from connection to other people."[4] Thus, it is possible to comment briefly on the second thesis concerning the availability of altruistic childrearing practices—by noting that it may soon be possible for parents to consciously choose to nurture their children to become altruistic persons. That is, our knowledge of the origins of altruism in family interactions during early childhood may soon be adequate enough to generate recommendations of sufficient detail to specify a coherent "strategy" for altruistic child-rearing. Summarizing the implications for a "pattern of parental practices," based on the study of three decades of empirical re-

search, psychologist Ervin Staub is already prepared to identify "schemata" for parental behaviors and can report on the favorable results of experiments in training parents in specific skills of childrearing.[5] In anticipation of this possibility, we return to the main issue posed for debate: ought parents to feel morally obligated to choose such a strategy?

I want to answer this question in the affirmative, but before a more specific presentation of my argument, it is important to look more closely at the main reservation against raising children to be altruistic: the concern about autonomy. Emphasizing the "absence of concern for the self"— as reflected in condition 4 of the definition of altruism, a critic might suggest the danger that altruism is associated with weak "ego strength," low self-esteem, or "self-regard," and lack of self-direction. Such concerns probably explain why some might fear that altruistic individuals will be "walked all over," or taken advantage of by "users" or abusive persons, and will be unable to stand up for their own rights.

But the psychological research of the Oliners and others provides absolutely *no basis* for this suspected connection between altruism and spinelessness. On the contrary, there is considerable evidence for a positive correlation between altruism and personality characteristics associated with strength of character and effectiveness such as courage and assertiveness. People behave altruistically, it appears, because they *choose* to care, or to act on their values or principles, not (as might be feared) because they are "suckers" or suffer from a learned or inherited tendency to give in to the needs of others.[6]

These considerations indicate that, contrary to the critic's expectations, altruistic persons are often (non-abusively) assertive and generally possess a strong sense of self worth. Nevertheless, an apparent paradox persists: inasmuch as altruism is "selfless"—that is, action without regard to (or overriding concern with) consequences (often very drastic) for the self—how is altruism compatible with the evidence for the altruist's strongly "centered" and "bounded" self? Seeking a solution to this puzzle leads to a richer, more revealing way of understanding "selves." The altruistic "self" can be tightly defined and strongly bounded, as it is for example, when an altruist—rather like a "rugged individualist"—relies on her own judgment to stand up for what she thinks is right, come what may. But that same self can simultaneously extend its boundaries, and through *identification,* "feel" the fear and pain of the other.

Perhaps the best way of understanding how these apparent opposites co-exist in creative tension is to be found in the Oliners' theorizing about the difference between "extensive" and "constricted" persons. The Oliners propose that the altruist is a person whose life experiences "propel" her toward extensive relationships with others, "relationships in which ego boundaries [are] sufficiently broadened so that other people [are] experienced as part of the self."[7] More specifically, extensive persons have two salient personality dimensions: *attachment,* the propensity to attach oneself to others in committed interpersonal relationships, and *inclusiveness,* the propensity towards the "breadth" of feelings of interpersonal connectedness. The opposite of the extensive person is—at the extreme—the "constricted" person. "As *extensivity* implies reaching out and integrating, *constrictedness* implies dissociation, and detachment. As extensivity implies attachment and inclusiveness, constrictedness implies a propensity to avoid committed and responsible . . . relationships." Constrictedness signifies as well an *exclusiveness* that "implies the deliberate expulsion of particular individuals or groups from consideration"[8] as well as "an ego that perceives most of the world beyond its own boundaries as peripheral."[9]

Altruism as a Foundation for Happiness

. . . [W]e are now better positioned, I believe, to answer definitively the initial question with which we began this inquiry—ought parents to raise their children to become "extensive," altruistic persons? There are two perspectives from which to respond to this question, both of which yield an affirmative answer.

One perspective considers the development of extensivity as providing foundations for happiness. Taking this perspective, we might feel ourselves in a position comparable to that of Plato and Aristotle when they faced the question, why should we be moral? Both Plato and Aristotle believed, although obviously on different grounds, that living the good life was simply impossible without morality. By analogy, if we can rely on what has been said above about the connections between the altruistic personality and moral autonomy, then those aspects of care and inclusiveness definitive of the extensive person are also integral to moral autonomy. They are perhaps not psychologically necessary in quite the same way that Plato and Aristotle believed morality to be logically necessary for happiness. There may well be other ways to attain moral autonomy . . . [b]ut a very good case can be made, I believe, for the view that the nurturing of extensive persons is at least one route to moral autonomy. If what has been presented here is true, then extensivity may be *sufficient* for moral autonomy. Furthermore, there is no reason to fear that extensive persons are more likely than their altruistic, constricted, counterparts to fall prey to the vicious and evil among us. Indeed, as we have seen, the evidence suggests the reverse—that altruists may be better prepared to protect themselves from victimization and manipulation.

Will extensive persons be happy as well as autonomous? A lot depends on how we choose to understand happiness. Very probably extensive persons will not crave the material trappings of our culture, nor assess their sense of well being in terms of popularity or social approval. But this is far from a persuasive reason for choosing not to adopt altruistic child-rearing practices. Just because the happiness extensive people seek is so entirely different, it must be defined in terms of the quality of relationships, opportunities for effective care, the thriving of the persons for whom one extends one's self, and self-insight and understanding. A skeptic might be tempted to protest that if everyone became altruistic, then opportunities for helping others would be diminished as well as the happiness derived therefrom. But this would be an objection without merit. As Aristotle has convincingly shown for friendship, true friends benefit each other the greater their equality and the more virtuous they both become.[10] There is no reason for supposing that the same would not be true for altruism. There is no ground for supposing some "upper limit" on beneficence, and in any case, only a utopian visionary would assume universal choice of altruistic child-rearing, the perfect fruition of this nurturing, and a world in which the need for help would miraculously vanish. Finally, it might be asked why parents can't fulfill their moral obligations by just being "good enough"; why must they strive to do more? Well, the issue is not whether they will succeed psychologically in finding the motivation to provide appropriate interactive care, but whether they should *aspire* to be parents who do. Despite the fact that some of the best intentioned might nevertheless fail, one cannot set one's sights on "muddling through" for the simple reason that in raising children, as with many other practical arts, one must aim for the best to have even a reasonable chance of obtaining a "good enough" outcome. So much for the first perspective.

Altruism and Autonomy

The second perspective invites us to take a closer look at the moral obligations of parents and suggests that developing extensive persons may be the best way for parents to meet these obligations. The overriding objective of parenting is to raise to adulthood persons who are not only healthy and happy, but also capable of giving and receiving genuine love and living their lives as self-directing, autonomous persons. But the research on the difference between extensive and constricted persons, as well as studies of early childhood relationships, shows that these objectives enabling our children to be loving (and lovable) and enhancing their autonomy, are—given the practical circumstances of life—often at odds.

This much is familiar to us all from our individual experiences of life in a fast paced, materialistic, semi-liberal and competitive society. But there is no reason to suppose that there is any inherent aspect of moral autonomy resulting in freedom (independence) that is inimical to deep love (attachment). On the contrary, it appears that our experiences of tension between independence and attachment result from beliefs and practices, including our family interactions and child-rearing methods, that falsely presuppose that the attainment of one requires some sacrifice or rejection of the other. It is notorious, for example, that boys are taught that "being a man" requires not only repressing emotions but also exclusivity and domination, whereas girls are raised to believe that their roles as caretakers require deference to men as well as suppression of both independent judgment and pursuit of their own visions of the good. But as the analyses of feminists have shown, these gender related oppositions are artificial and socially constructed. They arise out of false assumptions and beliefs, not only about men (boys) and women (girls), but also about love (as dependence and need) and autonomy (as separation and indifference). Yet, as we have seen, if the results of research on altruistic personality are correct, then we have strong reasons for believing that altruists live lives characterized by the reconciliation of care and independence, attachment and separation, and unconditional acceptance and critical discernment. Extensive persons overcome the apparent opposition between deep love and moral autonomy. And for this very reason, raising children to become extensive persons will be the very best way—and perhaps the only really consistent way—of fulfilling our parental obligations to do our best at raising persons who love to be free and are truly free to love.

Trust and Punishment in the Family

David A. Hoekema

David Hoekema is academic dean at Calvin College in Grand Rapids, Michigan. He is the author of *Rights and Wrongs: Coercion, Punishment and the State* (Selinsgrove, PA: Susquehanna University Press, 1986).

Family relationships are not only among the most profoundly influential but also among the least voluntary of all our social interactions. We cannot choose our parents; nor, except in unusual circumstances such as adoption and remarriage, can we choose our children. In modern Western societies we have a good deal of freedom in choosing spouses, but our choices are deeply influenced by class, economic status, and community expectations. Yet the influence of our families on educational achievement, emotional health, and vocational choices far exceeds the influence of other social institutions.

The role of the family in society has not received the attention it merits from philosophers, however—an omission that the essays in this volume help to remedy. In this discussion I wish to draw attention to an aspect of the family that has not been addressed by the other essays and is seldom mentioned by philosophical writers: the establishment and maintenance of *trust* among family members. To understand the nature and the importance of trust, I believe, is essential to any moral assessment of family relationships. Although in this brief discussion I cannot articulate such a theory fully, I will illustrate it by describing a specific episode involving the imposition of punishment. Punishment of children, which on first impression appears antithetical to trust, can be seen in this case to be not only a result of trust but a necessary condition for its maintenance.

Trust and Personal Risk

"The distinctively moral value of life begins in the sphere of those who trust one another," wrote Nicolai Hartmann in his survey of ethics.[1] In Hartmann's interpretation, trust is an attitude of faith in others that entails taking the risk of disappointment and loss. The attitude is extended in response to the truthfulness and reliability of the person trusted. Thus these two virtues give rise to the morally valuable trait of trust. In Hartmann's schema, trust is a "complementary value." Justice and charity are moral virtues when they are displayed by an individual, and those who are benefited by their exercise need not exercise any particular character traits in return. But one person's reliability cannot demonstrate itself unless others extend their trust. Trust thus entails personal risk:

> All trust, all faith, is an adventure; it always requires something of moral courage and spiritual strength. It is always accompanied by a certain commitment of the person. . . . The one who loves does not surrender himself; he stakes nothing; he gives only from himself, his own personality remains untouched. The trustful person, on the contrary, puts himself into the hands of him whom he trusts; he stakes himself. In this way his gift is morally the higher, and presupposes a greater moral strength.[2]

Hartmann captures a central element of trust—the element of deliberate and personal risk—that distinguishes it among the categories of moral action. Few other philosophers have addressed the topic of trust explicitly, and when they have, their focus has often been of limited relevance to the context of the family. Sissela Bok's engaging study of *Lying,* for example, is concerned with trustworthiness in the sense in which it is opposed to deceit.[3] In the chapter of her recent book entitled "The Grounds of Social Trust," Virginia Held is concerned not with the general character of trust but with conditions that make trust justifiable in society, especially those that make it reasonable for the disadvantaged to place their trust in social institutions.[4]

From David Hoekema, "Trust and Punishment in the Family," in R. C. L. Moffett, J. Grcic, and M. D. Bayles, eds., *Perspectives on the Family* (Lewiston, NY: Mellen Press, 1990). Published by permission of Mellen Press.

Perhaps the most helpful discussion of trust in general of recent decades can be found in two recent articles by Annette Baier.[5] Baier takes the family as a paradigm for the trust that underlies and informs moral behavior. It is absurd to suppose that children and parents have entered into a contractual agreement of mutual care, for children are not capable of committing themselves to such agreements at a young age. But from the earliest stages of consciousness and deliberative action, Baier observes, children trust their parents and others. Only against this background do the more nuanced and more intentional relationships of later life begin to form.

Baier suggests, as a preliminary definition, that trust is "accepted vulnerability to another's possible but not expected ill will (or lack of good will) toward one."[6] She observes:

> We do in fact, wisely or stupidly, virtuously or viciously, show trust in a great variety of forms, and manifest a great variety of versions of trustworthiness, both with intimates and with strangers. . . . Trust is always an invitation not only to confidence tricksters but also to terrorists, who discern its most easily destroyed and socially vital forms. Criminals, not moral philosophers, have been the experts at discerning different forms of trust.[7]

In every city and at every time of day, we trust others on the street not to assault us, other drivers not to use their vehicles as battering rams, other customers in the restaurant to refrain from slipping poison in our pie. Variations in trust are visible in the way women carry their purses—and themselves—in large cities and in small towns, in the comparative difficulties of cashing checks, in the number of locks on our doors. But even in the most dangerous and mistrustful of environments, we rely on each other in countless ways. The trust that obtains within the family is similar in character to our accepted vulnerability in these larger and looser contexts.

Trust is at its strongest within the family, particularly between husband and wife, parent and child. But events may strain or destroy it. Spouses lose each other's trust through infidelity or inattention, through acts of open hostility or merely

through the omission of acts of kindness. Relationships between parent and child are strengthened or weakened by actions and words, by promises made and kept or made and broken. Past patterns of action similarly influence the degree to which we are willing to extend our trust to neighbors, fellow workers, and others whose actions can help or harm us.

Trust between Adults and Children

The trust that concerns us here, however, is not trust among adults, who are able within limits to choose whom they will trust, but trust between adults and children, where choices are very limited. Consider first children's trust in their parents.[8] It arises at least as early as conscious and deliberate action begins, during the first year of life, in infants' implicit but inescapable reliance on their parents' help and concern. The child is unable to recognize or reflect on her own vulnerability until linguistic and conceptual abilities become developed—until she becomes able to move about in the world of the abstract and the intentional as well as that of the concrete and physical. But the trust that she extends is none the less real, her vulnerability no less significant.

Children's trust in parents, in its earlier stages, arises from an interplay between natural impulses, plain necessity, and love. Held's article cited above is concerned with "voluntary trust, the trust that is possible between conscious, autonomous persons who are able to trust or not to trust and able to betray or not to betray."[9] The trust of children for their parents falls outside her scope, for it is voluntary only in a prospective and partial sense.

But isn't it possible—one might argue in reply—for children to be suspicious and mistrustful at an early age? And if children are capable of withholding trust, then the trust they normally extend to parents must be the result of voluntary choice after all.

But the conclusion does not follow from the observation cited. It is true that, if children's trust in their parents is betrayed, their instinctual reliance on their parents can be diminished or destroyed even in early infancy. Child psychologists report that many infants subjected to abuse or neglect adapt to their situation by withdrawing within themselves, with potentially devastating results for emotional and cognitive development.

Yet the possibility that children's trust in parents can be sabotaged does not imply that trust itself must arise in the first place from voluntary choice. A child may deliberately and consciously cease to speak, for an hour or a day; but this does not imply that he made a deliberate choice in initially acquiring language. Children trust their parents by instinct and by necessity, unless catastrophic circumstances show their trust to be misplaced. They extend their trust before they possess any conscious and reflective awareness of their action or of the possibility of mistrust, and their trust is no more a consequence of voluntary choice than is their ability to say and understand a language.

Equally important in the family is parents' trust in their children. The element of choice here is far larger. A certain measure of trust is as essential for parents to lead an ordinary human life as for children, but the necessity in this case is practical, not developmental or psychological. A suspicious and overzealous parent can, after all, hire servants to keep children under close surveillance around the clock from cradle to adulthood. One need not trust a child whose every movement is watched and controlled. Needless to say, a sane parent is willing to take some of the risks that trust entails—with the second and third child, at least.

Trust is extended to children in stages, as age and behavior warrant. A toddler can learn to stay away from a hot stove but cannot be trusted to put away fine china. At four a child may be given the privilege of riding a bike around the block without a parent in attendance; at six, of crossing the street; at eight, of biking to the store for baseball cards; and so on into adolescence and growing self-reliance. Circumstances determine the details of the expanding stages of trust: the age at which a child can be trusted to cross the street depends on whether the street is in a small farming town or in midtown Manhattan. Such factors alter the particulars but not the pattern of widening boundaries of responsibility. Gradually and by numerous small steps, parents trust that an infant

will not throw himself from the changing table grows into a relationship of trust between adults.

Trust Versus Utility and Rights

I now turn to the implications of trust for moral action in the family, and its advantages over utility or rights as a ground of morality. Rather than advance my case at this point by philosophical argument, however, I offer instead a story. A true story.

Two children of early school age, playing by themselves, were experimenting with a candle, studying the black smudge that appears when they hold a paper napkin just above the flame for a moment. Inadvertently they set a napkin afire and dropped it, damaging a plastic tablecloth and, thankfully, nothing more.

Evidently frightened both of their parents' anger and of their close brush with danger, they answered the questions put to them truthfully. Their guilt for the careless and potentially destructive experiment was undeniable—even a teenager would have found it difficult to devise an innocent explanation for the smoldering remains. As soon as the sentence was pronounced against them, the forfeiture of two dollars apiece for the tablecloth, the children ran quickly to bring their banks. They counted out their dollar bills not grudgingly but eagerly. As they did so they relaxed visibly, breathing easily again.

Thus punishment was quickly borne with a sense of relief, even of gratitude: this, they seemed to sense, is how we can put things right again. Without a penalty the burden of the offense would have been too great to bear. The accident evidently frightened them, and they needed no adult authority to tell them how close they came to starting a serious and damaging fire. As soon as a parent arrived, the immediate danger was gone—the fire was out and an adult would know what to do if it rekindled. A nervous fear remained in the children's eyes. But counting out the penalty diminished it. Not only did the children not protest or resent the punishment inflicted, they seemed to welcome it.

The example may not be typical of punishments imposed in the family. Guilt is seldom so unambiguous, and penalties are usually more complex and more resented. All the same, the particular features of this episode suggest three general observations about punishment and its place in the morality of the family.

1. *The function of punishment is not adequately accounted for by the consequences it achieves.* The utilitarian justification of punishment is not completely irrelevant or without force. Undeniably, punishment is needed in many contexts in order to secure compliance with rules, and a system of punishment that brings about general compliance while minimizing arbitrary suffering is to be preferred. But in this case, as in many similar situations in the family, utilitarian considerations alone do not account for the importance of appropriate punishment.

Punishment in the case described achieves an important future good—fire prevention—by reinforcing implicit and explicit rules about dangerous play. But that end could be even more effectively achieved by strict and constant supervision, by locking up all matches, or by any number of other direct constraints on behavior.

The trust that makes dangerous acts possible requires that punishment be imposed when children do not live up to the trust placed in them. And a system in which parents allow children a degree of freedom that may be abused, and children bear the risk of being punished, is better on two counts than a system of behavioral control to prevent any risky acts: it instills in children a concrete awareness of responsibility for their acts, and it permits the maintenance and expansion of an atmosphere of trust. These advantages—not reducible to preference satisfaction or any other single interpersonal measure of utility—have to do not with the quantifiable consequences of action but with the agents' capacity for action and the character of the relationships in which future actions will take place.

2. *Considerations of individual rights do not explain the importance of punishment.* To identify just what rights are at stake in the example described would be difficult. We might cite children's right to reasonable freedom and to due process, parents' right to set rules, and property rights not to have one's house burned down. Some of these have direct bearing and obvious moral import. It would be unfair for the parents to punish if there were not clear evidence of guilt, for example. But if, as in the case described, there has been no gross breach of fairness, the appeal to rights becomes so indirect, and so clouded by the unequal status of children and adults, that it offers no clear guidance. Moreover, to attribute rights to children—whether natural rights or rights established by contract—is to presuppose a sphere of free, and autonomous action that children do not yet fully possess.

It simply does not help us in understanding the inherent appropriateness of punishment in the episode described to ground our sense of rightness in an appeal to the child's right to autonomy or the parent's right to control. The child has no general right to autonomy, given his limited but growing capacity for voluntary choice and action, nor does the parent have an abstract right to punish. The rights of each party are rights to certain kinds of treatment within the context of the parent-child relationship. But then the appeal to rights must rest in the end on the presumed legitimacy of a certain kind of relationship.

A radical egalitarian might challenge any differentiation between rights of children and rights of adults. Why should children not be given just as much voice in setting rules and imposing punishment as are parents? Such a challenge cannot be met on the moral ground of rights alone. It can be met only by appealing to the capacities of the child and to the ultimate benefit for parent and child alike of a relationship of mutual, but not strictly reciprocal, vulnerability. We have then moved beyond deontological reasons and into the realm of trust.

3. *Punishment, far from undermining trust, both reflects and reinforces it.* Punishment and trust appear initially to be at odds with each other. When the members of a family trust each other, it might appear, punishment is not needed. If punishment must be invoked, it is only because trust has broken down, and the imposition of penalties substitutes coercive enforcement for the trust that is now lost.

There is an element of truth in this picture, but in the end it is inaccurate. The imposition of punishment in the family does characteristically result from a betrayal of trust, as is the case in the episode described. The children's carelessness was just the sort of danger that their parents willingly risked by permitting the children to play without constant supervision.

But the punishment imposed on the children not only reflects the violation of trust but also makes possible its restoration. The two-dollar fine is a concrete enactment of the importance of the rule that was violated and a resetting of the scales so that trust can be extended once again. Had there been no punishment, the children would have been left with the burden of having betrayed their parents' expectations. Punishment partially lifts that burden and in doing so reestablishes the possibility of trust.

The reality of the burden that punishment removes was evident in the children's faces, even if its precise nature is difficult to articulate. If it is partly psychological, it is also partly metaphysical. Counting money from the bank brought a sense of relief simply because it was a concrete action releasing the children from silent contemplation of their parents' angry faces and the ashes on the table. But it was also a righting of the balance in a more than psychological sense, the sense that is the grounding for Kantian and Hegelian theories of the justice of punishment.[10]

I cannot attempt here to explicate just what phenomenon ties the children's sense of release to Hegel's theory of punishment as expressive of the criminal's will. I make only the initial suggestion that the function and the importance of punishment are illuminated by the relationships of trust within which punishment is imposed. In the family, in particular, it is impossible to sustain the sense of openness and risk that characterize trust between parents and children unless violations meet with appropriate punishment. Certainly there are many ways in which punishment may undermine rather than enhance trust. If it is arbitrary or capricious, cruel or excessive, children will learn not to trust but merely to fear. But when rules are reasonable and penalties fair, the practice of punishment encourages the development and expansion of trust by marking its outer bounds.

Trust requires punishment in order to show that the trust is genuine and not mere indifference. The practice of punishment enhances the normal development of trust, as categorical prohibitions give way, with the increasing maturity of the child, to wider spheres of discretion. Parents make themselves vulnerable in extending their trust to their children. In doing so, and in imposing punishment when it is appropriate, they make possible a richer and more fully voluntary relationship of trust in the future.

QUESTIONS FOR THOUGHT AND DISCUSSION

1. According to William Ruddick, what "general concepts of parenthood" arise in disputes about pediatric, educational, and other child-related matters?

2. Describe the three principles mentioned by Ruddick which may be invoked to resolve matters when the general concepts of parenthood come into conflict.

3. Why should we prefer Ruddick's Life-Prospect principle (LPP) to other principles of childrearing mentioned in his essay?

4. What does the LPP imply about the childrearing practices of the Down's parents (described in the chapter introduction)?

5. What does the LPP imply about the practice of a subculture living in America who permanently scar the faces of their male children as a sign of tribal identity?

6. According to Robert Paul Churchill, what is altruism? What attitudes and behavior are characteristic of an altruistic person?

7. What are some of the reasons why some would argue that parents should recognize a moral obligation to raise their children as budding altruists?

8. What are some of the reasons why others would argue that parents have an obligation to raise their children as egoists?

9. How does Churchill describe the difference between "extensive" and "constricted" persons? Will extensive persons be autonomous? Will they be happy?

10. Is it morally permissible for parents to punish children for wrongdoing? What justification of punishment explains this? Deterrence? Retribution?

11. Why does Hoekema reject both deterrence and retribution as justifications of the parental practice of punishing children for wrongdoing?

12. Why does Hoekema believe that parental punishment is necessary to restore trust between parent and child?

13. If parents have a moral obligation to raise their children as budding altruists, are they justified in using punishment as a means to achieve this goal?

14. How much and what type of punishment are parents justified in using to restore trust? In Chapter 8, bell hooks argues that parents are never justified in using corporal punishment. Why does she say this? Do you agree?

FURTHER READING

Edmund Leites, "Locke's Liberal Theory of Parenthood." In Onora O'Neill and William Ruddick, *Having Children: Philosophical and Legal Reflections on Parenthood*, 306–318. New York: Oxford University Press, 1979.

Edgar Page, "Parental Rights." *Journal of Applied Philosophy* 1, 2 (1984): 187–203.

Ferdinand Schoeman, "Parental Discretion and Children's Rights: Background and Implications for Medical Decision-making." *The Journal of Medicine and Philosophy* 10 (1985): 45–61.

———, "Adolescent Confidentiality and Family Privacy." *The John Marshall Law Review* 20, 4 (Summer 1987): 641–660.

Herbert Spencer, *The Principles of Ethics*, vol. 1, 575–580. Indianapolis: Liberty Classics.

NOTES

William Ruddick

1. Traditionally, girls become mature when old enough to gain a husband's protection, and boys when capable of self-protection. In the Middle Ages, male majority was set by adding the 2 years needed for military training to 19, the age at which boys were judged strong enough to wear and wield armor.

2. In an earlier essay, "Parents and Life-Prospects," (in *Having Children: Philosophical and Legal Reflections on Parenthood*, eds., Onora O'Neill & William Ruddick, New York: Oxford University Press, 1979, section 2) I contrasted guardians with gardeners. I was not thinking of routine watering, feeding and spraying, but rather of gardeners' horticultural work of pruning, training, and shaping plants. Horticulture is clearly

more akin to the raising of children, the second parental concept I take up shortly.

3. Robert Frost's famous lines caught these aspects: "Home is the place where, when you have to go there, / They have to take you in," says the farmer as he watches a former worker returning across a field. Or, as his less quoted wife replies, "I should have called it / Something you somehow haven't to deserve." —"Death of a Hired Man," first published in *North of Boston* (London, 1914).

4. Henceforth I'll use "family-making" to cover both adding children (by birth, adoption, or remarriage) and family-maintaining. Since family ties need constant adjusting, mending, altering, and reviving, this expansion is apt. (Compare the theological view that God sustains the world through constant recreation.)

5. See Michelle Barrett & Mary McIntosh, *The Anti-Social Family* (London: Verso/New Left Books, 1982).

6. Plato, *Republic,* Bk. V [reprinted in Chapter 5 above.—Ed.]

7. Militaristic rhetoricians get the connection. Witness, the recruiter's call for men to fight abroad against a foreign enemy who, if undefeated, would invade the "Homeland," rape wives and daughters, and leave families with alien, unwanted children of mixed-race.

8. Despite its high cure rate, the parents sought to spare him the "torture" of further leukemia chemotherapy. Defying the order, they fled with him to Mexico for an unproved, but less toxic treatment with the extract of apricot pits. The boy subsequently died.

9. *In re Sampson,* 317 N.Y.S. 2d 641. Although a Jehovah's Witness, she did not think that blood transfusion would imperil her son's prospects for heaven, if imposed by the physicians.

10. "A Child's Right to an Open Future," in *Whose Child?,* eds. William Aiken and Hugh LaFollette (Totowa, NJ: Rowman and Littlefield, 1980).

11. *Ibid.,* p. 130.

12. *Ibid.,* p. 142.

13. A slight revision of the principle as I first proposed it in "Parents and Life Prospects," *op. cit.,* section 3.

14. A better term might be the *psychosocial* sense of "life" for those attitudes, aims, and social relationships need not have the coherence or distinctive, unifying themes that biographies, as narrated stories, require. Children's lives develop within, and often remain intertwined with, their parents' lives in ways that do not provide such literary features, let alone the highly individualistic, even careerist features that some philosophers presuppose in their use of "biographical life." It is this partial identity of the lives of parents and children that is both the aim of family-makers and maintainers, as well as the opportunity for parents' excessive, coercive, or unrealistic attempts at control.

15. One doctor estimates that 1 in 5 classical ballet dancers suffer eating disorders, 20 times the incidence in white middle-class (girls and) women. *New York Times,* 7/16/97, C15.

16. I take up these matters in an essay for a project on prenatal testing for genetic disability at the Hastings Center (Garrison, New York), sponsored by the NIH National Human Genome Research Institute's ELSI (Ethical, Legal, and Social Implications) Program. A collection of these papers will be published in 1998/9.

17. See James Rachels and William Ruddick, "Lives and Liberty," in *The Inner Citadel: Essays on Individual Autonomy,* ed. John Christman, New York: Oxford University Press, 1989.

18. This theme is most prominent in the work of Carol Gilligan (*In a Different Voice*) and Nel Noddings (*Caring*), as well as in more recent unpublished work by Hilde Lindemann Nelson and Sara Ruddick.

Robert Paul Churchill

1. *The Altruistic Personality: Rescuers of Jews in Nazi Europe* (New York: Free Press, 1988).

2. Pearl M. Oliner, Samuel P. Oliner, Lawrence Baron, Lawrence A. Blum, Dennis L. Krebs, and M. Zuzanna Smolenska (eds.), *Embracing the Other: Philosophical, Psychological, and Historical Perspectives on Altruism* (New York: New York University Press, 1992).

3. "Altruism and the Moral Value of Rescue: Resisting Persecution, Racism, and Genocide" in *Embracing the Other* (1992), pp. 30–47.

4. "The Origins of Caring, Helping, and Nonaggression: Parental Socialization, The Family System, Schools, and Cultural Influence" in *Embracing the Other* (1992), pp. 390–412, quoted at p. 400.

5. *Id.*

6. See *The Altruistic Personality,* pp. 173–175.

7. *Id.,* p. 183.

8. Pearl M. Oliner and Samuel P. Oliner, "Promoting Extensive Altruistic Bonds: A Conceptual Elaboration and Some Pragmatic Implications," in *Embracing the Other,* pp. 369–389, quoted at 373.

9. *The Altruistic Personality,* p. 186.

10. *Nicomachean Ethics,* Books VIII and IX, esp. Book VIII, Secs. 4–8, and Book IX, Secs. 1-2, and 4-9.

David Hoekema

1. Nicolai Hartmann, *Ethics,* trans. Stanley Coit (New York: Macmillan, 1932), Vol. II, p. 294.

2. Hartmann, *Ethics,* II, p. 292.

3. Sissela Bok, *Lying* (New York: Pantheon Books, 1978).

4. Virginia Held, *Rights and Goods: Justifying Social Action* (New York: Free Press, 1984), chap. 5.

5. Annette Baier, "Trust and Anti-Trust," *Ethics,* 96 (1986): 231–260; "What Do Women Want in a Moral Theory?" *Nous* 19 (1985): 53–63.

6. Baier, "Trust and Antitrust," p. 235.

7. Ibid., p. 234.

8. Although for simplicity I speak of "children and their parents," I do not intend any presumption that a social unit consisting of two parents and their biological children is either normal or normative in contemporary society, nor is the relevance of my discussion in any way limited to such situations. Such a "nuclear family," once the dominant arrangement in American society, composes a diminishing share of American households. In the past the family unit commonly included grandparents; today homosexual and lesbian partners, shared custody following divorce, and other more complex relationships are increasingly common. Yet the fundamental need for trust, and its determination by parents' and children's behavior, persist in families of every kind.

9. Held, *Rights and Goods,* p. 65.

10. Immanuel Kant, *The Metaphysical Elements of Justice,* trans. John Ladd (Indianapolis: Bobbs-Merrill, 1965); G. W. F. Hegel, *Philosophy of Right,* trans. T. M. Knox (Oxford: Oxford University Press, 1942).

12

The Obligations
of Grown Children
to Their Parents

Introduction
John Locke, "The Perpetual Obligation to Honor One's Parents"
Jane English, "What Do Grown Children Owe Their Parents?"
Jan Narveson, "What Do We Really Owe Our Parents, and Why?"

Historians of the family say that a persistent myth in Western societies is that before the twentieth century old people always lived with their grown children and were lovingly cared for by them. In fact, family historians report, the old of the past lived in circumstances remarkably similar to those of the elderly of today. Either they lived alone, or with other elderly persons, or with a married couple to whom they may or may not have been related. The only generalization that can be made about the difference between the elderly of the past and contemporary elderly persons is that there are so many more elderly in the current population than in the past. The second difference is that today's elderly who do not live with their children are more likely than the elderly of the past to be living in institutions than in other types of accommodation.

Even if historians succeed in dispelling the myth about the living conditions of the elderly in times past, grown children continue to feel ambivalent about their moral obligations to their parents. The central ethical questions that are raised when thinking about "filial obligation" are: What are the reasons for thinking that grown children have an obligation to "honor and respect" their parents? Do grown children owe their parents more than honor and respect—for example, should they assume the physical and financial responsibility to care for their parents when their parents become unable to care for themselves? What kind of obligation is this? For example, is it an obligation based on gratitude? On debt? What creates this debt?

John Locke argued in 1690 that grown children have a "perpetual obligation" to honor their parents. The duty, he said, is God given. The word "honor" implies not only a (negative) duty not to injure the happiness or life of one's parents, but also a (positive) duty to defend, relieve, assist, and comfort them. This does not mean, however, that a grown child has a duty to obey the commands of his parents. Once the child comes into the age of his majority, he is "as free from subjection to the will and commands of his father, as he himself is free from subjection to the will of anybody else."

Although Locke refers to filial duties as "God given," he also derives them from "the benefits received by and from" one's parents. We should be grateful when we have received benefits from our parents, and we show our gratitude by honoring them in the ways just indicated. In this respect, the reader should compare Locke's justification of filial duty with that offered by the Chinese philosopher Lin Yutang in Chapter 3.

Jane English disagrees with Locke's claim that children owe their parents honor, not because she thinks that grown children owe them something besides honor, but because she thinks that grown children owe their parents nothing at all! Her argument is that what parents do for their children while they are young is not a favor but, at most, a voluntary sacrifice. Voluntary sacrifices lay the ground for friendship between parents and children but do not make the children indebted to their parents. If parents and children are not friends at the time that parents need the help of their children, then the children are under no obligation to give them aid.

In saying this, English also rejects the idea that the mere fact of a biological relationship between child and parent gives rise to a duty of the child to care for her parent. For example, a man whose relationship with a child is only that he was a sperm donor for the artificial insemination of the child's mother has no right to the child's help if he should become needy in his old age. Nor can he base a right to her help on the fact that he later volunteered to pay for her college education. According to English, this would have been a voluntary sacrifice on his part. "His" child owes him nothing for this act of beneficence, although it may lay the ground for their future friendship.

In the final essay in this chapter, Jan Narveson argues that there may be room to speak of the obligation of a grown child to her parents even if the child does not love them nor regard them as friends. If she agrees that her parents have benefitted her, then she should see to it that they are benefitted in turn to "at least the degree that renders it non-irrational for the parents to have done this." Narveson's argument is that a rational ethics would include a moral rule requiring that grown children honor and care for their parents if parenting is itself to be a worthwhile occupation. At the same time, Narveson rejects the idea that filial duty can be grounded in the fact that their parents "gave them life." Something is a benefit for someone only if that person exists to receive the benefit. Hence, if life itself was a benefit, the child would have had to exist in order to receive it. As Herbert Spencer one said in another context, this would constitute "a curious compound of truism and absurdity."[1]

The Perpetual Obligation to Honour One's Parents

John Locke

John Locke studied and later taught at Oxford University, England. He is credited with being one of the originators of the empiricist approach to philosophy. His philosophical fame in ethics and political theory is mainly due to his *Two Treatises of Government,* first published in 1690.

66. But though there be a time when a child comes to be as free from subjection to the will and command of his father, as he himself is free from subjection to the will of anybody else, and they are each under no other restraint but that which is common to them both, whether it be the law of nature or municipal law of their country, yet this freedom exempts not a son from that honour which he ought, by the law of God and nature, to pay his parents. God having made the parents instruments in His great design of continuing the race of mankind, and the occasions of life to their children, as He hath laid on them an obligation to nourish, preserve, and bring up their offspring, so He has laid on the children a perpetual obligation of honouring their parents, which containing in it an inward esteem and reverence to be shown by all outward expressions, ties up the child from anything that may ever injure or affront, disturb, or endanger the happiness or life of those from whom he received his; and engages him in all actions of defence, relief, assistance, and comfort of those by whose means he entered into being, and has been made capable of any enjoyments of life. From this obligation no state, no freedom, can absolve children. But this is very far from giving parents a power of command over their children, or an authority to make laws and dispose as they please of their lives or liberties. 'Tis one thing to owe honour, respect, gratitude and assistance; another to require an absolute obedience and submission. The honour due to parents, a monarch in his throne owes his mother, and yet this lessens not his authority, nor subjects him to her government.

67. The subjection of a minor places in the father a temporary government, which terminates with the minority of the child; and the honour due from a child, places in the parents a perpetual right to respect, reverence, support, and compliance too, more or less, as the father's care, cost, and kindness in his education has been more or less. This ends not with minority, but holds in all parts and conditions of a man's life. The want of distinguishing these two powers which the father hath, in the right of tuition during minority, and the right of honour all his life, may perhaps have caused a great part of the mistakes about this matter. For, to speak properly of them, the first of these is rather the privilege of children, and duty of parents, than any prerogative of paternal power. The nourishment and education of their children is a charge so incumbent on parents for their children's good that nothing can absolve them from taking care of it. And though the power of commanding and chastising them go along with it, yet God hath woven into the principles of human nature such a tenderness for their offspring that there is little fear that parents should use their power with too much rigour; the excess is seldom on the severe side, the strong bias of nature drawing the other way. And therefore God Almighty, when He would express His gentle dealing with the Israelites, He tells them that though He chastened them, He chastened them as a man chastens his son (Deut. viii. 5)—i.e., with tenderness and affection—and kept them under no severer discipline than what was absolutely best for them, and had been less kindness to have slackened. This is that power to which children are commanded obedience, that the pains and care of their parents may not be increased or ill rewarded.

68. On the other side, honour and support, all that which gratitude requires to return for the benefits received by and from them, is the indispensable duty of the child, and the proper privilege of the parents. This is intended for the parents' advantage, as the other is for the child's,

From John Locke, *Second Treatise of Government* (London: 1690).

though education, the parents' duty, seems to have most power, because the ignorance and infirmities of childhood stand in need of restraint and correction, which is a visible exercise of rule, and a kind of dominion. And that duty which is comprehended in the word honour requires less obedience, though the obligation be stronger on grown than younger children. For who can think the command, "Children, obey your parents," requires in a man that has children of his own the same submission to his father as it does in his yet young children to him, and that by this precept he were bound to obey all his father's commands if, out of a conceit of authority, he should have the indiscretion to treat him still as a boy?

69. The first part, then, of paternal power, or rather duty, which is education, belongs so to the father that it terminates at a certain season. When the business of education is over, it ceases of itself, and is also alienable before. For a man may put the tuition of his son in other hands; and he that has made his son an apprentice to another has discharged him during that time of a great part of his obedience, both to himself and to his mother. But all the duty of honour, the other part, remains, nevertheless, entire to them; nothing can cancel that. It is so inseparable from them both that the father's authority cannot dispossess the mother of this right, nor can any man discharge his son from

honouring her that bore him. But both these are very far from a power to make laws, and enforcing them with penalties that may reach estate, liberty, limbs, and life. The power of commanding ends with nonage; and though after that, honour and respect, support and defence, and whatsoever gratitude can oblige a man to, for the highest benefits he is naturally capable of, be always due from a son to his parents, yet all this puts no sceptre into the father's hand, no sovereign power of commanding. He has no dominion over his son's property or actions, nor any right that his will should prescribe to his son's in all things, however it may become his son in many things not very inconvenient to him and his family to pay a deference to it.

70. A man may owe honour and respect to an ancient or wise man, defence to his child or friend, relief and support to the distressed, and gratitude to a benefactor, to such a degree that all he has, all he can do, cannot sufficiently pay it; but all these give no authority, no right of making laws to any one over him from whom they are owing. And 'tis plain all this is due not only to the bare title of father, not only because, as has been said, it is owing to the mother, too, but because these obligations to parents, and the degrees of what is required of children, may be varied by the different care and kindness, trouble and expense, which are often employed upon one child more than another.

What Do Grown Children Owe Their Parents?

Jane English

Jane English (1947–1978) taught philosophy at the University of North Carolina, Chapel Hill. She wrote several essays on contemporary moral problems and edited the anthology, *Sex Equality* (Englewood Cliffs, NJ: Prentice-Hall, 1977).

What do grown children owe their parents? I will contend that the answer is "nothing." Although I agree that there are many things that children *ought* to do for their parents, I will argue that it is inappropriate and misleading to describe them as things "owed." I will maintain that parents' voluntary sac-

rifices, rather than creating "debts" to be "repaid," tend to create love or "friendship." The duties of grown children are those of friends and result from love between them and their parents, rather than being things owed in repayment for the parents' earlier sacrifices. Thus, I will oppose those philosophers who use the word "owe" whenever a duty or obligation exists. Although the "debt" metaphor is appropriate in some moral circumstances, my argument is that a love relationship is not such a case.

From Jane English, "What do Grown Children Owe Their Parents?" *Having Children: Philosophical and Legal Reflections on Parenthood* (New York: Oxford University Press, 1979), 351–356.

Misunderstandings about the proper relationship between parents and their grown children have resulted from reliance on the "owing" terminology. For instance, we hear parents complain, "You owe it to us to write home (keep up your piano playing, not adopt a hippie lifestyle), because of all we sacrificed for you (paying for piano lessons, sending you to college)." The child is sometimes even heard to reply, "I didn't ask to be born (to be given piano lessons, to be sent to college)." This inappropriate idiom of ordinary language tends to obscure, or even to undermine, the love, that is the correct ground of filial obligation.

Favors Create Debts

There are some cases, other than literal debts, in which owing, though metaphorical, is apt. New to the neighborhood, Max barely knows his neighbor, Nina, but he asks her if she will take in his mail while he is gone for a month's vacation. She agrees. If, subsequently, Nina asks Max to do the same for her, it seems that Max has a moral obligation to agree (greater than the one he would have had if Nina had not done the same for him), unless for some reason it would be a burden far out of proportion to the one Nina bore for him. I will call this a favor: when A, at B's request, bears some burden for B, then B incurs an obligation to reciprocate. Here the metaphor of Max's "owing" Nina is appropriate. It is not literally a debt, of course, nor can Nina pass this IOU on to heirs, demand payment in the form of Max's taking out her garbage, or sue Max. Nonetheless, since Max ought to perform one act of similar nature and amount of sacrifice in return, the term is suggestive. Once he reciprocates, the debt is "discharged"; that is, their obligations revert to the condition they were in before Max's initial request.

Contrast a situation in which Max simply goes on vacation and, to his surprise, finds upon his return that his neighbor has mowed his grass twice weekly in his absence. This is a voluntary sacrifice rather than a favor, and Max has no duty to reciprocate. It would be nice for him to volunteer to do so, but this would be supererogatory on his part. Rather than a favor, Nina's action is a friendly gesture. As a result, she might expect Max to chat over the back fence, help her catch her straying dog, or something similar—she might expect the development of a friendship. But Max would be chatting (or whatever) out of friendship, rather than in repayment for mowing the grass. If he did not return her gesture, she might feel rebuffed or miffed, but not unjustly treated or indignant, since Max has not failed to perform a duty. Talk of "owing" would be out of place in this case.

It is sometimes difficult to distinguish between favors and non-favors, because friends tend to do favors for each other, and those who exchange favors tend to become friends. But one test is to ask how Max is motivated. Is it "to be nice to Nina" or "because she did x for me"? Favors are frequently performed by total strangers without any friendship developing. Nevertheless, a temporary obligation is created, even if the chance for repayment never arises. For instance, suppose that Oscar and Matilda, total strangers, are waiting in a long checkout line at the supermarket. Oscar, having forgotten the oregano, asks Matilda to watch his cart for a second. She does. If Matilda now asks Oscar to return the favor while she picks up some tomato sauce, he is obliged to agree. Even if she had not watched his cart, it would be inconsiderate of him to refuse, claiming he was too busy reading the magazines. He may have a duty to help others, but he would not "owe" it to her. But if she has done the same for him, he incurs an additional obligation to help, and talk of "owing" is apt. It suggests an agreement to perform equal, reciprocal, canceling sacrifices.

The Duties of Friendship

The terms "owe" and "repay" are helpful in the case of favors, because the sameness of the amount of sacrifice on the two sides is important; the monetary metaphor suggests equal quantities of sacrifice. But friendship ought to be characterized by *mutuality* rather than reciprocity: friends offer what they can give and accept what they need, without regard for the total amounts of benefits exchanged. And friends are motivated by love rather than by the prospect of repayment. Hence, talk of "owing" is singularly out of place in friendship.

For example, suppose Alfred takes Beatrice out for an expensive dinner and a movie. Beatrice incurs no obligation to "repay" him with a goodnight kiss or a return engagement. If Alfred complains that she "owes" him something, he is operating under the assumption that she should repay a favor, but on the contrary, his was a generous gesture done in the hopes of developing a friendship. We hope that he would not want her repayment in the form of sex or attention if this was done to discharge a debt rather than from friendship. Since, if Alfred is prone to reasoning in this way Beatrice may well decline the invitation, request to pay for her own dinner, his attitude of expecting a "return" on his "investment" could hinder the development of a friendship. Beatrice should return the gesture only if she is motivated by friendship.

Another common misuse of the "owing" idiom occurs when the Smiths have dined at the Joneses four times, but the Joneses at the Smith's only once. People often say, 'We owe them three dinners." This line of thinking may be appropriate between business acquaintances, but not between friends. After all, the Joneses invited the Smiths not in order to feed them or to be fed in return, but because of the friendly contact presumably enjoyed by all on such occasions. If the Smiths do not feel friendship toward the Joneses, they can decline future invitations and not invite the Joneses; they owe them nothing. Of course, between friends of equal resources and needs, roughly equal sacrifices (though not necessarily roughly equal dinners) will typically occur. If the sacrifices are highly out of proportion to the resources the relationship is closer to servility than to friendship.[1]

Another difference between favors and friendship is that after a friendship ends, the duties of friendship end. The party that has sacrificed less owes the other nothing. For instance, suppose Elmer donated a pint of blood that his wife Doris needed during an operation. Years after their divorce, Elmer is in an accident and needs one pint of blood. His new wife, Cora, is also of the same blood type. It seems that Doris not only does not "owe" Elmer blood, but that she should actually refrain from coming forward if Cora has volunteered to donate. To insist on donating not only interferes with the newlyweds' friendship, but it belittles Doris and Elmer's former relationship by suggesting that Elmer gave blood in hopes of favors returned instead of simply out of love for Doris. It is one of the heart-rending features of divorce that it attends to quantity in a relationship previously characterized by mutuality. If Cora could not donate, Doris's obligation is the same as that for any former spouse in need of blood; it is not increased by the fact that Elmer similarly aided her. It is affected by the degree to which they are still friends, which in turn may (or may not) have been influenced by Elmer's donation.

In short, unlike the debts created by favors, the duties of friendship do not require equal quantities of sacrifice. Performing equal sacrifices does not cancel the duties of friendship, as it does the debts of favors. Unrequested sacrifices do not themselves create debts, but friends have duties regardless of whether they requested or initiated the friendship. Those who perform favors may be motivated by mutual gain, whereas friends should be motivated by affection. These characteristics of the friendship relation are distorted by talk of "owing."

Parents and Children

The relationship between children and their parents should be one of friendship characterized by mutuality rather than one of reciprocal favors. The quantity of parental sacrifice is not relevant in determining what duties the grown child has. The medical assistance grown children ought to offer their ill mothers in old age depends upon the mothers' need, not upon whether they endured a difficult pregnancy, for example. Nor do one's duties to one's parents cease once an equal quantity of sacrifice has been performed, as the phrase "discharging a debt" may lead us to think.

Rather, what children ought to do for their parents (and parents for children) depends upon (1) their respective needs, abilities, and resources and (2) the extent to which there is an ongoing friendship between them. Thus, regardless of the quantity of childhood sacrifices, an able, wealthy child has an obligation to help his needy parents more than does a needy child. To illustrate, suppose sisters Cecile and Dana are equally loved by their parents, even though Cecile was an easy child to care for, seldom ill, while Dana was often sick and caused some trouble as a juvenile delinquent. As adults, Dana is a struggling artist living far away, while Cecile is a wealthy lawyer living nearby. When the parents need visits and financial aid, Cecile has an obligation to bear a higher proportion of these burdens than her sister. This results from her abilities, rather than from the quantities of sacrifice made by the parents earlier.

Sacrifices have an important causal role in creating an ongoing friendship, which may lead us to assume incorrectly that it is the sacrifices that are the source of the obligation. That the source is the friendship instead can be seen by examining cases in which the sacrifices occurred but the friendship, for some reason, did not develop or persist. For example, if a woman gives up her newborn child for adoption, and if no feelings of love ever develop on either side, it seems that the grown child does not have an obligation to "repay" her for her sacrifices in pregnancy. For that matter, if the adopted child has an unimpaired love relationship with the adoptive parents, he or she has the same obligations to help them as a natural child would have.

The filial obligations of grown children are a result of friendship, rather than owed for services rendered. Suppose that Vance married Lola despite his parents' strong wish that he marry within their religion, and that as a result the parents refuse to speak to him again. As the years pass, the parents are unaware of Vance's problems, his accomplishments, the birth of his children. The love that once existed between them, let us suppose, has been completely destroyed by this event and thirty years of desuetude. At this point, it seems, Vance is under no obligation to pay his parents' medical bills in their old age, beyond his general duty to help those in need. An additional, filial obligation would only arise from whatever love he may still feel for them. It would be irrelevant for his parents to argue, "But look how much we sacrificed for you when you were young," for that sacrifice was not a favor but occurred as part of a friendship which existed at that time but is now, we have supposed, defunct. A more appropriate message would be, "We still love you, and we would like to renew our friendship."

I hope this helps to set the question of what children ought to do for their parents in a new light. The parental argument, "You ought to do x because we did y for you" should be replaced by, "We love you and you will be happier if you do x," or "We believe you love us, and anyone who loved us would do x." If the parents' sacrifice had been a favor, the child's reply "I never asked you to do y for me," would have been relevant; to the revised parental remarks, this reply is clearly irrelevant. The child can either do x or dispute one of the parents' claims: by showing that a love relationship does not exist, or that love for someone does not motivate doing x, or that he or she will not be happier doing x.

Seen in this light, parental requests for children to write home, visit, and offer them a reasonable amount of emotional and financial support in life's crises are well founded, so long as a friendship still exists. Love for others does call for caring about and caring for them. Some other parental requests, such as for more sweeping changes in the child's lifestyle or life goals, can be seen to be insupportable once we shift the justification from debts owed to love. The terminology of favors suggests the reasoning "Since we paid for your college education, you owe it to us to make a career of engineering rather than becoming a rock musician." This tends to alienate affection even further, since the tuition payments are depicted as investments for a return rather than done from love, as though the child's life goals could be "bought." Basing the argument on love leads to different reasoning patterns. The suppressed premise, "If A loves B, then A follows B's wishes as to A's lifelong career" is simply false. Love does not even dictate that the child adopt the parents' values as to the desirability of alternative life goals. So the parents' strongest available argument here is, "We love you, we are deeply concerned about your happiness, and in the long run you will be happier as an engineer." This makes it clear that an empirical claim is really the subject of the debate.

The function of these examples is to draw out our considered judgments as to the proper relation between parents and their grown children, and to show how poorly they fit the model of favors. What is relevant is the ongoing friendship that exists between parents and children. Although that relationship developed partly as a result of parental sacrifices for the child, the duties that grown children have to their parents result from the friendship rather than from the sacrifices. The idiom of owing favors to one's parents can actually be destructive if it undermines the role of mutuality and leads us to think in terms of quantitative reciprocal favors.

What We Really Owe Our Parents, and Why[1]

Jan Narveson

Jan Narveson is professor of philosophy at the University of Waterloo, Ontario, Canada. He is the author of The Libertarian Idea (Philadelphia: Temple University Press, 1988) and Morality and Utility (Baltimore, MD: Johns Hopkins Press, 1967).

1. Morality

Do we have significant and special duties to our parents, and if so, why? To make progress on this question, we must begin by defining more sharply the relevant kinds of obligation or duty in question . . . I propose a tripartite division as follows:

(a) Personal principles: these are those rules of action or attitudes toward life which are such that people in general may not hold the individual whose principles or attitudes they are to account for them—society may not insist on a person's having one rather than another from among the set of alternatives respecting the matter in question. Example: do you make it a matter of principle to keep in tip-top physical condition? Very well, that's your choice; the next person may reasonably opt for a life in which her physique receives only minor and necessary attention.

(b) Morality, or if you like, "public morality" (I believe these are really identical): these are the principles which ought to be universally reinforced upon and by everyone in the society in question, by the familiar devices of interpersonally administered praise and blame, criticism and assessment, reward and punishment.

(c) "Political": these are the principles which may properly be enforced by publicly appointed agencies empowered to invoke organized force, if need be, to secure compliance or effect.

Note that all of these are specified in terms of what "may" or "should" be done. It would also be possible to make a parallel set of de facto distinctions, between what is, in the society in question, left to the individual, what is approved or disapproved by the public, and what is done by the government. I shall be speaking only of the de jure senses here, but mention this point to ward off possible implications that I am claiming that certain things ought to be done a certain way simply because the acts in question are widely reinforced. This is an implication which never directly holds, in my view.

Now I take it that the question before us is primarily in domain (2), and not in either (1) or, at least for present purposes, in (3). Thus, regarding (3): whether the considerations advanced below would be usable to support a universal, tax-supported system of old-age pensions, for instance, is certainly an important and eligible question, but it is not taken up here. And regarding (1), on the other hand, what you happen to think of your mother, or of mothers in general, is also not at issue. What is at issue is whether we (all) should be criticizing people for "neglect" of their parents: should, for example, blame people who, following a personal rift with them, thereafter do nothing to support them, or who show generosity in respect of various causes but treat their own parents no better. This is an issue in public morality, in other words, but not necessarily an issue of public, meaning government, policy.

We settle issues on the personal level—if we settle them at all—by looking into our souls, by sensing the general drift to which the currents of our life experience give rise regarding the matter at hand. That seems to me all one can say about it,

From "On Honouring Our Parents," The Southern Journal of Philosophy, 25, 1 (1987): 65–78. Reprinted by permission.

and of course it is an utterly unhelpful thing to say, so far as it goes. But in any case, it is no way to settle a *moral issue*. When morality is in question, we must ask not what attitudes our personal life experiences incline us toward, but rather, which attitudes, among those we can garner any adherence to, it would be reasonable to expect *everyone* to adopt with respect to the matter at hand. We need to ask this, because morality consists of those principles which there is reason for everyone to reinforce with respect to everyone: everyone is to comply, and everyone is to direct his or her repertoire of behavioral influence so as to secure that universal compliance. People can't be expected to do this unless there is benefit, at least in the long run, to them, as seen from their point of view, from the prospect of universal compliance of the kind in question. A rational morality must, for this reason, be an agreement among all persons, or all persons with a possible influence on the issue at hand.

Very few principles, in my view, get the nod from such a strict framing of our subject. But some certainly will. One of them, I think, is the obligation to live up to one's voluntarily undertaken agreements and interpersonal commitments, and another is to refrain from pursuing one's interests by means harmful to the legitimate interests of others (thus requiring a further characterization of "legitimacy"). Neither of these take us very far in the present case, however. If there is a duty [to care for our parents], it is clearly not a duty arising from an agreement we have made, but rather a duty which may very well require us to make certain agreements. And neglecting my parents does not thereby necessarily harm them, apart from the "emotional" harm they might undergo upon the painful perception that their child does not love them. But whether they have a right to expect that love is precisely what is, in considerable part, in question here!

The general idea that we owe something to those who have done something for us, however, is certainly of potential importance here, for at least in typical cases, our parents have indeed benefited us. We must here pose two crucial questions. The first is whether there is any such principle at all, and if so, of what force. And the

second is whether what our parents do in the way of simply bringing us into existence in the first place, and thereby of contributing to our "genetic identity," may properly count as something they have, in the relevant sense, "done for us." These are both extremely interesting and difficult issues. I shall offer some thoughts on both, though I do not suppose the result will amount to a sufficient, let alone a definitive, treatment.

The Duty to Requite: Children as Beneficiaries of Services

Why might we do something for someone, apart from the special cases where we have an explicit commitment to do so? Out of good nature, for one thing. And good nature is in general a source of benefit to those toward whom it is directed. At an extreme, good nature can be pathological, a pattern of compulsive random benefitting of others that goes continually unrequited and erodes one's spiritual resources. It is in our interest that others not be disposed to encourage good nature to that level of self-disregard. And we must be wary that well-intentioned good-natured persons not become officious and annoying, attempting to benefit us where we'd prefer to be left on our own. Short of these extremes, however, we surely have ample reason to encourage good nature, and a principal way to do so is to see to it that those who show us good nature, whenever (as I take to be typical) it really is beneficial to us, do not suffer for their trouble. If we enjoy having people smile pleasantly at us rather than walking stolidly by, we shall return the smiles; when others are dour we shall try, somewhat gingerly, to cheer them up, and if we succeed are rewarded by their marginal increment in agreeableness. We shall hope that they do likewise. These things aren't done much on principle, and would be both less successful and less amiable if they were; but retrospective reflection will assure us that these tendencies are on the right track, and insofar as we can encourage them in ourselves, we have reason to do so.

Where good nature is not the (or the main) operative factor, we must turn to interests of other kinds. There is, of course, the special case of love. Much of what was said about good nature applies to this also, but with important caveats. A primary one among them is occasioned by the fact that we do not love "disinterestedly," with literally no thought of return. We want those we love to have certain attitudes toward us, and we are susceptible to bitter disappointment or frustration when they are not forthcoming. For this reason, it would, as Nietzsche so wisely observed, be a terrible mistake to encourage universal love. A very few loves are the most we can handle (there is a not implausible view that the magic number is just one); as indeed, the objects of our affection will not gladly view it should they find that only a scant bit of our attention comes to them as a result of this alleged love. What does have to be forthrightly denied is the suggestion that love is literally selfless—from which it does not follow that if someone loves you, then you have the duty to benefit that person. It does follow, however, that if someone loves you and you take him or her up on it, then you certainly do have such a duty, though the terms of benefit concerned must be a matter for rather nice definition by the persons concerned.

Finally, then, we come to the doing of good turns to persons toward whom you have no particular feelings of affection, and apart from, or even despite the absence of good nature. Here, it seems to me, the only rational motive can be that of, as we may say, *investment*. Even the dourest among us will, if they pay any attention to their interactions with others, be disposed to give a stranger directions if asked for them, to save a life when that can be done without great danger or much of tragedy. But the present point is that the sort of coin in which a parent wants to be repaid for his or her investment may be one that no amount of observing of anything that could plausibly be called a "duty" would equal. In that respect—surely not an unimportant one—the answer to our question is that parenting is a risky business, the most crucial aspects of which are simply beyond the reach of moral concepts. Period.

Luckily, that is not the whole story. The parents in question, for example, though they would have surely preferred the outcome in which their child is in no condition to be of material aid to them but loves them as well and truly as it is hu-

manly possible for an offspring to love a parent, may nevertheless be a lot happier with the situation in which the young one does take care of them, even though merely out of a sense of duty, than they would be if the child simply ignored their needs utterly. And here moral concepts can quite definitely be of use. One has only to note the typical differences between what Italian children do for their parents and what American children nowadays do for theirs to be convinced that custom is a genuine social force. Of course, it may also be a force that is not within the control of reason, and that is something that any moral theory of the sort I am inclined toward must reckon with if it can. Still, it is not obviously silly to ask what the rationale of one or another possible practice might be.

So we are back to the question of what and how much we should be requiring of children in relation to their parents, and why. The general answer, I have implied, is that parents do put themselves to much trouble to benefit their children, and if the children in question agree that the effects of those efforts really have been beneficial, then they should see to it that they are benefited in turn to at least the degree that renders it non-irrational for the parents to have done this. In different circumstances (e.g., in different cultures), this may be very easy to do or fairly difficult. If there are cases in which it is extremely onerous, however, then it seems to me seriously doubtful that a rational ethics could include such a duty.

Life and Genes as Benefits

Thus far, I have been speaking of "investments" and "benefits" of very much the general sort that *can* be instanced between people quite apart from such relations as that of parent to child, and have invoked a general principle that to a substantial extent applies to the parent-child relation only contingently: that is, only by virtue of properties of this situation other than those logically entailed by the notion of parenthood. And it seems to me that we do get real results from looking at it in this way. But obviously the other of the two points mentioned above is the most fundamental one here. Were it not for our parents' sexual activity, we would not exist at all. They have, we are inclined to say, "given us life." Is this, then, a benefit? And if it is, is it one for which we may have a duty of requital? They have also, in doing so, given us a genetic endowment, distinct for each individual. The one we got in particular may be exceptionally desirable in some respect or other. Do we owe them special gratitude for that, and if so does it eventuate in duties to requite?

Let's start with the first one: life. There are certainly questions to ask about regarding this as a benefit which our parents have given to us. For one thing, it is surely not just nit-picking to ask how this can be a benefit they have given "to us." After all, we weren't even born—in fact, not even conceived—when the alleged "gift" was bestowed. On whom, then, was it bestowed? At very least, we were certainly not the beneficiaries in the sense that *we* were made better off for getting it than *we* would otherwise have been: for we *would not* otherwise have been at all. . . .

There is also the question whether life as such is a "benefit." This is in part, to be sure, an "ultimate" question which each person must address for himself. But it seems hard to deny that in some cases, life is a burden, and that at any rate the answer to this question must very largely be determined on the basis of what sort of life it is. Thus in some cases it is plausible to suggest that the life a certain infant would end up with would foreseeably not be a benefit at all but rather a terrible burden. Finally, if we allow the possibility that a human life might be utterly indifferent—of no evident value whatever to its possessor—then I suggest that there just is no case for claiming that life as such is a benefit. Good lives are, and bad ones aren't, and that's that.

Which means, in effect, that the entire burden of this question is carried by its other leg: that of the genetic contribution made by the parent to the child. Now here, truly, we have "identity" being contributed by someone, though again it is that peculiar sense of "contribution" in which the recipient doesn't exist prior to the "contribution". Here too we must agree that no genetic benefit is so simply in the abstract. Thus A might endow B (usually unbeknownst to A) with fantastic musical talent, for instance, but alas, B's social environment includes none who could appreciate

and recognize, let alone nurture, this talent. When we say that someone has a desirable genetic endowment, then, we speak against a background of many conditions in the absence of which the judgment would make little sense. Nevertheless, it is clear enough that genetic components are essential to the realization of all sorts of personal attributes—being a human being rather than a member of some other species of animals being prominent among them.

But as I say, the parents who supply these rarely has much basis for predicting that their offspring will be so endowed, and not much in the way of credit is really appropriate in most cases. Cosmically speaking, it would seem, each of us is an absolute accident. And from that viewpoint it seems hard to give much credit to the bestowing of life or of enviable genotypes upon our offspring. Parents whose children, as we say, turn out well, are lucky, their opposite numbers unlucky, and that's pretty much the end of the matter. From there on in, it's all nurturing—where luck, though still a major factor, is no longer the only one at work, and parents are eligible for credit or, as the case may be, the reverse.

Now, people do on occasion have the thought that they are "glad to be alive," despite the utter absurdity of the idea that there might have been any other possibility. Moreover, we look about us and identify many whose situations we account it a matter of singular good fortune not to occupy. Is it appropriate to be grateful *to our parents* for this piece of good luck? In some depleted sense of the term, yes. But it must be admitted that not all the conditions for gratitude are fully realized there. All one can do is say that there, but for the grace of God, go I, filling in the blank in accordance with one's metaphysical proclivities—but not obviously with the names of one's parents. For in no sense were they in any position to do you the favor of getting you out of the unhappy conditions in question. In the first place, you were never in those conditions; so whatever else you may have to thank your parents for, it wasn't getting you out of them.

And there is a question whether you even could have been: could you have been in those "conditions" without actually being those other persons whose conditions they are? This would seem to depend on the condition. Could you have been you except that you happened to have imbecile intelligence instead of the at-least-normal mental capacity you have? However, it does seem possible I should have been me except club-footed, or with a genetic propensity for Hodgkin's disease, or with the pianistic potential of an Ashkenazy instead of the very modest amount I apparently have.

Apart from this, it must be pointed out that even if it would have been possible to be the person one is but without the unfortunate conditions in question, one's parents could not, normally, have intentionally done anything about it anyway, since they have virtually no control over the gene mix that will in fact be instantiated by their children. Perhaps what we should say they have done is, happily, to have mated with someone who had a reasonable antecedent probability of bringing normal children into existence rather than ones with unfortunate genetic inheritances. "Happily" is the right word, in most cases, for in those cases it is most unlikely that one's parents had any such thing in mind in selecting the mate they in fact did.

If we turn to the social question which, I conceive, is the only one that could plausibly be regarded as subject to much rational formulation here, what must be our result? A program of encouraging the genetically more fortunate to have children, and discouraging those less fortunate from doing so, perhaps? Perhaps; but the project is problematic, in too many well-known ways to need much recounting.

We must be aware that there may come a day when we know a good deal more than we do about what the probable children of a couple consisting of you and X, where X ranges over all known-to-be-possible mates, would be like. It would then be at least technically possible to encourage people to select mates in such a way that their offspring would likely fall within a certain range of values of certain genetic variables. There would then be the problem of deciding just which values of which variables were in question, and on what ground. And here, it seems to me, we can do no better than to analyze the probable cost to others of offspring of one sort rather than another, and insist that the particular couple in question foot the bill. They would then simply decide whether they were willing to pay that cost. This system would leave maximal scope for free decision on this matter to the parents. And if person A is the outcome, then A might have occasion to be grateful to those parents, if A is happy with his condition. But again, there is the possibility that A might be unhappy with her condition and in that case gratitude is not obviously indicated. Perhaps, indeed, the reverse!

Summing Up

. . . Rationally speaking, we have reason to be grateful to our parents for such good service to us as they may have rendered in childhood, and as far thereafter as may apply in the case. And we have reason, many of us, to breathe an existential sigh of relief that our genetic inheritance is as favorable as it is. But a duty to support our parents in old age, due simply and solely to the fact that they have "contributed to our identity," seems unsustainable. The "existential" factors exert themselves at the emotional and therefore subjective level, with the usual implication: they do not provide firm basis for general moral obligations. In this, I think, we have reason to cheer. Parents must earn their way in life, not only in relation to their neighbors but also to their children. With reasonable diligence and a bit of luck, they will usually do so. This, I suggest, is good enough.

QUESTIONS FOR THOUGHT
AND DISCUSSION

1. Why does John Locke argue that grown children have a "perpetual obligation" to honor their parents? (What does Locke mean by "honor"?)

2. If grown children have an obligation to honor their parents, then why don't they also have a perpetual obligation to obey them? (That is, why doesn't honoring one's parents extend to obedience?)

3. According to Jane English, what is the difference between doing a favor for someone and voluntarily sacrificing for that person?

4. Why does Jane English conclude that children owe nothing to their parents? What is the relevance of her distinction between favors and voluntary sacrifices to this conclusion?

5. Would English agree or disagree with Locke's claim that grown children have a "perpetual obligation" to honor their parents? Explain.

6. What is the difference between the rationales for filial obligation offered by Jane English and Jan Narveson? Would Narveson agree or disagree with English's claim that grown children owe nothing to their parents?

7. Why does Narveson claim that a rational ethics would include a moral rule requiring that grown children honor and care for their parents?

8. Suppose that a father says to his grown child that she has an obligation to take care of him because "I gave you life." Is this a plausible basis for filial duty?

FURTHER READING

Raymond A. Belliotti, "Honor Thy Father and Thy Mother and to Thine Own Self Be True." *The Southern Journal of Philosophy* 24, 2 (1986): 149–162.

Norman Daniels, *Am I My Parent's Keeper? An Essay on Justice Between the Young and Old.* New York: Oxford, 1988.

Nancy S. Jecker, "Are Filial Duties Unfounded?" *American Philosophical Quarterly* 26, 1 (1989): 73–79.

Christina Hoff Sommers, "Filial Morality." *The Journal of Philosophy* 83, 8 (August 1986): 439–456.

NOTES

Introduction

1. Cf. Herbert Spencer, *Social Statics* (New York: Robert Schalkenbach Foundation, 1954), p. 156.

Jane English

1. Cf. Thomas E. Hill, Jr., "Servility and Self-Respect," *Monist* 57 (1973). Thus, during childhood, most of the sacrifices will come from the parents, since they have most of the resources and the child has most of the needs. When children are grown, the situation is usually reversed.

Jan Narveson

1. [Jan Narveson:] I had the good fortune to be a tutor of Jane English's when she was an undergraduate and was saddened at the news of her untimely death in a mountaineering accident. I wish to dedicate this article to her memory.